he kept

THE LIFE RECORDS OF
John Milton

RUTGERS STUDIES IN ENGLISH

NUMBER 7

MILTON AT THE AGE OF 10
By Cornelius Janssen (Courtesy of the Pierpont Morgan Library)

THE LIFE RECORDS OF

John Milton

VOLUME I

1608-1639

EDITED BY J. MILTON FRENCH

RUTGERS UNIVERSITY PRESS

NEW BRUNSWICK, NEW JERSEY

1949

PR 3581
M6 F
v. 1

MANUFACTURED IN THE U.S.A.
BY THE PRINCETON UNIVERSITY PRESS

PREFACE

THE present work, to be completed in four volumes, is intended to fill a need which has long existed in the study of not only Milton but also most other great authors. It is a source book, designed to provide a day-by-day guide to the known facts in the life of a great poet. However useful it may possibly prove as a quarry for future biographers, it is not a biography in the ordinary sense, since it simply presents the records and allows them to speak for themselves. But within the limits of present knowledge, it attempts to reveal what Milton and the members of his family were doing each year, month, and even day during his lifetime.

The information assembled here, some of which has not previously been published, is therefore arranged in strictly chronological order, beginning with the day of the poet's birth and ending with that of his death. All material covering more than one date is divided into smaller units which can be presented day by day or month by month. Thus items from a biographical account like Milton's own autobiographical passages or the lives by Wood and Phillips appear piece by piece according to their dates throughout the work. When specific dating is not possible, items which can be assigned to months are gathered at the beginnings of those months; those which can be assigned only to years appear at the head of the entries for those years. The few which cannot be dated at all will be assembled at the end of the work.

The sources drawn on are almost exclusively those of the seventeenth century, since they provide almost all of the known facts, though when a later one gives what seems to be a reasonably likely tradition not found earlier, it is entered. For that matter, even unlikely traditions, early or late, when at all widespread, are included, if only to be exploded, so that readers will not think they have been overlooked. Contemporary records, books, and manuscripts, then, furnish most of the material. Though the basic assumption is that these are usually reliable, and though they are labeled when they are obviously undependable, no record is guaranteed to be true. It is guaranteed, to the best of the editor's ability, to be faithfully transcribed and labeled, but its accuracy or error is for the reader finally to determine.

For this reason the editor has made every effort to transcribe the originals scrupulously. So many biographies of Milton have distorted so many items so often that it is important to have a repository of them in accurate form. By this means some of the problems which harass the student may be avoided, since dates, names, and many other matters become garbled in the process of being handed down from second hand to third and later hands. The editor has therefore tried to see every text and record at first hand, and in a high percentage of instances has succeeded. In most of the other cases he has seen photographic copies of the originals. In the few cases where he has missed, he has so stated in a note.

For the sake of maximum fidelity the text follows the original spelling and punctuation except for printing long *s* as short *s* and silently correcting turned and imperfectly printed letters. Though in some ways facsimile reproduction might have been superior, as Dr. Harris Fletcher has shown in his splendid new text of Milton's poems, the originals are so varied and the manuscripts are often so difficult to read that the convenience of readable type may compensate for any loss of exactness.

The following abbreviations which appear frequently in the text are common in books and manuscripts of the seventeenth century:

-con, -c̄on	-tion
lī	pounds sterling
łł	ll plus case endings
p	per
ꝑ	pro
p̄	præ or pre
-q;	-que (usually on Latin words)
y	th
-z	-us or other final endings
ꝑ	-es

In addition, an apostrophe, a horizontal line over a letter, or the use of superscript letters indicates the omission of one or more letters. Very little practice will be required before the reader will be able to read this semi-shorthand easily, especially since its most concentrated use is in Latin, which, like all other languages, is followed by a translation within square brackets. The following made-up nonsense sentence illustrates the use of these abbreviations: "yᵉ ꝑp p̄scripc̄on for the oc̃as'n is to be brusq; wᵗʰ Parlmᵗ and ask yᵐ for a mandamz for 30ˡⁱ quos iłł hom̃ꝑ hēnt." Translated, this reads: "The proper prescription for the occasion is to be brusque with Parliament and ask them for a mandamus for 30 pounds which those men have [quos illi homines habent]."

Footnotes usually give (1) the location of the original record, (2) the standard modern edition of it when there is one, and (3) whatever additional comment seems to be needed. Titles of books frequently referred to are usually abbreviated as follows:

Aubrey   John Aubrey, biographical notes on Milton, Bodleian Library MS. Aubrey 8; transcribed in Darbishire (see below), pp. 1-15.

Brennecke   Ernest Brennecke, Jr., *John Milton the Elder and his Music*, Columbia University Press, 1938.

CBEL   *The Cambridge Bibliography of English Literature*, ed. F. W. Bateson, Cambridge, 1941.

CHEL   A. W. Ward and A. R. Waller, *The Cambridge History of English Literature*, Cambridge, 1907-1927.

CM   *The Works of John Milton*, ed. Frank A. Patterson and others, Columbia University Press, 1931-1938.

CSP   *Calendars of State Papers.*

Darbishire   Helen Darbishire, *Early Lives of Milton*, Constable, 1932.

DNB   Sir Sidney Lee and others. *The Dictionary of National Biography*, London and New York, 1885 ff.

Earliest   Anonymous life of Milton, Bodleian Library MS. Wood D 4, printed as "The Earliest Life of Milton," ed. Edward S. Parsons, *English Historical Review*, January,

1902; reprinted in Darbishire (see above), pp. 17-34, as by John Phillips.

Fletcher   Harris F. Fletcher, *Contributions to a Milton Bibliography*, University of Illinois, 1931.

Fletcher Facsimile   *John Milton's Complete Poetical Works*, ed. Harris F. Fletcher, University of Illinois, 1943-1948.

French   J. Milton French, *Milton in Chancery*, Modern Language Association, 1939.

Hamilton   W. D. Hamilton, "Original Papers Illustrative of the Life and Writings of John Milton," Publications of the Camden Society, LXXV (1859).

Hanford   James Holly Hanford, *A Milton Handbook*, fourth edition, Crofts, 1946.

Hunter   Joseph Hunter, *Milton. A Sheaf of Gleanings*, London, 1850.

Marsh   John F. Marsh, "Papers Connected with the Affairs of Milton and his Family," Chetham Society Miscellanies, Vol. I (1851).

Mackellar   *The Latin Poems of John Milton*, ed. Walter Mackellar, Cornell Studies in English, XV (1930).

Masson   David Masson, *The Life of John Milton*, Macmillan, 1859 ff.; when the first edition differs from the reprinted edition of 1946, the page numbers of the latter are added in parentheses after those of the first edition.

Parker   William R. Parker, *Milton's Contemporary Reputation*, Ohio State University, 1940.

Phillips   *Letters of State, Written by Mr. John Milton*, with a biographical introduction by Edward Phillips, London, 1694.

Raymond   Dora Neill Raymond, *Oliver's Secretary*, Minton Balch, 1932.

Richardson   Jonathan Richardson, *Explanatory Notes and Remarks on Milton's Paradise Lost*, London, 1734; reprinted in Darbishire (see above), pp. 199-330.

Sotheby   Samuel L. Sotheby, *Ramblings in the Elucidation of the Autograph of Milton*, London, 1861.

STC   A. W. Pollard and G. R. Redgrave, *A Short-Title Catalogue*, London, 1926.

Stern   Alfred Stern, *Milton und seine Zeit*, Leipzig, 1877-
1879.

Stevens   David H. Stevens, *Reference Guide to Milton*,
Chicago, 1930.

Thomason   G. K. Fortescue, *Catalogue of the . . . Books . . .
Collected by George Thomason*, British Museum, 1908.

Todd   *The Poetical Works of John Milton*, ed. H. J. Todd,
third edition, London, 1826.

Warton   John Milton, *Poems upon Several Occasions*, ed.
Thomas Warton, second edition, London, 1791.

Wing   Donald Wing, *Short-Title Catalogue . . . 1641-1700*,
Columbia University Press, 1945 ff.

Wood   Anthony Wood. *Athenæ Oxonienses*, Oxford, 1691-
1692. The life of Milton, which appears in the *Fasti Oxonienses*, I, 880-884, is reprinted in Darbishire (see above),
pp. 35-48.

The editor has received so much help from so many sources
that adequate expression of thanks is impossible. But in addition to many acknowledgements along the way, he wishes
especially to record here his indebtedness to the following good
Samaritans: to the Rutgers University Research Council for
generously subsidizing the publication of this volume and incidental expenses connected with it; to Mr. Earl S. Miers, former
Director of the Rutgers University Press, to his assistant Mrs.
Roy Yarborough, and to Mr. P. J. Conkwright, the designer
of the Princeton University Press, who have taken a warm
interest in this unusual venture and who have solved resource-
fully many perplexing problems involved in the evolution of
a difficult manuscript into a pleasing book; to Dr. Leslie Hotson
for contributing many valuable items from his phenomenal
collection; to Mr. Charles V. Bernau and Miss Nellie O'Farrell
for great assistance with research in the Public Record Office
and elsewhere in London; to Dr. Harris Fletcher for many
valuable suggestions for the improvement of the manuscript;
to Mrs. J. Wheeler Bird for patient and efficient work on the
index; to The Macmillan Company for kind permission to

quote extensively from Masson's *Life of Milton*; to Professor William R. Parker, Secretary of the Modern Language Association, for gracious permission to draw freely on the editor's *Milton in Chancery*; to many libraries, of which the Public Record Office, the British Museum, the Bodleian, the New York Public, the Huntington, the Pierpont Morgan, and those of Harvard, Yale, and Princeton Universities are the chief, for generously making available their vast resources; and finally to his wife for loyal, patient, inspiring help at all times. To all these the editor acknowledges his deep gratitude.

Finally, since the editor realizes that despite all his agonized efforts far too many errors are bound to have crept into this work, he will be grateful for any corrections which anyone can provide, and which can perhaps be included in the final volume. With their help he hopes to be able to follow, though at a great distance, in the steps of Bacon, who said of his researches: "So have I been content to tune the instruments of the muses that they may play that have better hands."

Rutgers University
June, 1949   J . MILTON FRENCH

THE LIFE RECORDS OF
John Milton

The Life Records of John Milton

December 9. Born in London.

John Milton was born the 9ᵗʰ of December 1608 die Veneris half an howr after 6 in the morning.

Milton's family Bible, British Museum Add. MS. 32,310; Darbishire, p. 336; Masson, I, 1 (3); cm, xviii, 274. The note is in Milton's hand.

Mr. John Milton, Authour of Iconoclastes, born. . . . Dec. 9°. 6ʰ. manè. 1608. Lat: London.

Bodleian Ashmole MS. 436, part 1, fol. 119. There are facsimiles immediately following in this manuscript and in the British Museum, Add. MS. 24,501, fol. 8. In the original (as of course in the facsimile) the text as quoted above is found in a small square set within a larger square, the whole being fully marked up with astronomical signs as usual in such horoscopes. In the facsimiles the work is ascribed to John Gadbury. See also cm, xviii, 348, 555.

The learned Mʳ John Milton, born about the yeer sixteen hundred and eight . . .

The "earliest" biography, fol. 140; Darbishire, p. 18.

He was borne A° Dnī . . . the . . . day of . . . about . . . a clock in the . . . John Milton was born the 9ᵗʰ of december 1608 die veneris half an howr after 6 in the morning. . . . Why do ye not set downe where Joh. Milton was borne? . . . ☞ q Mʳ Chr. Milton to see the date of his Bro: Birth. . . . his [the elder Milton's] son Jo: was borne in Bread street in London at ye Spread eagle, wᶜʰ was his house. . . .

Aubrey, ff. 63, 64, 65; Darbishire, pp. 1, 2, 11, 12, 13. The second section of this quotation is written in a hand identified by Miss Darbishire as that of the poet's widow; that of the third section in the hand of Anthony à Wood.

[1]

John Milton, was Born in Bread Street on Friday. the 9th day of December. 1608. and was Baptised in the Parish-Church of All-Hallows Bread-Street on Tuesday. the 20th day of December. 1608.

Tablet on the west side of the Church of St. Mary le Bow, Cheapside, 1936. Another tablet immediately below it states that it was placed there early in the nineteenth century on the original Church of All-Hallows, but was removed in 1876 on the demolition of that structure.

Milton. Born in Bread street 1608. Baptised in Church of. All Hallows. which stood here. ante 1878.

Tablet on the corner of Bread and Watling Streets, 1936.

He was born in *Breadstreet* within the City of *London*, between 6 and 7 a clock in the morning of the ninth of *Decemb.* an. 1608.

Wood, 1, 880; Darbishire, p. 35. Although C. M. Clode states (*Memorials of the Guild of Merchant Taylors*, London 1875, p. 284) that at the time of the poet's birth the house in Bread Street belonged to the Company of Merchant Taylors, it was actually owned by Eton College. See below under date of October 16, 1617.

DECEMBER 9. MILTON AN ALBINO?

This question was raised by Heinrich Mutschmann in his "Milton und das Licht," *Beiblatt zur Anglia*, xxx (1919), 320 ff. He amplified and defended his theory in *Der andere Milton*, Bonn, 1920; *The Secret of John Milton*, Dorpat, 1925; and elsewhere. For further references see Stevens, *Reference Guide to Milton*, index. Most students have refused to accept Mutschmann's theory. For various criticisms, see Stevens's index.

DECEMBER 20. BAPTIZED AT ALL HALLOWS CHURCH, LONDON.

The xx^{th} daye of Decēbe^r 1608./ was also baptized John the sonne of John Mylton scrivenor. [In the margin, printed by another hand, is the comment:] John Mylton Author of X Paradise Lost &c. &c.

Parish registers of All Hallows, Bread Street, London, which in 1936 were kept in the church of St. Mary le Bow, London. Transcribed in numerous places, among them being Masson, 1, 27 (39); J. P. Malcolm,

London Redivivum, 1803, III, 300; Publications of the Harleian Society, Registers, XLVII (1913), 16.

WORK ATTRIBUTED TO HIS FATHER.

A Sixe-folde Politician, 1609, STC 17,804, actually by Sir John Melton, is occasionally attributed to the father of the poet. The only reason for the mistake is the similarity of name. See CM, XVIII, 639; J. Milton French, "Mute Inglorious Miltons," *Modern Language Quarterly*, I (1940), 369. Melton's book was entered in the Stationers' Registers under date of December 15, 1608, as "*A Sixefold Polititian* by JOHN MILTON . . . vj^d."

FATHER TAXED 6 SHILLINGS.

Allhallowes parishe . . . John Milton—vj^{li}—vj^s.

Public Record Office, Subsidy Roll of 1610, Subsidies 146/470; this page is reproduced in facsimile in Kenneth Rogers, "Bread Street," *London Topographical Record*, XVI (1932), facing p. 74. Although Mr. Rogers does not use the customary classifications of the Record Office, I presume that this record falls within the Subsidy Rolls which are catalogued as E 179. The significance of the entry is not entirely clear. It may mean that Milton was taxed six shillings on holdings valued at six pounds.

JANUARY 9. FATHER'S SERVANT DIES.

The ixth Daye of January A° 1609 / Was buried Oliver Lowe s'vant to m^r John mylton.

Parish register, Church of All Hallows, Bread Street, London; Publications of the Harleian Society, Registers, XLIII (1913), 173.

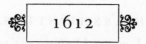

1611

FEBRUARY 26. MOTHER'S MOTHER, HELEN JEFFREYS, BURIED.

The xxvjth Daye of ffebruary A° 1610 / was buried in this churche m^{rs} Helyn Jefferys the mother of m^r John myltons Wyffe of this pishe.

Parish registers, Church of All Hallows, Bread Street, London; Publications of the Harleian Society, Registers, XLIII (1913), 174; Masson, I, 18-19 (30); Stern, I, i, 346. Both Masson and Stern misread the date as February 22, probably through mistaking xxvj for xxij. Joseph Hunter, in his *Chorus Vatum* (B. M. Add. MS. 24, 491, Vol. IV, p. 184 [or 334 by another numbering]), reads this entry: "1610. Feb. 26. buried Mrs Eliz. Jefferys, mother of the wife of John Milton, scrivener."

FATHER'S COMPOSITION.

I have been told, that the Father composed a Song of fourscore parts, for the Lantgrave of Hess, for wch Highnesse sent a medall of Gold or a noble present.

Aubrey, fol. 64; Darbishire, p. 10; Brennecke, pp. 34n, 66. The date is highly uncertain. William, Landgrave of Hesse, died about 1598. But Brennecke thinks Aubrey's note may be an error for the Polish Prince or for Prince Otto, son and heir of Landgrave Maurice of Hesse, who came as a suitor to the Princess Elizabeth in 1611. If the latter identification is correct, the date must be about 1611. The original composition has not been found. The Landgrave of Hesse was certainly in London in July and August of 1611; see *CSP Dom, 1611-1618*, pp. 59, 64.

1612

JULY 15. SISTER SARA BAPTIZED.

The xvth Daye of July 1612 / was baptized Sara the Dawghter of John Mylton scrivenor.

Parish register, Church of All Hallows, Bread Street, London; Publications of the Harleian Society, Registers, XLIII (1913), 17; Masson, I, 27 (40).

AUGUST 6. SISTER SARA BURIED.

The vj^th Daye of August 1612 / Was buried in y^e church Sara the Dawghter of John mylton.

Parish register, Church of All Hallows, Bread Street, London; Publications of the Harleian Society, Registers, XLIII (1913), 174; Masson, I, 27 (40).

1613

NOVEMBER 19. FATHER DEPOSES IN HARVEY-JONES SUIT.

19. Novembris. *1613.*   (Ex parte Thome Harvy quer' con'
A°. RR℘ Ja': 11°/   ffranciscū Johanes et āl dēftes testes
exā p Othon' Nicholson in Cancell'
Exaiator'/

[November 19, 1613, in the eleventh year of the reign of King James. Witness examined on the part of Thomas Harvey, plaintiff, against Francis Jones and others, defendants, by Otto Nicholson, Examiner in Chancery.]

John Milton of London Scr: dwelling in Bredstrete of the age of 47 yeres or thereab^te sworne &c vppon the. 1. 10. 11 & 12. Jnterrs. 1 Jnter. That he knoweth Thomas Harvy the Cōmplt 1 and John Harvy one of the dēft℘ and hath knowne them these last score yeres past and one of them longer tyme but more of the dēft℘ hee knoweth not.

That the s̄d Cōmplt before the yere of o^r Lord. *1605.* and in ⎰10 and after the same yere stode ingaged to dyvers and sundry ⎱11 psons wth the s̄d dēft John Harvy . . . and saythe that the sumēs of money for wch the p̄lt became so bounde for and wth the s̄d John Harvy were as followeth. viz. One hundred & fyve pound℘ due to Rychard Scudamore of London gent' by bond the 15. of November. *1606.* Three score and three pound℘ due to the s̄d Richard Scudamor by bond the 19. of May 1606 One hundred & fyve pound℘ due to Willm White of Puttney gent' by bond on the xvj^th of November *1605*. One other hundred & fyve poundȝ due to Thomas Willm̄s gent' by bond on the xvij^th of November *1605*. ffyftye two poundȝ and ten shillingȝ due by bond to John Cottoñ gent' the 2. day of December *1606*. ffyftye two poundȝ ten shillingȝ due by bond to John Cotten gent' the last day of November. *1605*. One hundred & fyve poundȝ due by bond to Thomas Williams gent' the ix^th of may 1605. ffyftye two poundȝ ten shillingȝ to m^rs Owen due by bond on the xviij^th of June *1603*. ffower score and three poundȝ sixe shillingȝ eight pence due by bond to Thomas Williams the 21. of May *1604*. And saith that he thinketh all and every the dettȝ aforeȳd were iust and due dettȝ for that he ffyndeth the bondȝ for the same entred in this deptȝ note booke and doth ṗtely rem̄ber them all to haue been lent. . . .

Public Record Office, Chancery Town Depositions, C24/386/41. This deposition, of which the important part is here given, and which has not before been published, was found by Mr. Charles A. Bernau; from his reference Miss Nellie O'Farrell procured the photostatic copy for me.

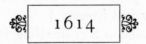

1614

FATHER'S MUSIC INCLUDED IN LEIGHTON'S "TEARES."

[1] Thou God of might . . .
[2] O Lord behold my miseries . . .
[3] O had I winges . . .
[4] If that a sinner sighes . . .

Sir William Leighton, *The Teares Or Lamentacions Of A Sorrow-fvll Sovle*, 1614; Warton, 1791, p. 523; Todd, 1826, VI, 336; Brennecke, pp. 69 ff.; Masson, I, 37 (51). The words of this collection had been published in 1613 without the music. There are copies of the 1613 edition in the British Museum, the Bodleian, and the Cambridge, Huntington, and New York Public Libraries; of the 1614 edition in the British Museum, Cambridge, and the Folger Library. Brennecke reproduces facsimiles of the titlepage of 1614 (facing p. 72) and the musical setting of Milton's "Thou God of Might" (facing p. 76). There is a manuscript copy of a German translation of this last song in the Nationalbibliothek at Vienna, MS. 19287, together with a copy of Henry Lawes's setting of "Lord Judge my Cause"; see *Tabvlae Codicvm Manv Scriptorvm Praeter Graecos et Orientales in Bibliotheca Palatina Vindobonensi Asservatorvm*, x (1899), 359. Brennecke (pp. 75-76) mentions other manuscript copies in the British Museum and in the Royal College of Music (MS. 1940). Leighton's *Teares* was entered in the Stationers' Registers under date of January 25, 1613.

JANUARY 30. SISTER TABITHA BAPTIZED.

The xxx^th of January 1613 / Was baptized Tabitha the Dawghter of m^r John mylton.

Parish register, Church of All Hallows, Bread Street, London; Publications of the Harleian Society, Registers, XLIII (1913), 18; Masson, I, 27 (40).

FATHER'S MUSIC IN COLLECTION.

[An undated manuscript collection of music of the early seventeenth century contains the following songs set by Milton's father:]

[f.   6:] Thou God of might hast chastned me . . .

[f. 20v:] O Lord behold my miseryes . . .

[f. 26v:] O had I winges like to a Doue, O . . .

[f. 29:]   If that a sinner sighes, if . . .

British Museum, MS Roy. App. 63; *British Museum Catalogue of Western Manuscripts in the Old Royal and King's Collections*, by Sir George F. Warner and J. P. Gilson, London, II (1926), 394. The manuscript, without definite title, is a form of Sir William Leighton's *Teares or Lamentations of a Sorrowfull Soule*, 1613. The date of the manuscript, though not given, is pronounced to be "after 1614" by the Catalogue.

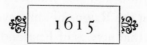

1615

ENTERS ST. PAUL'S SCHOOL (?).

The exact date of Milton's entrance into St. Paul's is not known, though the few facts that we do have are entered below under the year 1620. But Aubrey says that he was sent "very young," and M. F. J. McDonnell pointed out, in *A History of St. Paul's School, London*,

1909, p. 170, that in view of his precocity in writing verse, which was not ordinarily taught before the fourth form, "we may safely state that he went to school in 1615." Professor Donald L. Clark also (*John Milton at St. Paul's School*, Columbia, 1948, pp. 27-32) makes a strong case for 1615. He also quotes a line of verse (pp. 200-201) as having been written by Milton at this time: "The conscious water saw its God and blushed." Though the source of this tradition is not known, Milton is said to have produced this one-line theme when his schoolmaster, Alexander Gill, set his class to writing essays on the miracle at Cana, in which Christ turned water to wine. But since the greater part of the present volume was already in proof before Professor Clark's volume appeared, the main entry for Milton's going to St. Paul's has been left under the year 1620.

APRIL 14. FATHER MADE ASSISTANT IN COMPANY OF SCRIVENERS.

No original proof of this statement has been found. But Hyde Clarke, writing in the *Athenaeum*, 1880, 1, 760, quotes a Mr. Gribble, clerk of the Scriveners' Company, as saying that the elder Milton held such an office, which means that he was on the court of the company. Brennecke, p. 80, repeats this statement.

AUGUST 3. SISTER TABITHA BURIED.

The third Daye of August 1615 / Was buried here Tabitha the Daughter of m^r John mylton of this pish.

Parish register, Church of All Hallows, Bread Street, London; Publications of the Harleian Society, Registers, XLIII (1913), 175; Masson, 1, 27 (40).

AUGUST 5. FATHER WITNESSES (AND POSSIBLY PREPARES) WILL OF RALPH HAMOR, MERCHANT TAYLOR.

Jn the name Amen the ffiveth Daye of August in the Yere of oure Lord god one thowsand six hundred and fifteene and in the thirteenth Yere of the Raigne of our Soveraigne Lord James the Kynges Maiestie that now ys of England &c' and of Scotland the Nyne and fortith: J Raphe Hamor Citizen and Marchantaylor of London . . . Do make and ordayne this my last Will and Testament. . . . [Then follows a long list of legacies to relatives and friends, including £200 to "the Worshipfull Companye of Marchantaylors . . . to be lent out in free Loane to fower young men of the same Companye."] Signed sealed knowledged and published by the saide Raphe Hamor as and for his last will and Testament the saied fyveth Day of August one thowsand sixe hundred and fifteene Jn the presence of Richard Stocke. John Milton Scr' *Memorandum* that one Clause conteyning two Lynes and a halfe lyne or therabowtꝑ was stricken out by the sayed Raphe Hamor before thensealing hereof beyng in the third Leafe Richard Stocke John Milton Scr'

Prerogative Court of Canterbury, London, 78 Rudd. I owe this reference to the kindness of Dr. Leslie Hotson, who raises the question whether the elder Milton, in addition to witnessing the will, may also have prepared it and done the actual writing of it. An interesting connection between Milton and Hamor comes in the fact that Milton's apartment in Bread Street abutted on property of the Company of Merchant Taylors occupied by Hamor. See the entry below under October 16, 1617. Masson (1, 40 [54]) gives a brief account of Richard Stocke, the other witness to the will, who was minister of Milton's church, All Hallows Bread Street.

NOVEMBER 24 (?). BROTHER CHRISTOPHER BORN.

Christofer Milton was born on Friday about a month before Christmass at 5 in the morning 1615.

Milton's family Bible, British Museum Add. MS. 32,310; Darbishire, p. 336; CM, XVIII, 274. The entry is in Milton's own hand. In 1615 November 24 was a Friday.

DECEMBER 2. FATHER'S SERVANT WITNESSES SHELLEY-STONE BOND.

Nouerint vniūsi per pntes nos Thomam Shelley de Worminghurste in Com̄ Sussex Armiger, Johem̄ Alford de Assington in Com̄ predic̄ Armiger et Henricū Goring De Burton in Com̄ Sussex p̄d milit teneri et firmiter obligari Anne Stone de London Sempster in Quadringeñt libris Legalis monete Anglie, Soluend̄ eidem Anne Stone aut suo certo attorñ executor vel admīstrator suis, Ad quā quidem solucōnem bene et fideltr facieñd. Obligamus nos et Quemlibet nrūm per se pro toto et in solīd hered executor et admīssr nrōs et Cuiuslibet nrūm

[9]

firmiter p p̄ntes Sigillis nr̄is sigillat dat Secundo die Decembris
1615. Annoqz RRρ dnī nrī Jacobi Anglie &cρ Decimo tertio ac
Scotie Quadragesimo Nono:/

sigillat & deliber	Thomas Shelley
Edw. Jennye	Jhon Alford
Thomas Pattinson	Henry: Goringe
Et ρdcas Thomam in p̄ncia	[Seal] Mr Shelley 210^li
Jn°j: Wormay	the 27th of June
Tho: Church	1616
Et ρdes in p̄ncia	
Wm Bolde	

        servieñ Jo: milton sc.

The Condicōn of this obligacōn is such That if the wth in bound
Thomas Shelley John Alford and Sr Henry Goring their heires
executors admīstrators or assignes or any of them doe well and
truly pay or cause to be paid vnto the wth in named Anne Stone
her executors admīstrators or assignes the some of Two Hundred and Tenn powndρ of Lawfull money of England, At the
nowe dwelling house of John Milton Scrivener in Breadstreete
in London On the Sixte Day of June next ensuing the Date
wth in written, That then this obligacōn to be void, Or elles it to
stand in full force and vertue:/

    British Museum Cart. Harl. 112.D.19; *Athenaeum*, 1880, 1, 376;
Brennecke, p. 81. At the end is an endorsement, in another hand: "Sussex 1615. 13 Jac. 112.D.19."

[Know all men by these presents that we, Thomas Shelley
of Worminghurst in the county of Sussex, gentleman, John
Alford of Assington in the same county, gentleman, and Henry
Goring of Burton in the county of Sussex aforesaid, knight,
hold ourselves firmly bound to Anne Stone of London, semp-
stress, in four hundred pounds of lawful English money to be
paid to the said Anne Stone or her specified attorney or executor
or administrator, to which payment, well and faithfully to be
made, we oblige ourselves and each of us himself for all and
entirely, firmly by these presents, and also our heirs, executors,
and administrators, and those of each of us. Sealed with our

seals and given on the second day of December, 1615, and in the thirteenth year of the reign of our Lord James of England etc., and the forty-ninth of Scotland.

Sealed and delivered by	Thomas Shelley
Edward Jennye	John Alford
Thomas Pattinson	Henry Goring
And the aforesaid Thomas in the	[Seal] Mr. Shelley

presence of John Wormay, Thomas £210, June 27, 1616. Church, and the aforesaid in the presence of William Bolde, servant to John Milton, Scrivener.]

DECEMBER 3. BROTHER CHRISTOPHER BAPTIZED.

The third Daye of December 1615 / Was baptized Christopher the sonne of John mylton of this pishe scrivenor.

Parish register, Church of All Hallows, Bread Street, London; Publications of the Harleian Society, Registers, XLIII (1913), 18; Masson, I, 27 (40); Malcolm, *Londinum Redivivum*, II, 10; British Museum Add. MS. 19,142, fol. 78; Brennecke, p. 81. Brennecke erroneously states that Christopher was born on December 3, 1616.

MUSIC BY FATHER INCLUDED IN MYRIELL'S COLLECTION.

Tristitiæ Remedivm. Cantiones selectissimæ, diuersorū tū authorum, tum argumentorū; labore & manu exaratæ Thomæ Myriell. A.D. 1616. [Contains the following contributions by the elder Milton:]

[fol. 11v] Thou God of might hast chastned me.

[fol. 18] O Lord behold my miseries.

[fol. 18v] If that a sinners sighs.

[fol. 19] When Dauid heard that Absolon was slaine.

[fol. 19v] O Woe is me for thee, for thee.

[fol. 20] I am the resurrection, and the life, saith ye Lord.

[fol. 134v] Faire Orian in the Morne.

[fol. 135v] Precamur Sancte Domine.

[fol. 138v] How doth the holy City remaine solitary alas.

[fol. 139v] She weepeth continually, continually she.

British Museum Add. MS. 29,372; Brennecke, pp. 82 ff. and *passim*. The volume just named is the cantus part. Add. MSS. 29,373-29,377 contain, respectively, the altus, tenor, bassus, quintus, and sextus parts of the same selections. The paging agrees with that given in the altus, tenor, and bassus, but varies somewhat in the other two. There is some difference in the actual selections in the quintus, and the sextus is incomplete. Of the several sets of paging written, I use above that assigned to the volume by the British Museum.

Brennecke describes these volumes at pp. 82 ff., and gives several facsimiles at pp. 82 and 86. He also furnishes modern transcriptions of several songs at pp. 169, 171, 191, and 193.

Other song-writers included in the collection are Ward, Ferrabosco, Tompkins, Weelkes, Wilkins, Bull, Pierson, Ravenscroft, Byrd, Morley, and others.

Myriell was the minister who married Milton's daughter to Edward Phillips on November 22, 1623; see that entry.

MUSIC BY FATHER INCLUDED IN ANONYMOUS COLLECTION.

[The collection has no titlepage. The following contributions are by the elder Milton:]

[fol. 19] O Lord behould my miseries.

[fol. 21v] I am the resurrection & the life saith the Lord.

[fol. 22] O had I wings like to a dove.

[fol. 22v] If that a sinners sights.

[fol. 32v] When dauid hard that absolon was slaine.

[fol. 33] O woe is mee for thee.

[fol. 68] If that a Sinners sighs.

[fol. 68v] O woe is me for thee, for thee.

British Museum Add. MS. 29,427. The only title to the volume is "Altus." Although undated, it is placed under the year 1616 because of its close resemblance to Myriell's *Tristitiæ Remedivm* of that year. Though an entirely distinct work, it includes songs by many of the same authors, such as Wilbye, Tompkins, Pierson, Weelkes, Ward, and Ravenscroft.

JUNE 27. THOMAS SHELLEY PAYS A BOND AT FATHER'S SHOP.

[Seal] Mr Shelley 210 ^{li} the 27th of June 1616.

British Museum Cart. Harl. 112.D.19, attached to the Shelley-Stone bond of December 2, 1615.

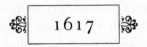

JANUARY 20. SCRIVENERS' COMPANY, TO, WHICH FATHER BELONGS, INCORPORATED BY LETTERS PATENT.

[The patent making them a royal corporation is dated:] apud Westm̄ vicesimo die Januarij [14 James I].

Public Record Office, C66/2093/5; Stern, I, i, 43; Masson, I, 47-48 (61-62); Brennecke, p. 81. Masson does not give the accurate date, but merely states that the company drew up a charter in 1616. Brennecke follows Masson, but gives the date as January, 1618/9. Masson goes on to say that the company prepared revised regulations for their government, which received the sanction of Sir Francis Bacon and the Chief Justices in January, 1618/9. The exact reference to the patent has, I think, not previously been given.

FATHER HAS SERVANT THOMAS BOWER.

. . . this Defendant [Thomas Bower] saith, That he was for the space of Eight yeares or thereaboutȝ now past servant to the said John Milton Scrivener . . . and hath beene for the space of Six yeares now past, or thereaboutȝ Partner with the said John Milton . . .

Public Record Office, C2 Charles I/D39/47 (Bower's answer to Rose Downer, May 3, 1631); French, *Milton in Chancery*, p. 243. By adding eight and six and subtracting the total from 1631, we arrive at 1617 as the year when Bower first became servant to Milton.

JULY 13 (OR EARLIER). FATHER WRITES SONNET TO JOHN LANE.

Johannes Melton, Londinensis Ciues, amico
suo viatico, in Poesis Laudem. S.D.P.

If virtewe this bee not! what is? tell quick!
    for, *Childhode, Manhode, Old age,* thow doost write,
Loue, warr, and *Lustes* quelled, by arm *Heroick;*
    instanced in *Gwy* of *Warwick* (knighthodes light.)
Heraltes recordę, and each sownd *Antiquarie,*
    for *Gwyes* trewe beinge, lief, death, eake hast sought,
to satisfye those w^ch *præuaricari:*
    Manuscript, Cronikel, (yf mote bee bought)
Coventries, Wintons, Warwickes monumentes,
    Trophies, Traditions delivered of *Guy,*
With care, cost, plume, as sweetlie thow presentę,
    toexemplifie the flawre of *Cheualrye.*
fro^m cradle to the sadle, And the biere;
    for *Christian* immitation, all are heere.

                   J. M.

[At end of poem, fol. 132] This poem containinge a corrected historie of *Guy Earle* of *Warwick* in 87 leaves [the present contains 132] of large quarto, written by m^r *John Lane,* hath licence to bee printed.
Jul; 13°. 1617

               John Tauerner.
                  as in ye original.

John Lane, *The Corrected historie of Sir Gwy, Earle of Warwick,* 1612, British Museum Harl. MS. 5243; Hunter, pp. 12-13; Todd, 1 (1826), 4; Brennecke, pp. 91-92. Todd suggests that the author may be Melton the astrologer. Brennecke transcribes "flawre" (line 12) as "powre," "plume" (line 11) as "paine," and "And" (line 13) as "to." In the original manuscript the words printed above in italics are in italic writing, the remainder in secretary hand. The writing may be Lane's. Joseph Hunter, in "Chorus Vatum," II (British Museum Add. MS. 24,489), 85 (143 by another numbering), calls this poem "really too bad to be quoted . . . very hobbling poetry indeed."

OCTOBER 16. FATHER'S HOUSE IN BREAD STREET SURVEYED.

A *Suruey* of ye House Called the Beare in Cheapeside And ye Tenem^ts therevnto belonging taken by Mr Thomas Wever Vice Prouost & Mr Daniell Collins sent by the [Eton] College

to Veiwe the same the xvi day of October A° RRρ Jacobi xv et
A° Dnī 1617. . . .

Tenem^{ts} & Shopps in Breedstreet [*sic*] pcell of the White
Beare. . . .

[1] The Litle Shopp a Scruen^{rs} shopp vnd^r ye Kitchin [1]
Length 3 yards North & South wanting halfe q^{tr}
Breadth v yards halfe Lack a naile
Hight 2 yards 3 q^{trs} Lack & [*sic*] inch

[2] The Seller Vnder ye Litle Shopp in pt to Mr Milton
[12]
Length iij yards & q^{tr}
hight iij yards
Breadth [blank]

[3] The Low Seller [11]
Length ij yards iij q^{trs} North & South
Breadth vj yardes & a halfe
Hight ij yards iij q^{trs}

The first Tenem^t in the occupacōn of Mr John Milton Scriv-
ener abutting vpon the house wch belongeth to the Marchant
Taylo^{rs} South late in ye occupacōn of Raph Hamer deceased
Marchand Tayler

[4] The Hall [2]
Length 7 yards North & South ⎫
Breadth vj yards iij q^{trs} & a halfe ⎬ Wenscotted
Hight iij yards Lacking ij inches ⎭

[5] To wch adjoyneth a litle Butterie West Congeining [*i.e.*,
containing] 3 yards 3 q^{trs} in Length & a yard 3 q^{trs} in Breadth

[6] The pler next Bredstreet West [3]
Length vj yards & halfe q^{tr}— ⎫
Breadth v yards & halfe q^{tr}— ⎬ Wenscotted
Hight iij yards Lacking iij inches ⎭

[7] The Kitchin North to the pler [4]
[8] A litle Counting house South
Length iij yards halfe & halfe q^{tr} North. South
Breadth vj yards & q^{tr}

Hight 2 yards halfe & halfe q^{tr}

[9] The Chamber oū ye hall Wenscott [5]

Length 5 yards halfe & halfe q^{tr} North-South

Breadth vj yards & q^{tr}

Hight iij yards

[10] A litle Buttry North from ye former Chamb^r

Length j yard & halfe North-South

Breadth v yards more or lesse East-West

Hight iij yards—

[11] The Chamber oū ye pler West vpon Bredstreet [6]

Length v yards & halfe North South.

Breadth vj yards

Hight ij yards halfe & q^{tr} wanting one inch

[12] A Lodging Chamber [between?] ye former 2 Chamb^{rs}

Length iiij yards North South.

Breadth 2 yards Lack 2 inches

Heigth vt Supra

[13] The New Chamb^r oū ye Hall Chamber [7]

Length vj yards 2 inches North & South ⎫

Breadth vj yards q^{tr} & halfe East & West ⎬ Wenscott

Height 2 yards & halfe ā naile ⎭

[14] The Chamb^r oū ye pler Chamber [8]

Length vij yards halfe q^{tr} North & South

Breadth vj yards East & West

Height ij yards & halfe lacking ij inches

[15] An house of Office

[16] The Garrett oū the new Chamber [9]

Length v yards iij q^{trs} North & South

Breadth viij yards & halfe Lack a naile

Hight ij yards & a foote

[17] The Greate Seller vnder ye great Shopp. [10]

Length vj yards & q^{tr} North & South.

Breadth xij yards

Height iij yards

The Tyth of the White Beare xxx^s a quart^r. . . .

The Whole measure in Breedstreete of the Tenem[ts] is xxij yards iij & a Naile

Records of Eton College, Vol. XVI, London, The White Bear, no. 42; Noel Blakiston, "Milton's Birthplace," *London Topographical Record*, Vol. XIX, No. 80, pp. 6-12. These records have recently been studied and catalogued by Mr. Blakiston, who described this and related material about the Bread Street house to the London Society of Antiquaries in January, 1945. The section concerning Milton is here reproduced through his kindness and that of the Provost and Fellows of Eton College.

For convenience of reference the description of each room is here preceded by a number in brackets and is followed by another number in brackets, both the addition of the present editor. The first set of numbers simply applies to the rooms as they come; the second set refers to the corresponding rooms in the list given below, taken from the floor plans here described under the same date. When no number follows a room, the floor plans, though showing a room, give no name or measurements.

Although Milton had many rooms, the large building had several other occupants. In addition to the White Bear itself, which occupied several large rooms, the tenants were a grocer named Sydway, a girdler named Thomas Hambleton, a milliner or leather-seller named Richard Westcomb, and a pointmaker named Richard Scales. The building was located on the southeast corner of Bread Street and Cheapside, with Milton's apartment opening on Bread Street.

The records show that this property was part of a grant made to Eton College by the Hospital of St. James in 1449. Since the survey shows that it was at the lower end of Bread Street, between Cheapside and Black Spread Eagle Court, Aubrey's statement that the poet was born at the Spread Eagle receives new support.

Two former ideas about Milton's house may now be revised in the light of this new information. Professor Brennecke (p. 52) says that "there is no difficulty in visualizing its main features. Within the entrance was the business office, with chairs for clients and desks for the master and his assistants. To the rear was a living room, furnished with a dining table, with books and music, and the kitchen; in the upper story, with its gable projecting over the street, were the sleeping apartments." Except that the office was on the ground floor, that there were a living room and a kitchen, and that the chambers were higher up, almost nothing in the survey corresponds to the fanciful picture.

A more serious error is Professor Brennecke's assertion (p. 53) that Milton was "the outright owner, not only of the Bread Street house, but also (according to Aubrey) of 'another house in that street, called The Rose, and other houses in other places.' " From the records it is obvious that Milton is the renter rather than the owner of his quarters here. Aubrey, moreover, does not say that Milton was the "outright owner";

he simply says that Milton "had" other houses, including the Rose, and that the Bread Street house at the Spread Eagle "was" his home. Aubrey would naturally not use such a term as "owner," since almost everybody who held property in Milton's day held it on lease for a term of years.

The assertion frequently made that the birthplace belonged to the Company of Merchant Taylors (see the entry above under December 9, 1608) probably comes from a confusion with the adjoining property. The survey states that Milton's tenement is "abutting vpon the house wch belongeth to the Marchant Taylo^rs South late in ye occupacōn of Raph Hamer deceased Marchant Tayler." Possibly Milton also had rooms in that neighboring house. A careful search of the records of the Company of Merchant Taylors might shed some light on this point.

OCTOBER 16 (?). FLOOR PLAN OF FATHER'S HOUSE IN
BREAD STREET.

White beare in Cheapeside

First storie
[1] m^r Miltons shope 11 fot ½ [N-S] 16 fot ½ [E-W] [1]

Second storie
[2] Mr Miltons Hall 21 fot [N-S] 20-0 [E-W] [4]
[3] parlor 14 fot 9 [N-S] 13 foot 4 [E-W] [6]
[4] Kitchine 11 fot ½ [N-S] 17 fot ½ [E-W] [7]

Third Storie
[5] 1 chamber ouer m^r Miltons Hall 16 foot [N-S] 20 foot
[E-W] [9]
[6] 1 chamber ou^r his parlor 21 fot [N-S] 15 foote [E-W]
[11]

ffourth Storie
[7] Second Chamber over m^r Miltons Hall 15 fot ½ [N-S]
20 fot [E-W] [13]
[8] Garret [measuring about 20 feet N-S by 16 feet E-W]
[14]

The Vppmost Storye of all the buldinge
[9] Garats ouer m^r Miltons Hall [measuring about 21 feet
N-S by 20 feet E-W] [16]

Vndergrounde
[10] A Sceller belongeing to Mr Milton 18 fot ½ [N-S] 35
fot ½ [E-W] [17]

[11] Mr Miltons [measuring about 7 feet N-S by] 17 fot [E-W] [3]

[12] sellers 21 fot [N-S] 14 fot [E-W] [2]

Records of Eton College, Vol. XVI, London, The White Bear, no. 44; Noel Blakiston, "Milton's Birthplace," *London Topographical Record*, Vol. XIX, No. 80, Plates I-VI. Mr. Blakiston's reproductions of these plans appear as inserts in the article in which the survey of the house is quoted. Although the drawings are not dated, they are here assumed to have been made at the same time as the survey. The items quoted above, which are only those concerning Milton selected from the plans of the whole house, are quoted here through the generosity of the Provost and Fellows of Eton College and of Mr. Blakiston.

Each item is numbered for convenience for reference, and is followed by a number in brackets which refers to the corresponding room as given in the survey. Thus the two can easily be compared. I have also added the points of the compass in brackets. The plans correspond reasonably well with the survey. The dimensions are not always identical, and several rooms mentioned in the survey are not labeled in the plans, though the plans show plenty of closets and cubby-holes, some of which are the ones given in the survey. The rooms omitted by name from the plans are the two butteries, the countinghouse, the lodging chamber, and the house of office.

A few further notes on the plan may be added:

1. Although several other tenants shared the building, Milton, except for the White Bear, held the largest portion.

2. The door to Milton's apartment was about 75 feet down the east side of Bread Street from Cheapside.

3. His apartment was five stories high, or six if we include the cellar.

4. The plan shows windows in the shop, the parlor, and the two chambers on the fourth story. Though other rooms also probably had them, they are not shown. Probably some of the rooms, at least those on the lower floors, had none because of adjoyning houses standing wall to wall.

5. Fireplaces are shown in the parlor, the kitchen, and the front chamber on the third story.

6. Stairways lead up on the first floor from the shop and from the corridor; on the second story from the hall and from the space between the hall and the parlor; and thereafter only above the last named. The only stairway to the cellar is between the shop and the corridor.

7. A break in the front wall of the large cellar may indicate an outside entrance from Bread Street.

8. The front chamber on the fourth story and the chamber on the fifth story seem to have sloping walls.

OCTOBER 28. WILL OF WILLIAM TRUELOVE, POET'S GREAT-UNCLE.

It seems unnecessary to give the text of this document since there is no mention of the Miltons directly in it. But William Truelove of Essex married Margaret Jeffrey, sister of the poet's grandmother Helen Jeffrey. It is dated October 28, 15 James I, and is called the will of William Truelove of Blankenham-vponn-the-hill, Co. Suffolk, gent. It was proved May 7, 1618, by Margaret Truelove, relict of the testator, and William, his son.

The will mentions lands in Tillingham, Hertford, and Hatfield Peverell, Essex. Persons named are the testator's wife Margaret, his eldest son William, his other sons Robert, Paul, Richard, and Henry, his daughters Katherine, Sara, Margaret, and Anne (formerly Drury, now Butler), and his cousin James Caston. Each son is to receive fifty pounds on reaching the age of twenty-four, and each daughter forty pounds at the age of twenty-one.

The original is in the Prerogative Court of Canterbury, London (23 Ayloffe). It is described by Joseph Lemuel Chester in the *Athenaeum*, 1897, II, 496-7, and in Masson, I (1881), 37-39.

1618

TUTORED BY THOMAS YOUNG; BEGINS TO WRITE POETRY.

A° D^{ni} 1619, he was ten yeares old, as by his picture: & was then a Poet. his schoolm̄ then was a puritan in Essex, who cutt his haire short.

Aubrey, fol. 63; Darbishire, p. 2. That Aubrey referred to Young is almost certain because of the tone of Milton's letters and poems to Young. If Milton was ten years old, the date was 1618-1619.

> Primus ego Aonios illo præeunte recessus
> Lustrabam, & bifidi sacra vireta jugi,
> Pieriosque hausi latices, Clioque favente,
> Castalio sparsi læta ter ora mero.

[First, under his guidance, I explored the recesses of the Muses, and beheld the sacred green spots of the cleft summit

of Parnassus, and quaffed the Pierian cups, and, Clio favouring
me, thrice sprinkled my joyful mouth with Castalian wine.]

Milton, *Elegia Quarta*, lines 29-32; CM, I, 186-187; Masson, I,
54 (72). See also Arthur Barker, "Milton's Schoolmasters," *Modern
Language Review*, XXXII (1937), 517 ff. The Elegy is addressed to
"*Thomam Junium præceptorem suum.*"

. . . that he had another Master possibly at his Father's house,
appears by the Fourth Elegy of his Latin Poems written in his
18th year, to *Thomas Young*, Pastor of the *English* Company
of Merchants at *Hamborough*, wherein he owns and stiles him
his Master . . .

Phillips, p. viii; Darbishire, p. 54. The sketch of Young in Warton,
1791, pp. 440-441, is reproduced in Todd, 1826, VI, 197-198.

EARLY EDUCATION AND ABILITY.

. . . after I had from my first yeeres by the ceaselesse diligence
and care of my father, whom God recompence, bin exercis'd to
the tongues, and some sciences, as my age would suffer, by sundry masters and teachers both at home and at the schools, it was
found that whether ought was impos'd me by them that had
the overlooking, or betak'n to of mine own choise in English,
or other tongue, prosing or versing, but chiefly this latter, the
stile by certain vital signes it had, was likely to live.

Milton, *The Reason of Church Government*, 1641, p. 37; CM, III,
235. Although this and several following entries cannot be precisely
dated, they must refer to approximately this period. They are therefore
grouped together at this point.

Pater me puerulum humaniorum literarum studiis destinavit;
quas ita avidè arripui, ut ab anno ætatis duodecimo vix unquam
ante mediam noctem à lucubrationibus cubitum discederem;
quæ prima oculorum pernicies fuit: quorum ad naturalem de-
bilitatem accesserant & crebri capitis dolores; quæ omnia cùm
discendi impetum non retardarent, & in ludo literario, & sub
aliis domi magistriis erudiendum quotidie curavit: ita variis instructum linguis, & percepta haud leviter philosophiæ dulcedine,
ad Gymnasium gentis alterum, Cantabrigiam misit.

Milton, *Defensio Secunda*, 1654, p. 82; CM, VIII, 118-121.

[My father destined me while yet a little boy for the study of humane letters, which I seized with such eagerness that from the twelfth year of my age I scarcely ever went from my lessons to bed before midnight; which, indeed, was the first cause of injury to my eyes, to whose natural weakness there were also added frequent headaches. All which not retarding my impetuosity in learning, he caused me to be daily instructed both at the grammar-school and under other masters at home; and then, when I had acquired various tongues and also some not insignificant taste for the sweetness of philosophy, he sent me to Cambridge, one of our two national universities.]

Masson, I, 66 (84-85). See also further similar selections given below under the topic of Milton's entry into St. Paul's School, 1620.

[Milton] had his institution to learning both under public, and private Masters; under whom, through the pregnancy of his Parts, & his indefatigable industry (sitting up constantly at his Study till midnight) hee profited exceedingly; and early in that time wrot several grave and religious Poems, & paraphras'd some of Davids Psalms.

The "earliest" biography, fol. 140v; Darbishire, p. 18.

EARLY STUDIOUSNESS.

. . . & ipse ab ineunte adolescentiâ iis eram studiis incensus, quæ me ad optima quæque si minùs facienda, at certè laudanda incitatum ferebant.

Milton, *Defensio pro Populo Anglicano*, 1651 (Madan's no. 1), p. 4; CM, VII, 8-9. See also the notes on his early education.

[. . . and I myself from earliest youth had been kindled to those studies which stirred me, if not to do the noblest deeds, at least certainly to praise them.]

EARLY MUSICAL ABILITY.

He had a delicate tuneable Voice & had good skill: his father instructed him: he had an Organ in his house: he played on that most.

Aubrey, fol. 63v; Darbishire, p. 6.

DESTINED TO CHURCH FROM A CHILD.

. . . the Church, to whose service by the intentions of my parents and friends I was destin'd of a child, and in mine own resolutions, till coming to some maturity of years. . . .

Milton, *The Reason of Church Government*, 1641, p. 41; CM, III, 242. Although impossible to date exactly, this item has been placed here because of its close connection with other notes about Milton's studies of this period.

PORTRAIT PAINTED BY CORNELIUS JANSSEN.

[Legend:] John Milton, ætatis suæ 10, Anno 1618.

The original painting is now in the Pierpont Morgan Library in New York. It seems to have been in the possession of Mrs. Milton as late as 1721, when the artist Vertue visited Milton's daughter Deborah and learned from her that Mrs. Milton had two paintings of the poet—one as a lad in school and the other "about twenty." Presumably the first was the present portrait and the second the original of the so-called Onslow portrait (see below under December 9, 1629). Among later owners were Charles Stanhope, Thomas Hollis, Thomas Brand Hollis, Edgar Disney, J. Passmore Edwards, and J. Pierpont Morgan.

This picture has been frequently reproduced. The best known is perhaps that etched by Cipriani for Hollis in 1760. An enamel copy said to have been made by William Essex in 1856 is in the Victoria and Albert Museum. Reproductions may be found in Masson, I, frontispiece; Williamson, *Milton Tercentenary The Portraits, Prints and Writings of John Milton*, Cambridge, 1908, facing p. 3; and CM, I, frontispiece. For information about it, see Masson, I, 50 (665-67); Williamson, pp. 2 ff.; *Notes and Queries*, II, xii (1861), 2; Darbishire, p. 333.

A print issued in 1823 bears the legend: "John Milton. Painted by C. Janssen. Engraved by Charles Pye. London. Pubd. for the Proprietor, March 1823." Although it might seem to stem from the Janssen portrait mentioned here, those who have seen it believe it does not in the least represent Milton. See Williamson, pp. 19, 86.

Although the original portrait does not bear the name of Janssen as painter, it has regularly been attributed to him since at least 1750.

A reproduction of this portrait serves as the frontispiece to the present volume.

OCTOBER 7. FATHER DEPOSES IN LEEDS-KNOLLES SUIT.

7° die octobris *1618*   Ex parte Johannis Leeds mīl quer:
Anº R Rℓ Jacobi 16°   verss Ricū Knolles et āl defen^tes
                                        Testes exaiāt p Othonem Nicholson
                                        in Cancellaria Exaiātorem

[October 7, 1618, in the 16th year of the reign of King James. On the part of John Leeds, knight, plaintiff, against Richard Knolles and others, defendants. The witness examined by Otto Nicholson, Examiner in Chancery.]

John Milton Cytyzen and Scrivener of London of the parrish of All S^ts als̄ Allhollowes breadstreete London Aged 50 yeares
1   yeares [*sic*] or theraboutꝑ sworne &c To the first Jnterr: sayth That he hath seene Sr John Leeds kn^t named for Comp^lt in this suite but hath no further knowledge of him, neyther doth this dep^t know anie of the def^tꝑ in this suite, named in the tytle of the Articles, But sayth that he did very well know Sr Thomas Leeds kn^t in the Article named, the sd Comp^ltꝑ ffather, And John Kinge in the Article likewise named, And did knowe the sd Sr Thomas Leeds for the space of manie yeares, before it was reported, that he was gonne beyonde the seas, And did know the sd John Kinge for divers yeares before his decease./. . .

Jo: Milton

Public Record Office, Chancery Town Depositions, C24/456/84. I found this document through Mr. Charles A. Bernau's lists of Chancery depositions. Milton's answers to the other questions are that he can depose nothing material to them. This document has not previously been published.

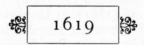

FATHER KNOWS RICHARD SHERATT.

Richard Sheratt Cittizen and Haberdasher of London dwelling within the p'cinct of bridwell . . . hath knowne the sd Milton some twelue yeares or theraboutꝑ. . . .

Public Record Office, Chancery Depositions, C24/574/40; French, *Milton in Chancery*, p. 252. By subtracting 12 from the date of Sheratt's deposition, September 26, 1631, we arrive at 1619 as the date of the beginning of the acquaintance. The context makes it quite clear that it is the elder Milton and not the poet who is concerned.

MAY 21. FATHER DEPOSES IN GOTTS-HICKS SUIT.

21. Maij. *1619* p   Luke Miles con' Gottᵱ testes exām p Othoñ
Aº RRᵱ Ja: *17º*   Nicholson in Cancellaria Examinatorem/

[May 21, 1619, in the 17th year of the reign of King James. In behalf of Luke Miles against Gotts. The witness examined by Otto Nicholson, Examiner in Chancery.]

John Milton Citizen and Scryvener of Londoñ dwelling in the parish of All hallowes in Bred Strete aged 50. yeres or therabtᵱ sworne &c' vppon the 1. & 7. Inter'

That he knoweth Sʳ Baptist Hickᵱ knᵗ the dēft and hath sene 1 Thomas Gottᵱ named for the Complt in this sute

That he was pʳsent at the dēftᵱ howse in Chepeside on the 7 fowerth day of December *1615*. being the day mencōed in the sd awarde in the Jnter' mencōed when the dēft by the same awarde was to seale the Relese to the p̄lt . . . and he furthʳ saith that the writing in paper dated the iiijᵗʰ day of December *1615*. purporting a Release and wᵗʰ waxe thervppon wᵗʰowte the print of anye seale ys the very same writing of Relese before mencōed to haue bene tendred to the p̄lt by the dēft as aforesd wᶜʰ this dēpt saith he knoweth to be true by the memorandū wᶜʰ ys therto subscribed yt being of this dep̄tᵱ owne handwriting and was written by this dep̄t at the tyme aforesd and certifyed by this dep̄t and others whose names apere thervnto subscribed as wytnesses of the aforesd tender   /   And more &c'

Capt' coram Nichō Robertᵱ   Jo: Milton./
in absenc' Mrī Nicholson./

[Taken before Nicholas Roberts in the absence of Master Nicholson.]

Public Record Office, Chancery Town Depositions, C24/461/55. This document was first found by Mr. Charles Bernau. Milton's father would naturally know Sir Baptist Hicks, since they lived at this time in the same house. See the survey of Milton's house entered above under date of October 16, 1617. This deposition has not previously been published.

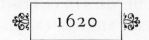

1620

WORK ATTRIBUTED TO HIS FATHER.

Astrologaster, or the Figure-caster, 1620, STC 17805, actually by Sir John Melton, is occasionally attributed to the father of the poet. See references under Melton's *Six-folde Politician*, 1609. This book was entered in the Stationers' Registers on April 8, 1620.

FATHER INVESTS MONEY FOR JOHN DOWNER.

. . . one John Downer the Complaynantᵱ late husband, having beene this Defendantᵱ [i.e., John Milton the elder] long acquaintance Did dispose of at this Defᵗᵉ. shopp at Jnterest, vpon securitie, to the good liking of him the said John Downer some moneys, But this Defᵗ doth not well remember the particuler soē or soēes soe lent, And the said John Downer dying long since . . .

Public Record Office, C2 Charles I/D39/47 (Milton's answer to Rose Downer, May 3, 1631); French, *Milton in Chancery*, p. 241. The date 1620 is merely conjectural, but since the relation presumably continued some time, and since the entry following this one indicates that probably John Downer was dead and the affairs being managed by his wife Rose by 1624, it seems reasonable to set some such date as 1620. By the tone of Milton's writing, we may guess that he had already known Downer for some time, though there is no way of telling how long.

. . . the husband of the Compˡᵗ. in his life time, had some moneys lent at Jnterest, at the shopp of the said Defendant John Milton, And further saith that true it is that the ffiftie poundᵱ in the bill mencōned, was by the said John Milton and this Defendant, by and with the consent, and good liking of the said Complaynant, putt to Jnterest for the vse of the said Complaynant, into the handᵱ of one Master Leigh vpon sufficient securitie by bond in November One thowsand six hundred Twenty & ffower . . .

Public Record Office, C2 Charles I/D39/47 (Bower's answer to Rose Downer, May 3, 1631); French, *Milton in Chancery*, p. 243.

Owns and annotates lodge's seneca?

A copy of the *Workes of Lucius Annæus Seneca*, 1620 (STC 22,214), edited by Thomas Lodge, is in the possession of Captain F. L. Pleadwell or W. H. Lowdermilk and Company of Washington, D.C. Since it has been thought that the initials "I.M." worked in the cover may stand for John Milton, it was included among the possible books from Milton's library catalogued in CM, XVIII, 579. There are a few unimportant annotations in a hand surely not Milton's. The chances of its having actually belonged to Milton are slight; and it is mentioned here simply for the sake of completeness. Even if actually Milton's, it may have been acquired by him at almost any time subsequent to the date of its publication; but it is put under this date because it is as likely as any other.

Begins study at St. Paul's School, London.

Equidem quoties recolo apud me tua mecum assidua pene colloquia (quæ vel ipsis Athenis, ipsâ in Academiâ, quæro, desideróq;) cogito statim nec sine dolore, quanto fructu me mea fraudârit absentia, qui nunquam à te discessi sine manifesta Literarum accessione, & ἐπιδόσει, plane quasi ad Emporium quoddam Eruditionis profectus.

[Indeed, as often as I recollect your almost constant conversations with me (which even in this Athens, the University itself, I long after and miss), I straightway think, and not without grief, of how much benefit my absence from you has deprived me—me, who never left your company without a manifest increase and growth of literary knowledge, just as if I had been to some emporium of learning.]

Milton, Letter to his former teacher at St. Paul's, Alexander Gill, dated July 2, 1628, in *Joannis Miltonii Angli, Epistolarum Familiarium Liber Unus*, London, 1674, p. 11; CM, XII, 10-13. The translation is David Masson's. For Gill, see *DNB* and Arthur Barker, "Milton's Schoolmasters," *Modern Language Review*, XXXII (1937), 517 ff.; a careful study of the two Gills, father and son, is given by Donald L. Clark in "Milton's Schoolmasters: Alexander Gil and his son Alexander," *Huntington Library Quarterly*, IX (1946), 121-147. St. Paul's School and its curriculum in the time of Milton are well described in M. F. J. McDonnell, *A History of St. Paul's School*, London, 1909, pp. 43-44. McDonnell shows that the list of subjects studied by Milton must have included the catechism in English, the accidence, Erasmus's *Institutum Christiani homines* and his *Copia*, Lactantius, Prudentius, Proba, Sedulius, Juvencus, and Mantuan. By 1672, if not earlier, there had been added the Hebrew Psalter or Grammar, Homer, Demosthenes, Persius, Juvenal, "moral themes or declamations," a "divine theme" on Saturdays, minor poets, Greek grammar, Horace, Apollodorus, Cicero's orations, the Greek Testament, Martial, Virgil, Sallust, the turning of the Psalms into Latin verse, Latin grammar, and Ovid (*ibid.*, p. 266). See also John Brinsley, *Ludus Literarius: or, The Grammar Schoole*, 1612, and *A Consolation for our Grammar Schools*, 1622, especially the section entitled "Contents in Generall of svch things as may (by Gods blessing) be easily effected in our ordinarie Grammar schooles" (pp. 52 ff.).

The date when Milton entered St. Paul's is not certain. For Mr. McDonnell's theory that it was 1615, see above under that year. Masson thinks (1, 56 [74]) that "the date of Milton's admission cannot have been later than 1620."

. . . scias, ex quo ludum vestrum relinquerim hoc me unicum atq; primum græce composuisse. . . .

[. . . understand that, since I left your school, this is the first and only thing I have composed in Greek. . . .]

Milton, *Epistolarum Familiarium Liber Unus*, London, 1674, p. 14, letter to Alexander Gill, December 4, 1634; CM, XII, 16-17.

. . . I had from my first yeeres by the ceaselesse diligence and care of my father, whom God recompence, bin exercis'd to the tongues, and some sciences, as my age would suffer, by sundry masters and teachers both at home and at the schools . . . .

Milton, *The Reason of Church Government*, 1641, p. 37; CM, III, 235.

[Milton] had his institution of learning both under public, and private Masters . . .

The "earliest" biography, fol. 140v; Darbishire, p. 18.

He went to schoole to old Mr Gill at Paules schoole . . . .

from his Bro: Chr: Milton. When he went to Schoole, when he was very young he studied very hard and sate-up very late, comonly till 12 or one a clock at night, & his father ordered yᵉ mayde to sitt-up for him, and in those years composed many Copies of Vses: wᶜʰ might well become a riper age.

Aubrey, ff. 63, 64; Darbishire, pp. 2, 10.

... he the said *John Milton* the Author was educated mostly
in *Pauls* School under *Alex. Gill* senior . . . .

Wood, I, 880; Darbishire, pp. 35-36.

John our Author, who was destin'd to be the Ornament and
Glory of his Countrey, was sent, together with his Brother, to
Paul's School, whereof Dr. *Gill* the Elder was then Chief Master; where he was enter'd into the first Rudiments of Learning,
and advanced therein with that admirable Success, not more by
the Discipline of the School and good Instructions of his Masters, (for that he had another Master possibly at his Father's
house, appears by the Fourth Elegy of his Latin Poems written
in his 18th year, to *Thomas Young*, Pastor of the *English* Company of Merchants at *Hamborough*, wherein he owns and stiles
him his Master), than by his own happy Genius, prompt Wit
and Apprehension, and insuperable Industry; for he generally
sate up half the Night, as well in voluntary Improvements of
his own choice, as the exact perfecting of his School-Exercises:
So that at the Age of 15 he was full ripe for Academick Learning.

Phillips, p. viii; Darbishire, pp. 53-54.

STUDIES, GROWTH OF WRITING ABILITY, POETIC AMBI-
TION, AND GENERAL TENOR OF LIFE DURING YOUTH.

I had my time Readers, as others have, who have good
learning bestow'd upon them, to be sent to those places, where
the opinion was it might be soonest attain'd: and as the manner
is, was not unstudied in those authors which are most com-
mended; whereof some were grave Orators & Historians;
whose matter me thought I lov'd indeed, but as my age then
was, so I understood them; others were the smooth Elegiack
Poets, whereof the Schooles are not scarce. Whom both for the
pleasing sound of their numerous writing, which in imitation I
found most easie; and most agreeable to natures part in me,
and for their matter which what it is, there be few who know
not, I was so allur'd to read, that no recreation came to me better
welcome. For that it was then those years with me which are

excus'd though they be least severe, I may be sav'd the labour
to remember ye. Whence having observ'd them to account it the
chiefe glory of their wit, in that they were ablest to judge, to
praise, and by that could esteeme themselves worthiest to love
those high perfections which under one or other name they took
to celebrate, I thought with my selfe by every instinct and pres-
age of nature which is not wont to be false, that what imboldn'd
them to this task might with such diligence as they us'd im-
bolden me, and that what judgement, wit, or elegance was my
share, would herein best appeare, and best value it selfe, by how
much more wisely, and with more love of vertue I should
choose (let rude eares be absent) the object of not unlike praises.
For albeit these thoughts to some will seeme vertuous and com-
mendable, to others only pardonable, to a third sort perhaps
idle, yet the mentioning of them now will end in serious. Nor
blame it Readers, in those yeares to propose to themselves such
a reward, as the noblest dispositions above other things in this
life have sometimes preferr'd. Whereof not to be sensible, when
good and faire in one person meet, argues both a grosse and
shallow judgment, and withall an ungentle, and swainish brest.
For by the firme setling of these perswasions I became, to my
best memory, so much a proficient, that if I found those authors
any where speaking unworthy things of themselves; or unchaste
of those names which before they had extoll'd, this effect it
wrought with me, from that time forward their art I still ap-
plauded, but the men I deplor'd; and above them all preferr'd
the two famous renowners of *Beatrice* and *Laura* who never
write but honour of them to whom they devote their verse, dis-
playing sublime and pure thoughts, without transgression. And
long it was not after, when I was confirm'd in this opinion, that
he who would not be frustrate of his hope to write well hereafter
in laudable things, ought him selfe to bee a true Poem, that is,
a composition, and patterne of the best and honourablest things;
not presuming to sing high praises of heroick men, or famous
cities, unlesse he have in himselfe the experience and the prac-

tice of all that which is praise-worthy. These reasonings, together with a certaine nicenesse of nature, an honest haughtinesse, and self-esteem either of what I was, or what I might be,
(which let envie call pride) and lastly that modesty, whereof
though not in the Title page yet here I may be excus'd to make
some beseeming profession, all these uniting the supply of their
naturall aide together, kept me still above those low descents
of minde, beneath which he must deject and plunge himself,
that can agree to salable and unlawfull prostitutions. Next, (for
heare me out now Readers) that I may tell ye whether my
younger feet wander'd; I betook me among those lofty Fables
and Romances, which recount in solemne canto's the deeds of
Knighthood founded by our victorious Kings; & from hence had
in renowne over all Christendome. There I read it in the oath
of every Knight, that he should defend to the expence of his best
blood, or of his life, if it so befell him, the honour and chastity
of Virgin or Matron. From whence even then I learnt what a
noble vertue chastity sure must be, to the defence of which so
many worthies by such a deare adventure of themselves had
sworne. And if I found in the story afterward any of them by
word or deed breaking that oath, I judg'd it the same fault of
the Poet, as that which is attributed to *Homer*; to have written
undecent things of the gods. Only this my minde gave me that
every free and gentle spirit without that oath ought to be borne
a Knight, nor needed to expect the guilt spurre, or the laying of
a sword upon his shoulder to stirre him up both by his counsell,
and his arme to secure and protect the weakenesse of any attempted chastity. So that even those books which to many others
have bin the fuell of wantonnesse and loose living, I cannot
think how unlesse by divine indulgence prov'd to me so many
incitements as you have heard, to the love and stedfast observation of that vertue which abhorres the society of Bordello's.
Thus from the Laureat fraternity of Poets, riper yeares, and
the ceaselesse round of study and reading led me to the shady
spaces of philosophy, but chiefly to the divine volumes of *Plato*,

and his equall, *Xenophon*. Where if I should tell ye what I learnt, of chastity and love, I meane that which is truly so, whose charming cup is only vertue which she bears in her hand to those who are worthy. . . .

Milton, *An Apology against a Pamphlet*, 1641, pp. 15-17; CM, III, 302-305. Although undated, this passage seems to fit best with the period of Milton's attendance at St. Paul's and is therefore placed with it. The situation undoubtedly prevailed without much change during much of his university career.

JANUARY. MILTON'S FUTURE FATHER-IN-LAW, RICHARD POWELL, PURCHASES WHEATLEY FROM SIR GEORGE SIMEON.

[Concord of fine between Richard Powell of Forest Hill near Oxford and Sir George Simeon, by which Powell acquires two messuages, cottages, eighty acres of land, and other appurtenances in Wheatley for £120. Dated Hilary term (January), 17 James I.]

Public Record Office, CP 25 (2) Oxon., Hil 17 Jac. Milton was to take over this property in 1647.

. . . Richard Powell did purchase ye Messuage in this Jnterrīe [interrogatory] mencōned to him & his heires from Sr George Symeon in this Jnterrīe mencōned & also one Cottage & ye moetye of one yard Land & a halfe wth. Thappteñces in Whately aforesaid. . . .

Deposition of George Ball in Milton-Ashworth suit, January 11, 1655/6, Public Record Office, C22/759/17; French, *Milton in Chancery*, p. 314.

MAY 2. FATHER NAMED IN WILL OF WILLIAM PRIESTLEY, MERCHANT TAYLOR.

Jn the name of God, Amen. The seconde daye of May 1620. . . . J William Pristley Cittizen, and Merchanttaylo^r of London, beinge of good, and perfect memory, thanks be given to God, doe make and declare this my p^rsent Testament in manner, and forme following. . . . My bodie to be buried in Allhallowes Church Breadstreete, in the Jsle where my two wives lye buried. [Then follows a long list of legacies to relatives and friends, of which a few which have some bearing on Milton are given.] . . . Jtem J doe giue and bequeath vnto the M^rs. and Wardens of Merchanttaylo^rs, the some of Two hundred & ffifty pounds in trust, and confidence, for the mayntenñce of eight poore men forever. . . . Jtem, J doe giue and bequēth to Richarde Stocke, and [blank] Culverwell, Preachers of God's worde, the some of Thirty poundes, to be distributed, by them, to poore preache^rs, aboute the Cittye of London. . . . Jtem J doe giue to John Milton, and his wife to buy them Ring℘, the some of Three pound℘. . . . Jn witnesse whereof to this my last will, J the sayde Willyam Preistlye, haue set my hand and seale Dated the day and yeare first abouewritten. William Preistley. . . .

Prerogative Court of Canterbury, London, 39 Soames. I owe this reference to the kindness of Dr. Leslie Hotson. Two interesting connections between the elder Milton and Priestley, in addition to the legacy, appear here. First, Milton's house in Bread Street abutted on a house owned by the Company of Merchant Taylors, of which Priestley was a member. Second, Milton also held, or was to hold, another house called the Rose, also in Bread Street, from the Company of Goldsmiths, from whom Priestley also held a house in Bread Street. On Richard Stocke see Masson, I, 40 (54).

This will was proved on May 31, 1620, by the testator's son William Priestley and his son-in-law John Cason.

MAY 18. FATHER ARRANGES SANDYS-COTTON BOND.

S^r Wm Sandys & oth^rs ℘ obl' Dat' xviij° Maij 1620 . . . 100^li

Thomas Bower's schedule of Cotton's bonds made out by himself and Milton's father; see below under date of November 25, 1630. The original bond has not been found.

. . . Sr Willm Sandys and others by bond dated h^e Eighteenth of [May One thousand] six hundred Twentie, One hundred pound℘ principall debt . . . .

Sir Thomas Cotton's bill; see below under date of May 28, 1636.

MAY 23. FATHER DEPOSES IN WARWICK-SEARLE SUIT.

23. die Maij. *1620* ℘ Warwick
Ano' RR℘. Jac: 18./

John Milton of the parishe of All Saint℘ āls All Hallowes in

Breadstreet London scrivenoʳ, aged 52. yeares, or theraboutₚ sworne &c. by direccōn, vpoñ the 2. & 4ᵗʰ Jnterˢ.

That he doth knowe xp̄fēr Warwick named for the complᵗ: in this Suyte, And this depᵗ sayth he thinketh that he hath heretofore seene all the other ₚsons & parties named in this Jnt. But hath not any certaine knowledge of them, or of any of them, to his now Rem̄brance./

That he knoeth not when the five hundred poundₚ mencōned in this Jnt. was borrowed, or payd againe, Nor when the now Complt: was a Sutor vnto the Company of ffeltmakers of London, to be admitted, & sworne Clerck of the sd Company. But this depᵗ sayth he doth knowe That the Complᵗ: was heretofore accepted of, to be the sd Companies Clercke, But whether vpōn Condicōn That he should pay the sd Sum̄e of five hundred poundₚ, vnto the Late Lo: Harrington, and discharge such as were bound for the same, or not, this depᵗ sayth he doth not knowe, Neyther doth this depᵗ knowe That the complt: was to lend yt five hundred poundₚ, or any other, vnto the sd Company, *gratis*, for a yeare, to bee imployed in their Stocke. And whether that the complᵗ: before he was sworne clercke in the sd Office of Clerckship did deposite the sd five hundred poundₚ, or any other and discharge, and take vp the Security form̄ly given for the same, by the sd Company, wherin any of the sd Company stood bound vnto the sd Lo. Harrington, for the sd five hundred poundₚ, Or whether the Complᵗ: did ₚcure any discharge, vnder the hand and seale of the sd Lo. Harrington, for Banister Loe, Sondₚ, & Sadler, in this Jnᵗ. named, or not this depᵗ sayth, he doth not knowe. Neyther doth this depᵗ knowe any thing els whereof he can materially depose, for satisfying the further Contentₚ of this Jnt.

Jo: Milton

Public Record Office, Chancery Town Depositions, C24/467/97. I owe this reference to the kindness of Dr. Leslie Hotson. The signature is presumably that of the poet's father.

NOVEMBER 19. FATHER ARRANGES CHARNOCK-COT-
TON BOND.

Mr Charnock & oth^{rs} p obl' Dat' xix° Novembr' 1620 . . .
200^{li}

Thomas Bower's schedule of Cotton's bonds made out by himself and
Milton's father; see below under date of November 25, 1630. The
original bond has not been found.

. . . Mr Charnock & others by bond dated the Nynteenth of
November One thowsand six hundred & Twentie Two hundred
pound℘ principall [debt] . . . .

Sir Thomas Cotton's bill; see below under date of May 28, 1636.

DECEMBER 1. FATHER ARRANGES HEATH-COTTON
BOND.

Sr Robt Heath & oth^{rs} p obl' Dat' j Decembr' 1620 . . . 100^{li}

Thomas Bower's schedule of Cotton's bonds made out by himself and
Milton's father; see below under date of November 25, 1630. The
original bond has not been found.

. . . Sr Robert Heath & others by bond dated the Tenth of
December One thowsand six hundred & Twentie One hundred
pound℘ principall [debt] . . . .

Sir Thomas Cotton's bill; see below under date of May 28, 1636.
The schedule and the bill disagree as to date.

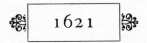

1621

JOHN LANE'S TRIBUTE TO THE POET'S FATHER.

. . . warblinge, dividinge, tewninge, relishinge,
accentinge, airinge, curbinge, orderinge,
those sweet-sweet partes *Meltonus* did compose,
as wonders selfe amazd was at the [c]lose,
wch in a counterpoint mayntaininge hielo,
gann all sum^m vp thus *Alleluia Deo*.

British Museum MS. Reg. 17 B xv, fol. 179v; Hunter, p. 10; Sir
Sidney Lee, "Lane, John," *DNB*; Brennecke, p. 92. Hunter gives the

title as "Triton's Triumph to the Twelve Months," Lee as "Triton's Trumpet to the sweet monethes," and Brennecke as "Triton's Trumpet to the Twelve Months." Brennecke reads "dividinge" as "dicidinge." The word at the end of the fourth line, as written in the manuscript, is almost certainly "lose," but it seems almost sure that the poet must have meant "close," as Hunter reads it. Lee states that there is another manuscript of it at Trinity College, Cambridge—MS. O.ii.68. He also gives the date of completion as 1621 (it was not published), and says that the present copy was dedicated and presented to Charles I when Prince of Wales.

Hunter's "Chorus Vatum," ii (British Museum Add. MS. 24, 489), 85 (143 by another numbering), calls the British Museum copy the dedication copy to Prince Charles, and says that the Trinity copy had also belonged to him. He here entitles it: "Triton's Trumpets to the Twelve Months, husbanded and moralized &c. 1621." He quotes most of the above passage on p. 85v.

FATHER CONTRIBUTES TO RAVENSCROFT'S BOOK OF PSALMS.

[Thomas Ravenscroft, *The Whole Book of Psalmes*, 1621, contains the following numbers set to music by the elder Milton:]

[p. 30, #5] Incline thine eares vnto my vvords.

[p. 62, #27] The Lord is both my health and light.

[p. 106, #55] O God give eare, and doe apply.

[p. 120, #66] Yee men on earth in God reioyce.

[p. 174, #102] O Heare my prayer Lord.

[p. 242, #138] Thee will I praise with my whole heart.

Ravenscroft, *The Whole Book of Psalmes*, 1621; Masson, 1, 38 (51); Brennecke, pp. 98 ff. The two tunes used here are "York" (#27, 66, 138) and "Norwich" (#5, 55, 102). Among "THE NAMES OF THE Authors which Composed the *Tunes*," sig. A3, is "*Iohn Milton.*" Brennecke gives some facsimiles and reproductions. There was a later edition of Ravenscroft's book in 1633.

SCRIVENERS APPRENTICED TO MILTON'S FATHER.

1621 ... Wᵐ Bower—of John. Milton—1599

Ricᵈ. Milton—of John Milton—1599.

Bodleian Library, MS. Rawl. Miscell. 51, fol. 29; *Athenaeum*, 1880, 1, 565; Brennecke, p. 110. The title of the manuscript book is "An Annual Catalogue ... of the Company of Scriveners."

MAY 13. FATHER ARRANGES LEA-COTTON BOND.

Mr Lea & oth^{rs} p obl' Dat' xiij° Maij 1621 . . . 100^{li}

Thomas Bower's schedule of Cotton's bonds made out by himself and Milton's father; see below under date of November 25, 1630. The original bond has not been found.

. . . M^r [Lea and others by bond dated the thirteenth] of May One thousand Six hundred Twentie & one One hundred pound℈ principall debt . . . .

Sir Thomas Cotton's bill; see below under date of May 28, 1636.

MAY 25. FATHER AND JOHN LANE BUY ESTATE FROM LEONARD POE.

This Indenture made the five and twentith day of May in the yeare of our lord god one thousand six hundred twenty and one and in the nyneteenth yeare of the raigne of our soveraigne lord James by the grace of God king of England ffraunce and Ireland defendor of the faith &c and of Scotland the foure and fiftith Betweene leonard Poe of london Doctor of Phisicke of the one part And John Milton Cittizen and Scrivener of london and John lane of london gent of the other part witnesseth that the said leonard Poe for and in consideracōn of the soᵐe of one hundred tenn pound℈ and tenn shilling℈ of lawfull money of England to him the said leonard Poe by the said John Milton at and before thensealing and delivery of theis p̄sent℈ well and truly satisfied and paid the receipt whereof the said leonard Poe doth by theis p̄sent℈ acknowledge and for other good causes and consideracōns him the said Leonard Poe therevnto moving hath geven graunted bargained sold enfeoffed and confirmed and by theis p̄sent℈ doth give graunt bargaine seℓℓ enfeoffe and confirme vnto the said John Milton and John lane and to their heires and assignes forever aℓℓ and singuler the messuag℈ teñt℈ land℈ hereditament℈ good℈ and chattells hereafter in theis p̄sent℈ menc̄oned and expressed that is to say the moytie or one halfe of aℓℓ that one messuage or teñte with the hereditament℈ and app^{r}tenanc℈ therevnto belonging now or late in the occupac̄on of one William Atkins Currier scituate and being neare

the north end of Graies Inne lane in the County of Midd And
also all that one piece or pcell of ground or garden plott sett
lying and being neare vnto the said teñte And alsoe all the
moytie or one half of all that teñte with the hereditam^te and
app^rtenanc̹ therevnto belonging as the same now standeth late
being in the tenure or occupaçon of one [blank] Colt widowe
and now being in the tenure or occupaçon of one William hill
his assignee or assignes scituat and being nere Graies Inne lane
aforesaid vpon the south side of the foote way or passage there
leading betweene Graies Inne lane toward̹ Clarkenwell And
alsoe all that shedd on the backside of the same last mençoned
teñte together with the wast ground lying betweene the same
shedd and the ditch there on the south part thereof And alsoe
one garden or garden plott belonging to the same And alsoe all
that messuage or teñte with the hereditam^te and app^rtenanc̹
therevnto belonging And alsoe the garden on the backside of
the same messuage scituate and being in Aldersgate streete in
the parish of Saint Buttolphes without Aldersgate london now
or late in the tenure or occupaçon of one Thomas Stutevill gent
together alsoe with all such good̹ ymplement̹ and household
stuffe as are mençoned and expressed in an Inventory or Scedule
annexed to an Indenture of lease made to the said Thomas
Stutevill by and from one Ceward Balbie sometime owner of
the p̄misses and alsoe all the right title estate interest vse possession reverçon remainder ꝑperty clayme and demaund whatsoever which he the said leonard Poe his heires or assignes now
hath or hereafter may can might should or ought to have clayme
or demaund of in or to the said messuag̹ tent̹ hereditam^te and
all singuler other the p̄misses with thapp^rtenanc̹ aboue mençoned to be bargained and sold and every part and pcell thereof
And alsoe all and singular deed̹ fynes evidenc̹ charters writ-
ing̹ script̹ and myniment̹ concerning the p̄misses and every
or any of them or any part thereof All and singuler which said
p̄misses were granted to the said leonard Poe by and from one
Thomas Ord of west Ord in the County of Duresme Esquire
To have and to hould all and singuler the said moieties or halfe

[38]

partꝑ of the said twoe first messuageꝑ or tenementꝑ hereditamͭꝑ
and p̄misses aboue bargained and sould or menc̄oned meant or
intended to be hereby bargained and sold with their and every
of their appʳtenancꝑ and every part and pcell thereof scituate
neare Graies Inne lane aforesaid And aƚƚ that the said messuage
or teñte with the appʳtenancꝑ scituate and being in Aldersgate-
streete without Aldersgate aforesaid And all gardens garden
plottꝑ hereditamͭꝑ and aƚƚ and singuler other the p̄misses above
by theis p̄sentꝑ graunted bargained and sould with their appʳtenancꝑ and every part and pceƚƚ thereof vnto the said John
Milton and John lane their heires and assignes to the only and
ꝑper vse and behoofe of them the said John Milton and John
lane their heires and assignes forever And the said leonard Poe
for him his heires executors and administrators and for every
of them doth covenant and graunt to and with the said John
Milton his heires and assignes and to and with every of them
by theis psentꝑ that he the said John Milton his heires and assignes shall or may from henceforth peaceably and quietly haue
hould occupy possesse and enioy aƚƚ and singuler the p̄misses
with thappʳtenancꝑ and every part and pceƚƚ thereof And the
rentꝑ issued and ꝑffitꝑ thereof and of every part thereof shall
or may receave and take to the only vse and behoofe of him the
said John Milton his heires and assignes forever without any
lett trouble interrupc̄on denyaƚƚ or disturbance of or by the said
Leonard Poe his heires or assignes or of or by any other ꝑson
or ꝑsons clayming or which shall or may clayme or p̄tend to
haue any estate or interest in or to the p̄misses or any part
thereof by from or vnder him the said leonard Poe his heires
or assignes cleerly acquited and discharged or sufficiently saued
and kept harmeles of and from aƚƚ manner of former and other
bargaines sales guiftꝑ grauntꝑ Joynctures dowers estates iudg-
mentꝑ execuc̄ons chargꝑ titles trouble and incumbrancꝑ whatsoever by him the said leonard Poe his heires or assignes had made
com̄itted done or suffered or to be had made com̄itted done or
suffered to the contrȳ In witnes whereof the parties abouesaid to

theis p̄sent Jndentures interchangeably haue set their handꝑ and seales yeoven the day and yeare first aboue written.

Et memorand qd die et ann̄ sup'script praefat' leonardus Poe venit coram dtō dnō Rege in Cancellaria sua & recognovit Jndentur' predtam̄ ac omnia & singula in eadem content & spīficat' in forma sūpdtā./ Inᵈ tc̄io die Septembris Ann' p̄dict.

Public Record Office, C54/2477/34; photostatic copies in Harvard College Library (shelf-mark 14495.58PF); Stevens, *Milton Papers*, p. 1; Brennecke, p. 110 (dated May 2); French, *Milton in Chancery*, p. 13. The Latin endorsement at the end of the document bears the name "Bird" in the left-hand margin and the notation "ex'" in the right.

[Translation of Latin endorsement at end:] And be it noted that on the day and year above written the aforesaid Leonard Poe came before the said Lord King in his Chancery and acknowledged the aforesaid indenture and all and every thing contained and specified in the same in the form above written. Indented on the third day of September in the year aforesaid.]

SEPTEMBER 2. FATHER'S INDENTURE WITH JOHN LANE COMPLETED.

Inᵈ tc̄io die Septembris Ann' p̄dict.

This is the endorsement on the document of May 25, *q.v.*

OCTOBER 2. FUTURE FATHER-IN-LAW POWELL ACQUIRES FOREST HILL FROM EDMUND BROME.

. . . one Edmund Brome Esqʳ. by deede dated October 2° 19° Jac. did demise vnto Richard Powell Esqʳ. yᵉ Mannor of fforesthill in yᵉ County of Oxoñ for yᵉ Terme of 20 yeares . . . .

Public Record Office, S P Dom 23/109, p. 521 (John Pye's petition of August 23, 1650); Hamilton, p. 85.

In a bill dated April 19, 1651, John Pye stated that on Oct. 2, 19 James I (which is 1621), he had by indenture transferred the manor and appurtenances of Forest Hill to Richard Powell for twenty years for a consideration of five pounds a year; see the reference for that date. There may, however, be a mistake in the date; see also the entry under November 21, 1621. See French, *Milton in Chancery*, p. 73.

OCTOBER 31. FUTURE FATHER-IN-LAW POWELL TAX-COLLECTOR.

hundr̄ de Bullington dorchester, Thame dī hundr̄ de Ewelme, hundr̄ de lukenor Pirton Bynfeild, et langtræ et Vill de Henley in Com̄ Oxoñ Oct 31, 1621

Com̄pus Richī Powell geñ Coll̄ prim̄ Coluc Scdi Subsid dñor integrz Subsid dño Regi nuc̄ Jacobo . . . apud Westm̄ in Anno regñ s̄ xviij^{no} concess̄ levand et colligend iuxta form̄ et effect Dctūs pliam^t Ac ad re^t : Sttij dcī dnī Rp solvend ad vel ante prim̄ diem Novembr̄ 1621 Sicut coñt in quibusdm̄ Extractp indent inde p Genr̄ Poole mi^1 Johem Doyly et al comissz dnī Rp ibm̄ Thess et Baron huius Sttij Certificat Ac in quadm̄ baga de pticlīs huius Compī in Custod Remem̄ dcī dnī Rp remañ viz de prim̄ Coluc Scdi Subsid p̄d./

Vt Inferius . . . .

Public Record Office, E179/289/31, m. 2; Hunter, p. 29. For another section of the same document, see under date of January, 1621/2. The handwriting of the document is so difficult to read that some letters may be erroneous; and some words after "Jacobo" near the beginning are illegible.

[In abstract form rather than exact translation, the substance of this document is that it is the account of Richard Powell, gentleman, appointed collector of taxes under a statute of King James through Parliament in the eighteenth year of King James for the raising and collecting of money to be paid before November 1, as stated in the statute and signed by the commissioners and on file in the Treasurer's office. The localities concerned are Dorchester, Thame, Ewelme, Lukenor, Pirton Bynfield, Langtrae, Henley, and Bullington.]

NOVEMBER. FUTURE FATHER-IN-LAW POWELL LEASES FOREST HILL.

[Reading's report of January 1, 1650/1, mentions] a former Lease thereof for 20. yeares, which did expire, the first of Nouember 1641. ffor and vnder the yearly rent of 5^{li}.

See entry for January 1, 1650/1. The date, though apparently settled by this reference, may not be correct; see also the entry under October 2, 1621. The original record of the transfer of this property has not been found.

FATHER AS "ASSISTANT" IN SCRIVENERS' COMPANY.

Peter Blower .... Master

W^m. Child ⎫
Jn°: Woodward ⎬..Wardens

John Milton ⎫
Geffery Bower ⎬.........................Assistants taken in

John Warren ⎫
Leon^d. Walworth ⎬..Stewards

Bodleian Library, MS. Rawl. Miscell. 51, fol. 29 ("An Annual Catalogue . . . of the Company of Scriveners"); *Athenaeum*, 1880, I, 565-566, 760-761; Brennecke, p. 110. Hyde Clarke explains the term "assistant" as meaning that Milton was "on the Court of the Company."

LETTERS TO THOMAS YOUNG.

[In a letter to Young dated March 26, 1625, he apologizes to Young:] Quod autem hoc plusquam triennio nunquam ad te scripserim . . . [Of the letters which he has written:] Quereris tu vero (quod merito potes) literas meas raras admodum & perbrevis ad te delatas esse. . . .

[That I should never have written to you for now more than three years. . . . . You complain, indeed, as justly you may, that my letters to you have been as yet few and very short. . . .]

Milton, *Epistolarum Familiarium Liber Unus*, 1674, p. 8; CM, XII, 4-5; CM, XVIII, 526. William R. Parker (*Modern Language Notes*, LIII, 1938, 399 ff.) dated the letter 1627 rather than 1625, and hence dates these previous letters 1624. The letters here referred to have not been found.

JANUARY. FUTURE FATHER-IN-LAW POWELL ASSESSED IN FOREST HILL.

> hillaꝝ bea' tnno xix°.
>
> Rꝑ Jacobi R° R

hundꝝ de Bullington . . .

Reᵗ: Denaꝝ./ Idem ꝝ Compiñ de cc xxviiiˡⁱ xvijˢ pdcū CoꝈ reᵗ de prim̄ Coluc Scdī Subsid p̄d in hundꝝ pred assessat et taxat ac ad reᵗ Sttiȷ̄ (vt p̄d est Solvend Sicut continet in p̄d Extract indentat inde sup hunc Compiñ libāt et exaiat iuxta form̄ et effect Dctus pliamᵗ p̄d xxxviijˡⁱ xvjˢ . . . ꝓvenien de p̄d pm̄a Coluc Scdi Subsid p̄d assessat et taxat Sup dm̄s ꝑson sequeñ Viz . . .

Ricū Powell de fforresthill geñ xxixˢ iijᵈ

Public Record Office, E179/289/31, m. 2; Hunter, p. 29; French, *Milton in Chancery*, p. 73. This is a part of the same document from which another extract was quoted under date of October 31, 1621.

[The substance of this document, in abstract, is that of the £228-17-0 subsidy described above in the same writing, Richard Powell of Forest Hill has the share of 29s. 3d.]

FEBRUARY 9. FATHER LENDS FIFTY POUNDS TO EDWARD RAYMOND.

. . . whereas one Edward Raymonde in or about the Moneth of ffebruarie in the ninetenth yeare of the Raigne of our Soueraigne the Kingꝑ māᵗⁱᵉ that now is did borrowe and take vp at interest of one Joh Milton a Scriuener in London the sūme of ffiftie powndꝑ for sixe moneths for securitie whereof your Orator at the instance and requeste of the said Edward Raymonde . . . was Content to become bounde wᵗʰ the said Edward Raymonde as his suerty . . . by their Obligacōn beareing date vppon or about the ninthe day of ffebruarie in the said nynetenth yeare of his Maiesties raigne . . . to one John llane in whose name the said Milton now affirmes he took the said bonde. . . .

Public Record Office, C2 James I/A6/35 (James Ayloffe's bill against the elder Milton); French, *Milton in Chancery*, pp. 23, 221.

. . . in or aboute the time in the bill of Complainte mencōned One Edward Raymond . . . together wth the said Comp^{lt}. Ayloffe became bound by obligacōn to one John Lane in the sōme of One hundred poundȝ for paym^{t}. of ffiftie two poundȝ. and Tenn shillingȝ On or aboute the Eleaventh daie of August then following. . . .

Public Record Office, C2 James I/A6/35 (Milton's answer to Ayloffe); French, *Milton in Chancery*, pp. 25, 224.

MARCH 6. FATHER DEPOSES IN FREERE SUIT.

6. Marcij 1621.   p ffreere Baronett'
A° Jacobi Rȝ xix°.

[March 6, 1621/2, in the 19th year of King James. On behalf of Freere, Baronet.]

1   *John Milton* of the parrish of All hollowes in Breadstreet London Scriveñ of the age of 57. yeares or thereaboutȝ sworne and exaīed &c'. That he doth knowe Sr Edward ffreere Baronett named for Complt and thinketh he hath seene the deft when he was a youth and saieth he doth also very well knowe Phillippe Pittȝ of Iffly and the Close or ground neare Stow wood in the Countye of Oxoñ Comonly called Stowford Close belonging to Oriall Colledge in Oxford in the arcle enquired of./

2.   That he doth verie well rem̄ber that about some five or six yeares agone as he thinketh but this dept doth not certeinly rember the tyme, the now Complt Sr Edward ffrere as suertye for the sd Phillippe Pittȝ did enter into one bond wth the s̄d Phillip Pittȝ and for his the sd Phillips debt togather wth Symon Pittȝ in the arcle menconed sonne of the s̄d Phillip in the penall som̄e of CC^{li}. Condiconed for the paym̄t of 105^{li}. at a certeine daye in the Condicon of the sd bond mencōned vnto William Campion of Gowdhurst in the County of Kent then gentlmañ and now kn^{t}, for he saieth that the same bond was made at his this dept^{ȝ} shoppe and the hundred poundes so lent vppon that securitie was delivered at his this dept^{ȝ} s̄d shoppe vnto the s̄d Phillipp Pittȝ whoe was principall in the s̄d bond and whoe had that mony and not the now Complt, and tuching the other bond

of 160ˡⁱ. in the arc̄le enquired of this dept saieth that he never knew nor heard of any such before now to his now rem̄brance and therefore cannot further satisffie this Jnter'./

To the rest of the Jnterrs' he is not to be exaīed by direccoñ

Jo: Milton:

Public Record Office, Chancery Town Depositions, C24/486/28. This record was found by Mr. Charles A. Bernau. It has not previously been published.

APRIL 3. FATHER SELLS LAND IN LONDON TO JAMES KENT.

Milton et Kent 32

This Indenture made the third day of Aprill Anno dñi 1622 and in the twentith yere of the reigne of our soūeigne lord James by the grace of god king of England ffraunce & Ireland defendor of the faith &c and of Scotland the five and fiftieth Betweene John Milton Citizen and Scrivenor of london and John lane of london gent of thone part And James Kent Citizen & Barbor-chirurgeon of london of the other part witnesseth that the said John Milton & John lane for and in consideracōn of the some of forty and five poundᵽ of lawfull money of England to him the said John Milton by the said James Kent at and before thensealing & delivery of theis p̄sentᵽ well and truly satisfied & paid the receipt whereof the said John Milton doth by theis p̄sentᵽ acknowledge & thereof and of every part thereof they the said John Milton and John Lane and either of them doe & doth clerely acquite exonāte & discharge the said James Kent his heires executors & assignes and every of them forever by theis p̄sentᵽ haue bargained sold enfeoffed & confirmed and by theis p̄sentᵽ doe fully & absolutely bargaine selł enfeoffe & confirme vnto the said James Kent and to his heires & assignes foreū the moytie or one halfe of ałł that one mesuage or teñte with the hereditamᵗᵽ and appʳtenn̄cᵽ therevnto belonging now or late in the occupacōn of one William Atkins Currier scituate and being neare the north end of Graies Jnn lane in the County of Midd. And alsoe the moytie or one halfe of one peece

or pcell of ground or garden plott sett lying & being neare vnto
the said teñte And alsoe aɫɫ the moytie or one halfe of aɫɫ that
teñte with the hereditamᵗꝑ & appʳtenñcꝑ therevnto belonging
as the same now standeth late being in the tenure or occupacōn
of one [blank] Cowlt widowe and now being in the tenure or
occupacōn of one Richard Hiɫɫ his assignee or assignes scituate
& being neere Grayes Jnn lane aforesaid vpon the south side of
the foote way or passage there leading from Graies Jnn lane
towardꝑ Clarkenwell And alsoe the moytie or one halfe of all
that shedd on the backside of the same last mencōned teñte
togeather with the wast ground lying betweene the same shedd
& the ditch there on the south part thereof & also the moytie
or one halfe of one garden or garden plott belonging to the
same And alsoe all the right title estate interest vse possession
revercōn remainder pperty rent and rentꝑ & clayme & demaund
whatsoeū which they the said John Milton and John lane or
either of them haue or hath or may can might should or ought
to have clayme or demaund of in or to the said moyties of the
said teñtꝑ & p̄misses with thappʳtenñcꝑ above mencōned to be
hereby bargained & sold and every part & pceɫɫ thereof And
alsoe aɫɫ and singuler deedꝑ evidencꝑ charters writingꝑ scriptꝑ
& minimentꝑ concerning the p̄misses only or only any part thereof Aɫɫ and singuler which said p̄misses were heretofore graunted
bargained & sold by and from Thomas Ord of west Ord in the
County of Durham Esquier to leonard Poe of london Doctor
of Phisick and by and from the said leonard Poe to them the
said John Milton and John lane As by the severaɫɫ Jndentures
of bargaine & sale thereof wherevnto relacōn being had more
at large it doth & may appeare To have & to hold aɫɫ & singuler
the said moyties or halfe partꝑ of the said twoe mesuagꝑ or
teñtꝑ hereditamᵗꝑ & aɫɫ other the p̄misses hereby bargained &
sold or herein mencōned ment or intended to be hereby bargained & sold with their and every of their appʳtenñcꝑ and
every part & pcell thereof vnto the said James Kent his heires
& assignes to thonely & pper vse & behoofe of the said James
Kent and of his heires and assignes foreū And the said John

Milton for him and his heires executors & administrators doth
covennt & graunt to and with the said James Kent his heires
and assignes and to and with every of them by theis p̄sentꝑ in
manner & forme following that is to say that he the said James
Kent his heires & assignes shałł or may from henceforth peaceably & quietly haue hold occupy possesse & enioy ałł & singuler
the p̄misses with thappʳtenncꝑ and every part and ꝑcell
thereof and the rentꝑ issues & ꝑfittꝑ thereof and of every part
thereof shall or may receive & take to thonly vse & behoofe of
him the said James Kent his heires and assignes foreū without
any lawful let trouble interrupcōn denyall or disturbance of
or by the said John Milton & John lane or either of them their
or either of their heires or assignes or of or by the said leonard
Poe his heires or assignes or of or by any other ꝑson or ꝑsons
clayming or which shall or may clayme or p̄tend to haue any
estate or interest of in or to the p̄misses or any part thereof by
from or vnder them the said John Milton John lane & leonard
Poe or any of them or by or from or vnder their or any of their
act or actꝑ meanes consentꝑ or ꝑcurementꝑ And that the same
p̄misses hereby bargained & sold or herein mencōned ment or
intended to be hereby bargained & sould & every part & ꝑcell
of the same now at the tyme of thensealing & delivery hereof
are & be & doe from henceforth forwardꝑ foreū shall or may
remayne contynue endure & be vnto the said James kent his
heires & assignes cleere & free & cleerly & freely acquited ex-
oñated & discharged or by the said John Milton his heires or
assignes saved & kept harmeles of & from all & all manner of
former & other bargaines sales guiftꝑ grauntꝑ leases ioyntures
dowers estates iudgmtꝑ execucōns chargꝑ titles troubles & incombrancꝑ whatsoeū by them the said John Milton John lane
and leonard Poe or any of them their or any of their heires or
assignes had made committed done or suffered to the contr̄y
And the said John Milton for himselfe his heires executors &
administrators doth further covennt ꝑmise & graunt to and with
the said James kent his heires & assignes by theis p̄sentꝑ that he
the said John Milton and Sara his wife & either of them and

the heires of the said John Milton for and during the tyme &
space of seaven yeres next ensueing the date of theis p̃sentꝑ shaℓℓ
and wiℓℓ vpon the reasonable request & at the costꝑ & chargꝑ in
law of the said James kent his heires or assignes make doe
acknowledge execute & suffer & cause to be made done acknowledged executed & suffered aℓℓ & every such further & other act
& actꝑ thing & thingꝑ devise & devises assurance & assurancꝑ in
the law for the further better & more absolute conveying assur-
ing & setling of aℓℓ and every the p̃misses above hereby bargained & sold or herein mencōned ment or intended to be hereby bargained & sold to the said James kent his heires & assignes
to the only vse & behoofe of him the said James kent & of his
heires & assignes forever be it by deed or deedꝑ enrolled or not
inrolled the acknowledging & enrolemᵗ of theis p̃sentꝑ fyne
feoffemᵗ recovery with single or double voucher or vouchers
with warranties only against the said John Milton & his heires
or without warranty as by the said James kent his heires or assignes or by his or their Councell learned in the lawes of this
realme of England shalbe reasonably devised advised & required so as the said John Milton & Sara his wife be not compelled to traveℓℓ or go further then to the Citties of London
& Westm̃ in the County of Midd for the executing or doinge
of the same assurance or assurancꝑ And lastly it is covenñted
graunted agreed & declared by and betweene the said pties to
theis p̃sentꝑ that aℓℓ & every such fyne & fynes recovery & recoveries conveyance & conveyancꝑ assurance & assurancꝑ as by
and betweene the said parties to theis p̃sentꝑ or either of them
their or either of their heires or assignes shalbe had made
knowledged levied executed or passed of for touching or con-
cñing the p̃misses hereby bargained & sould or any part or pcell
thereof shalbe & invre and shalbe adiudged deemed & taken to
be & invre to and for the only ꝑper vse & behoofe of the said
James Kent and of his heires & assignes forever and to and for
none other vse intent or p̃pose Jn witneš whereof the said pties
to theis indentures sonderly haue set their handꝑ & seales dated
the day & yeares first above written

Et memorand qd die et ann' suꝑscript' prefat' Johēs Milton venit coram dtō dnō Rege in Cancellar' sua & recognouit Jndentur' pred ac oīnia & singula in eadem content' & spīficat' in forma sūpdtā Ac etiam memorand qd octauo die Julij ann' sūpscript' prefat' Johēs Lane gener' venit coram dtō dnō Rege in Canc' sua & recognouit Jndentur' pred ac oīnia & singula in ead content' & spīfic' in forma sūpdtā Jnd vndecimo die Julij Ann' pdict' ex^r

Public Record Office, C54/2525/m.32; photostatic copies in the Harvard College Library (shelf-mark 14495.58PF); French, *Milton in Chancery*, p. 13. In the margin of the Latin endorsement at the end appear the names "Bird" and "Hayward."

[Be it noted that on the day and year abovewritten the aforesaid John Milton came before the said Lord King in his Chancery and acknowledged the aforesaid indenture and all and singular contained and specified in it in the form above written. And also be it noted that on the eighth day of July in the year above written the aforesaid John Lane gentleman came before the said Lord King in his Chancery and acknowledged the aforesaid indenture and all and singular contained and specified in the same in the form above written. Indented on the eleventh day of July in the year aforesaid.]

AUGUST. FATHER RECEIVES INTEREST AND CONTINUES BOND OF EDWARD RAYMOND.

... the said Milton ... Did at the ende of those six moneths ... receaue the interest then due for the said money and contynued the said money at interest for six moneths longer vpon the said securitye. ...

Public Record Office, C2 James I/A6/35 (bill of James Ayloffe); French, *Milton in Chancery*, pp. 21, 221.

And this def^t doth also denie y^t for anie reward giuen to him by the said Raymond, or by anie aggreem^tº. between them (other then the consideracōn for the said Six monethes paste) he did continue the said money at interest. ...

Public Record Office, C2 James I/A6/35 (Milton's answer); French, *Milton in Chancery*, pp. 21-22, 224.

OCTOBER 16. EDWARD, THOMAS, AND ROBERT WIL-
LOUGHBY GIVE BONDS TO WILLIAM SMITH.

. . . Edwardus Willughby . . . smn' fuit ad respondend' Willō
Smith de plīto qd' reddat ei ducentas libras quas ei debet &
iniuste detinet &c vnde idem Will's p henricum hodgkinson'
Attorn' suu' dic' qd' cum p'dcus Edrus' decimo sexto die Octobris Anno regni dnī Regis nunc Angli &c vicesimo . . . [Simi-
larly to Thomas and Robert Willoughby]

Public Record Office, Plea Rolls, 21/22 James I, CP40/2137/
m.3030 (judgment granted in Hilary term, 1623/4, to William
Smith); French, *Milton in Chancery*, pp. 28, 228. The purport of this
entry, of which only a fragment is given here, is that the Willoughbys
gave bond to William Smith on October 16, 1622, for £200. It seems
possible that one provision of the bond was that payment should be made
at the shop of Milton's father, and perhaps that the elder Milton drew
the bond. At any rate, the transaction was the beginning of a process
which eventually culminated in a Chancery suit of Samuel Burton against
Milton on May 10, 1626, *q.v.*

It seems highly likely that this is the bond referred to in Burton's bill
under the following terms: ". . . whereas [about] Three Yeares laste
paste one Robert Willoughbie late Citizen and Grocer of London Together wth Thomas Willoughbie the elder of Sutton Colefield in the
Countie of Warrwicke gentleman, and [Edward] Willoughbie the
Yonger Citizen and Linnen Draper of London became bound vnto one
William Smith by his addition styled to bee Citizen and Mercer of London in the penall somme of two hundred pounds [condicōned] for the
paim^t of one hundred Pounds wth the Jnterest therevppon due at a Day
now past . . ." (For fuller text, see below under date of May 10, 1626.)

[Edward Willoughby was summoned to reply to William
Smith about a plea that he should repay him two hundred
pounds which he owes him and unjustly detains, etc. Whereupon the same William (Smith) by his attorney Henry Hodgkinson says that whereas the aforesaid Edward on the sixteenth
day of October in the twentieth year of the reign of our Lord
the now King of England, etc. . . .]

NOVEMBER 6. EDWARD AND THOMAS WILLOUGHBY
GIVE BOND TO THOMAS PARADINE.

. . . Edwardus Willughby nup de london' Ar alias dcus'

Edwardus Willughby de Sutton' Coldfeild' in Com' Warr'
Armig' . . . dic qd' cum p'dcus Edwardus sexto die Novembris
Anno regnī dnī Regis nunc Angl' Etc vicesimo apud london'
in parochia bē marie de Arcubz in Warda de Cheape p queddam
scriptum suī obligatorū concessisset se teneri' eidem Thome
[Paradine] in p'dcis trescentis libris soluend' eidem Thome
cum inde requisit' fuisset. . . . [This form is repeated for
Thomas Willoughby.]

Public Record Office, Plea Rolls, 21/22 James I, CP40/2137/
m.3030 (judgment granted in Hilary term, 1623/4, to Thomas Paradine); French, *Milton in Chancery*, pp. 28, 227. On the possible connection of Milton's father with this transaction, see the similar entry
for October 16, 1622.

[Edward Willoughby, late of London, gentleman, alias
Edward Willoughby of Sutton Coldfield, co. Warwick, gentleman . . . says that whereas the aforesaid Edward on the sixth
day of November in the twentieth year of the reign of our Lord
now King of England etc. at London in the parish of St. Mary
of the Arches in the ward of Cheapside by a certain writing of
his obligations granted that he held himself indebted to the
same Thomas Paradine in the aforesaid three hundred pounds,
to be paid to the said Thomas whenever it should be demanded.
. . .]

AUTUMN? FATHER DEMANDS REPAYMENT OF RAY-
MOND LOAN AND THREATENS COURT ACTION.

. . . Mīchas terme then folloing [i.e., after the payment of
the first interest on the loan, namely in August, 1622], and then
this Defᵗ. sente to the said Raymond, and pressed him that in
freindly and Curtuous mañ he wold repaie the said ffiftie
poundꝗ or otherwise he should be compelled to comence suite
both against him the said Raymond, and against the said Compˡᵗ.
Ayloffe. And the said Defᵗ. haueing often called and sent vnto
the said Raymond for his said Money. . . .

Public Record Office, C2 James I/A6/35 (Milton's answer to
Ayloffe's bill); French, *Milton in Chancery*, p. 224.

NOVEMBER 28. FATHER ARRANGES CARRENT-COTTON BOND.

Mr Carrent & oth^{rs} p obl' Dat' xxviij° Novembr' 1622 . . . 100^{li}

Thomas Bower's schedule of Cotton's bonds made out by himself and Milton's father; see below under date of November 25, 1630.

. . . Mr Carrent & others by bond dated the Eight & twentieth of November One thowsand six hundred Twentie Two One hundred pound₡ principall debt.

Sir Thomas Cotton's bill; see below under date of May 28, 1636.

OWNS OVID'S "METAMORPHOSES" (?)

The late Hugh C. H. Candy owned a copy of *Iohan. Posthii Germershemii Tetrasticha in Ovidii Metamor. Lib. XV*, Frankfurt, 1563, in which many stanzas had been written in manuscript. He was convinced that the writing was Milton's, and that the book had been Milton's property. If so, the likeliest period for him to have acquired the book and written such verses would have been fairly early, probably during his years in the university. Though few scholars have accepted Candy's thesis, the book is included here on the chance that he may have been correct. For bibliography, see Stevens, #2484, 2569, 2672-74; J. M. French, "The Autographs of John Milton," *ELH*, IV (1937), 301 ff., #56; CM, XVIII, 601.

ALLEGED PORTRAIT.

Ao. 1623. aet. suae 12.

The *Gentleman's Magazine* carried in 1787 (Vol. LVII, pp. 758-759, 892) a description and a poor reproduction of a drawing on wood bearing the inscription quoted above. The writer believed that it was a portrait of Milton. The subject of the picture has red hair and bears a copy of Homer's *Iliad*. The later history of the drawing is unknown, and Dr. Williamson (*Milton Tercentenary*, 1908, p. 3) doubts its authenticity.

JANUARY-FEBRUARY. FATHER ENTERS ACTION AGAINST RAYMOND AND AYLOFFE.

And the said Def.^t haueing often called and sent vnto the said Raymond for his said Money, and finding that he cold not haue it by faire meanes in Hillary terme then following deliuered the said obligacōn to an Attorney in his said Maties. Co^{rt}. of Comon pleas at Westm' to comence sute against the said Raymond, and the said Cōmp^{lt}. Ayloffe.

Public Record Office, C2 James I/A6/35 (Milton's answer to Ayloffe's bill); French, *Milton in Chancery*, p. 224. For the course of this action and its later abandonment, see Milton's complete answer as given under date of May 10, 1624, below. The action was dropped because of a compromise arrangement by which Raymond paid part of the amount due and gave new surety for the remainder. The date is made clear by (1) the fact that Hilary term extends from January 23 to February 12, and by (2) the phrase "then following," which refers to an interest payment by Raymond in the summer of 1622 and conferences between him and Milton shortly afterwards.

FEBRUARY 7. FRIEND CHARLES DIODATI MATRICULATES AT TRINITY COLLEGE.

Collegium Trinitatis Vicecancellario D^{ore} Peirs Anō.
Dnī: 1622°. . . . febr: 7°. . . . Carolus Deodatus:
Middlesexia: fil: Theodori Deōd: de London in Medicina Do^{ri}. an: nat' - - - - - - - - - - - - - - - - } —13

Cambridge University Matriculation Register, p. 126. I owe to my friend Professor Donald Dorian the courtesy of allowing me to see the photostatic copy of this entry in his possession. There has previously been an extraordinary amount of argument and disagreement about this date, which could have been settled once for all by resort to the register, which is unequivocal. The date has previously been placed all the way from 1621 (Warton, Todd), through 1622 (Masson, Gardiner, Venn), to 1623 (Masson [1881 edition of *Life*], Foster, Blakiston). It is interesting to note that the entry of Nathaniel Gill, son of Milton's former teacher Alexander Gill of London, occurs on the same page.

[Trinity College, Dr. Peirs, Vice-Chancellor, A.D. 1622 (i.e., 1622/3), February 7: Charles Diodati of Middlesex, son of Theodore Diodati of London, M.D., at the age of 13.]

MARCH 26. FATHER BRINGS ACTION AGAINST RAYMOND IN LORD MAYOR'S COURT AND SECURES JUDGMENT.

. . . the said Edward Raymonde vppon or about the sixe and twentieth day of March in the one and twentieth yeare of his ma^ties said raigne haueing before that payed a great pte of the said debte to the said Milton . . . did acknowledge a Judgment before the Lord Mayor and aldermen of the Citie of London in the Chamber of Gin-hale London to the said John llane for one hundred pownd℔ debt and one penny cost℔ wch the said John llane remitted to ffourty pownd℔. . . . And the said John Milton according to the said former agreement did agree vnder his hand by way of defeazancing of the said Judgment to stay execution for the residue of the said debte . . . to be payd at ffower seuerall dayes then to Come . . . after the accknowleging of wch Judgment the said Raymond satisfied and payd to the said Milton all or w^thin a small deale of the residue. . . .

Public Record Office, C2 James I/A6/35 (bill of James Ayloffe); French, *Milton in Chancery*, p. 222.

. . . this def^t . . . did accordingly bring an accōn in the Lorde Maio^rs. Co^rt. in the Citie of London vpon the said obligacōn. . . . He the said Raymond intreated the def^t . . . that he would grante him some respite of time for the paym^t . . . where vpon this def^t . . . was content to accepte of Tenn pownd℔ in hand, and the remainder being ffourtie pownd℔ to take by Tenn pownd℔ a quarter. . . .

Public Record Office, C2 James I/A6/35 (Milton's answer); French, *Milton in Chancery*, p. 225.

MAY? BOND OF EDWARD, ROBERT, AND THOMAS WILLOUGHBY TO WILLIAM SMITH.

See above under date of October 16, 1622, note. Although the wording of the reference from Burton's bill of May 10, 1626 ("Three Yeares laste paste"), would seem to place the bond in May of 1623, there is sufficient latitude and inaccuracy in most such references to make it quite normal that a note of October 16, 1622, should be mentioned in May 10, 1626, as being dated "about three years ago." Furthermore, it is likely that the bill was prepared some weeks before it was actually presented, a fact which would bring the two dates more closely together.

MAY 17. FATHER ARRANGES MOLINEUX-COTTON BOND.

Sr Ric' Molineux & oth^rs p obl' Dat' xvij° Maij 1623 . . . 100^li

Thomas Bower's schedule of Cotton's bonds made out by himself and Milton's father; see below under date of November 25, 1630. The original bond has not been found.

. . . Sr Richard Molineux & others by bond dated the Seventeenth of May One thousand [six] hundred Twentie & three [one hundred pound℥ principall debt].

Sir Thomas Cotton's bill; see below under date of May 28, 1636.

MAY 21. FATHER ARRANGES BANNESTER-COTTON BOND.

Mr Bannester & oth^rs p obl' Dat' xxj° Maij 1623 . . . 100^li

Thomas Bower's schedule of Cotton's bonds made out by himself and Milton's father; see below under date of November 25, 1630. The original bond has not been found.

. . . Mr Bannister & others by bond dated ye One & Twentieth [of] May One thowsand Six [hundred twenty three] One hundred pound℥ principall debt.

Sir Thomas Cotton's bill; see below under date of May 28, 1636.

MAY 26. FATHER'S SERVANTS WITNESS COPINGER-RANDOLPH INDENTURE.

This Indenture made the Six and twentith daie of Maie in the yeare of our Lord God One thowsand six hundred twentie and three . . . [an indenture of contract to title of houses and property in Fishtoske, Lincolnshire, sold by Edward Copinger of Kirtlington, Nottinghamshire, to Ambrose and Robert Randolph of London] Seald and deliũed in ye pnce of

John Hutton
Thomas Bower svants to Jo: Milton Sr.

Public Record Office, SP 14/145/36; Hamilton, pp. 44-45; Masson, I (1881), 62-63; Brennecke, p. 110. Since Milton did not witness the document himself, it has not seemed necessary to give the complete text. Brennecke transcribes Hutton's name as Hatton.

SUMMER? FATHER RECEIVES TEN POUNDS MORE FROM RAYMOND, WHO SOON DIES.

And this defd^t saith That the said Raymond made paym^t. of the said first Tenn pound$_e$ of the said remainder of ffourtie pound$_e$ and dyed verry shortely after . . . .

Public Record Office, C2 James I/A6/35 (Milton's answer); French, *Milton in Chancery*, p. 225. Though the time is not specified, this payment followed shortly after the action of March 26, 1623, in the Lord Mayor's Court, and presumably on or about the date agreed on for the first payment of ten pounds, namely Midsummer Day.

JUNE 11. FATHER DEPOSES IN BOLD-LEEKE SUIT.

11° die Junij *1623*   ꝑ Bould
An° R R$_e$ Jacobi 21°

[June 11, 1623, in the 21st year of the reign of King James. On behalf of Bold.]

John Milton Cyttyzen & Scrivener of london of the parish of Allhallowes Breadestrete, Aged 58 yeares or thereabout$_e$
1.   sworne &c To the first Jnterr: sayth That he knoweth Edward Bould named for the Comp^{lt} in this suite, And hath heretofore seene S^r ffrancis Leeke kn^t named for one of the def^{te} in this suite, but he should not knowe hym if he should now see hym, nor doth this dep^t knowe any of the other def^{te} in this suite, nor doth this dep^t knowe the manno^r in the Jnterr. menc̄oned./

[He knows nothing in answer to any of the other questions asked him.] . . .   Jo: Milton

Public Record Office, Chancery Town Depositions, C24/499/15. Mr. Charles Bernau found this document for me. This is the first publication of it.

JULY 4. FATHER ARRANGES A BOND FROM EDWARD EWER TO SIR PETER TEMPLE AND OTHERS.

Novīnt vniūsi ꝑ p̄ntes me Edrūm Ewer de Bucknell in Com̄ Oxoñ Armiger' Teneri et firmiter obligari Thome Temple de Stowe in Com̄ Buck$_e$ Milit' et Baronet' Petro Temple Milit' filio et herēd apparen̄ Dc̄i Thome et Joh̄i Lentall de Blechindon in Com̄ Bērkᵽ Milit' in Cent' et quinquagint' libris legl̄is monet' Anglie Solvēnd eīsd Thome Petro et Joh̄i aut eorū vni sive eorū cert' Attorn Executor' vel Adm̄istr' suis Ad qm̄ quidem solu-coēm bene et fidelr' facien̄d Obligo me herēd executor' et ad-m̄istrator' meos firmiter p pn̄tes Sigillo meo sigillat' Dat' Quarto die Julij *1623* Annoqz RRᵽ dn̄i nr̄i Jacobi Anglie &c' vicesimo primo ac Scotie quinquagesimo sexto:./

The Condicōn of this obligacōn is such That whereas the above named Sʳ Thomas Temple Sʳ Peter Temple and Sʳ John Lentall at the request and for the only debt of the above bound Edward Ewer by one obligacōn of the date above written stand bound vnto John Palmer Citizen & Habērd of London in One Hun-dred poundᵽ for the paymᵗ of ffifty Twoe poundᵽ and Ten shillingᵽ At the nowe dwelling howse of John Milton Scriven̄ Scituat in Breadstreete London On the Sixt day of January next ensueing the date above written If therfore the said Edward Ewer his heires executoʳs adm̄istratoʳs or assignes or any of them doe well & truly pay or cause to be paid to the said John Palmer his executoʳˢ, adm̄istratoʳˢ or assignes the sōm of ffifty Twoe poundᵽ and Ten shillingᵽ of lawfull money of England On the day and at the place of paymᵗ thereof aforesaid in dis-charge of the recited obligacōn And doe at all times save and keepe harmeles the said Sʳ Thomas Temple Sʳ Peter Temple & Mʳ John Lentall theire heires executoʳˢ & adm̄istratoʳˢ & eūy of them Of and from the said recited obligacōn That then this obligacōn to be voyde Or else to stand & abyde in full force and vertue./

p me Edwardū Ewer.

Sealed & deliūed in the pn̄ce of
Henry Gibbs
Jo: Smith

Henry E. Huntington Library; French, "John Milton, Scrivener, The Temples of Stowe, and Sir John Lenthall," *The Huntington Li-brary Quarterly*, IV (1941), 303-305. Since the terms of the bond as quoted mention Milton's house in Bread Street as the place where the debt is to be settled, it seems likely that he arranged the transaction. The bond between the Temples and John Palmer mentioned here, also probably arranged by Milton, has not been found.

[Know all men by these presents that I, Edward Ewer of Bucknell in Co. Oxford, gentleman, hold and firmly obligate myself to Thomas Temple of Stowe in Co. Bucks, knight and baronet, to Peter Temple, knight, son and heir apparent of the said Thomas, and to John Lenthall of Blechindon in Co. Berks, knight, in one hundred fifty pounds of lawful money of England, to be paid to the said Thomas, Peter, and John or their or any of their designated attorneys, executors, or administrators, for which payment, well and faithfully to be made, I oblige myself, my heirs, executors, and administrators firmly by these presents. Sealed with my seal. Given this fourth day of July, 1623, and in the twenty-first year of our Lord James, King of England, and of Scotland the fifty-sixth.]

JULY 4. FATHER ARRANGES BOND BETWEEN SIR PETER TEMPLE AND SIR THOMAS TEMPLE AND OTHERS.

Noverint vniūsi per p̄ntes me Petrū Temple Milit' filiū et Herēd apparent' Thome Temple de Stowe in Cõm Buckₚ Milit et Baronet', teneri et firmiter obligari p̄'dict' Thome Temple et Johī Lentall de Blechindon in Cõm Oxoñ Milit.' in Sexcent' libris legalīs monet' Anglie Solveñd eisdem Thome Temple, et Johī Lentall, aut eorū alteri siue eorū certo Attorñ, executor' vel admīstrator' suis, Ad qm̄quidem solucōnem bene et fidelr' facieñd, Obligo me hered, executor', et admīstrator' meos firmiter p p̄ntes, Sigillo meo sigillat' Dat' quarto die Julij 1623. Annoqz RRₚ dnī nrī Jacobi Anglie &c Vicesimo primo et Scotie quinquagesimo Sexto:./

The condicōn of this obligacōn is such; That whereas the aboue named Sʳ. Thomas Temple, and Sʳ. John Lentall at the request and for thonely debte of the aboue bound Sʳ. Peter Temple by Two obligacōns of the date aboue written, standeth bound wᵗʰ the said Sʳ. Peter Temple, That is to saie by one of the same obligacōns vnto Rōbte Hassard of London gentleman, in Two hundred pounds, Condicōned for the paym^t. of One hundred and five poundȝ At the now dwelling house of John Milton Scriven' scituate in Breadstreete London, On the Sixte daie of January next ensueing the date aboue written, and by thother of the same obligacōns vnto George Sheires of the citie of Westm' Esquio^r in Two hundred poundȝ, Condicōned for the paym^t. of One hundred & ffive poundȝ At the place of paym^t. thereof aforesaid, On the said Sixte daie of January next, If therefore the said S^r. Peter Temple his heires, executo^{rs}. admīstrato^{rs}. or assignes, or anie of them doe well and truly paie or cause to be paid to the said Rōbte Hassard, and George Sheires theire executo^{rs}. admīstrato^{rs}. or assignes seūally and respectiuely the seūall somes aboue specified on the daie and at the place of paym^t. thereof aforesaid according to the seūall condicōns of the seūall recited obligacōns indischarge of the same obligacōns, And doe at all times saue and keepe the said S^r. Thomas Temple, and S^r. John Lentall their heires, execanto^{rs}, & admīstrato^{rs}. and all their landȝ, tēntȝ, goodȝ, and chattellȝ and eūy of them, of and from the said seūall obligacōns and of and from all accōns, suitȝ, costȝ, losses, paiem^{tȝ}. and damagȝ concerning the same or either of them, That then this obligacōn to be voyde or else to stand in full force and vertue:./

Sealed and deliūed in ye pñce of

[signed] Peter Temple
[seal]

Henry E. Huntington Library; French, "John Milton, Scrivener, The Temples of Stowe, and Sir John Lenthall," *The Huntington Library Quarterly*, IV (1941), 303-306. The space left for the signatures of witnesses has not been filled in. The other obligations mentioned in this bond, to Robert Hassard and George Sheires, have not been found.

[Know all men by these presents that I, Peter Temple, knight, son and heir apparent of Thomas Temple of Stowe in Co. Bucks, knight and baronet, hold and firmly obligate myself to the aforesaid Thomas Temple and John Lenthall of Blechindon in Co. Oxford, knight, in six hundred pounds of lawful money of England, to be paid to the said Thomas Temple and John Lenthall or their or either of their specified attorneys, executors, or administrators. To which payment, well and truly to be made, I oblige myself, my heirs, my executors, and my administrators firmly by these presents. Signed with my seal. Given on the fourth day of July, 1623, and in the twenty-first year of the reign of our Lord King James of England, and of Scotland the fifty-sixth.]

JULY 21. FUTURE FATHER-IN-LAW BUYS FOREST HILL.

I finde . . . . That Edmond Browne Esqz by Indenture dated 21° Iuly 1623 bargained and sold to Richard Powell Esqz. The Mannor of fforesthill, with the appurtennances in the County of Oxoñ; with the Rectory impropriate, and other lands there, for the tearme of 31. yeares, to commence from the expiracōn of a former Lease thereof for 20. yeares, which did expire, the first of Nouember 1641. ffor and vnder the yearly rental of 5ˡⁱ.

. . . one Edmund Brome . . . by an other deede dated 21° Julij 21° Ja: did demise vnto yᵉ said Richard yᵉ same pʳmīses for 31 yeares to cōmence after yᵉ ende of 20 yeares, vnder yᵉ yearly rent of 5ˡⁱ . . . .

Public Record Office, SP 23/109/517, 521 (Reading's report of January, 1650/1, and Pye's petition of August 23, 1650); Hamilton, p. 55; French, *Milton in Chancery*, p. 73. See also above under October 2, 1621. For a history of Forest Hill, see *The Journal of the British Archeological Association*, v (1850), 418-419. Part of Powell's house was still standing in 1850, the property of Lincoln College at that time. For a picture of the house in the nineteenth century, see *Milton in Chancery*, facing p. 100. For further confusion as to date and title, see the entry below under date of September 1, 1623.

SEPTEMBER 1. PATENT TO EDMUND BROME TO SELL FOREST HILL [TO RICHARD POWELL?].

licen' ał int' Rex Omībz ad quos &c saltm̄ Sciatis qd' nos
Brome & de grā nrā spiāli ac ꝑ octoginta solid' solut
Chesterman ffirmar' nrīs virtute łrar ñrar paten' conces-
40 simˢ & licentiam dedimˢ ac ꝑ nōb hered' &
Successoribz ñris quantum in nōb est ꝑ p̄sentes concedimˢ &

licentiam damˢ dīlcis nōb Edmundo Brome Armigō & Elizabēth uxj eius qd' ipī maner' de fforresthiłł ałs fforesthiłł ałs
ffosthiłł cum ptin' ac decem mesuag' decem Cotag' Centum &
sexaginta acras terr' viginti acras prati & centum acras pastur'
cum ptin' in fforresthiłł ałs fforsthiłł ałs ffosthiłł & Caddesden
necnon Rcōriam de fforresthiłł ałs fforesthiłł ałs ffosthiłł cum
ptin in Cоm̃ nrō Oxon' Que de nōb tentent' in Capite vt dicit'
dare possint & concedere alienare aut cognoscere p finem vel p
recuperacōem in Cur' nrā coram Justic' nrīs de Banco aut aliquo
alio modo quocumqz ad libit' ipōr Edmundi & Elizabēth diłcis
nōb Jacobo Chesterman genōso & Willō hearne habend' & tenend' eisdem Jacobo & Willō ac hered' & assign' ipiūs Jacobi ad
opus & vsum ipōr Jacobi & Willī ac hered' & assign' suor' imppm̃
de nōb hered' & Successoribz p suīcia p̄dcā inde debit & de iure
consuet' Et eisdem Jacobo & Willō qd' ipī pdīct' manēr mesuag'
terr' ten' & cetā p̄missa cum ptin' a p̄fat' Edmundo & Elizabēth
recipē possint & tenere sibi ac hered' & assign' ipīus Jacobi ad
opus & vsum p̄dict' de nōb hered' & Successoribz nrīs p sūicia
p̄dtā sicut p̄dcm̃ est imppm̃ tenore p̄senciū similit' licenciam
dedimˢ ac p nōb hered' & Successoribz nrīs p̄dcīs damˢ spīalem
Nolentes qd' p̄dcī Edmundus & Elizabēth vel hered' sui aut
pfāt' Jacobus & Willṡ vel hered' sui rōne p̄missor p nos hered'
vel Successores nrōs aut p Justic' Escaet' vicecomit' Ballinos
alios Officiar' seu ministros nrōs aut dcōr hered' vel Successor
nrōr quoscunqz inde occonent' molestent' impetant' vexent' in
aliquo seu gñent' nec eor aliquis occonet' molestet' impetat'
vexet' in aliquo seu gñet' Jn cuius rei &c T R apud Westm̃ primo
die Septembris.

Public Record Office, Patent Rolls, C66/2318/40. This document
has not, to my knowledge, previously been published. The final *r* of
genitive plurals in this document, as in others of its class, is made with
a crossed line through it so that it closely resembles an *x*; the modern
druggist's sign is much like it.

[License to alienate, between Brome and Chesterman. The
king to all to whom etc., greeting. Know that we of our
peculiar favor and for eighty pounds paid to our treasurers, by

virtue of our letters patent grant and give license and for us and our heirs and successors, as much as lies in us, grant by these presents and give license to our beloved Edmund Brome, Esq., and to Elizabeth his wife that they may give the manor of Forest Hill with its appurtenances and ten messuages, ten cottages, 160 acres of land, 20 acres of meadow, and 100 acres of pasture with their appurtenances in Forest Hill and Cuddesdon, together with the rectory of Forest Hill with its appurtenances in our county of Oxford, which are held of us in chief, as it is called—that they may give, concede, alienate, or acknowledge them by fine or recovery in our court before our Justices of the Bench or in any other way whatsoever at the pleasure of the said Edmund and Elizabeth, to our beloved James Chesterman, gentleman, and to William Hearne; to have and to hold to the same James and William and the heirs and assigns of the same James for the benefit of the said James and William and their heirs and assigns forever, from us and our heirs and successors by the aforesaid service as owed and accustomed by law. And to the said James and William we grant that they may receive the aforesaid manor, messuages, lands, tenements, etc., with their appurtenances, from the said Edmund and Elizabeth, and hold them for themselves and the heirs and assigns of the said James for the use aforesaid from us, our heirs, and our successors for the service aforesaid as described above forever. By a copy of these presents similarly we give, and for us, our heirs, and our successors aforesaid we give special license; not wishing that the aforesaid Edmund and Elizabeth or their heirs or the aforesaid James or William or their heirs by virtue of promises from us or our heirs or successors or from justices, sheriffs, viscounts, bailiffs, or our other officers or ministers or of any of those of our said heirs or successors whatsoever should be troubled, molested, bothered, vexed, or in any way harmed, nor any of them be troubled, molested, bothered, vexed, or in any way harmed. In which thing, etc. Witness the King at Westminster on the first day of September.]

SEPTEMBER 25. FATHER DEPOSES IN WILLIAMS-POW-LETT SUIT.

25°. Septembris 1623.   Ex parte Thome Williams gen' quer'
A° Jacobi R℘. xxj°.   verss Thomã Powlett ar' def^t Testes
exaiati p Mchm̃ Robert℘ in Canc'
Exaiãtorem/

[September 25, 1623, in the 21st year of King James. On behalf of Thomas Williams, gentleman, plaintiff, against Thomas Powlett, Esquire, defendant. The witness examined by Michael Roberts, Examiner in Chancery.]

John Milton of the parrish of Allhollowes in Breadstreet   1
London Scriveñ of the age of 58. yeares or thereabout℘ sworne and exaied &c'. That he doth verie well know Mr Thomas Williams named for Complt and hath knowne him about these xx yeares and saieth that about some sixtene yeares agone as he rembreth the tyme he this dep^t did see Mr Thomas Powlett whoe is named for def^t in this suite but hath no great knowledge of him/

That he doth knowe it to be true that the reversoñ of the   4 Lease and house in the third Jnterr' menconed and the rent in the s̃d Lease reserved, did by lawfull & meane Conveyaunce come vnto the Complt Thomas Williams and was accordingly vested in him before the expiracoñ of the six yeares in the said Lease menconed, ffor this dept saieth that he this dept did drawe the same Conveyaunce and caused the same to be engrossed and this dept saieth that he doth knowe that the deed now shewed to him this dept at this the tyme of his exanicoñ bearing date the Twelveth daye of Maye *1607*. in the fiveth yeare of the king℘ Ma^{te} reigne that now is over this his realme of England is a true deed for this dept saieth it is the same wch he did both drawe and caused to be drawne & to be engrossed and was a witnes amongst others to the sealing and delivering of the sd deed or Jndrē and doth knowe his name thereto sett as a witnes to be of his the dep^{ts} owne hand writing

but for more certeinty of the Content℈ of the sd Jñdre or deed
this dept saieth he referreth himself thereunto./ ...
Capt. corā Martino Basill./.   Jo: Milton.
                [Taken before Martin Basill.]

Public Record Office, Chancery Town Depositions, C24/501/99.
This document, first found by Mr. Charles Bernau, is now first published.

MICHAELMAS TERM. CONCORD OF FINE FOR SALE OF
FUTURE FATHER-IN-LAW RICHARD POWELL'S RESI-
DENCE, FOREST HILL.

Hec est finalis Concordia fta' in Cur' dni' Regis apud Westm'
in Octavis sci' Mich[ās] Anno regnoru' Jacobi' Dei' gra' Anglj
Scotie ffranc' & Hibnīe Regis fidei' Defens' &c Anglj ffranc'
& hibnīe vicesimo primo & Scotie quinquagesimo septimo coram
henr' hobarte humfro' Winchē Rico' Hutton' & Willō Jones
Justic' & alijs dni' Regis fidelibz tunc ibi' p̄sentibz Jnt Jacobum
Chesterman' Gen'osum & Willm̄' hearne quer' et Edmundum
Broome Armig'um & Elizabēth vxem' [eju]s deforc' de
man'io de fforesthiłł alias fforsthiłł alias ffosthiłł cum ptin' Ac
de decem [mesu]agijs decem Cotagijs Centum & quadraginta
acris tre viginti' acr' prati' & Centum [acris pastur]ijs cum ptin'
in fforresthiłł alias fforsthiłł alias ffosthiłł & Cuddesden' necnon'
[Rc̄oriam de] fforresthiłł alias fforsthiłł alias ffosthiłł cum ptin'
vnde Plītm' Comen'cois [sūm fuit inter eos] in eadem Cur'
Scīlt qd p̄dti' Edūs & Elizabēth recogn' p̄dta man'm ten' &
[terras] esse ius ipiūs Jacobi' vt iłł que ijdem Jacobus & Willš
hēnt de dono [predict' Edmundi et] Elizabēth Et iłł remiser'
& quietclam' de ipīˢ Edō' & Elizabēth & hered[ibus ipsius Edī
p̄dtī] Willō & hered ipiūs Jacobi' Jmpp̄m' Et p̄tea ijdem Edmundus & Elizabēth [concedunt pro se et hered'] ipiūs Edmundi' qd' ipi' Warant' p̄dtiš Jacobo & Willō & hered ipiūs
[Jacobi prēd messuagium & cotagios & acras] & Rc̄oriam cum
ptin' cont^r om̄es' hoīes Jmpp̄m Et p̄ hac recogn' [remissione
quiet' clam' War]ant' fine & Concordia ijdem Jacobus & Willš
deder' p̄dtis' [Edō & Elizabēth—libras] sterlingor'.

[Endorsed as follows:]
Prima pclam' fat'[   ]
Anno vicesimo primo Reg[   ]
t'nno' sti hillarij Anno vicesimo [   ]
die Aprilis t'nno' Pasche Anno vicesimo [   ]
vicesimo nono die maij t'nno' ste' Trinitatie [   ].

Public Record Office, Concords of Fines, CP 25. (2). 340. 21 James
I. Mich. The brackets indicate blanks and illegible words in the original
document, most of which are tentatively filled in from analogous documents. From other related records there can be no doubt that Milton's
future father-in-law Richard Powell was concerned in this transaction.

[This is a final concord made in the court of our Lord the
King at Westminster in the eight days of Michaelmas in the
year of the reigns of James, by the grace of God King of England, France, and Ireland the twenty-first, and the fifty-seventh
of Scotland, before Henry Hobart, Humphrey Winch, Richard
Hutton, and William Jones, Justices, and other faithful servants
of our Lord the King then present; between James Chesterman,
gentleman, and William Hearne, plaintiffs, and Edmund
Brome Esq. and Elizabeth his wife, defendants; about the
manor of Forest Hill with its appurtenances and ten messuages
and ten cottages and 140 acres of land and 20 acres of meadow
and 100 acres of pasture with their appurtenances in Forest
Hill and Cuddesdon; also the rectory of Forest Hill with its
appurtenances, about which a suit has arisen between them in this
court; namely, that the aforesaid Edward and Elizabeth acknowledge the aforesaid manor and tenements and lands to be the
property of the said James as that which the same James and
William hold by gift of the said Edmund and Elizabeth. And
they remit and quitclaim these for the said Edmund and Elizabeth and their heirs to the said William and the heirs of the
same James forever. And further the said Edmund and Elizabeth grant for themselves and the heirs of the said Edmund
that they guarantee to the said James and William and the heirs
of the said James the aforesaid messuages and cottages and lands
and rectory with appurtenances against all men forever. And for
this recognizance, remission, quitclaim, warrant, fine, and con-

cord the said James and William have given the said Edmund and Elizabeth (blank) pounds.

Endorsements: The first proclamation was made (   ) in the twenty-first year of King James. The second proclamation was made in the term of St. Hilary in the twenty-first year of King James. The third proclamation was made on the (   ) day of April in Easter term in the twenty-second year of King James. The fourth proclamation was made on the twenty-ninth day of May in the term of Holy Trinity in the twenty-second year of King James.]

AUTUMN? FATHER CONFERS WITH JAMES AYLOFFE ABOUT RAYMOND DEBT.

... the Cōmp^lt. Ayloffe as this def^t. is informed by his svant͜ꝑ, shortly after the death of the said Raymond of his owne accord came to this def^tꝑ shopp, and desired to know whether he were discharged of the said debte, or no, and he was then answered that he was not discharged thereof . . . .

Public Record Office, C2 James I/A6/35 (Milton's answer to Ayloffe); French, *Milton in Chancery*, p. 226.

OCTOBER 8. FATHER DEPOSES IN WALTHEW-SHERES SUIT.

viij° octobr' A°. xxj° Jacobi Rꝑ. 1623.

John Mylton of the pishe of Allhallowes in Breadstreete London scryvener aged 60. yeres or thereabout͜ꝑ sworne & exd

1.1. That he doeth well knowe Mr Sheres & Mr Walthewe named for the ꝑtyes complt & defft to this suyte and hath knowen them these xx yeres past or thereabout͜ꝑ

12. That true it is that he doeth fynd a note in a booke wch he keepeth for such purposes that the Defft Robert Walthewe by an obligacōn dated the xxvij^th day of ffebruary Aō Dnī 1607. did become bound to the plt in the penall somme of fower hundred pound͜ꝑ condicōned for the paymt of CCxx^li to the complt at the shoppe of the depont in Breadstreete london vpon the first day of March Ao Dnī 1608. as by the said booke may appeare wherevnto for more certenty he

doeth referre himself And sayth that he verely beleeueth that the defft or some for him did afterward℈ satisfy and pay to or to the vse of the complt the said CCxxˡⁱ in discharge of the said bond or obligacōn at or about the tyme lymitted for the payment thereof in & by the condicōn of the said obligacōn And more or otherwise he sayth he can depose nothing certen or materiall to any the other questions of the Jnterr' vpon his nowe pʳsent rēmbrance To the rest not exd by direccōn

[*Signed*] Jo: milton

Public Record Office, C24/501; French, *Milton in Chancery*, p. 399. I am indebted to Miss N. O'Farrell for her kind assistance in procuring a copy of this document for me.

NOVEMBER 22. SISTER ANNE MARRIES EDWARD PHILLIPS.

The 22th of november 1623 weare maried Edward Phillips And Ann Miltoñ the Daughter of John Miltonn by lycence.

Registers of St. Stephen's, Walbrook, and of St. Benet Sherehog, London (from the St. Stephen's section); Publications of the Harleian Society, Registers, XLIX (1919), 60; Brennecke, p. 111. Brennecke unaccountably dates it 1624.

The will of an Edward Phillips of Braden Heath, Hampton, co. Salop, dated May 16, 1623, and proved Nov. 27, 1623, is catalogued as 117 Swann in Somerset House, London. But though it was proved by Edward Phillips, presumably his son, it seems to have no connection with the present family of that name, and is therefore mentioned here only for completeness.

William R. Parker ("Thomas Myriell," *Notes and Queries*, CLXXXVIII [1945], 103) points out that the clergyman who married them was Thomas Myriell, rector of St. Stephen's, Walbrook, presumably the author of *Tristitiae Remedium*, 1616, which contained compositions by the elder Milton.

NOVEMBER 27. WITNESSES MARRIAGE SETTLEMENT BETWEEN SISTER ANNE AND EDWARD PHILLIPS.

This Jndenture tripartite made the Seaven & twentith day of November Jn the yeare of oʳ Lord God One Thowsand Six Hundred Twenty and Three. And in the One and Twentith yeare of the raigne of oʳ Soveraigne Lord James by the grace of God King of England ffraunce and Jreland defendor of the faith &c. And of Scotland the Seaven and ffiftith Betweene Edward Phillipps of London Gentleman of the first parte Katherine Phillipps of the towne of Shrewsbury in the County of Salop Widdowe and mother of the said Edward of the Seacond parte. And John Milton Citizen and Scrivener of London and James Hodgkinson of London Gentleman of the Third parte Witnesseth That whereas a marriage was [lately] had and solempnized Between the said Edward Phillipps and Anne hys nowe wife daughter of the said John Milton And whereas the said John Milton at and before th'ensealing and delivery of thes pñtɋ hath paid and delivered vnto the said Edward Phillipps the soṁe of Eighte Hundred Poundɋ of lawfull money of England and vpwards [as a] Childɋ parte and porc̄on given to the said Edward Phillipps in marriage wᵗʰ the said Anne his wife and for the marriage porc̄on of the said Anne And whereas the [said] Edward Phillipps and Katherine for and in considerac̄on of a Jointure to be had made and perfected to and for the said Anne wife of the said Edward and for the estat[ing and] setling of the Messuages landɋ and hereditamᵗɋ herein hereafter menc̄oned to and for the vses intentɋ and purposes herein hereafter expressed have agreed to suffer Twoe severall [recove]ries (that is to saie) One recovery wherein the said John Milton and James Hodgkinson shalbe demaundantɋ and the said Edward Phillipps and Katherine shalbe Tenantɋ according [to th]e Course of Coṁon recoũies in such behalf vsed of for and concerning Twoe Mesuages or Tenemᵗɋ wᵗʰ thappʳtenñce Scituate and being in the towne of Shrewsbury aforesaid wᵗʰin the said County of S[alop in] a certaine place there Coṁonly called Milkestreete The one of them nowe or late in the tenure or occupac̄on of the said Katherine Phillipps her assignee or assignes Thother of them (adioyning to the said fo[rmer] mesuage) is nowe or late was in the tenure or occupac̄on of one Randall Thomas his assignee or assignes, One other mesuage or tenemᵗ and a Brewhowse therevnto belonging and one other Mesuage or tenemᵗ and a Tan-

ning howse therevnto apperteyning scituat in the towne of
Shrewsbury aforesaid in a certaine place there Comonly called
Mardall nowe or late in the tenure or occupacon of one Richard
[Alvie?] his assignee or assignes, ffower other mesuages or
tenem$^{t\rho}$ wth thapp^{r}tenñcρ scituate in Shrewsbury aforesaid in a
certaine place there Comonly called Dogg lane nowe or late
in the severall tenures or occupacons of Richard Hurst John
Sankey and Mary Lewys Widdowe theire assignee or assignes,
One other mesuage or tenem^t wth thappurtenñcρ in the towne of
Shrewsbury aforesaid nowe or late in the tenure or occupacon
of one Phillipp Hussie his assignee or assignes All wch mesuages
tenem$^{t\rho}$ hereditam$^{t\rho}$ and p^{r}misses before expressed by what
name or names place or places soever the same or any of them
is or are vsually called knowne or distinguished by scituat lying and being in the towne and County of Salop aforesaid or
in one of them And the other recovery wherein the said John
Milton and James Hodgkinson shalbe demandantρ and only
the said Edward Phillipps shalbe Tenannt according to the
said Course of Comon recoveries of for and concerning one
other Mesuage or tenement wth the Landρ hereditamentρ and
appurtanñcρ therevnto belonging scituat lying and being in
Caersowse ats Caerwis in the County of Mountgomery or by what
name or names soever the same is or are vsually called knowne
or distinguished by nowe or late in the severall tenures or occupacons of one Robert Phillipps and Anne Symes Widdowe
theire or one of theire assignee or assignes Nowe it is mutually
Covenñted condicõned and agreed by and betweene all the said
parties to thes p^{r}sentρ And the said Edward Phillipps and
Katherine for themselves theire heires and assignes and for
every of them doe Covenñt and graunt to and wth the said John
Milton and James Hodgkinson theire heires and assignes and
to and wth every of them by thes p^{r}sentρ in manner and forme
following (that is to saie) That they the said John Milton
and James Hodgkinson theire heires and assignes shall from
and imediatly after the executing and perfecting of the said
recoveries stand and be seized of and in all and singuler the

said Messuages or tenem^{te} howses brewhowse Tanning howse
and hereditament^ρ wth thapp^{r}tenñc$ρ$ therevnto belonging scituat and being in the towne of Shrewsbury aforesaid or elsewhere in the said County of Salop to the vses intent$ρ$ and
purposes hereafter in thes present$ρ$ limited expressed and declared (that is to saie) to and for the vse and behoof of the
said Katherine Phillipps for and during her naturall life and
after her decease then to the vse and behoof of the said Edward Phillipps and Anne his wife for and during theire Twoe
naturall lives and the naturall life of the longer liver of them
and after the decease of the said Edward and Anne and the
longer liver of them Then to the vse and behoof of the first
sonne of the bodies of them the said Edward and Anne lawfully to be begotten and to the heires males of the body of
such first sonne lawfully to be begotten And for default of
such issue then to the vse and behoof of the seacond sonne of
the bodies of them the said Edward Phillipps and Anne his
wife lawfully to be begotten and to the heires males of the body
of such seacond sonne lawfully to be begotten And for default
of such issue then to the vse of every other sonne of the bodyes
of the said Edward and Anne lawfully to be begotten and to the
heires males of the body of every such other sonne lawfully to
be begotten successively one after another theldest for the time
being and the heires males of his body being always p^{r}ferred
before the yonger or the heires males of his body and for default
of such issue then to the vse and behoof of the right heires of
the said Edward Phillipps forever And it is further Covenñted
and agreed by and betweene the said parties to thes p^{r}sent$ρ$
And the said Edward Phillipps for himself his heires and assignes doth Covenñt and graunt to and wth the said John Milton and James Hodgkinson theire heires and assignes and to
and wth every of them by theis p^{r}sent$ρ$ in manner and form following (that is to saie) That they the said John Milton and
James Hodgkinson theire heires and assignes shall stand and
be seized of and in the said mesuage or tenem^t land$ρ$ and here-
ditam^{te} wth thapp^{r}tenñc$ρ$ in Caersowse aforesaid to the iñediat

vse and behoof of the said Edward Phillipps and Anne his wife
for and during theire Twoe naturall lives and the naturall life
of the longer liver of them And after the decease of them the
said Edward and Anne and the longer liver of them Then to
the vse and behoof of the first sonne of the bodies of them the
said Edward and Anne lawfully to be begotten and to the heires
males of the body of such first sonne lawfully to bee begotten
And for default of such issue then to the vse and behoof of the
seacond sonne of the bodies of them the said Edward Phillipps
and Anne his wife lawfully to be begotten and to the heires
males of the body of such seacond sonne lawfully to be begotten
And for default of such issue then to the vse and behoof of every
other sonne of the bodies of the said Edward and Anne lawfully
to be begotten and to the heires males of the body of every such
other sonne lawfully to be begotten successively one after
another theldest for the time being and the heires males of his
body being alwayes p^rferred before the younger or the heires
males of his body And for default of such issue then to the vse
and behoof of the right heires of the said Edward Phillipps
forever And the said Edward and Katherine Phillipps for
them selves theire heires executo^{rs} admīstrato^{rs} and assignes and
for every of them doe Covenñt and graunt to and wth the said
John Milton his heires executo^{rs} admīstrato^{rs} and assignes and
to and wth every of them by thes pñtꝑ in manner and forme
following (that is to saie) That they the said Edward Phillipps
and Katherine Phillipps or one of them at the time of thensealing
and deliūy of thes pñtꝑ are or one of them is lawfully rightfully
and absolutely seized of a good and perfect estate of inheritance
in fee simple or fee taile in possession or reverčon wthout any
reverčon or remaynder in the Crowne of and in the said mesuages or tenemtꝑ landꝑ hereditamtꝑ and all and singuler other
the p^rmisses wth thapp^rtenñcꝑ and every parte and parcell thereof
And likewies That they the said Edward and Katherine Phil-
lipps have or one of them hath full power good right true title
and lawfull authority to graunt and assure the p^rmisses to the

vses [here]in before limited and expressed And further That
they the said Edward and Katherine Phillipps theire heires and
assignes and all and every other person and persons and theire
hei[res ha]veing or clayming or wch shall or may have or clayme
or pretend to have any lawfull estate right title interest or other
thing in to or out of the same premisses or any parte thereof
shall a[nd wil]l from time to time and at all times hereafter
vpon every request in that behalf to be made make doe acknowledge execute and suffer or cause to be made donne acknowl-
edg[ed exe]cuted and suffered All and every such further and
other acte and actꝑ thing and thingꝑ device and devices assurance and assurances in the lawe for the further better and more
perfecte [   ] and suerty and sure making of all and
singuler the p^rmisses wth thappurtenñcꝑ to the vses and intentꝑ
herein before limited and expressed As by the said John Milton
his heires or assig[nes or by his] or theire Counsell learned in
the lawe shalbe resonablie devised or advised and required And
moreover That shee the said Anne Phillipps and her assignes
for and during her [naturall] life iṁediatly from and after the
decease of them the said Edward and Katherine Phillipps shall
or may peaceably and quietly have hold occupy possesse and
enioy All and singuler the said mesuages or ten[emtꝑ her]edit-
amtꝑ and p^rmisses in Shrewsbury aforesaid or in the said County
of Salop or in either of them And allsoe That shee the said Anne
Phillipps and her assignes for and during her naturall life
[iṁed]iatly from and after the decease of her said husband
Edward Phillipps shall or may peaceably and quietly have hold
occupy possesse and enioy the said mesuage tenem^t landꝑ
hereditamtꝑ and premisses in Ca[erwi]s aforesaid w^thout any
lett troble deniall or interrupc̄on of or by the said Edward and
Katherine their heires or assignes or of or by any other person
or persons by or by reason of theire or either o[r any of]
theire actꝑ meanes consent default or procurement And laste-
lie it is concluded and agreed by and betweene the said parties
to thes p^rsentꝑ That all fines feoffementꝑ re[coveries] convey-

ances and assurances whatsoever of the premisses or any parte thereof by what name or names soever the same have beene are or hereafter shalbee had levied made or suffered by and [be-tw]eene the said parties to thes presentɛ or by or betweene any other person or persons whatsoever shalbe and envre and shalbe expounded adjudged and taken to bee and envre to the only vses in[terests] and purposes herein before limited and expressed and to none other vse intent or purpose whatsoever Jn witnes whereof the parties abovesaid to thes present Jndentures Jnter-chang[eably have] sett theire handɛ and seales Yeoven the day and yeares first above written

[Signed] Edw. Phillipps

[Endorsed:] Sealed and deliūed in the pñce of

Anne [?] Milton

John Milton Junior

James Hodgkinson

Thomas Bower

John Hutton

} sʳvantɛ to the wᵗʰⁱⁿ named John Milton

[Below in another hand:] Tho Owen Esqz of Powle & Lath-wood

[Below:] 27.ᵗʰ Nov. 1623

Mʳ.: Phillipps his Covennte Leading the vse of his recoverie. on the Marriage of Edwᵈ. Phillips & Ann the Daughter of John Milton

Milk Street

[Below:] Writeingɛ of yᵉ houses in Milkestrᵗᵉ & Sellerɛ Vnder yᵉ Shearmanɛ Hall

Pierpont Morgan Library, New York; *Review of English Studies*, IX (1933), 58-60; British Museum Add. MS. 24,501, f. 76 (Hunter's notes); French, "The Autographs of John Milton," *ELH*, IV (1937), 325, #96; CM, XVIII, 624. The brackets indicate illegible places in the manuscript, filled in as well as possible from the demands of the context. The signatures are in various hands, presumably those of the names concerned, though the handwriting of the name of the elder Milton looks almost identical with that of John Hutton. Now first published in its entirety by the kind permission of the Pierpont Morgan Library.

Ann, the onely Daughter of the said *John Milton* the Elder, had a considerable Dowry given her by her Father, in Marriage with *Edward Philips*, (the Son of *Edward Philips* of *Shrewsbury*,) who coming up Young to Town, was bred up in the Crown-Office in Chancery, and at length came to be Secondary of the Office under Old Mr. *Bembo*; by him she had, besides other Children that dyed Infants, two Sons yet surviving, of whom more hereafter. . . .

Phillips, pp. vii-viii; Darbishire, p. 53.

NOVEMBER 27. FATHER ARRANGES CHETWODE-COTTON BOND.

Mr Chetwode & oth^rs p obl' Dat' xxvij° Novembr' 1623 . . . 100^ll

Thomas Bower's schedule of Cotton's bonds made out by himself and Milton's father; see below under date of November 25, 1630. The original bond has not been found.

. . . [Mr Chetwode] & others by bond dated the seven & Twentieth of November One thowsand six hundred Twentie three One hundred pound♙ principall debt.

Sir Thomas Cotton's bill; see below under date of May 28, 1636.

1624

PARAPHRASES OF PSALMS 114 AND 136.

A Paraphrase on *Psalm* 114.

This and the following *Psalm* were don by the Author at fifteen years old. . . .

Psalm 136.

Poems, 1645, pp. 12-16; CM, I, 11-15. Though the date of composition is uncertain, the year during which Milton was fifteen years old extended from December 9, 1623, to December 8, 1624. Thus most of it falls in the year 1624. Though editors are divided in their dating, Hughes favors 1624.

FATHER'S APPRENTICES ADMITTED TO COMPANY OF SCRIVENERS.

1624 . . . James Hodgkinson - - - of John Milton - - - 1599
   Tho. Bower - - - of John: Milton - - - 1599.

 Bodleian Library, Rawl. MS. Miscell. 51, f. 29; *Athenaeum*, 1880, 1, 566.

WINTER. FATHER SUES EDWARD RAYMOND'S ESTATE.

 . . . this def[t]. [Milton] endeavouring to haue eased the said Comp[lt]. Ayloffe of the paym[t]. of this debte did sue the admīstratrix of the said Raymond vpon the said Judgem[t]. and her Attorney (as he affirmeth) had instruccōns to plead that she had satisfied as farr as the goodɤ came vnto vpon other Judgem[tɤ]. before the said Def[t]. did sue out his scire facias vpon his Judgem[t]. . . .

 Public Record Office, C2 James I/A6/35 (Milton's answer to Ayloffe's bill, May 10, 1624); French, *Milton in Chancery*, pp. 21 ff., 221 ff. See also the closely related entry under the same date as this and under the heading, "Father and John Lane sue James Ayloffe."

WINTER? FATHER AND JOHN LANE SUE JAMES AYLOFFE.

 . . . the said John Milton and John llane p[r]tending that all or the greatest pte of the said debte for w[ch] your Orator stood bound as suerty for the said Raymond as is aforesaid is yet vnsatisfied . . . the said Milton hath ꝓcuered an action to be therevppon brought in the name of the said Lane against your Orator at the Comon lawe and intendɤ to recouer the penalty there . . . .

 [The elder Milton] . . . comēnced his accōn against the said Ayloffe at y[e] Comon lawe . . .

 Public Record Office, C2 James I/A6/35; French, *Milton in Chancery*, pp. 21 ff., 221 ff. The first quotation is from Ayloffe's bill of May 1, 1624, the second from Milton's answer of May 10, 1624. The action at common law here referred to has not been found, but there seems no doubt of its actuality, since both parties agree on it. It seems highly likely that this action is identical with that referred to elsewhere in Milton's bill as one against Edward Raymond's estate (*q.v.*), though the two are entered separately in this volume since they are not specifically identified by Milton.

MARCH 2. FATHER WITNESSES WEBBER-COWPER BOND.

Norint vniuersi per pntes me Margarett [Webber] de Londoñ Spinster teneri et firmiter [obligari] Jacobo Cowper de poch' scī Petri apud Paul[s] Wharf Londoñ in Quatuor libris leglis monet' Anglie solveñd eidem Jacobo Cowp̱ aut suo [certo] Attorñ, bene et fidēlr' faciend, Obligo me herēd, executor', et admīstrator' meos firmiter p̱ pntes', Sigillo meo sigillat' Dat' Secundo die Marcij. 1623. Annoqz RR̥ Dnī nrī Jacobi Anglie &c Vicesimo primo, et Scotie quinquagesimo Septimo.

The Condicōn of this obligacōn is such, That if the aboue bound Margaret Webber her heires, execūto^rs. admīstrato^rs. or assignes, or anie of them Doe well and truly paie or cause to be paid to the aboue named James Cowp̱ his executo^rs. admīstrato^rs. or assignes, the some of ffourtie and ffoure shilling̥ of lawfull money of England At the now dwelling house of the said James Cowp̱ scituate in the p̱ish of St. Peter aboue mencōned, On the ffourth daie of March wch shalbe in the yeare of our Lord God One thowsand Six hundred Twentie and ffoure, That then this obligacōn to be voyde, or else to stand in full force, and vertue:. Sealed & deliūed in ye p̄nce of

Jo: milton: scr   ye mk. X of Margaret
John Hutton svante to y^e   Webber
       said Scr
     vlt Aprilis 1634   [seal]

[Endorsed:] Mar: Webber
        44s. March 4 1624.

Records of the Corporation of London, Historical Papers, Guildhall, London, Vol. I, #11; *Athenaeum*, 1884, I, 20. One or two words, illegible through time or torn spots, have been supplied from elsewhere in the document or from similar forms.

[Know all men by these presents that I, Margaret Webber of London, Spinster, hold myself firmly obligated to James Cowper of the parish of St. Peter at Paul's Wharf, London, in the sum of four pounds of lawful money of England, to be paid to the same James Cowper or his designated attorney, for the good and faithful performance of which I oblige myself, my heirs, my executors, and my administrators firmly by these presents. Sealed with my seal. Given the second day of March, 1623/4, and in the twenty-first year of our Lord King James of England, and of Scotland the fifty-seventh.]

APRIL-MAY. FATHER ARRANGES BURTON-PECKHAM-SMITH BOND (?).

. . . Robert Willoghbie and Thomas Willoughbie the elder or one of them about Two Yeares since were arrested at the suite of the sayd William Smith, who therevppon tolde them that if they Could procure any other securitye They should not onley bee inlarged but allso absolutely Released of the sayd debt And therevppon the sayd Robert Willoughbie became a sutor vnto Your sayd Subiect [Burton] to ioyne wth one Sr George Peckham of Shipley in the Countie of Derbie Knight to secure vnto the sayd William Smyth the sayd Somme of One hundred pound... . . . And so At the length Your Subiect being thus wrought vppon about May in the two and twentieth Yeare of our late Soueraigne Lord King James entred into a Bonde of the penall Summe of Two hundred pounds vnto the sayd Smyth Condicōned for the payment of one hundred and Tenn pounds at the now dwelling house of John Milton Scriuenor scituate in Broadstreete London on the Twentieth day of Aprill which then should bee in the Yeare of our Lord God One Thousand sixe hundred twentie & fiue . . . and which sayd Bond as Your Subiect taketh it beareth date the eighteenth day of Aprill in the sayd Two and twentieth Yeare of the Raigne of our Late Soveraigne Lord King James. . . .

From Samuel Burton's bill, May 10, 1626, *q.v.* The original bond has not been found. Since Burton says it was made payable at Milton's house, it seems likely that he drew it up. In his answer of November 15, 1626 (*q.v.*), Milton denies having known Smith personally at this time and denies all charges of fraud, complicity, compulsion, and the like, but he does not specifically deny having made this bond.

The history of this transaction is briefly as follows. On October 16, 1622, Edward, Thomas, and Robert Willoughby, of London and Warwickshire, gave bond to William Smith for £200, probably as security for a loan of about £100. Similarly on November 6 Edward and Thomas Willoughby gave bond to Thomas Paradine for £300. Evidently they failed to pay the usual interest on these loans at the appointed times, because in Hilary term (January-February), 1624, both Paradine and Smith brought suit against them at the common law for recovery of their debt with interest. By judgment of the court they were awarded the repayment of their principal debt with, respectively, 100s. and 80s. damages. Though the original bonds have not been found, the story is found in the documents of the suit: Public Record Office, Common Pleas records, C.P. 40/2137, m. 3030; French, *Milton in Chancery*, pp. 27 ff., 227 ff.

It is after these difficulties that the Willoughbys apparently succeeded in inducing Burton and Peckham to come to their aid and assume the indebtedness to Smith, probably for some consideration not mentioned in these records.

MAY 1. JAMES AYLOFFE BRINGS ACTION AGAINST MILTON'S FATHER.

Primo Maij 1624   To the right honorable John Lord Bishopp
Euelyn   of Lincolne Lord Keeper of the great seale
                             of England.

Humbly complayning sheweth vnto your good Lordshipp your dayly Orator James Ayloffe of Melditch in the Countie of Cambridge Esquier That whereas one Edward Raymonde in or about the Moneth of ffebruarie in the ninetenth yeare of the Raigne of our Soueraigne the kingꝑ māᵗⁱᵉ that now is did borrowe and take vp at interest of one Joh Milton a Scriuener in London the sume of ffiftie powndꝑ for sixe moneths for securitie whereof your Orator at the instance and requeste of the said Edward Raymonde and for his only and ꝓper debte and vppon his Confident affirmacōns to saue and keepe your Orator harmeles was Content to become bounde wᵗʰ the said Edward Raymonde as his suerty for the said money for six moneths onely and noe longer And accordingly the said Edward Raymonde together wᵗʰ your Orator as his surety did by their Obligacōn beareing date vppon or about the ninthe day of ffebruarie in the

said nynetenth yeare of his Maiesties raigne become bound to
one John llane in whose name the said Milton now affirmes he
tooke the said bonde wth Condicōn for repayment of the said
fiftie powndp wth interest at the ende of the sixe months then
next following or there aboutp vppon the sealeing of wch bonde
Your Orator did declare to the said Milton that hee would not
stand bounde as surety for that debte longer then only for sixe
moneths and willed him that the said money might not be Contynued at interest vppon that bonde any longer then onely for
that tyme when yf the said Raymond fayled to make paymente
he desiered him to make him accquainted therew^th to the ende
your Orator might haue p^rssed the said Raymonde to haue
satisfied that money and haue discharged him. But the said
Milton for some rewarde given to him by the said Raymonde
and by some agreementp betweene them Did at the ende of those
sixe moneths notw^thstanding your Orators said Declaration receaue the interest then due for the said money and contynued
the said money at interest for sixe moneths longer vpon the said
securitye and bonde w^thout the privitye or knowledge and
exp^rsly against the good will and likeinge of your Orator whoe
for that the said Raymonde tould him that the said money was
then payed And for that the said Milton neuer acquainted him
wth the Contrarye hee thought the same had bin satisfied by the
said Raymonde soe as by reason thereof your Orator resting
secure that he was discharged did not as otherwise he would
haue done presse the said Raymonde to satisffie the same but
the same as your is since given to vnderstande being by like
agreement betweene the said Raymond and Milton and for the
like rewarde by the said Raymond given to the said Milton as
aforesaid at the ende of those sixe months Continued at interest
for sixe months longer and your orator whoe in the meane tyme
had notice that the said Debte was vnpayed at the ende of those
last sixe moneths pressing the said Raymond to make satisfaction
of the said debte the said Edward Raymonde and John Milton
fell to a newe agreement concerning the said debte w^thout the

privitie knowledge or assent of your Orator whereby the said
Raymonde agreed to pay pte of the said money in hand or wthin
a fewe dayes after and to accknowledge a iudgment for the residue
and the said Milton did agree to deliuer vpp the said obligacōn
vppon the acknowledging of the said Judgm^t and to give the
said Raymonde longer dayes for the payment of soe much of
the said debte as was then vnpayd and to discharge your Orator
from the same or to such or the like effecte and accordingly the
said Edward Raymonde vppon or about the sixe and twentieth
day of March in the one and twentieth yeare of his ma^{ties} said
raigne haueing before that payed a great pte of the said debte
to the said Milton or to some other to his vse did acknowledge
a Judgment before the Lord Mayor and aldermen of the Citie
of London in the Chamber of Gin-hale London to the said John
llane for one hundred powndę debt and one penny costę wch the
said John llane remitted to ffourty powndę wch iudgment though
it were in the name of the said llane yet as the said Milton nowe
affirmeth yt was for the benifyte and behallf of the said Milton
and yt was by him taken and accepted as in full discharge of the
said Obligacōn and debte therevppon And the said John Milton
according to the said former agreement did agree vnder his
hand by way of defeazancing of the said Judgment to stay execution for the residue of the said debte then vnpayd wch came not
to ffowerty powndę to be payd at ffower seuerall dayes then to
Come according to the former agreement and nowe all past in
the life tyme of the sayd Raymond by equall porcōns vppon the
accknowledgeing of wch Judgment allsoe the said obligacōn
wherein your Orator stood bound as suerty wth the said Raymonde was according to the said agreement deliuered vp to the
said Raymond whoe shewed the same to your Orator and tould
him the same was discharged after the accknowleging of w^{ch}
Judgment the said Raymond satisfied and payd to the said
Milton all or wthin a small deale of the residue of the said debte
for wch the said Judgment was defeazanced as aforesaid vppon
or very neere to the dayes agreed vppon soe as your Orator

neither is nor ought in equity to be Charged wth the said debte
for wch he stood originally bound wth the said Raymond as
aforesaid But nowe soe yt is may it please your good Lordshipp
That not w^thstanding the said Judgment was taken and accepted
by the said Milton in full discharge of the said Obligacōn
wherein your Orator as a suerty for the said Raymond stood
ingaged as aforesaid And that vppon acknowleging of the said
Judgment the said Raymond and Milton came to the said newe
agreement for the said debte as aforesaid And notw^thstanding
that all or the most pte of the said debte for wch the said Judgment was defeazanced as aforesaid either was or if yt were not
might haue bin satisfied in the life tyme of the said Raymond yf
the said Milton either had or would haue psecuted execution
against him vppon the said Judgment yet the said John Milton
and John llane p^rtending that all or the greatest pte of the said
debte for wch your Orator stood bound as suerty for the said
Raymond as is aforesaid is yet vnsatisfied knoweing that the
said Raymond is lately deade soe as your Orator cannot make
proofe of the said agreement or paymentȝ and haueing gotten
into their or one of their handȝ the said obligacōn wch was formerly deliuerd vp the said Milton hath pcuered an action to be
therevppon brought in the name of the said Lane against your
Orator at the Comon lawe and intendȝ to recouer the penalty
thereof against him contrary to all right equitie and good Conscience, the p^rmisses Considered And fforasmuch as your Orator
Cannot plead anything in barre to the said accōn nor can be re-
lieued against the same at the Comon lawe nor otherwise but in
equitie before your good Lordshipp in this honorable Court,
nor hath any securitie from the said Raymond or otherwise to
saue him harmlesse from his said ingagement May it therefore please your Lordshipp to relieue your Orator in equitie and
to graunt vnto him his Maties most gracious writt of subp^a to be
directed to the said John Milton and John llane thereby Cō-
manding them and either of them at a certayne day and vnder a
certayne paine therein to be limitted to be and psonally to appeare before your Lordshipp in his Maties most high Court of

Chauncerie then and there to aunswere the p^rmisses and to stand
and abide such further order and direccōn therein as to your
Lō^p in equitie shalbe thought fitt/ And your Orator shall pray
for your Lō^p longe lieff and happines/

Wm Gilbert. J

Public Record Office, C2 James I/A6/35; French, *Milton in
Chancery*, pp. 21 ff., 221 ff.

MAY 10. FATHER ANSWERS JAMES AYLOFFE'S BILL.

Jurat.' Maij. 10. 1624.	The answere of John Milton Def^t.
Jacobus Hussey	to the Bill of Complainte of James
Saunders	Ayloffe Complaynñte./

The said Def^t. saveing vnto himselfe all advantages of excepcōn to the incertaynetie, and insufficiency of the said Bill for
answere therevnto saith; That true it is, That in or aboute the
time in the bill of Complainte mencōned One Edward Raymond
in the said Bill of Complainte named, and now deceased to-
gether wth the said Cōmp^{lt}. Ayloffe became bound by obligacōn
to one John Lane in the sōme of One hundred poundꝑ for
paym^t. of ffiftie two poundꝑ. and Tenn shillingꝑ On or aboute
the Eleaventh daie of August then following. And this Def^t.
beleeveth it to be true. That the said debte was the proper debte
of the said Edward Raymond. and that the said Def^t. Ayloffe
was onely bound as suertie for the same, And likewise saith that
the said debte is truly and iustly due to him this Def^t. and that
he vsed the name of the said John Lane as obligee in the said
obligacōn only in trust for this Def^{tꝑ}. vse, But he this Def^t. doth
absolutely denie, That the said Ayloffe did declare to him this
Def^t That he would not stand bound as suertie for y^t debte longer
then onely for Six monethes, or y^t he willed him this Def^t. that
the said money might not be continued at interest vpon that bond
anie longer then onely for that time as in the said Bill of Complainte is most vntruely suggested. And this def^t doth also denie
y^t for anie reward giuen to him by the said Raymond, or by anie
agreem^{tꝑ}. betweene them (other then the consideracōn for the
said Six monethes paste) he did continue the said money at in-

terest, but the money being payable on or aboute the Eleaventh daie of August in ye Nineteenth yeare of his Maties. raigne that now is of England, The said Def^t. was informed he colde haue no accōn in his Maties. Co^rt. of Comon pleas at Westm' against the said Raymond, and Ayloffe vntill Mīchas terme then folloing, and then this Def^t. sente to the said Raymond, and pressed him that in freindly and Curtuous mann he wold repaie the said fiftie pound℈ or otherwise he should be compelled to comence suite both against him the said Raymond, and against the said Cōmp^lt. Ayloffe. And the said Def^t. haueing often called and sent vnto the said Raymond for his said Money, and finding that he cold not haue it by faire meanes in Hillary terme then following deliuered the said obligacōn to an Attorney in his said Maties. Co^rt. of Comon pleas at Westm' to comence suite against the said Raymond, and the said Cōmp^lt. Ayloffe But the said Attorney acquainting the said Raymond therew^th (he the said Raymond being an Attorney in the same Co^rt.) intreated the said Attorney to make stay thereof for that he intended to giue this def^t. p^rsent satisfaccōn. And shortly afterward℈ sent to this def^t. and entreated him either to forbeare his money, or otherwise y^t he would bring his accōn in some Co^rt. w^thin the Citie of London to avoyde extraordinarie expences in suite of lawe, And this def^t. (willing to spare the said Ayloffe as longe as he could conveniently and to put the said Raymond to as litle charge as might be) did accordingly bring an accōn in the Lorde Maio^rs. Co^rt. in the Citie of London vpon the said obligacōn aboute the time in the bill mencōned and pressing ye said Raymond either to haue a plea, or a Judgem^t. He the said Raymond intreated the def^t to accepte of his Judgement, and that he would grante him some respite of time for the paym^t. of the said debte in respect (as he alleged) That if execucōn were sued out against him, he should be forced to lye in prison, wch would be his vtter ouerthrowe, and vndoeing. where vpon this def^t. (pittieing his complainte) was content to accepte of Tenn pound℈ in hand, and the remainder being fourtie pound℈ to take by Tenn pound℈ a quarter, and to loose the the forbearance, or in-

terest thereof, (that is to saie) at Midsomer laste Tenn poundƿ
at Michās then following Tenn poundƿ at Xrīmas laste, Tenn
poundƿ, and the rest at the feast of Thannunciacōn of the blessed
virgin Marie then next following. and as this def^t. thinketh
there is a note entred vpon the said Judgem^t. but not anie de-
feizance at all that if defaulte were made in anie of these paym^{tƿ}.
then execucōn to be prosecuted, And this defd^t saith That the said
Raymond made paym^t. of the said first Tenn poundƿ of the said
remainder of ffourtie poundƿ and dyed verry shortely after and
soe there hath not beene anie other paym^t. made sithence, And
this def^t. doth absolutely denie, that he did euer agree to deliuer
vpp the said obligacōn vpon the acknowledging of the said
Judgem^t. or to discharge the said Cōmp^{lt}. of or from the same,
as is in the said bill of complainte most vntruely alledged how-
beit he saith that there was such a request made, but vpon ad-
visem^t. of the weaknes of the said Raymondƿ estate, he absolutely denied it, and sent for the said obligacōn from his Attorney, and hath kepte the same euer since himselfe, And this def^t.
is verily pswaded in his conscience y^t the said Cōmp^{lt}. Ayloffe
doth certenly know, that he is not discharged of the said obliga-
cōn; And this defendant veriely beleeveth that the same obligacōn, neuer came to the handƿ of the said Ayloffe or that the
said Raymond euer shewed him the same, or tolde him, that
it was discharged, for that the same obligacōn to this Def^{tƿ}.
knowledge was neuer delieuered to anie, saueing to his svantƿ
to carry to his Attorney to prosecute the suite, and he is the
rather induced to beleeue it to be true for that the Cōmp^{lt}.
Ayloffe as this def^t. is informed by his svantƿ, shortly after the
death of the said Raymond of his owne accord came to this def^{tƿ}
shopp, and desired to know whether he were discharged of the
said debte, or no, and he was then answered that he was not discharged thereof, And this Def^t. thinketh that the said Cōmp^{lt}.
would neuer haue sought after him this Def^t. if his Conscience
had not accused him, or at leaste pswaded him y^t he was not discharged, And this def^t taketh it, That the said Cōmp^{lt}. Ayloffe
doth offer him great wronge to put him to these vnnecessary

vexacōns, and charge of suite for y^t. allwayes in loving and curteous mann̄ he required but the iuste somē that was due, and the interest & reasonable charge expended in & aboute the recouery of the same, and this Def^t made the said Ayloffe this offer before anie charge was expended, and is still willing, and ready to pforme the same, and to discharge the said Ayloffe of the said bond vpon paym^t. of the remainder of the said debte being Thirtie pounde wth interest, and of ye Charge wch this def^t. hath expended in and aboute the getting of his money, And this def^t. doth much marvell that the said Ayloffe doth still psiste in his obstinate refusall of this def^{te} offers, and to put both himselfe, and this Def^t to such vnnecessarie Charge, for that as the said Ayloffe confessed, he hath in his hande of the estate of the said Raymond to the value of Sixteene pounde or thereaboute, and likewise for y^t this def^t. was allwaies willing that the said Ayloffe might releeve himselfe vpon the said Judgem^t. recouered in the Lord Maio^{rs}. Co^{rt}. against ye admīstratrix of the said Raymond: And this def^t. endeavouring to haue eased the said Cōmp^{lt}. Ayloffe of the paym^t. of this debte did sue the admīstratrix of the said Raymond vpon the said Judgem^t. and her Attorney (as he affirmeth) had instruccōns to plead that she had satisfied as farr as the goode came vnto vpon other Judgem^{te}. before the said Def^t. did sue out his scire facias vpon his Judgem^t. and for that it would haue beene Chargeable to haue brought the same to a tryall, He desired the said Ayloffe to pay the said debte, and take an assignem^t. of the said Judgem^t. wch he refused to doe, and therefore this def^t. comēnced his accōn against the said Ayloffe at ye Comōn lawe, as it was lawfull for him soe to doe (as he thinketh) wthout that that anie other matter, or thing in the said Bill of Complainte conteyned matteriall or effectuall in the lawe for this def^t. to Answere vnto, and herein and hereby not before sufficiently answered vnto, confessed, or avoyded, trauersed, or denyed is true, All wch matters, and thinge this deft is and wilbe readie to averr, and prove as this hono^{ble}. Co^{rt}. shall award, and humbly prayeth to be hence dismissed wth his reason-

able cost℈ and Charg℈ in this behalfe most wrongfully susteyned:./

Edm. Breres

Public Record Office, C2 James I/A6/35; French, *Milton in Chancery*, pp. 21 ff.; 224 ff.

MAY 11. FATHER ARRANGES ERDISWICK-COTTON BOND.

Mr Erdiswick & others p obl' xj° Maij 1624 ... 200^{ll}

Thomas Bower's schedule of Cotton's bonds made out by himself and Milton's father; see below under date of November 25, 1630. The original bond has not been found.

... Mr Erdiswick & others by bond dated the Eleventh of May One thowsand six hundred Twentie ffoure Two hundred pound℈ principall debt.

Sir Thomas Cotton's bill; see below under date of May 28, 1636.

JULY 26. FATHER SIGNS RECORDS OF SCRIVENERS' COMPANY AS AUDITOR?

In the *Athenaeum* for 1880, 1, 760-761, Hyde Clarke states that the elder Milton was an auditor for 1624 and that he signed the book of the company in that capacity on July 26. I have however not been able to find any trace of such an activity in Bodleian MS. Rawl. Miscell. 51, which is the annual catalogue of the Company.

NOVEMBER. FATHER ARRANGES LEIGH-DOWNER BOND FOR FIFTY POUNDS.

... the ffiftie pound℈ in the bill mencōned, was by the said John Milton and this Defendant, by and with the consent, and good liking of the said Complaynant, putt to Jnterest for the vse of the said Complaynant [Rose Downer], into the hand℈ of one Master Leigh vpon sufficient securitie by bond in November One thowsand six hundred Twenty and ffower ....

Public Record Office, C2 Charles I/D39/47 (Bower's answer to Rose Downer, May 3, 1631); French, *Milton in Chancery*, p. 243.

NOVEMBER 30. FATHER ARRANGES LEIGH-COTTON BOND.

S^r ffrancis Leigh & oth^{rs} p obl' Dat' vltimo Novembr' 1624 ... 100^{ll}

Thomas Bower's schedule of Cotton's bonds made out by himself and Milton's father; see below under date of November 25, 1630. The original bond has not been found. This Leigh may have been the same man who, some time in the same month, borrowed fifty pounds from Rose Downer through Milton's shop. See entry above under date of November, 1624.

. . . [Sir Francis] Leigh & others by bond dated the Last of November One thowsand Six hundred Twentie ffoure One hundred poundȩ principall debt . . . .

Sir Thomas Cotton's bill; see below under date of May 28, 1636.

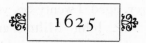

1625

LATIN VERSE AND PROSE ESSAYS.

(1) [Title:] Carmina Elegiaca.   [Johann]es Milton
    [First begins:] Surge, age surge, leues, iam convenit, excute somnos . . . .
    [Second begins:] Ignavus satrapam dedecet inclytum . . . .

(2) [Title:] Mane citus lectum fuge.
    [Begins:] Tritum est vetustate proverbium . . . .

The original sheet on which these pieces were written has disappeared. It was found by A. J. Horwood in the same package as Milton's Commonplace Book, but was not included by him in the photographic facsimile of that work which he published in 1876. He did, however, make photographs and deposit them in the Public Record Office and the British Museum. At least, he so states in his introduction to that volume. Actually no copy seems to be known in the Public Record Office, and that in the British Museum (MS. Add. 41063 1) was deposited much later, the gift of Hugh C. H. Candy. See Horwood's introduction to the revised edition of the reprint of the Commonplace Book in the Camden Society Publications, New Series, 1877, 61-63; French, "The Autographs of John Milton," #1; Mackellar, pp. 361-365; CM, I, 326-327, 596-598; CM, XVIII, 643; Masson, I (1881), 303-305. The date is very uncertain.

FATHER TAKES THOMAS BOWER INTO PARTNERSHIP.

. . . this Defendant saith, That he . . . hath beene for the space of Six yeares now past, or thereaboutǫ Partner with the said John Milton in the Profession which he now vseth, and hath within the said time beene a meanes of putting out many somēs of money at Jnterest. . . .

Public Record Office, C2 Charles I/D39/47 (Bower's answer to Rose Downer, dated May 3, 1631); French, *Milton in Chancery*, p. 243.

FATHER ACQUAINTED WITH OLIVE STREET.

Oliue Street of the parish of St: Andrewes in the Wardorb London Embrowderer, aged Twenty Six yeares or thereaboutǫ . . . hath knowne . . . John Milton and Thomas Bower named for deftǫ, for these Six yeares and vpwardes . . . .

Public Record Office, Chancery Depositions, C 24/574/40 (Street's deposition, dated September 19, 1631); French, *Milton in Chancery*, p. 245.

FATHER AND HIS PARTNER THOMAS BOWER INVEST MONEY FOR JOHN COTTON.

. . . John Cotton vncle of yoʳ sᵈ subiect being an old decripitt weake man of the age of fourscore yeares and vpwards did heretofore about five yeares sithence put into the hands off one John Milton of Breadstreet in yoʳ maᵗⁱᵉˢ city of Londō scrivener and Tho: Bower seruant to the sayd John Milton dīv great sumēs of money, in trust to be lett out at interest aftʳ yᵉ rate of eight in the hundred by the sayd John Milton and Tho: Bower which sayd somes were by seuerall specialtyes put out by the sayd John Milton and Tho: Bower viz . . . .

From Sir Thomas Cotton's bill of May 28, 1636, *q.v.* The date as given by Cotton is patently wrong. Five years before the date of his bill would be 1631, whereas we know from Bower's receipt that John Cotton had turned over the whole group of bonds to Bower as early as November, 1630; and by Cotton's own admission, Milton and Bower had collected interest on them and turned it over to Cotton "for some yeares" before this transfer took place. So this entry is placed in 1625 merely as an approximation to the true date. Possibly 1620, the earliest date on the list of bonds, would be more accurate.

FATHER AND HIS PARTNER BOWER COLLECT INTEREST ON JOHN COTTON'S INVESTMENTS AND TURN IT OVER TO HIM.

[Milton and Bower invested £3,600 for Cotton,] for which sayd somes the sayd John Miltō and Tho: Bowre did bring to the sayd John Cotton your subiects said vncle halfe yearly the interest after the rate of 8 p cent for some yeares and did often renew call in and put out the sayd sumes as they thought best themselues . . . .

Sir Thomas Cotton's bill against Milton, dated May 28, 1636, *q.v.* Since 1625 has been used arbitrarily as the date of the investment of the money by Milton and Bower for Cotton, the collection of interest has been filed under the same year. Obviously it must have continued for a considerable time, but the dates are so vague that this single entry is used to cover the whole. The process must have ended before November 25, 1630, when John Cotton turned over the whole group of bonds to Bower.

FATHER STEWARD OF COMPANY OF SCRIVENERS.

1625 . . . Tho: Hill - - - ⎱ Stewards
    Jnº: Milton ⎰

  Bodleian Library, MS. Rawl. Miscell. 51, "An Annual Catalogue . . . of the Company of Scriveners," f. 29; *Athenaeum*, 1880, I, 565; Brennecke, p. 113.

JANUARY 16. NEPHEW JOHN PHILLIPS BAPTIZED.

[Baptisms] Januarii 1624 [*i.e.*, 1624/5] . . . 16 . . . Johannes Phillips fs. Edwardi, gen'osi, et Anne.

  The Register of St. Martin-in-the-Fields London 1619-1636, ed. J. V. Kitto, 1936 (Publications of the Harleian Society, Vol. LXVI), p. 35. I have not seen the original parish record. This and the five succeeding records of the children of this family, entered under the dates of January 12, 1626, January 22, 1628, April 9, 1628, March 15, 1629, and February 19, 1631, were published by William R. Parker in the London *Times Literary Supplement* for December 17, 1938, and repeated by James Holly Hanford in *A Milton Handbook*, 1939, p. 139. This John Phillips appears to have died on March 15, 1629, *q.v.* His more famous namesake was born in August, 1630.

[John Phillips, son of Edward, gentleman, and Anne, was baptized January 16, 1624/5.]

JANUARY 24. FUTURE WIFE, MARY POWELL, BAP-
TIZED.

Marie Powell the daughter of Richard Powell baptized the
the [*sic*] xxiiij[th] day of Januarie, 1625.

Forest Hill Parish Register; Masson, II, 499. Masson interprets this
date, naturally enough, as January 24, 1625/6; but the way in which
the year is written and the preceding and following entries seem to prove
that the proper year is 1624/5. Both this entry and the one immediately
preceding it were first written 1624, and then the 4 was changed to 5;
the item before this is November, 1624. The several entries following
that of Mary Powell are dated respectively March 13, 1625; April,
1625; May, 1625; July, 1625; and various other items also in 1625.
It seems undeniable, in the light of this evidence, that Mary must have
been born in 1625, modern dating. The date of her birth should therefore be changed from 1626 to 1625 in my *Milton in Chancery* in the
genealogical chart facing p. 167.

FEBRUARY? RECEIVES GIFT OF HEBREW BIBLE FROM
TUTOR THOMAS YOUNG (AND ALSO A LETTER?).

Biblia Hebræa, pergratum sane munus tuum, jampridem
accepi.

Milton, *Epistolarum Familiarium Liber Unus*, 1674, p. 9; CM, XII,
6-7; XVIII, 526, 562. The Bible has not been traced in modern times.
The date given here is of course only approximate. It seems likely that
the Bible was accompanied by a letter, since Milton's letter of March 26,
here quoted, is partly in answer to one or more letters by Young. By
inference from Milton's writing, we can be sure that Young complained
that Milton's letters had been few and short. Harris Fletcher thinks that
the Bible was the Bomberg rabbinical Bible, edited by Johann Buxtorf
and published at Basle about 1620; see his *Milton's Semitic Studies*,
Chicago, 1926, pp. 74-75.

[The Hebrew Bible, your truly most acceptable gift, I received some time since.]

FEBRUARY 12. ADMITTED TO CHRIST'S COLLEGE, CAM-
BRIDGE.

Johannes Milton. Londinensis filius Johannis institutus fuit
in literarū elementis sub M[ro] Gill Gymnasij Paulini præfecto.
admissus est pensionarius minor. ffeb. 12. 1624. sub M[ro] Chappell. Soluitqz pro ingressu . . . 10[s].

Christ's College, Cambridge, Admission Register; Masson, I, 88 (112); French, "The Autographs of John Milton," *ELH*, IV (1937), #98. There is a facsimile in Williamson's *Milton Tercentenary*, p. iii.

[John Milton of London, son of John, instituted in the elements of letters under Master Gill, prefect of St. Paul's School, was admitted as a minor pensioner on February 12, 1624/5, under Master Chappell. He paid for entrance ten shillings.]

MARCH 26. LETTER TO THOMAS YOUNG.

Thomæ Junio *Præceptori suo.*

1. Quanquam statueram apud me (Præceptor optime) Epistolium quoddam numeris metricis elucubratum ad te dare, non satis tamen habuisse me existimavi, nisi aliud insuper soluto stylo exarassem; incredibilis enim illa & singularis animi mei gratitudo, quam tua ex debito vendicant in me merita, non constricto illo, & certis pedibus ac syllabis angustato dicendi genere experimenda fuit, sed Oratione liberâ, immo potius, si fieri posset, Asiaticâ verborum exuberantiâ. Quamvis quidem satis exprimere quantum tibi debeam, opus sit meis viribus longe majus, etiamsi omnes quoscunq; Aristoteles, quoscunq; Parisiensis ille Dialecticus congessit Argumentorum τόπους exinanirem, etiamsi omnes elocutionis fonticulos exhaurirem. Quereris tu vero (quòd merito potes) literas meas raras admodum & perbreves ad te delatas esse; ego vero non tam doleo me adeo jucundo, adeoq; expetendo defuisse officio, quam gaudeo & pene exulto eum me in amicitia tua tenere locum, qui possit crebras à me Epistolas efflagitare. Quod autem hoc plusquam triennio nunquam ad te scripserim, quæso ut ne in pejus trahas, sed pro mirifica ista tua facilitate & candore, in mitiorem partem interpretari digneris. Deum enim testor quam te instar Patris colam, quam singulari etiam observantiâ te semper prosecutus sim, quamq; veritus chartis meis tibi obstrepere. Curo nempe cum primis, cum Tabellas meas nihil aliud commendet, ut commendet raritas. Deinde, cum ex vehementissimo, quo tui afficior desiderio, adesse te semper cogitem, teq; tanquam præsentem alloquar &

intuear, doloriq; meo (quod in amore fere fit) vanâ quâdam præsentiæ tuæ imaginatione adblandiar; vereor profecto, simulac literas ad te mittendas meditarer, ne in mentem mihi subito veniret, quam longinquo à me distes terrarum intervallo; atque ita recrudesceret dolor absentiæ tuæ jam prope consopitus, somniúmq; dulce discuteret. Biblia Hebræa, pergratum sane munus tuum, jampridem accepi. Hæc scripsi Londini inter urbana diverticula, non Libris, ut soleo, circumseptus: Si quid igitur in hac Epistola minus arriserit, tuamque frustrabitur expectationem, pensabitur aliâ magis elaboratâ; ubi primum ad Musarum spatia rediero.

Londino, Martii 26. 1625.

Milton, *Epistolarum Familiarium Liber Unus,* 1674, pp. 7-9; CM, XII, 4-7; XVIII, 526. William R. Parker (*Modern Language Notes,* LIII, 1938, 399 ff.) questions the date 1625 and suggests that 1627 would be more likely. The evidence which he presents is of considerable weight, but I have placed the letter here because of its date in the original edition.

[Although I had resolved with myself, most excellent Preceptor, to send you a certain small epistle composed in metrical numbers, yet I did not consider that I had done enough, unless I also wrote something in prose; for truly the boundless and singular gratitude of my mind, which your deserts justly claim from me, was not to be expressed in that cramped mode of speech, straitened by fixed feet and syllables, but in a free oration, nay rather, were it possible, in an Asiatic exuberance of words. Albeit, 'tis true, to express sufficiently how much I owe you were a work far greater than my strength, even if I should call into play all those commonplaces of argument which Aristotle or that Dialectician of Paris has collected, or even if I should exhaust all the fountains of oratory. You complain (as justly you may) that my letters have been to you very few and very short; but I, on the other hand, do not so much grieve that I have been remiss in a duty so pleasant and so enviable, as I rejoice, and all but exult, at having such a place in your friendship as that you should care to ask for frequent letters from me. That I should never have written to you for now more than three years, I pray you will not misconceive, but, in accordance with your wonderful indulgence and candour, put the more charitable construction upon it. For I call God to witness how much as a Father I regard you, with what singular devotion I have always followed you in thought, and how I feared to trouble you with my writings. In sooth I make it my first care that since there is nothing else to commend my letters, their rarity may commend them. Next, as out of that most vehement desire after you which I feel, I always fancy you with me, and speak to you and behold you as if you were present, and so (as almost happens in love) soothe my grief by a certain vain imagination of your presence, it is in truth my fear, as soon as I meditate sending you a letter, that it should suddenly come into my mind by what an interval of earth you are distant from me, and so the grief of your absence, already nearly lulled, should grow fresh, and break up my sweet dream. The Hebrew Bible, your truly most acceptable gift, I have already received. These lines I have written in London in the midst of town-distractions, not, as usual, surrounded by books: if, therefore, anything in this epistle should please you less than might be, and disappoint your expectation, it will be made up for by another more elaborate one, as soon as I have returned to the haunts of the Muses.]

Masson, I, 122-123 (147-148); CM, XII, 5-7.

APRIL 9. MATRICULATES AT CAMBRIDGE.

1625 April 9 . . . Lesser Pensioners . . . John Milton.

Cambridge University, Matriculation Books; Masson, I, 124 (149); Stern, I, i, 308. There are copies of this entry in two British Museum manuscripts: Harl. 7036 and 7041. The form of this note is taken from Masson since unfortunately I do not have a copy of the original.

APRIL 9. ARRIVAL AT CHRIST'S COLLEGE; STUDIES; TUTORS; REPUTATION AT CAMBRIDGE.

went at his own Chardge only to Christs College in Cambr: at fifteen whre he stayed eight yeares at least: . . . And was a very hard student in the University, & pformed all his exercises there wth very good Applause. His 1st Tutor there was M^r

Chapell, from whom receiving some unkindnesse (whip't him), he was afterwards (though it seemed / yᵉ Rules of yᵉ Coll: transferred to the Tuition of one Mʳ Tovell, who dyed Parson of Lutterworth.

Aubrey, ff. 63, 64; Darbishire, pp. 2, 10. The phrase "at his own Chardge only" is added over a caret; "at fifteen" is written above cancelled "very young sc. about thirteen was the most"; "whip't him" is written above "unkindnesse," a situation which I have tried to suggest by the use of parentheses; the diagonal bar after "it seemed" appears in the manuscript as a bar with a tiny circle at each end, and seems to be Aubrey's shorthand for "contrary to."

A description and picture of Milton's room is given by David Masson in "Local Memories of Milton," *Good Words*, xxxiv (1893), 39 ff. For Wordsworth's excitement at living in the rooms once occupied by Milton, and his rare adventure into inebriety as a result, see "The Prelude," Book iii, lines 293-302.

At about eighteen Yeers of age hee went to Christs College in Cambridge; where for his diligent study, his performance of public exercises, and for choice Verses, written on the occasions usually solemniz'd by the Universities, as well as for his virtuous and sober life, hee was in high esteem wᵗʰ the best of his time.

The "earliest" biography, f. 140v; Darbishire, pp. 18-19.

... at the Age of 15 he was full ripe for Academick Learning, and accordingly was sent to the University of *Cambridge*; where in *Christ's College*, under the Tuition of a very Eminent Learned man, whose Name I cannot call to mind, he Studied Seven years, and took his Degree of Master of Arts; and for the extraordinary Wit and Reading he had shown in his Performances to attain his Degree, (some whereof spoken at a Vacation-Exercise in his 19th. year of Age, are to be yet seen in his Miscellaneous Poems) he was lov'd and admir'd by the whole University, particularly by the Fellows and most Ingenious Persons of his House.

Phillips, pp. viii-ix; Darbishire, p. 54.

... *Pauls* School ... thence at 15 years of age was sent to *Christs* Coll. in *Cambridge*, where he was put under the tuition of *Will. Chappell*, afterwards Bishop of *Ross* in *Ireland*, and there, as at School for 3 years before, 'twas usual with him to sit up till midnight at his book, which was the first thing that brought his eyes into the danger of blindness. By this his indefatigable study he profited exceedingly, wrot then several Poems, paraphras'd some of *David's Psalms*, performed the collegiate and academical exercise to the admiration of all, and was esteemed to be a vertuous and sober person, yet not to be ignorant of his own parts.

Wood, I, 880; Darbishire, p. 36. Milton's career at Cambridge is described in some detail by John Peile in *Christ's College*, 1900, pp. 145-149. Peile points out the unlikelihood that his tutor would have whipped him. On Milton's tutor Chappell, see Masson, I, 104 (128); Stern, I, i, 56.

APRIL 9 FF. STUDIES GREEK, FRENCH, ITALIAN, AND HEBREW AT THE UNIVERSITY.

> . . . tuo pater optime sumptu
> Cùm mihi Romuleæ patuit facundia linguæ,
> Et Latii veneres, & quæ Jovis ora decebant
> Grandia magniloquis elata vocabula Graiis,
> Addere suasisti quos jactat Gallia flores,
> Et quam degeneri novus Italus ore loquelam
> Fundit, Barbaricos testatus voce tumultus,
> Quæque Palæstinus loquitur mysteria vates.

Milton, "Ad Patrem," *Poems*, 1645, part ii, p. 67.

[At your expense, best of fathers, when mastery of the language of Romulus and the Latin graces had come to me, and when the sublime speech of the eloquent Greeks, which graces the lips of Jove, lay open to me, you persuaded me to add the flowers of language which France glories in and the modern Italian pours from his degenerate mouth, testifying by his voice to barbarian upheavals, and the mysteries which the Palestinian prophet speaks.]

STUDIES THEOLOGICAL WORKS, AND MAKES THEOLOGICAL NOTEBOOK.

Coepi igitur Adolescens . . . cum ad libros utriusqz Testamenti lingva perlegendos assiduus incumbere, tum Theologorum Systemata aliquot brevior sedulo percurrere: ad eorum deinde exemplum, locos communes digerere, ad quos omnia quæ ex scripturis haurienda occurrissent, expromenda cum opus esset, referrem. Ad uberiora deinde Theologorum volumina et disputantes in utramqz partem de capitibus quibusdam fidei quæstiones, fidentius demum me contuli . . . nihil mihi tutius neque consultius visum est, quam ut ipse aliquid huius modi quod ad manum mihi esset, labore ac lucubratione propriâ ex ipso adeoqz solo Dei verbo, et fidelissimè quidem, nisi mihimet fortè infidus esse volebam, de integro componeram. Quod cum per aliquot annos agere attentissimè perseverassem . . .

Milton, *De Doctrina Christiana,* preface; CM, XIV, 4-7. The original notebook mentioned here by Milton has not been found. But a few scattered phrases and titles from it, under the heading of "Index Theologicus," were brought together in CM, XVIII, 227, 510. It should be remembered, however, that Milton may very well have kept more than one book of this nature, and that not all references to such a volume are necessarily to the same one.

[I entered upon an assiduous course of study in my youth, beginning with the books of the Old and New Testament in their original languages, and going diligently through a few of the shorter systems of the divines, in imitation of whom I was in the habit of classing under certain heads whatever passages of Scripture occurred for extraction, to be made use of hereafter as occasion might require. At length I resorted with increased confidence to some of the more copious theological treatises, and to the examination of the arguments advanced by the conflicting parties respecting certain disputed points of faith . . . . I deemed it therefore safest and most advisable to compile for myself, by my own labor and study, some original treatise which should be always at hand, derived solely from the word of God itself, and executed with all possible fidelity, seeing that I could have no wish to practice any imposition on myself in such a matter.

After a diligent perseverance in this plan for several years. . . .]

Milton, *Prose Works,* Bohn edition, 1861, IV, 2-4.

LEARNS TO FENCE.

When he was Young he learnt to Fence, probably as a Gentlemanly Accomplishment, and that he might be Able to do Himself Right in Case of an Affront . . . though it does not appear he ever made This Use of his Skill.

Richardson, p. v; Darbishire, p. 204.

RELATIONS WITH THE UNIVERSITY; FRIENDSHIP WITH FELLOWS; OPINION OF THE UNIVERSITY; INTEGRITY.

[He scorns Hall's charge of an "inordinat and riotous youth spent at the *Vniuersity*," only then to be *"vomited out thence*,"] for it hath given me an apt occasion to acknowledge publickly with all gratefull minde, that more then ordinary favour and respect which I found above any of my equals at the hands of those curteous and learned men, the Fellowes of that Colledge wherein I spent some years: who at my parting, after I had taken two degrees, as the manner is, signifi'd many wayes, how much better it would content them that I would stay; as by many Letters full of kindnesse and loving respect both before that time, and long after I was assur'd of their singular good affection towards me . . . those ingenuous and friendly men who were ever the countnancers of vertuous and hopefull wits.

Milton, *Apology for Smectymnuus*, 1642, p. 12; CM, III, 297-298. None of the letters from the fellows to Milton can now be found.

[The actors in University plays] thought themselves gallant men, and I thought them fools; they made sport, and I laught.

Milton, *Apology for Smectymnuus*, 1642, p. 14; CM, III, 300.

[Milton scorns] those places, which were intended to be the seed plots of piety and the Liberall Arts, but were become the nurseries of superstition, and empty speculation.

Milton, *Apology for Smectymnuus*, 1642, pp. 37-38; CM, III, 335-336.

Illîc disciplinis atque artibus tradi solitis septennium studui; procul omni flagitio, bonis omnibus probatus, usquedum Magistri, quem vocant, gradum, cum laude etiam adeptus . . .

[Here I passed seven years in the usual course of instruction and study, with the approbation of the good, and without any stain upon my character, till I took the degree of Master of Arts.]

Milton, *Defensio Secunda*, 1654, p. 60; CM, VIII, 120; translation from Bohn, I, 254.

APRIL (?) ARRANGES TO VISIT DIODATI.

Ἡ μὲν παροῦσα κατάστασις τοῦ ἀέρος δοκεῖ φθονερώτερον διακεῖσθαι πρὸς ἃ ἡμεῖς πρωὴν διαλυόμενοι ἐθέμεθα, χειμά- ζουσα, καὶ ταρασσομένη δύο ἤδη ὅλας ἡμέρας. . . . ἀλλά σύ θάρσει ὦ φίλε, καὶ ἔμμενε τῷ δόξαντι συναμφοῖν, καὶ ἀνα- λάμβανε διάθεσιν τῆς ψυχῆς ἑορταστικήν, καὶ φαιδροτέραν τῆς καθημερινῆς. καὶ γὰρ ἐσαύριον ἔσται πάντα καλῶς.

From Diodati's letter to Milton, 1625 (?), given below.

→[The present state of the weather seems to be too unfavorable for what we planned when we parted the day before yesterday, since it has been wintry and stormy now for two whole days. . . . But take courage, my friend, and be with me as agreed, and put on a festive frame of mind and one gayer than usual. Tomorrow everything will go well. . . .]

APRIL (?) LETTER IN GREEK FROM CHARLES DIODATI.

Θεόσδοτος Μίλτωνι εὐφράινεσθαι

Ἡ μὲν παροῦσα κατάστασις τοῦ ἀέρος δοκεῖ φθονερώτερον διακεῖσθαι πρὸς ἃ ἡμεῖς πρωὴν διαλυόμενοι ἐθέμεθα, χειμά- ζουσα, καὶ ταρασσομένη δύο ἤδη ὅλας ἡμέρας, ἀλλ᾽ ὅμως τοσοῦ- τον ἐπιθυμῶ τῆς σῆς συνδιαιττήσεως, ὥσθ᾽ ὑπὸ ἐπιθυμίας ἤδη εὐδίαν, καὶ γαλήνην καὶ πάντα χρυσᾶ εἰς τὸν αὔριον ὀνειρώττειν, καὶ μονονοὺ μαντένεσθαι, ἵνα λόγων φιλοσόφων, καὶ πεπαιδευ- μένων ἐνωχώεθα ἔξ ἀλλήλιον διὰ τοῦτο οὖν ἠβουλόμην πρὸς σὲ γράφειν τοῦ προκαλεῖσθαί καὶ ἀναθαρσύνειν χάριν, δείσας μὴ πρὸς ἕτερα ἄττα νοῦν προσέχῃς ἀπελπίσας ἡλιασμοὺς, καὶ ἡδυπαθείας, εἰς τὸ παρόνγε. ἀλλά σύ θάρσει ὦ φίλε, καὶ ἔμμενε τῷ δόξαντι συναμφοῖν, καὶ ἀναλάμβανε διάθεσιν τῆς ψυχῆς ἑορταστικήν, καὶ φαιδροτέραν τῆς καθημερινῆς. καὶ γὰρ ἐσαύ- ριον ἔσται πάντα καλῶς, καὶ ὅ ἀὴρ, καὶ ὁ ἥλιυς, καὶ ὅ ποταμὸς,

καὶ δένδρα, καὶ ὀρνίθια, καὶ γῆ, καὶ ἄνθρωποι ἑορτάζουσιν ἡμῖν
συνγελάσουσιν, καὶ συγχορεύσουσι. τὸ δὴ ἀνεμεσήτως λελέχθω.
μόνον σὺ ἕτοιμος γίνου ἢ κληθεὶς ἐξορμάσθαι, ἢ καὶ ἄκλητος
ποθοῦντι ἐπελθείν. αὐτόματος δὲ ὃι ἦλθε βοὴν ἀγαθὸς μενέλαος.
ἔῤῥωσο.

British Museum, Add. MS. 5016*, f. 71; Stern, I, 310; Milton,
Prose Works, ed. Mitford, I (1851), cxciii-iv; CM, XII, 292; Milton,
Works, ed. Toland, 1698, I, 10; French, "The Autographs of John
Milton," *ELH*, IV (1937), no. 97. The contractions of the original
manuscript have been expanded to allow printing. The thirteenth word
is a correction in the margin in a hand which Mitford thinks Milton's.
Together with Diodati's later Greek letter of 1626 (?), this letter was
in the hands of Toland when he wrote his biography, and it bears on
f. 3 another note: "Found in the 1st Vol. of Milton's Works in 40."
In its original form this note began: "Found in Newton's Milton Vol. 1,"
but everything after the first word was then erased, and even now some
of the words are dubious. On the verso of the second letter is written
an unsigned note: "These 2 Greek Epistles of the famous *Diodati* to
Milton were given me by Mr. Toland who writ the life of said J M."
The letter bears no date, signature, or address, but is usually dated 1625.

[Diodati to Milton, to cheer up.

The present state of the weather seems to be too unfavorable
for what we planned when we parted the day before yesterday,
since it has been wintry and stormy now for two whole days.
But I am so anxious to see you that in my eagerness now I dream
of and prophesy everything warm and calm and golden for to-
morrow, so that we may regale ourselves with each other's
philosophical and scholarly talk. So I wanted to write this to
you in order to invite and encourage you, lest you should turn
your mind to other things after giving up hope of sunshine and
luxury for the present. But take courage, my friend, and be
with me as agreed, and put on a festive frame of mind and one
gayer than usual. To-morrow everything will go well; and the
air and the sun and the river and trees and birds and earth and
men will make holiday with us, and laugh with us. I say this
without offence. But be ready to come out when called, and
even uncalled, to meet me who yearn for you. "But Menelaus,
good at the battle-cry, came uninvited." Farewell.]

Partly from Masson, I, 137-138 (162), which is fragmentary, supplemented by the present editor.

APRIL (?) LEGEND OF MILTON AND THE FAIR CHARMER.

It is well known that, in the bloom of youth, and when he pursued his studies at Cambridge, this poet was extremely beautiful. Wandering, one day, during the summer, far beyond the precincts of the University, into the country, he became so heated and fatigued, that, reclining himself at the foot of a tree to rest, he shortly fell asleep. Before he awoke, two ladies, who were foreigners, passed by in a carriage. Agreeably astonished at the loveliness of his appearance, they alighted, and having admired him (as they thought) unperceived, for some time, the youngest, who was very handsome, drew a pencil from her pocket, and having written some lines upon a piece of paper, put it with her trembling hand into his own. Immediately afterwards they proceeded on their journey. Some of his acquaintances, who were in search of him, had observed this silent adventure, but at too great a distance to discover that the highly-favoured party in it was our illustrious bard. Approaching nearer, they saw their friend, to whom, being awakened, they mentioned what had happened. Milton opened the paper, and, with surprise, read these verses from Guarini:

[Madrigal xii. ed. 1598.]

> '*Occhi, stelle mortali,*
> '*Ministre de miei mali,—*
> '*Se chiusi m' uccidete,*
> '*Aperti che farete?*'

'Ye eyes! ye human stars! ye authors of my liveliest pangs! If thus, when shut, ye wound me, what must have proved the consequence had ye been open?' Eager, from this moment, to find out the fair *incognita*, Milton travelled, but in vain, through every part of Italy. His poetick fervour became incessantly more and more heated by the idea which he had formed of his unknown admirer; and it is, in some degree, to *her* that his own times, the present times, and the latest posterity must feel themselves indebted for several of the most impassioned and charming compositions of the Paradise Lost.

Milton, *Poetical Works*, ed. Todd, I (1826), 29-31; CM, XVIII, 535. Todd gives the origin of his version of this tale as an undated newspaper excerpt given to him by Mr. Bindley, who in turn had it from M. Whish, Esq. Todd also points out that a very similar story appears, though without reference to Milton, in the *Poesies* of Marguerite-Eleanore Clotilde de Vallon-Chalys, depuis, Madame de Surville (Paris, 1803, pp. xl-xli); the story is here almost word for word, though told of Justine de Lévis and Louis de Puytendre. In his *Curiosities of Literature* (edition of 1881, III, 299) Isaac Disraeli comments on the story as applied to Milton and says that Steevens invented it or at least adapted it to Milton from newspaper accounts stemming from the *Poesies*. There seems to be no reason for regarding it as having any true biographical connection with Milton.

APRIL (?) READS AND STUDIES DU BARTAS?

G. C. Taylor's book, *Milton's Use of Du Bartas*, Cambridge, Massachusetts, 1934, makes a strong case for Milton's having drawn on Du Bartas for materials for *Paradise Lost*, and also for his earliest poems. If Taylor's argument is sound, Milton must have been reading and studying his predecessor about this time.

APRIL (?) PROLUSION 5.

In Scholis Publicis.

Non dantur formæ partiales in animali præter totalem.

[In the public schools. There are no partial forms in an animal beyond the whole.]

Milton, *Epistolarum Familiarium Liber Unus*, 1674, 106-112; CM, XII, 190 ff. Since there is no clue to the date of this piece, it is filed under this year for convenience.

APRIL 14. FATHER ARRANGES BOLD-COTTON BOND.

Mr Bold & oth^{rs} p obl^{con} Dat' xiiij^{to} April' 1625 . . . 100^{ll}.

Thomas Bower's schedule of Cotton's bonds made out by himself and Milton's father; see below under date of November 25, 1630. The original bond has not been found.

. . . M^{r}. Bold & others by bond dated the ffourteenth of Aprill One thousand six hundred Twentie & ffive One hundred pound℈ [prin]cipall debt.

Sir Thomas Cotton's bill; see below under date of May 28, 1636.

JULY 16. WILL OF BROTHER CHRISTOPHER'S FUTURE WIFE'S FATHER.

John Webber, tailor, made his will on this date. He mentioned in it his children William, Anne, Isabel, Thomasin (wife of Christopher), and Katherine. He died and was buried at St. Clement Danes on June 5, 1632. His will was proved on June 11, 1632, by his relict Isabel. The record is in the Prerogative Court of Canterbury, 67 Audley. See *Notes and Queries*, XI, vii (1913), 21.

DECEMBER 10. FRIEND CHARLES DIODATI RECEIVES B.A.

The original record of this event is not immediately available, but it is recorded in Andrew Clark's *Register of the University of Oxford*, Oxford, 1888, II, part iii, p. 444. See also Donald C. Dorian, "Charles Diodati at Geneva," *PMLA*, LIX (1944), 589-591.

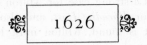

1626

POEM ON DEATH OF NIECE.

Anno ætatis 17.

On the Death of a fair Infant dying of a Cough.

Milton, *Poems*, 1673, 17-21; CM, I, 15-18. Most editors date this poem in the winter of 1625-26, though there is some question and a good deal of uncertainty about it. Milton was seventeen between December 9, 1625, and December 8, 1626. The infant mentioned seems without much doubt to have been the child of the poet's sister Ann and Edward Phillips, who were married in November, 1623. William R. Parker, and following him James Holly Hanford, favor a date after January 22, 1628, since on that day occurred the first recorded death of a child of this couple, Anne, who had been born on January 12, 1626. But it seems difficult to suppose that Milton or his printer would have headed a poem "Anno ætatis 17" which was written when Milton was actually over 19. On the other hand, such a mistake could occur. Parker's discussion is found in the *Times Literary Supplement*, December 17, 1938; Hanford's in his *Milton Handbook* (1946), pp. 138-140.

FUTURE FATHER-IN-LAW OBTAINS LEASE IN FOREST HILL FROM ALL-SOULS COLLEGE.

[When Richard Powell obtained a new lease in 1641, it was] upon his giving in of the said old Lease made in the yeare of our Lord, 1626.

[It is referred to elsewhere as] a Lease for years before that time [1634] made by *All-soules* Colledge.

Bodleian Library, MS. Wood 515, pp. 2, 3. This document is an eight-page printed account of a suit brought by William Powell alias Hinson against the warden and fellows of All-Souls College in the Chancellor's Court of the University of Oxford in 1656. It is described by David Stevens in his *Milton Papers*, p. 10.

JANUARY 12. NIECE ANNE PHILLIPS BAPTIZED.

[Baptisms] January 1625 [i.e., 1625/6] . . . 12 Ann Phillipps d. of Edward & Ann.

The Register of St. Martin-in-the-Fields London 1619-1636, ed. J. V. Kitto, 1936 (Publications of the Harleian Society, Vol. LXVI), p. 40. I have not seen the original parish record.

WINTER OR SPRING? FATHER AND OTHERS BRING COMMON LAW ACTION AGAINST SAMUEL BURTON FOR DEBT(?).

. . . the sayd William Smith and Sr George Peckham having vnder these p^rtences gotten your Subiect to stand bound as a surety for the sayd moneyes as aforesayd doe Combine and Confederate together wth one John Milton a Scrivenor in London and a Broker for the letting out of the moneyes of the sayd Smithe how they may lay the whole penaltie of the sayd Bond of Two hundred pounds vppon Your sayd Subiect, or at least the s'd somme of one hundred pound℘ wth Jnterest, whereas Your sayd Subiect hopeth to proue that the sayd Smith never lent one pennie of the sayd some of one hundred pound℘ and so in all equitie ought to have noe benefit of the sayd Bond nor to prosecute sute at Law therevppon, And Your Subiect hopeth allso to proue that the sayd Smith well knowing that hee depteth wth noe money vppon the sayd Bond doth not Beare the charges of the sayd sute at ye Common Law, nor disburse money in the same, but the sayd sute is meerelye prosecuted by the sayd Sr George and the sayd John Milton or one of them hoping thereby to gaine and make some advantage vnto themselues of Your sayd Subiect. . . .

From Samuel Burton's bill against Milton, May 10, 1626, *q.v.* The original proceedings at common law have not been found.

. . . this Def^t: Mylton confesseth that he hath heard that one Thomas Paradyne Cittizen & Haberdasher of London did vse the said William Smyths name in trust in such A bonde, for such a some of one hundred pound? . . . [and Burton now merely tries to] perplex & hinder some lawfull Course wch the said Thomas Paradyne in the name of the said Smyth hath taken against the Cōmp^lt, & the other Def^te Sr George Peckham, for Recouery of his Just Debte Due by the said bond W^th Costs & Damadges by him susteyned therein, wch this Def^t; John Mylton beleeueth the said Thomas Paradyne hath Done . . . this Def^t: John Mylton vtterly Denyeth that he pscuteth the said suite or any suite at all against the said Cōmp^lt, or hath any hand in the pscutinge of any suite whatsoeuer against the said Cōmp^lt, sauinge this same, wherein he is thus vniustly constrayned to make Defence. . . .

From Milton's answer to Burton, November 15, 1626, *q.v.* From Milton's vigorous denial of Burton's assertion it seems likely that he was not directly engaged as one of the plaintiffs in the present common law suit; but he was probably at least indirectly involved.

MAY? LETTER FROM CHARLES DIODATI; HARD STUDY.

Θεόδοτος Μίλτωνι χαίρειν.

Οὐδὲν ἔχω ἐγκάλειν τῇ νῦν διαγωγῇ μου, εκτὸς τούτου ἑνὸς, ὅτι στερισκομαι ψυχῆς τινος γενναίας λόγον ἄιτειν, καὶ διδόναι ἐπισταμένης τοίην τοι κεφαλὴν ποθέω, τὰ δ'ἄλλα ἄφθονα πάντα ὑπάρχει ἐνταῦθα ἐν ἀγρῷ. τί γὰρ ἂν ἔτι λείποι, ὁπόταν ἤματα μακρὰ, τόποι κάλλιστοι ἄνθεσι, καὶ φύλλοις κομῶντες, καὶ βρύοντες ἐπὶ παντὶ κλάδῳ ἀηδὼν, ἤ ἀκανθὶς, ἤ ἄλλο τι ὀρνίθιον ᾠδαῖς, καὶ μινυρισμοῖς ἐμφιλοτιμειται, περίπατοι ποικιλώτατοι, τράπεζα οὔτε ἐνδεὴς. οὔτε κατάκορος, ὕπνοι ἀθόρυβοι; ἐι εσθλὸν τινα ἑταίρον τούτεστι πεπαιδευμένον, καὶ μεμνημένον ἐπὶ τούτοις, ἐκτωμην, τοῦ τῶν περσῶν βασιλέως εὐδαιμονέστερος ἂν γενοί- μην. ἀλλ᾽ ἐστὶν ἀεί τι ἐλλιπὲς ἐν τοῖς ανθρωπίνοις πράγμασι, πρὸς ὅ δεῖ μετριότητος. σὺ δὲ ὦ θαυμάσιε, τί καταφρονεῖς τῶν τῆς φύσεως δωρημάτων; τί καρτερεῖς ἀπροφασίστως, βιβλίοις, καὶ λογιδίοις παννύχιον, πανῆμαρ προσφυόμενος; ζῆ, γέλα, χρῶ τῇ νεότητι, καὶ ταῖς ὥραις, καὶ πανοῦ ἀναγινώσκων τάς σπουδας καὶ τὰς ἀνέσεις καὶ ῥαστώνας τῶν πάλαι σοφῶν αὐτὸς κατατριβόμενος τέως. ἐγὼ μὲν ἐν ἄπασιν ἄλλοις ἥττων σοῦ ὑπάρχων, ἐν τούτῳ, τῷ μέτρον πόνων εἰδέναι κρείττων καὶ δοκῶ ἐμαυτῷ, καὶ εἰμι. ἔρρωσο, καὶ παῖζε, ἀλλ᾽ ὀυ κάτα σαρδανάπαλον τὸν ἐν σόλοις.

British Museum, MS. Add. 5016*, f. 5; Milton, *Prose Works*, ed. Mitford, I (1851), cxciv; CM, XII, 294. Dated in the spring of 1626 in the Columbia Milton.

[I have no fault to find with my present mode of life, ex- cept that I am deprived of any mind fit to converse with. I long for such a person. In other respects all passes pleasantly here in the country; for what else is wanting, when the days are long, the scenery around blooming with flowers, and waving and teeming with leaves, on every branch a nightingale or goldfinch or other bird of song delighting with its warblings, most varied walks, a table neither scant nor overburdened, and sleep un- disturbed? If I could only add to all these gifts a noble com- panion, well educated, with a good memory for all things, and select, I should be happier than the King of Persia. But there is always something missing in human affairs; hence moderation is needed. But you, wondrous youth, why do you despise the gifts of nature; why do you persist inexcusably in tying yourself night and day to your books? Live, laugh, enjoy your youth and the present hour; and stop studying the zeals and licenses and recreations of the wise men of old, meanwhile wearying your- self. I, in all things your inferior, both think myself and am superior to you in this, that I know a moderation in my labours! Farewell, and rejoice, but not like Sardanapalus in Soli.]

Masson, I, 138 (163), incomplete but filled in by the present editor.

SPRING? RUSTICATED FROM CAMBRIDGE.

Ajunt hominem Cantabrigiensi Academia ob flagitia pulsum. . . .

Moulin, *Regii Sanguinis Clamor*, Hague, 1652, p. 8. Moulin, it must be remembered, is trying in this book to make out the strongest and most unfavorable case he can against Milton, so that we need not accept his testimony literally.

[They say that the man, having been expelled from the University of Cambridge for his profligacy. . . .]

Masson, IV, 456. The chief first-hand evidence of this experience is the mention of "forbidden rooms," "the threats of a harsh master," "exile," "the hoarse-murmuring school," and a few other similar phrases used in Milton's first elegy to Diodati, quoted subsequently. Apparently there was a quarrel between Milton and the authorities, which resulted in his temporary separation from the school. We know that after his return he worked with a different tutor.

Aiunt, inquis, *hominem Cantabrigiensi Academiâ ob flagitia pulsum, dedecus & patriam fugisse, & in Italiam commigrasse* . . . hîc enim & te & illos impudentissimè mentiri . . . .

Milton, *Defensio Secunda*, 1654, p. 57; CM, VIII, 112.

[You say, that "the fellow having been expelled from the university of Cambridge, on account of his atrocities, had fled his country in disgrace and travelled into Italy" . . . the most abominable falsehood. . . .]

Bohn, I, 252.

MAY? FATHER AGAIN INVESTS MONEY FOR ROSE DOWNER.

Rose Downer . . . about fiue Yeares since having in her handꝑ of her owne moneys the greatest ꝑte of her estate being the sume of ffiftie poundꝑ and the same being come to the knowledge of John Milton of London Scrivener he repaired to yoʳ. said Oratrixe about the said time and advised her to put out the said ffiftie poundꝑ at interest . . . by meanes whereof yoʳ. Oratrixe was drawne to consent . . . and afterwardꝑ within a very short time after the said conference . . . the said John Milton . . . did nominate vnto yoʳ. said Oratrixe a Principall and twoe suerties. . . .

Public Record Office, C2 Charles I/D39/47, Rose Downer's bill, dated April 26, 1631; French, *Milton in Chancery*, p. 236. Milton's answer of May 3, 1631, and that of his partner Bower of the same date point out that previous to this time the two scriveners had invested money for Rose Downer's husband John, so that the present action was merely a continuation of a customary activity.

MAY. LATIN ELEGY TO CHARLES DIODATI, DESCRIBING EXPERIENCES IN LONDON AND RETURN TO CAMBRIDGE.

Elegia prima ad *Carolum Diodatum.*

Tandem, chare, tuæ mihi pervenere tabellæ,
    Pertulit & voces nuntia charta tuas,
Pertulit occiduâ Devæ Cestrensis ab orâ
    Vergivium prono quà petit amne salum.
Multùm crede juvat terras aluisse remotas
    Pectus amans nostri, tamque fidele caput,
Quòdque mihi lepidum tellus longinqua sodalem
    Debet, at unde brevi reddere jussa velit.
Me tenet urbs refluâ quam Thamesis alluit undâ,
    Meque nec invitum patria dulcis habet.
Jam nec arundiferum mihi cura revisere Camum,
    Nec dudum vetiti me laris angit amor.
Nuda nec arva placent, umbrasque negantia molles,
    Quàm male Phoebicolis convenit ille locus!
Nec duri libet usque minas perferre magistri
    Cæteraque ingenio non subeunda meo,
Si sit hoc exilium patrios adiisse penates,
    Et vacuum curis otia grata sequi,
Non ego vel profugi nomen, sortemve recuso,
    Lætus & exilii conditione fruor.
O utinam vates nunquam graviora tulisset
    Ille Tomitano flebilis exul agro;
Non tunc Jonio quicquam cessisset Homero
    Neve foret victo laus tibi prima Maro.
Tempora nam licet hîc placidis dare libera Musis,
    Et totum rapiunt me mea vita libri.
Excipit hinc fessum sinuosi pompa theatri,
    Et vocat ad plausus garrula scena suos.

Seu catus auditur senior, seu prodigus hæres,
    Seu procus, aut positâ casside miles adest,
Sive decennali fœcundus lite patronus
    Detonat inculto barbara verba foro,
Sæpe vafer gnato succurrit servus amanti,
    Et nasum rigidi fallit ubique Patris;
Sæpe novos illic virgo mirata calores
    Quid sit amor nescit, dum quoque nescit, amat.
Sive cruentatum furiosa Tragœdia sceptrum
    Quassat, & effusis crinibus ora rotat,
Et dolet, & specto, juvat & spectasse dolendo,
    Interdum & lacrymis dulcis amaror inest:
Seu puer infelix indelibata reliquit
    Gaudia, & abrupto flendus amore cadit,
Seu ferus e tenebris iterat Styga criminis ultor
    Conscia funereo pectora torre movens,
Seu mæret Pelopeia domus, seu nobilis Ili,
    Aut luit incestos aula Creontis avos.
Sed neque sub tecto semper nec in urbe latemus,
    Irrita nec nobis tempora veris eunt.
Nos quoque lucus habet vicinâ consitus ulmo
    Atque suburbani nobilis umbra loci.
Sæpius hic blandas spirantia sydera flammas
    Virgineos videas præteriisse choros.
Ah quoties dignæ stupui miracula formæ
    Quæ posset senium vel reparare Iovis;
Ah quoties vidi superantia lumina gemmas,
    Atque faces quotquot volvit uterque polus;
Collaque bis vivi Pelopis quæ brachia vincant,
    Quæque fluit puro nectare tincta via,
Et decus eximium frontis, tremulosque capillos,
    Aurea quæ fallax retia tendit Amor.
Pellacesque genas, ad quas hyacinthina sordet
    Purpura, & ipse tui floris, Adoni, rubor.
Cedite laudatæ toties Heroides olim,
    Et quæcunque vagum cepit amica Jovem.

Cedite Achæmeniæ turritâ fronte puellæ,
    Et quot Susa colunt, Memnoniamque Ninon.
Vos etiam Danaæ fasces submittite Nymphæ,
    Et vos Iliacæ, Romuleæque nurus.
Nec Pompeianas Tarpëia Musa columnas
    Jactet, & Ausoniis plena theatra stolis.
Gloria Virginibus debetur prima Britannis,
    Extera sat tibi sit fœmina posse sequi.
Tuque urbs Dardaniis Londinum structa colonis
    Turrigerum latè conspicienda caput,
Tu nimium felix intra tua mœnia claudis
    Quicquid formosi pendulus orbis habet.
Non tibi tot cælo scintillant astra sereno
    Endymioneæ turba ministra deæ,
Quot tibi conspicuæ formáque auróque puellæ
    Per medias radiant turba videnda vias.
Creditur huc geminis venisse invecta columbis
    Alma pharetrigero milite cincta Venus,
Huic Cnidon, & riguas Simoentis flumine valles,
    Huic Paphon, & roseam posthabitura Cypron.
Ast ego, dum pueri sinit indulgentia cæci,
    Mœnia quàm subitò linquere fausta paro;
Et vitare procul malefidæ infamia Circes
    Atria, divini Molyos usus ope.
Stat quoque juncosas Cami remeare paludes,
    Atque iterum raucæ murmur adire Scholæ.
Interea fidi parvum cape munus amici,
    Paucaque in alternos verba coacta modos.

Milton, Elegy I, *Poems*, 1645, part ii, p. 11; Mackellar, pp. 68 ff.;
CM, I, 168. The date here used is Tillyard's (p. 137).

Elegy the First, to *Charles Diodati.*

At length, dear friend, your letter has reached me, and the
messenger-paper has brought me your words—brought me them
from the western shore of Chester's Dee, where with prone
stream it seeks the Vergivian wave. Much, believe me, it delights me that foreign lands have nurtured a heart so loving of

ours, and a head so faithfully mine; and that a distant part of
the country now owes me my sprightly companion, whence,
however, it means soon, on being summoned, to send him back.
Me at present that city contains which the Thames washes with
its ebbing wave; and me, not unwilling, my father's house now
possesses. At present it is not my care to revisit the reedy Cam;
nor does the love of my forbidden rooms yet cause me grief.
Nor do naked fields please me, where soft shades are not to
be had. How ill that place suits the votaries of Apollo! Nor
am I in the humour still to bear the threats of a harsh master,
and other things not to be submitted to by my genius. If this
be exile, to have gone to my father's house, and, free from cares,
to be pursuing agreeable relaxations, then certainly I refuse
neither the name nor the lot of a fugitive, and gladly I enjoy
the condition of exile. O that that poet, the tearful exile in the
Pontic territory, had never endured worse things! Then had he
nothing yielded to Ionian Homer, nor would the supreme
reputation of having surpassed him be yours, O Maro! For it
is in my power to give my leisure up to the placid Muses; and
books, which are my life, have me all to themselves. When I
am wearied, the pomp of the winding theatre takes me hence,
and the garrulous stage calls me to its noisy applauses—whether
it be the wary old gentleman that is heard, or the prodigal heir;
whether the wooer, or the soldier with his helmet doffed, is
on the boards, or the lawyer, prosperous with a ten years' law-
suit, is mouthing forth his gibberish to the unlearned forum.
Often the wily servant is abetting the lover-son, and at every
turn cheating the very nose of the stiff father; often there the
maiden, wondering at her new sensations, knows not what love
is, and, while she knows not, loves. Or, again, furious Tragedy
shakes her bloody sceptre and rolls her eyes, with dishevelled
locks, and it is a pain to look, and yet it is a pleasure to have
looked and been pained; for sometimes there is a sweet bitter-
ness in tears. Or the unhappy boy leaves his untasted joys, and
falls off, a pitiful object, from his broken love; or the fierce
avenger of crime recrosses the Styx from the shades, perturbing

guilty souls with his funeral torch. Or the house of Pelops or that of noble Ilium is in grief, or the palace of Creon expiates its incestuous ancestry. But not always within doors nor even in the city, do we mope; nor does the season of spring pass by unused by us. The grove also planted with thick elms has our company, and the noble shade of a suburban neighbourhood. Very often here, as stars breathing forth mild flames, you may see troops of maidens passing by. Ah! how often have I seen the wonders of a worthy form, which might even repair the old age of Jove! Ah! how often have I seen eyes surpassing all gems and whatever lights revolve around either pole; and necks twice whiter than the arms of living Pelops, and than the way which flows tinged with pure nectar; and the exquisite grace of the forehead; and the trembling hair which cheating Love spreads as his golden nets; and the inviting cheeks, compared with which hyacinthine purple is poor, and the very blush, Adonis, of thy own flower! Yield, ye so often praised heroic daughters of old, and whatever fair mistress fixed the fancy of wandering Jove! Yield, ye Persian girls with the turbaned brows, and all that dwell in Susa and Memnonian Ninos. Ye also, nymphs of Greece, bend low your honours, and ye young matrons of Troy and nurses of Rome. Nor let the Tarpeian Muse boast of the portico of Pompey and the theatre crowded with beauties in their trains. The first glory is due to Britain's virgins; enough for you, fair foreigners, to be able to follow next! Thou, London, city built by Dardanian colonists, raising thy head of towers to be seen far and wide, thou, too happy, enclosest within thy walls, whatever of beauty this pendent orb contains! Not over thee in the clear sky do there glitter so many stars, the attendant crowd of Endymion's goddess, as through the middle of thy streets there shine, brilliant in beauty and gold, maidens worthy to be seen. Hither, borne by her twin-doves, gentle Venus, girt with her quiver-bearing soldiery of Cupids, is believed to have come, resolved evermore to prefer it to Cnidus, and the valleys watered by the river of Simois, and to Paphos itself, and to rosy Cyprus. But for me, while the forbearance of the blind boy allows it, I prepare as soon as possible to leave these happy walls, and, using the help of divine all-heal, to flee far from the infamous dwellings of the sorceress Circe. It is fixed that I do go back to the rushy marshes of Cam, and once more approach the murmur of the hoarse-murmuring school. Meanwhile accept the little gift of your faithful friend, and these few words forced into alternate measures.

Masson, I, 139-141 (164-165).

MAY 10. FATHER SUED BY SAMUEL BURTON.

To the Kings most excellent Maiestie./.

Jn all humblenes sheweth vnto Your most excellent Maiestie Your most loyall and dutifull Subiect Samuell Burton Arch-deacōn of the Diocesse of Gloucester That whereas [about] Three Yeares laste paste one Robert Willoughbie late Citizen and Grocer of London Together wth Thomas Willoughbie the elder of Sutton Colefield in the Countie of Warrwicke gentle-man, and [Edward] Willoughbie the Yonger Citizen and Linnen Draper of London became bound vnto one William Smith by his addition styled to bee Citizen and Mercer of Lon-don in the penall somme of two hundred pounds [condicōned] for the paim^t of one hundred Pounds wth the Jnterest there-vppon due at a Day now past and vnknowne vnto Your sayd Subiect The sayd William Smith being a Common Vsurer and one that employes great Sommes of money in that vsurious Course and practise, Vppon which sayd Bonde of Two hundred pounds as Your Subiect hath bin informed, the sayd Robert Wil-loughbie and Thomas Willoughbie the elder or one of them about Two Yeares since were arrested at the suite of the sayd William Smith, who therevppon tolde them that if they Could procure any other securitye They should not onely bee inlarged but allso absolutely Released of the sayd debt And therevppon the sayd Robert Willoughbie became a sutor vnto Your sayd Subiect to ioyne wth one Sr George Peckham of Shipley in the Countie of Derbie Knight to secure vnto the sayd William Smyth the sayd Somme of One hundred poundǫ affirming vnto

Your sayd Subiect that hee and the sayd Sr George Peckham
woulde satisfie the sayd debt, And that Your sayd Subiect should
onely enter Bond to satisfie the Curiositie of the sayd Smyth,
which seemed the more probable And that the sayd Smith allsoe
did Conceiue the sayd hundred pound sufficientlie secured by
the sayd Robert Willoughbie and the sayd Sr George for that
the sayd Smith accepted of their securitie onely by the space of
Two moneths or thereabouts before Your sayd Subiect became
bound for the same which induced Your sayd Subiect the more
willinglie and securely to enter into the sayd Bonde And so At
the length Your Subiect being thus wrought vppon about May
in the two and twentieth Yeare of our late Soueraigne Lord
King James entred into a Bonde of the penall Summe of Two
hundred pounds vnto the sayd Smyth Condicōned for the payment of one hundred and Tenn pounds at the now dwelling
house of John Milton Scriuenor scituate in Broadstreete London on the Twentieth day of Aprill which then should bee in
the Yeare of our Lord God One Thousand sixe hundred twentie
& fiue Jn which sayd Bonde the sayd Robert Willoughbie as
first and principall and the sayd Sr George Peckham as suerty
together wth your sayd Subiect as another suerty doe stand bound
ioyntlie and severallie for the paym^t of the sayd debt aforesayd,
and which sayd Bond as Your Subiect taketh it beareth date the
eighteenth day of Aprill in the sayd Two and twentieth Yeare
of the Raigne of our Late Soveraigne Lord King James But
now so it is May it please Your most excellent Maiestie That the
sayd William Smith and Sr George Peckham having vnder these
p^rtences gotten your Subiect to stand bound as a surety for the
sayd moneyes as aforesayd doe Combine and Confederate together wth one John Milton a Scrivenor in London and a Broker
for the letting out of the moneyes of the sayd Smithe how they
may lay the whole penaltie of the sayd Bond of Two hundred
pounds vppon Your sayd Subiect, or at the least the s'd somme
of one hundred poundȝ wth Jnterest, whereas Your sayd Subiect
hopeth to proue that the sayd Smith never lent one pennie of
the sayd sōme of one hundred poundȝ and so in all equitie

ought to have noe benefit of the sayd Bond nor to prosecute sute at Law therevppon, And Your Subiect hopeth allso to proue that the sayd Smith well knowing that hee depteth wth noe money vppon the sayd Bond doth not Beare the charges of the sayd sute at ye Common Law, nor disburse money in the same, but the sayd suite is meerelye prosecuted by the sayd Sr George and the sayd John Milton or one of them hoping thereby to gaine and make some advantage vnto themselues of Your sayd Subiect who conceiveth allso that the sayd Smith is dead and that the same is knowne vnto the sayd Milton or otherwise that he the sayd Smith by the advise of the sayd Milton concealeth the place of his lodging or dwelling from Your Subiect, so that hee cannot possiblie enquire out where the sayd Smith lodgeth or dwelleth to the intent hee might serue him wth the proces of this Court Albeit the sayd Milton hath every day allmost re-course to the sayd Smith, if hee bee living, and knoweth where hee dwelleth or lodgeth, and by Messengers sent by your Sub-iect to him for that purpose, hath bin earnestlie intreated to shew & declare vnto Your subiect when and where Your Subiect might haue Conference wth the sayd Smith Yet doth hee for the Rea-sons aforesayd vtterlie Refuse to acquaint Your Subiect with his sayd dwelling endeavoring by all meanes to stripp and de-priue Your subiect of all meanes for his Reliefe heerein, and indeede minding nothing else but with all speede possible to obtaine a Judgement against Your Subiect at the Comōn Law for the sayd penaltie of Two hundred poundǫ And Your Sub-iect further sheweth that the sayd Sr George Peckham by the Combinacōn aforesayd hath practised wth the sayd Smith and John Millton to forbeare all prosecution of Law vppon the sayd Bonde against him the sayd Sr George, Who thereuppon [*here follows a passage, later cancelled*: the sayd Smith hath secretlie receaued some recompence and Consideracon from the sayd Sr George, vppon which the sayd Smith hath promised him not to take any extreame Course against him by law but onelie to Colour their vniust designes doth make seeme thereof suing the sayd Sr George Peckham to an vtlarie, but purposeth to pro-

ceede further therein in such fauorable manner as hee intendeth
shall not bee p^rudiciall to him, nor any way Compell him to
make paim^t of the sayd debt, by reason whereof the sayd S^r
George] resteth so secure that hee vtterlie neglecteth the pai-
ment of the sayd p^rtended debt. Jn tender Consideracōn whereof
and forasmuch as Your sayd Subiect was drawne into the sayd
ingagements by the perswasions and faire pretences of of the
sayd [*cancelled*: William Smyth, and] Robert Willoughbie
and Sr George Peckham And forasmuch as the security of the
sayd Sr George Peckham was principallie & Chiefely aimed at &
regarded by the sayd William Smith at the sealing of the said
Bonde and was at the first accepted of in satisfaction of the first
bonde w^thout Your Subiect's sealing of the sayd second Bonde
And yet the sayd first bond is not deliuered vpp by the sayd
Smith according to his promise made vnto the sayd Robert Willoughbie as Yo^r subiect is informed [*cancelled*: as your Subiect,]
but by him [*cancelled*: the sayd Smith keepeth both the sayd
Bondǫ] kept on foote, & wth intent to take benefitt vppon both
the sayd securities; And forasmuch as the sayd Sr George Peckham is a man of great ability and sufficiencie having Lands worth
at the leaste One thowsand pounds p annū and noe Charge of
Children, and therefore verie well able to satisfie the sayd debt,
And in respect the sayd Sr George Peckham was of neere affinitie
to the sayd Willoughbie having married his the sayd Willough-
bies owne naturall Sister both by the ffathers and Mothers side,
Jt is most iust and Conscionable that the sayd William Smith
might bee ordered to take his remedie by the Lawe for the
Recouerie of the sayd debt against the sayd Sr George Peckham,
& not against Your Subiect And to the intent and purpose that
the sayd Sr George Peckham may vppon his oathe set forth
whether hee knoweth of the paymente or receit of any moneyes
receaued by the him selfe or the s'd Robtē Willoughbye of the
s'd Smith and whether the s'd former bonds of the s'd Willoughbie were [given] vpp or no and to shew cause if hee can
why hee should not satisfie the sayd debt, and disengage Your
s'd Subiect therefrom, And to the intent & purpose the sayd John

Milton may vppon his Aunswere set forth whether vppon the sayd Bond so entred into by your subiect, the sayd Smith payd any moneyes vnto the sayd Willoughbie or noe, or whether the sayd Smith bee living or dead, and in Case hee bee living where hee dwelleth, And to the intent and purpose the sayd William Smith and Sr George Peckham and John Milton may make true Aunswere to the premisses, May it please Your most excellent Maiestie the p^rmisses Considered to graunt vnto Your Subiect Your Maiesties most gratious wrytt of priuie Seale to bee directed vnto the sayd William Smith Sr George Peckham and John Milton Cōmaunding them thereby at a Certaine day and vnder a certaine paine therein to bee limited personallie to bee and appeare before yor Matie and your Highnes Counsaile in Your Maiesties Court of Whitehall then and there to aunswere the p^rmisses and also to stand to and abide such further order and direccōn as to Your Maiestie and Your highnes Counsaile shall seeme fitt As allso your Ma^te most gratious wrytt of Jniunction to bee awarded against the sayd William Smith his Counsellors Attorneyes sollicitors and ffactors in the Law to stay all further proceedingꝑ in his sayd suite at Lawe And Your Subiect shall allwayes pray for Your Maiesties long and prosperous Raigne ouer vs

Richard Townesend

[*Endorsed*] x° die Maij Anno Rñd Rꝑ Caroli Anglie Scotie fr et hibñie secundo Defend Nncī ꝑ Nñt Camer

[*Endorsed elsewhere*] Burton plea' q' v^rss Peckham mil Smith et Milton Defts

Public Record Office, Req 2/387; French, *Milton in Chancery*, pp. 228 ff. Described at some length by Joseph Hunter in "Chorus Vatum," IV (British Museum Add. MS. 24,489), 185v (336). Hunter says that Mr. Birt pointed it out to him in January, 1853.

[Endorsement 1: On the tenth day of May in the second year of the reign of our reverend Charles, King of England, Scotland, France, and Ireland, the defendants were notified by the messenger of the Chamber.

Endorsement 2: The plea of Burton, plaintiff, against Peckham, knight, Smith, and Milton, defendants.]

MAY 24. FATHER ARRANGES VEALE-COTTON BOND.

Mr Veale & oth^{rs} p obl' Dat' xxiiij^{to} Maij 1626 . . . 100^{li}

Thomas Bower's schedule of Cotton's bonds made out by himself and Milton's father; see below under date of November 25, 1630.

. . . Mr Veale & others by bond dated the ffoure & Twentieth day of May One thowsand six hundred Twentie six One hundred pound$\wp$ principall debt.

Sir Thomas Cotton's bill; see below under date of May 28, 1636.

JUNE (?). FATHER SUMMONED TO COURT OF REQUESTS TO ANSWER BURTON.

. . . upon consideracōn had of two seūall Affīd made in the said cause whereby it doth appear that th[e said De]f^t Milton being warned by the Messenger of this Court to appeare & answere at a day now past hath not appeared accordingly, And likewise that the Def^t Smith is not found whereby he may be serued wth any proces of this court to answere the said Compl$^{t\wp}$: Bill. . . .

Public Record Office, Req 1/32, p. 966 (Court of Requests order of June 27, 1626); French, *Milton in Chancery*, p. 232. The probability is that, although the summons here is not dated, it was issued not long before the order here quoted, which is June 27. The original summons has not been found.

JUNE 21. FATHER ARRANGES CLOPTON-COTTON BOND.

Mr Clopton & oth^{rs} p obl' Dat' xxj^o Junij 1626 . . . 100^{li}

Thomas Bower's schedule of Cotton's bonds made out by himself and Milton's father; see below under date of November 25, 1630. The original bond has not been found.

. . . Mr Clopton & oth^{rs} by bond dated the One & Twentieth day of June One thousand [six hundred] Twentie six One hundred pound$\wp$ principall debt.

Sir Thomas Cotton's bill; see below under date of May 28, 1636.

JUNE 27. COURT OF REQUESTS ISSUES INJUNCTION AGAINST MILTON'S FATHER.

P: xxvij^o die Junij A^o: &c. secundo./

Burton   Jn the matter of variance brought before the
[Peckham]   Kingᵽ Maᵗⁱᵉ: & his highness Counsaill in his
ho^{ble}: Court of Whitehall at Westmʳ by Samuel
Burton Archdeacon of Gloucester Comp^{lt} against Sʳ. George
Peckham Knight Willm' Smith & John Milton defᵗᵽ, Being
in effect for the stay of the defᵗᵽ proceedingᵽ at the Comōn
lawe vpon a Bond or Bill obligatorie of the penaltie of CC^{li}
entred into by the Comp^{lt} togeather with Sʳ. George Peckham Knight and one Rob't Willoughby gent vnto the said
Willm' Smith wth Condicōn for the payment of CX^{li} at a
day now past, Jnto wch Bond the Comp^{lt} was drawne by the
ᵽswasions of the said Robt Willoughby wth out receauin[g
any consideration] in respect thereof, and the same [upon a
bond] of the said John Milton, being [made out also] in the
name of the other Def[endants who are] altogeather vnknowne
vnto the C[omplainant] Sʳ George Peckham & Robt W[il-
loughby] & kindred ought to satisfie [the penalty of the] said
Bond if any were [Now the Complainant show]eth the said
Def^t Milt[on ha]th attempted suit at t[he Common Law
against the said Co]mp^{lt} intending to recouer the penaltie [of
the said bond against] him contrary to all equitie & conscience
As in & by [the said Co]mp^{ltᵽ}: Bill is more at lardge sett forth
& declared [Now therefore upon] the opening of W^{ch} same
matter by Mʳ. Townesend of Counsell wth the Comp^{lt} & upon
consideracōn had of two seūall Affīd made in the said cause
whereby it doth appear that th[e said De]f^t Milton being warned
by the Messenger of this Court to appeare & answere at a day
now past hath not appeared accordingly, And likewise that the
Def^t Smith is not found whereby he may be serued wth any
proces of this court to answere the said Comp^{ltᵽ}: Bill It is therefore by his Maᵗᵽ: said Counsaill of this Court ordered that they
the defᵗᵽ theire Councellorᵽ Atturneis & Sollicitorᵽ & euʳy of
them shall surcease & stay & noe further ᵽsecute or ᵽceede at
[Com]mon Lawe against the Comp^{lt} vpon the said bond in
question vntill such tyme as they the said defᵗᵽ shall haue appeared & answered the Comp^{ltᵽ}: Bill in this court & other & fur-

ther order bee had & made by his Maiesties said Counsaill of this court to the contrary And it is lastly ordered that an Jniunccōn vnder his Ma^te: Privie Seale vpon payne of CC^li. to be levied &c be furthw^th awarded & directed vnto the said def^te Willm' Smith & John Milton theire Counsello^re Atturnies & Sollicito^re & eu^ry of them for the due pformance of this order./

Public Record Office, Req 1/32, p. 966; French, *Milton in Chancery*, p. 232. Words in brackets are conjectural readings where part of the original page is torn away.

JUNE 28. FATHER APPEARS IN COURT TO ANSWER SAMUEL BURTON.

xxviij° die Junij A p^rdict. . . .
Johēs Milton psoñ compet corā cōm Rρ p mandat Nuñ Camer. Ad sect Samuelis Burton Theologie doct.

Public Record Office, Appearance Book of Court of Requests, Req 1/111, part 2, fol. 6; French, *Milton in Chancery*, p. 233.

[The 28th day of June in the year aforesaid. . . . John Milton personally appears before the commissioner of the King by command of the messenger of the chamber at the suit of Samuel Burton, Doctor of Theology.]

AUGUST. FATHER COLLECTS ROSE DOWNER'S MONEY FROM LEIGH BOND AND REINVESTS IT WITH SIR FULKE GREVILLE.

Rose Downer of London widdowe . . . about fiue Yeares since having in her handρ of her owne moneys the greatest pte of her estate being the sūme of ffiftie poundρ and the same being come to the knowledge of John Milton of London Scrivener he repaired to yor. said Oratrixe about the said time and advised her to put out the said ffiftie poundρ at interest . . . and afterwardρ within a very short time . . . he the s[aid John] Milton did nominate vnto yor. said Oratrixe a Principall and twoe suerties . . . and [she] willed the said John Milton to prepare the bondρ and take the securitie and the money should be deliūed, All which was done accordingly and yor. said Oratrixe was well pleased and did acc[ept] of the same . . . .

Public Record Office, C2 Charles I/D39/47 (Rose Downer's bill of April 26, 1631); French, *Milton in Chancery*, p. 236. The bracketed portion about half way through this quotation is a conjectural reading of a portion illegible in the original.

Master Leigh . . . bond . . . continued till about August One thowsand Six hundred Twenty & Six And then with all Jnterest paid in, And not long after by and with the privity and consent of the Plaintiffe, the said ffiftie poundẹ was lent at Jnterest vnto Sʳ. ffulke Grevill Knight vpon good securitie. . . .

Public Record Office, C2 Charles I/D39/47 (Bower's answer to Rose Downer, May 3, 1631); French, *Milton in Chancery*, p. 243. For further references to this transaction, less definite than the above, see *ibid.*, pp. 241, 246, 248, 250, 252.

AUGUST 7. FATHER ARRANGES DIGBY-COTTON BOND.

Sʳ Kenelme Digby & othʳˢ p obl' Dat' vij° Augustj 1626 . . . 200ˡˡ

Thomas Bower's schedule of Cotton's bonds made out by himself and Milton's father; see below under date of November 25, 1630. The original bond has not been found.

. . . Sʳ Kenelm Digby & others by bond dated the Seventh of August One thowsand six hundred Twentie six two hundred poundẹ [principall debt.]

Sir Thomas Cotton's bill; see below under date of May 28, 1636.

SEPTEMBER? LATIN ELEGY ON THE BISHOP OF WINCHESTER.

Elegia tertia, Anno ætatis 17.

In obitum Præsulis Wintoniensis.

[Elegy the Third, Written in His Seventeenth Year.

On the Death of the Bishop of Winchester.]

Milton, *Poems*, 1645, part 2, p. 16; CM, I, 178 ff.; Mackellar, pp. 74 ff. Mackellar notes that Lancelot Andrewes, Bishop of Winchester, died on September 26, 1626; Milton's elegy must have been written shortly thereafter.

OCTOBER? LATIN ELEGY ON BISHOP OF ELY.

Anno ætatis 17. In obitum Præsulis Eliensis.

Adhuc madentes rore squalebant genæ,

Et sicca nondum lumina;

Adhuc liquentis imbre turgebant salis,
　　Quem nuper effudi pius,
Dum mæsta charo justa persolvi rogo
　　Wintoniensis præsulis. . . .

Milton, *Poems*, 1645, part 2, p. 56; CM, I, 254 ff.; Mackellar, p. 132. The subject of this elegy, Nicholas Felton, died on October 6, 1626 (*D.N.B.*). Milton's elegy must therefore have been written shortly afterwards. That it followed soon after that on the Bishop of Winchester is evident from the selection given.

[In his seventeenth year. On the death of
the Bishop of Ely.

My cheeks were still damp and soaked with moisture, and my eyes not yet dry; they still flowed with the rain of the salt tears which I recently piously shed, while I paid my sorrowful tribute at the dear grave of the Bishop of Winchester. . . .]

OCTOBER? LATIN ELEGY ON VICE-CHANCELLOR GOSTLIN.

Anno ætatis 16. In obitum Procancellarii medici.

Milton, *Poems*, 1645, part 2, p. 44; CM, I, 232; Mackellar, p. 116. John Gostlin, the vice-chancellor, died October 21, 1626 (*D.N.B.*).

[In the sixteenth year of his age. On the death of the Vice-Chancellor, a physician.]

NOVEMBER? LATIN ELEGY ON RICHARD RIDDING, BEADLE OF CAMBRIDGE.

Elegia Secunda, Anno ætatis 17.
In obitum Præconis Academici Cantabrigiensis.

Milton, *Poems*, 1645, part 2, p. 15; CM, I, 176; Mackellar, p. 74. Mackellar notes that Ridding must have died probably in October, 1626, since his will was proved on November 28 of that year. Stern (I, i, 310) gives November 8 as the date of proving the will.

[Second Elegy, written in his seventeenth year. On the death of the Beadle of the University of Cambridge.]

NOVEMBER? LATIN POEM ON THE GUNPOWDER PLOT.

In quintum Novembris, Anno ætatis 17.

Milton, *Poems*, 1645, part 2, p. 46; CM, I, 236; Mackellar, pp. 118 ff. The most common year assigned for the writing of this poem is 1626.

[On the Fifth of November, in the seventeenth year of his age.]

NOVEMBER? EPIGRAMS ON THE GUNPOWDER PLOT.

[1] *In Proditionem Bombardicam.*
[2] *In eandem.*
[3] *In eandem.*
[4] *In eandem.*
[5] *In inventorem Bombardæ.*

Milton, *Poems*, 1645, pp. 40-42; CM, I, 222; Mackellar, pp. 108 ff. None of these poems is dated, but they are so closely joined in thought to the *In Quintum Novembris* that it seems likely he worked on them at nearly the same time. A statement in number 2, "Ille quidem sine te consortia serus adivit Astra" (He indeed lately without you reached the friendly stars), indicates that King James is dead, but probably recently so. Thus November, 1626, is the most likely date. Harris Fletcher suggests to me that each poem was written for and in a different year of Milton's student days at Cambridge.

[On the Gunpowder Plot, On the same, On the discoverer of gunpowder.]

NOVEMBER 7. FATHER ARRANGES STRANGE-COTTON BOND.

The Lord Strange & oth^{rs} p obl' Dat' vii° Novembr' 1626 ... 300^{ll}

Thomas Bower's schedule of Cotton's bonds made out by himself and Milton's father; see below under date of November 25, 1630. The original bond has not been found.

... The Lord Strang and others, by bond dated 7 of Novemb 1626 300 principall debt &c.

Sir Thomas Cotton's bill; see below under date of May 28, 1636.

NOVEMBER 15. WILLIAM SMITH AND MILTON'S FATHER APPEAR IN COURT TO ANSWER SAMUEL BURTON.

xv° die Novembris A°: &c. secundo. ...

Willūs Smith et Johēs Miltōn ꝑsoñ comꝑent corā cōm Rꝓ ꝓ
mañdat Nuntij Camer Ad sect Samuel Burton. cler, Et suꝓ
Respoñ Admissi sunt comꝑere ꝓ Petrū Langley Geñ Atturñ
suū cū cōm Mꝵi Hakewill/

Public Record Office, Court of Requests Appearance Book, Req
1/111, part 2, fol. 10v; French, *Milton in Chancery*, p. 233. The
answer will be found filed under the same date.

[On the 15th day of November in the second year (of King
Charles) . . . William Smith and John Milton personally appear before the King's Council by order of the messenger of the
court at the suit of Samuel Burton, clergyman. On their reply
they are allowed to appear through Peter Langley, Gentleman,
their attorney, with the help of Mr. Hakewill.]

NOVEMBER 15. FATHER ANSWERS BURTON'S BILL.

Langley ꝓ deftꝓ/	xv^{to} die Novembris Anno RRꝓ Caroli Angl &c. secundo 1626 Sydney Moun-tague	The Joynt & seuerāll An-sweare of William Smyth & John Mylton def^{ts}: to the bill of Cōmp^{lt} of Sam-uell Burton Clerke Cōmp^{lt}:/

The said Def^{nts} nowe & att all tymes hereafter sauinge to themselues & either of them all advantages of excepcōn vnto the
vncerteyntyes & Jnsufficiencies of the said Bill of Cōmp^{lt} for
Answeare therevnto the said Deft^{ts} saye & eyther of them for
himselfe seuerally sayth, that they conceaue the said Bill to bee
exhibited against them Causlessly, & of purpose to putt theis
Def^{te}: to vnnecessary suits & Chardges for the said Def^{te}: William Smyth sayth that he Did not or Doth knowe the said Rob-
ert Willoughby & Thomas Willoughbye in the bill named or
either of them neither what bond or bondꝓ they or either of
them entred into vnto this Def^{te}: William Smyth nor for what
some or somes money the same were soe made, nor whether the
said Robert Willoughby & Thomas Willoughby or either of
them, were Arrested therevpon, neither Did this Def^{te}: Smyth
euer tell the said Robert & Thomas therevpon, that if they

Could p̃cure any other securitye, they should not only be enlarged butt absolutely Released of the said Debte, for this Def^te:
Smyth sayth that to his knowledge he neuer had any Conference
either wth the said Robert Willoughby, Thomas Willoughbye,
Sr George Peckham in the bill named, or the said Cōmp^lt, or
any of them, And this Def^t: Smyth vtterly Denyeth that he is
a Comōn vserer as in the said Bill is scandalously alleadged, And
both theis Def^ts: William Smyth & John Mylton Doe Deny
that they or either of them, or Sr George Peckham in the bill
named (to their knowledge) Did vnder the p^rtences in the bill
named, or any other, gett the said Cōmp^lt: to stand bound as
suerty for the said moneys, And they Doe likewise Denye that
they haue Combined & Confederated togeather to laye the
whole penaltye of the said bond of twoe hundred poundę in the
bill named vpon the said Cōmp^lt: or att least the some of one
hundred poundę, wth interest, as in the bill is vntruely alleadged,
And Yett theis Def^ts: knowe noe Reason (vnder the fauo^r of this
Hō^ble Courte) if any such bond were made, why the same should
not be sued aswell against the said Cōmp^lt, as thother Def^ts in
the Bill named & the P^lt therein to take his Remedy against
wch of them he may soonest recouer his Debte, And this Def^t
John Mylton for his parte sayth that he putteth out noe money
or euer Did for the said Smyth, neither euer knewe any such
man till they nowe mett togeather to putt in this their aunswere
or of the said bond of twoe hundred poundę, for the paym^t. of
one Hundred poundę made as aforesaid, howbeitt this Def^t:
Mylton cōnfesseth that he hath heard that one Thomas Paradyne Cittizen & Haberdasher of London did vse the said William Smyths name in trust in such A bonde, for such a some of
one hundred poundę, And this Def^t verely beleeueth the said
Cōmp^lt hath beene longe ere this told soe much, & as this Def^te
beleeueth he well knoweth the same to be true, & although the
said Cōmp^lt (as this Def^te beeleeueth) well knoweth the same
to be a Just & true Debte, Yett nowe will not he seeme to take
notice thereof, butt vniustly molesteth & troubleth these Def^ts
aboute the same, thinking thereby (as theis Def^ts conceaue) to

perplex & hinder some lawfull Course wch the said Thomas
Paradyne in the name of the said Smyth hath taken against the
Cōmp^{lt}, & the other Def^{te} Sr George Peckham, for Recouery of
his Just Debte Due by the said bond Wth Costs & Damadges by
him susteyned therein, wch this Def^{t}; John Mylton beleeueth
the said Thomas Paradyne hath Done, & that he hath beene soe
farr from any Combynācon Wth the said Sr George Peckham to
laye the said Debte vpon the said Cōmp^{lt}, as the said Cōmp^{lt}
vntruely Chardge theis Def^{ts} John Mylton & William Smyth
therewth, whoe knoweth little or nothinge of the same, nor Doth
the same any whitt them concerne, that (as this Def^{t} John Mylton hath heard) he the said Thomas Paradyne hath sued aswell
the said Sr George Peckham, as the said Cōmp^{lt}, & that the said
Sr George hath beene soe stirred thereby that he hath paid fiftye
poundℓ of the said some of one hundred poundℓ, And this Def^{t}:
John Mylton vtterly Denyeth that he ℓsecuteth the said suite or
any suite at all against the said Cōmp^{lt}, or hath any hand in the
ℓsecutinge of any suite whatsoeuer against the said Cōmp^{lt},
sauinge this same, wherein he is thus vniustly constrayned to
make Defence. And this Def^{t} John Mylton further Denyeth
that to his knowledge the said Smyth is Dead, butt verylye
thinketh the contrary, or that the said Smyth by this Def^{tes}.
aduice concealeth the place of his lodginge, or Dwellinge from
the Cōmp^{lt} so that hee cannot serue ℓces vpon him. Butt this
Def^{te}: John Mylton sayth that the Cōmp^{lt} as he hath heard
hath beene often told where the said Thomas Paradyne Dwelt,
& that the said bond concerneth him, & that the said Cōmp^{lt}
accordinglie sente his man or some other vnto the said Thomas
Paradynes house, & as it should seeme conferred wth him, or
his man aboute the said bond, And this Def^{t}. John Mylton
Denyeth that he hath Dayly Recourse or any Recourse at all
to the said Smyth for he hath not known, neither him, or
his dwellinge till nowe this Def^{t} hath mett wth him to putt
in this their Answer as aforesaid And theis Def^{ts}: William
Smyth & John Mylton doe vtterly Deny that they or eyther of
them haue or hath Combined wth the said Sr George Peckham

to forbeare all psecucōn against him the said Sr George & only to psecute the said Cōmp^{lt} vpon the said bond, or any wise to meddle wth him att all, for theis Def^{ts} say they haue nothinge to Doe either wth the said Sr George, or him the said Cōmp^{lt} And this Def^{te}: Smyth further Denyeth that he pmised to Deliuer vp the said first bond in the bill named vnto the said Roberte Willoughby, or that he keepeth the same on foote wth an intent to take benefitt vpon both the said securityes, as in the said bill is vniustly alleadged, for this Def^{te}: Smyth sayth as formerly he hath, said, that he neither knoweth, or euer Did knowe of any such bond, or man, wthout that that any other matter or thinge materiall or effectuall in the lawe for theis Def^{ts}: or either of them to Answeare vnto, & herein either not sufficiently Answeared vnto, confessed & avoided trauersed or Denied is true, all wch matters or things theis Def^{ts}, & either of them are ready to auerr Justifye mayntayne & pue as this Hō^{ble} Courte shall award, & therefore humblye pray to be hence Dismissed wth their Reasonable Costs & Chardges in this behalfe wrongefully & wthout Cause susteyned./

W: Hakewill

Public Record Office, Req 2/387; French, *Milton in Chancery*, pp. 32, 233.

[Langley for the defendants. The fifteenth day of November in the second year of the reign of Charles, King of England, etc., 1626.]

NOVEMBER 18. FATHER ARRANGES NORRIS-COTTON BOND.

Sr Wm Norres & oth^{rs} p obl' Dat' xviij° Novembr' 1626 ... 100^{li}

Thomas Bower's schedule of Cotton's bonds made out by himself and Milton's father; see below under date of November 25, 1630. The original bond has not been found.

... Sr Will'm Norris & others by bond dated ye the Eighteenth of November One thousand six hundred Twentie & Six One hundred poundp principall debt.

Sir Thomas Cotton's bill; see below under date of May 28, 1636.

DECEMBER 12. FATHER ARRANGES LEIGH-COTTON AND RODNEY-COTTON BONDS.

Mr Leigh & oth^{rs} p obl' Dat' xij Decembr' 1626 . . . 050^{li}

Mr Rodney & oth^{rs} p obl' Dat' xij° Decembr' 1626 . . . 050^{li}

Thomas Bower's schedule of Cotton's bonds made out by himself and Milton's father; see below under date of November 25, 1630. The original bonds have not been found.

. . . Mr Leigh & others [by] bond dated ye Twelueth of [December One thousand] six hundred Twentie six ffiftie pound℘ principall debt.

. . . Mr Rodney & others by bond dated the Twelueth of December [One tho]wsand six hundred Twentie six, ffiftie pound℘ principall debt.

Sir Thomas Cotton's bill; see below under date of May 28, 1636.

DECEMBER 19. FATHER ARRANGES HORSEY-COTTON BOND.

Sr Geo: Horsey & oth^{rs} p obl' Dat' xix° Decembr' 1626 . . . 100^{li}

Thomas Bower's schedule of Cotton's bonds made out by himself and Milton's father; see below under date of November 25, 1630.

. . . Sr George Ho[rsey & others by] bond dated the Nyneteenth day of December One thowsand six hundred Twentie six One hundred pound℘ principall debt.

Sir Thomas Cotton's bill; see below under date of May 28, 1636.

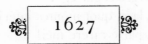

1627

SUPPOSED SONNET ON CAMBRIDGE UNIVERSITY LIBRARY.

ON THE LIBRARIE AT CAMBRIDGE

In that great maze of books I sighed and said,—
It is a grave-yard, and each tome a tombe;
Shrouded in hempen rags, behold the dead,

Coffined and ranged in crypts of dismal gloom,
Food for the worm and redolent of mold,
Traced with brief epitaph in tarnished gold—
Ah, golden lettered hope!—ah, dolorous doom!
Yet mid the common death, where all is cold,
And mildewed pride in desolation dwells,
A few great immortalities of old
Stand brightly forth—not tombes but living shrines,
Where from high sainte or martyr virtue wells,
Which on the living yet work miracles,
Spreading a relic wealth richer than golden mines.

J.M. 1627.

Notes and Queries, I, iii (1851), 37, 142, etc.; CM, XVIII, 600. In *Notes and Queries* these verses are said to have appeared first in *A Collection of Recente and Witty Pieces by several eminente hands*, 1628. Since no such title is known, it seems likely that the article of 1851, together with the poem, is a hoax.

LATIN ELEGY TO THOMAS YOUNG.

Elegia quarta. Anno ætatis 18. *Ad Thomam Junium præceptorem suum, apud mercatores Anglicos Hamburgæ agentes Pastoris munere fungentem.*

Curre per immensum subitò mea littera pontum . . .
   Ditis ad Hamburgæ mœnia flecte gradum . . .
Vivit ibi antiquæ clarus pietatis honore
   Præsul Christicolas pascere doctus oves;
Ille quidem est animæ plusquam pars altera nostræ,
   Dimidio vitæ vivere cogor ego.
Hei mihi quot pelagi, quot montes interjecti
   Me faciunt aliâ parte carere mei!
Charior ille mihi quam tu doctissime Graium
   Cliniadi, pronepos qui Telamonis erat.
Quámque Stagirites generoso magnus alumno
   Quem peperit Libyco Chaonis alma Jovi.
Qualis Amyntorides, qualis Philyrëius Heros
   Myrmidonum regi, talis & ille mihi.
Primus ego Aonios illo præunte recessus

Lustrabam, & bifidi sacra vireta jugi,
  Pieriosque hausi latices, Clioque favente,
  Castalio sparsi læta ter ora mero.
Flammeus at signum ter viderat arietis Æthon,
  Jnduxitque auro lanea terga novo,
Bisque novo terram sparsisti Chlori senilem
  Gramine, bisque tuas abstulit Auster opes:
Necdum ejus licuit mihi lumina pascere vultu,
  Aut linguæ dulces aure bibisse sonos. . . .
Hæc quoque paulum oculos in humum defixa modestos,
  Verba verecundo sis memor ore loqui. . . .
Accipe sinceram, quamvis sit sera, salutem
  Fiat & hoc ipso gratior illa tibi. . . .
Jamque diu scripsisse tibi fuit impetus illi,
  Neve moras ultra ducere passus Amor. . . .
Te tamen intereà belli circumsonat horror,
  Vivis & ignoto solus inópsque solo. . . .

Milton, *Poems*, 1645, part ii, p. 19; CM, I, 184; Mackellar, p. 80. Harris Fletcher (London *Times Literary Supplement*, January 21, 1926, p. 44) wishes to date this elegy 1625, previous to Milton's letter to Young of March 26, which he thinks refers to this. William R. Parker, however (*Modern Language Notes*, LIII, 1938, 403) feels sure it should be dated 1627, and probably between March 21 and April 28.

[Fourth Elegy. In his eighteenth year. To Thomas Young, his teacher, performing the duty of pastor among the English merchants doing business at Hamburg.

Run swiftly, my letter, through the immense ocean. . . . Turn your steps to the walls of sumptuous Hamburg. . . . There lives a bishop famous by reason of his old-fashioned piety, taught to feed the sheep of Christ. He indeed is the other half of my life; I am compelled to live only half a life. Alas, how many seas and mountains, thrust between, make me forego this other half of myself! Dearer he to me than thou, most learned of the Greeks, to Cliniades, who was the descendant of Telamon; and than the great Stagirite to his generous pupil whom the loving Chaonis bore to Libyan Jove. Such as Amyntorides and the Philyreian hero were to the king of the Myrmidons, such is he also to me. First, under his guidance, I explored the recesses of the Muses, and beheld the sacred green spots of the cleft summit of Parnassus, and quaffed the Pierian cups, and, Clio favouring me, thrice sprinkled my joyful mouth with Castalian wine. But flaming Aethon saw the sign of the Ram three times, and three times clothed his fleecy back with new gold; and you, Chloris, twice sprinkled the aged earth with new grass; and twice Auster took away your wealth; and still it was not permitted me to feast my eyes on his face or to drink in with my ear the sweet sounds of his voice. . . . Fixing modest eyes also on the ground for a little while, remember to speak these words with reverent mouth. . . . "Accept this greeting, sincere though belated; may it by this very fact be the more welcome to you. . . . For a long time now it has been his impulse to write you, and Love has not allowed him to delay longer. . . . But meanwhile the horror of war sounds about you, and you live alone and poor in an unknown land."

Masson, 1, 54 (72) (in part), supplemented by the present editor.

FATHER APPOINTED WARDEN OF SCRIVENERS' COMPANY BUT DECLINES.

1627 . . .	Wm. Child	Master
	ffran. Mosse	Vp. Warden
	Tho. Hill*	
	John Milton*	
	Jeffery Bower	Rent^r: Warden
	John Smith	} Ass^{ts}: taken in.
	W^m. Audley	

Bodleian Library, MS. Rawl. Miscell. 51 ("An Annual Catalogue . . . of the Company of Scriveners"), f. 29; Henry J. Sides, in *Athenaeum*, 1880, 1, 565; Brennecke, p. 113. An asterisk after the names here given indicates that those named paid a fine rather than serving in the office mentioned. Hence we may assume that Milton never accepted the appointment.

FATHER BECOMES ACQUAINTED WITH FRANCES STACY.

ffraunces *Stacy* of the parish of S^t. Andrewes in the Wardorb London Spinster, aged Twenty Two yeares or thereaboutp . . .

John Milton and Thomas Bower named for dēftꝑ, this depᵗ
saieth shee hath knowne for these ffower yeares or thereaboutꝑ. . . .

Public Record Office, Chancery Depositions, C 24/574/40 (Frances
Stacy's deposition of September 23, 1631); French, *Milton in Chancery*, p. 250.

FOURTH PROLUSION.

In Collegio, &c. Thesis.

*In Rei cujuslibet interitu non datur resolutio ad Materiam
Primam.*

[A thesis delivered in the college, etc. In the destruction of
anything there is no resolution to primal matter.]

Milton, *Epistolarum Familiarium Liber Unus*, 1674, p. 96; CM, XII,
172. The date is uncertain.

MAY 25. INDENTURE BETWEEN MILTON AND HIS FATHER AND ANTHONY RUDD CONCERNING ST. MARTIN-IN-THE-FIELDS.

This indenture made the five and twentith day of May in
the yeare of our lord god one thousand six hundred twenty and
seaven And in the Third yeare of the raigne of our soveraigne
lord Charles by the grace of god king of England Scotland
ffrance and Ireland defender of the faith &c Betweene Anthony
Rudd Citizen and Pewterer of London and Johane his wife of
thone parte and John Milton thelder Citizen and Scrivener of
London and John Milton the younger of the Vniūsitie of Cambridge sonne of the said John Milton thelder of thother part
witnesseth that the said Anthony Rudd and Johane his wife
aswell for and in consideracōn of the sōme of Twoe hundred
and fiftie poundꝑ of Lawfull money of England to them at or
before thensealing and delivery hereof by the said John Milton
thelder and John Milton the younger or one of them weꝇ and
truely paid whereof they the said Anthony Rudd and Johane
his wife doe by theis ꝑsentꝑ acknowledge the receipt As also for
divers other good causes and consideracōns them the said Anthony and Johane therevnto moving have given granted bar-

gained sold enfeoffed and confirmed And by theis p̃sentꝑ doe
fully cleerely and absolutely give grant bargaine sell enfeoffe
and confirme vnto them the said John Milton thelder and John
Milton the younger their heires and assignes forever All that
mesuage or teñte with thapꝑtenancꝑ scituate in the parish of St
Martins in the feildꝑ in the County of Midd betweene the now
or Late dwelling house of the right honurable the Lady Adelyn
Nevill on the east part and the mesuage or teñte now or late in
the occupacōn of John Reynoldꝑ on the west the Covennte garden on the north and the Kingꝑ high way on the south which
said bargained mesuage or teñte and p̃misses or the ground
wherevpon the same mesuage or teñte and p̃misses now standeth
was heretofore in the tenure or occupacōn of Peter Brickston or
his assignes and since in the tenure or occupacōn of John Johnson Coachmaker or his assignes and now or late in the tenure
or occupacōn of Mathew Lyster Doctor of Physick or of his
assignes or undertenñtꝑ Together with all houses edifices buildingꝑ shopps cellors sollers chambers romes lightꝑ yardꝑ gardens
easementꝑ ꝑfittꝑ comodities and apꝑteñcꝑ whatsoeū to the said
mesuage or teñte hereby bargained and sold belonging or in any
wise apꝑteyning or with the same demised vsed or occupied as
part or ꝑcell thereof And the revercōn and revercōns remainder
and remainders and all the rent issues and ꝑfittꝑ of all and
singuler the before bargained p̃misses and of every part and
parcell thereof and all thestate right title interest inheritance
clayme and demaund of them the said Anthony Rudd and
Johane his wife and either of them in and to the said mesuage
teñte and p̃misses and of in and to every part and parcell
thereof with thapꝑtenñcꝑ And all deedꝑ evidences chr̃es and
writingꝑ concerning the said mesuage and p̃misses or any parte
thereof to have and to hold the said mesuage teñte houses edifices buildingꝑ shopps cellors sollers yardꝑ gardens rentꝑ issues
ꝑfittꝑ comodities and all other the p̃misses before by theis
p̃sentꝑ bargained and sold or meant or mencōned to be hereby
bargained and sold and every parte and ꝑcell thereof with

thapptennͨᵱ vnto the said John Milton thelder and John Milton the younger their heires and assigns to thonely vse and
behoofe of them the said John Milton thelder and John Milton
the younger their heires and assignes forever In witness whereof
the said parties to theis p̄sent Indentures intͨchangeably have
sett their handᵱ and seales the day and yeare first above written/

Et memorand' qd' qvartodecimo die Junii anno sup̄script'
prefat' Anthonius & Johēs Rudd venerunt coram dtō dnō Rege
in Canc' sua & recognouerunt Jndentuꝛ' predict' ac oม̄ia &
singula in eadem content' & specificat' in forma sūpdtā./ Inᵈ
vicesimo tͨio die Junij Anno p̄dict'.

exʳ

Public Record Office, C54/2715/20; Stevens, *Milton Papers*, pp.
2, 39; CM, XVIII, 622. There are photographic facsimiles in the Harvard College Library (shelf-number 14495.58PF); also in the University of Chicago Library. In the margin opposite the beginning of the
document is the notation, "Rudd et Milton 20." Opposite the final paragraph is the name of the clerk, "Eden." A photographic copy serves as
the frontispiece to Stevens's *Milton Papers*.

[And be it remembered that on the fourteenth day of June
in the year above written the aforesaid Anthony and Joan Rudd
came before the same Lord King in his Chancery and acknowledged the said indenture and all and singular contained and
specified in the same in the form aforesaid. Indented on the
twenty-third day of June in the year aforesaid.]

JUNE 10? FINAL CONCORD BETWEEN THE MILTONS AND THE RUDDS.

Hec est finalis Concordia fat' in Curꝛ Dni' Regis apud
Westm' a die sce' Trinitatis in tres septimanas Anno regnor
Caroli' dei' gra' Anglz Scotie ffrancie & hibnie Regis fidei'
defens' &c' Aconqu' t'cio coram Thoma Richardson' Rico'
Hutton ffrancisco Haruye Georgio Croke & Henrz Yelverton'
Justic' & aliis dni' Regis fidelibz tunc ibi' psentibz Jnt Johēm
Milton seniorem & Johēm Milton Juniorem querz et Antonm'
Rudd & Johannam Vxem' eius deforc' de vno mesuagio cum
ptin' in parochia sci' martini' in campis vnde plitm' Convenco'rs

sum' fuit int' eos in eadem Curz Scilt qd p̄dci' Antonius & Johanna recogn' p̄dcm' mes' cum p̣tin' esse ius ipiūs Johīs Milton
sen' vt iłł quod ijdem Johēs & Johēs Milton Jun' Hēnt de
dono p̄dcor Antonij & Johanne Et iłł remiserz & quiet'clam' de
ipīs Antonio & Johanna & Hered suis p'dco' Johi' & Johi' &
hered' ipius Johīs Milton' sen' Imppm' Et p̄t'ea ijdem Antonius
& Johanna concesserz p̣ se & hered' ipiūs Antonij qd' ipī Warant' p̄dcīs Johī & Johī & hered ipiūs Antonij imppm̄ Et vlt'mo'
ijdem Antonius & Johanna concesserz p̣ se & hered' ipiūs Johanne qd ipi' Waranti' p̄dcis' Johī' & Johī' & hered' ipius Johīs
sen p̄dcm' mesuagm' cum p̣tin' cont' p̄dcōs Antonm & Johannam
& hered ipiūs Johanne Imppm̄' Et p̣ hac recogn' remissione
quiet' clam' Waranti' fine & Concordia ijdem Johēs & Johēs
dederz p̄dcīs Antonio & Johanne Centum libras sterlingor:./

ex' Midd':./

[Endorsed:] Scdm̄' formam statuti'./
Prima p̣clam' fcā fuit tcīodecimo die Junij tñno' sce' Trinitatie
Anno tc̄io Regis infrascrz Scdā p̣clam' fca' fuit vicesimo primo
die Novembris tñnō sce' Michis Anno tc̄io Regis infrascrz Tcia
p̣clam' fcā fuit sexto die ffebruarij tñno' sce' Hillarij Anno tc̄io
Regis infrascrz Quarta p̣clam' fca' fuit septimo die tñno' Pasche
Anno quarto Regis infrascrz:./

ex'

Public Record Office, CP25/2/457, Midd. 3 Chas. I. Trin. The
date is obtained as follows. Easter Day in 1627 fell on March 25, and
Trinity Sunday on May 20. Three weeks from Trinity would therefore be June 10. The proclamations recorded in the endorsement must
have been made on June 13, November 21, February 6, and May 7.

[This is a final concord made in the court of our Lord the
King at Westminster in the three weeks from the day of Holy
Trinity in the third year of the reign of Charles by the grace
of God king of England, Scotland, France, and Ireland, de-
fender of the faith, etc., before Thomas Richardson, Richard
Hutton, Francis Harvey, George Croke, and Henry Yelverton,
Justices, and other faithful servants of our Lord the King then
present in the same place, between John Milton Sr. and John

Milton Jr., plaintiffs, and Anthony Rudd and Joan his wife, deforciants, concerning one messuage with appurtenances in the parish of St. Martin-in-the-Fields from which the suit arose between them in this same court. Know that the aforesaid Anthony and Joan admit the aforesaid messuage with appurtenances to be the property of the said John Milton Sr. and that the said John and John Milton Jr. hold it by the gift of the aforesaid Anthony and Joan. And the former have given and quitclaimed from the said Anthony and Joan and their heirs to the aforesaid John and John and the heirs of the said John Milton Sr. forever. And furthermore the said Anthony and Joan have conceded for themselves and the heirs of the said Anthony that they have guaranteed to the aforesaid John and John and their heirs forever. And finally the said Anthony and Joan have conceded for themselves and the heirs of the said Joan that they have guaranteed to the aforesaid John and John and the heirs of the said John Sr. the aforesaid messuage with appurtenances against the aforesaid Anthony and Joan and the heirs of the said Joan forever. And in return for this recognizance, remission, quitclaim, guarantee, fine, and concord the said John and John have given to the aforesaid Anthony and Joan one hundred pounds sterling.

(Endorsed:) According to the form of the statute. The first proclamation was made on the thirteenth day of June in Holy Trinity term in the third year of the king written below. The second proclamation was made on the twenty-first day of November in Holy Michaelmas term of the same third year of the king written below. The third proclamation was made on the sixth day of February in the term of St. Hilary in the third year of the king written below. The fourth proclamation was made on the seventh day of Easter term in the fourth day of the king written below.]

JUNE 11. LENDS RICHARD POWELL, FUTURE FATHER-IN-LAW, £500 ON STATUTE STAPLE.

Noūint vniu'si p pn̄tes nos Ricūm Powell de fforest Hill in

Cōm Oxōn gen'osum et Will[mum] H[earne] Aurifabr' Londoñ, teneri et firmiter obligari Johī Milton de vniūsitat Cantabr'
geños' [in] Qu[ingentas libras de] legalis monete Anglie solveñd eīd Johī, aut suo certo Attorñ hoc script ostendeñ heredibus
vel executor' suis in festo Natiuit꙯: scī Johīs bāpte ꝑx' futur'
post dat' pñciū, Et si defecerimus in solūcoe debit p'd volumus
et [concedimus quod tunc] Currat suꝑ nos et utrumqz ñrum
heredes et executor' ñros pena in Statuto Staplē de debit ꝑui-
candiss in eād [empt] recupañd ordinat' et ꝑviss Dat' vndecimo
die Junij, Anno regni dnī nrī Caroli [dei grā re]gis Anglie
S[cotie] ffranc' et Hibñie fidei defensor' &c Tercio.

Ric Powell'   [*seal*]

William Hearne [*seal*]

[*blank*]   [*seal*]

Ni: Hyde   [*seal*]

[On dorso:] Cert' in Canc' Dnī regis per me Thomā Hampson Barronettū Clīcu &c Decimo Sexto Die Decembris Año
xxij^do Caroli Regni.

[Further endorsed:] Memorañd that vpon the nyne and
Twentieth day of November in the yeare of our Lord one thousand six hundred ffiftie and nyne Before the keepers of the liberty of England by authority of Parliament did come the within
named John Milton and did acknowledge himselfe to be fully
satisfied the within mencōned ffiue hundred pounds and all the
damages costs and expences any waies susteined in and aboute
the recovery thereof And therevpon he the said John Milton
instantly requireth that this wryteing obligatory may be Cancelled and made voide Att whose instance this said wryteing
obligatory is altogether Cancelled vacated and made voide.

J know the aboue named John Milton

Tho: Gemm'/

[Further endorsed:] Discharged the [29th day of Novem-
ber] 1659: because J saw [the said recognizance] in the hands
of Richard Powell [esquire]

John Milt[on]

Public Record Office, Certificates and Recognizances, C 152/61;

[136]

J. M. French, "The Powell-Milton Bond," *Harvard Studies and Notes in Philology and Literature*, xx (1938), 62; CM, XVIII, 419, 617; French, *Milton in Chancery*, pp. 100 ff., 292. Illegible spots in the manuscript are supplied within square brackets from similar documents or from names mentioned elsewhere here. Though the transaction had long been known, the document had never been printed before 1938.

[Know all men by these presents that we, Richard Powell of Forest Hill in the county of Oxford, gentleman, and William Hearne, goldsmith of London, hold ourselves firmly bound to John Milton of the University of Cambridge, gentleman, in five hundred pounds of lawful English money to be paid to the said John (or to his specified attorney on presentation of this writing), his heirs or executors, on the feast of the Nativity of St. John the Baptist next ensuing after the date of these presents. And if we fail to pay the aforesaid debt, we are willing and consent that there shall fall on us and both our heirs and executors the penalty ordained and provided in the Statute of the Staple, in case of debts, for the recovery of the said sum. Given this eleventh day of June, in the third year of the reign of our Lord Charles, by the grace of God King of England, Scotland, France, and Ireland, Defender of the Faith, etc.

Richard Powell
William Hearne
Nicholas Hyde

Certified in the Chancery of our Lord the King by me, Thomas Hampson, Baronet, Clerk, etc., on the 16th day of December, in the twenty-second year of the reign of King Charles.]

Masson outlined the history of this transaction (*Life*, II, 492-496); Brennecke, pp. 114-115. For some reason which does not seem clear he assumed (p. 495n.) that it represented a transfer of land from Milton to Powell. He queries: "Can any of the property of the old Roman Catholic yeoman, Richard Milton of Stanton St. John's, have come, by will or otherwise, to his grandson John in his own right? If so, and the property were near Forest Hill, there may have been a sale of it to Mr. Powell, and hence the recognizance." But there seems to be no need of any such explanation, which merely complicates the situation. Powell undoubtedly needed money, as he constantly did, and was able to borrow it of Milton; the statute staple was simply the security for the loan.

Whereas Richard Powell of fforresthill in the Countie of Oxford geñt and William Hearne late Cittizen and Goldsmith of London deceased, By their writing or recognizance of the nature of a statute staple beareing date the eleaventh day of June wch was in the third yeare of the raigne of the late King Charles of England &c made and provided for the recoũy of debts And taken acknowledged & sealed before S^r: Nicholas Hide, K^t: then Lord cheife Justice of the Court then called the Kings Bench at Westm^r did acknowledge themselues to owe unto John Milton then of the University of Cambridge geñl sonne of John Milton Cittizen and Scrivener of London the soñe of fiue hundred pounds of lawfull money of England, Which said statute or recognizance is by a writing beareing even date therewith defeazanced for the payment of the soñe of three hundred and twelue pounds of like money unto the said John Milton the sonne his Executors Adm^{rs} or Assignes on the twelueth day of December then next ensuing, As by the said statute or recognizance and defeazance therevpon where-vnto relañon being had more att large may appeare.

Public Record Office, SP 23/101, p. 931; Hamilton, p. 95.

I have examined, and find—The 11th of June 1627, Richard Powell of fforrest Hill in the County of Oxford Gent, and W^m. Hearne of London Citizen, and Goldsmith, acknowledged a Statute Staple of 500^{li} unto John Milton, the Petitioner Defeazanced by John Milton the Petitioners ffather, on the behalfe of the Petitioner, upon paym^t. of 312^l the 12th of December: then next ensuing. As by a Copie of the said Statute, deposed by Thomas Gardner, and by the Counterpart of the Defeazance, produced by the Petitioner, appeares . . .

4° Mar: 1650

[signed] Pet: Brereton.

Public Record Office, SP Dom 23/101, p. 923 (Brereton's report of March 4, 1650/1); Hamilton, p. 48.

The Lands belonging to ye s^d. Richard Powell lying in ye County of Oxford, were mortgaged before ye late vnhappy warres: The Freehold lying in Wheatley in ye s^d County, to M^r. John Milton. . . .

Anne Powell.   Richard Powell.

Public Record Office, SP Dom 1st series, vol. 1, p. 525; Hamilton, p. 112.

. . . Richard Powell and one William Hearne by a wryting or Recognizance in the nature of A statute Staple bearing date the Eleventh day of June in the Third yeare of the late King Charles . . . became bound vnto this Def^t in the Some of fiue hundred pounds of lawfull English money defeazanced for the payment of Three hundred povnds principall debt and Twelue pownds Jnterest for the same vpon the Twelueth day of December then next following Which said Three hundred pownds principall was for the like some then iustly and truely lent vnto the said Richard Powell by John Milton deceased ffather of this Def^t in his life time. . . .

Public Record Office, C10/44/2 (Milton's answer to Elizabeth Ashworth, February 22, 1653/4); French, *Milton in Chancery*, p. 304. In other papers of the Powell family are similar references to this transaction; *ibid.*, pp. 71 ff.

[Anne Powell testified in 1656] That shee doth beleiue that the said John Milton ye father did in or about June 1627 lend vnto this dēpts said late husband Richard Powell the summe of 300^li. att Jnterest and that for secureinge the Repayment thereof the said Richard Powell together with Wm Hearne since deceased in this Jntērr named did acknowledge a statute of 500^li. vnto the said dēft beareinge date ye Eleauenth day of June 1627. and y^t the said John Milton the father did defeasance the said statute by deed Jndented beareinge date on the said Eleauenth day of June 1627. made betweene the said John Milton of the one pte and the said Richard Powell and Wm Hearne of the other pte, and that the writeinge Jndented nowe shewed to this dēpt of the date aforesaid is the Counterpte of the said Jndenture . . . .

From Anne Powell's deposition in the Ashworth-Milton suit, June 4, 1656, *q.v.*

JUNE 11. POWELL'S STATUTE STAPLE RECORDED.

[Powell vndecimo die Junii Anno regni dnī nrī Caroli
Hearne dei grā regis Anglie Scotie ffranc et hibnīe fidei
H: defensor &c Tercio Ricūs Powell de fforrest Hill
cancelled] in Cōm Oxoñ geñ et Willmūs Hearne Ciuis et
Aurifabr' London, Coram Nichō Hide mīl &c Recogñ st debere
Johī Milton de vniūsitat Cantabr' geñ Quingentas Libras sō¹
in festo Natiuiᵗᵉ. sci Johīs bapte px' Et si &c./

Public Record Office, Lord Chamberlain's Recognizance Book, L.C.
4/200, f. 265; French, *Milton in Chancery*, p. 292.

[On the eleventh day of June in the third year of the reign
of our Lord Charles, by the grace of God king of England,
Scotland, France, and Ireland, defender of the faith, etc., Richard Powell of Forest Hill in Co. Oxford, gentleman, and William Hearne, citizen and goldbeater of London, came before
Nicholas Hyde, Knight, etc., and acknowledged that they owed
John Milton of the University of Cambridge, gentleman, five
hundred pounds, to be paid at the feast of the Nativity of St.
John the Baptist next ensuing. And if etc.]

M'd q'd xj° die Junij Anno p'd Ricūs Powell de fforest Hill
in Cōm Oxōn geñ et Willmūs Hearne Civis et Aurifabr' London. Coram Nīchs Hide mīl &c Recogñ se debere Johī Milton
de vniūsitat Cantabr' gen Quingentas libras sōl in festo Natiuiᵗˢ:
sci Johīs Baptē px':/ [*marginal note:*] 91

Public Record Office, Recognizance Roll, L.C. 4/56; French, *Milton in Chancery*, p. 293.

[Memorandum, that on the eleventh day of June in the year
aforesaid Richard Powell of Forest Hill in Co. Oxford, gentleman, and William Hearne, citizen and goldbeater of London,
came before Nicholas Hyde, Knight, etc., and acknowledged
that they owed John Milton of the University of Cambridge,
gentleman, five hundred pounds, to be paid at the feast of the
Nativity of St. John the Baptist next ensuing.]

JUNE 13. MILTON-RUDD CONCORD OF FINE PRO-CLAIMED.

Prima ꝑclam' fcā fuit tc̄iodecimo die Junij t̄n̄o' sce' Trini-tatie Anno tc̄io Regis infrascrz.

Endorsement on final concord of June 10, 1627.

[The first proclamation was made on the thirteenth day of June in the term of Holy Trinity in the third year of the king written below (Charles I).]

JUNE 14. FINE BETWEEN THE MILTONS AND THE RUDDS.

Midd ss Pr Antonio Rudd & Johanne vxi' eius qd iuste &c red' Johī Mylton sen' & Johī Milton Juni' con' &c de vno mesu-agio cum ꝑtin' in parochia sci' Martini' in Campis Et nisi &c./

Et est concordia tlīs scīlt qd pcdi' Antonius & Johanna recogn' pdcm' messuagm' cum ꝑtin' esse ius ipius' Johīs Miltōn' sen' & vt iłł que ijdem Johēs Milton sen' & Johēs Milton Juni' hēnt de dono pdcōr Antonij & Johanne Et ill remiser' et quiet clam' de se & hered eius p'dcis Johī Milton sen' & Johī Milton Juni' & hered ipius' Johīs Milton sen' imppm' Et p'tea ijdem An-tonius & Johanna concesser' ꝑ se & hered ipius' Antonij qd ipi' War' p'dcis Johī Milton sen' & Johī Milton Juni' & hered ipius' Johīs Milton sen mesuagm' cum ꝑtin' cont' ipos' Antonm' & Johannam & hered ipius' Antonij imppm' Et ult'ius ijdem An-tonius & Johanna concesser' ꝑ se & hered ipius' Johanne qd ipi' War' pdcis' Johī Milton sen' & Johī Milton Juni' & hered ipīus Johīs Milton sen' p'dcm' mesuagm' cum ꝑtin' con'   ipos' Antonm' & Johannam & heredes ipius' Johanne imppm' Et ꝑ hac &c./

Capt & cognit' xiiijo die Junij Anno t'cio Caroli Regis coram me   Tho Rychardson

[Endorsed:] ꝑclam' Trin' tcio Caroli &c.

[Middlesex county. Know that Antony Rudd and Joan his wife lawfully yield to John Milton Senior and John Milton

Junior in one messuage with appurtenances in the parish of St. Martin-in-the-Fields. And unless etc. And the agreement is as follows: namely, that the aforesaid Anthony and Joan recognize the aforesaid messuage with the appurtenances to be the property of this same John Milton Senior and to be things which the same John Milton Senior and John Milton Junior hold by gift of the aforesaid Anthony and Joan. And the latter have yielded and quit claim for themselves and their heirs to the aforesaid John Milton Senior and John Milton Junior and the heirs of the same John Milton Senior forever. And further the same Anthony and Joan have yielded for themselves and the heirs of the same Anthony that they guarantee to the aforesaid John Milton Senior and John Milton Junior and the heirs of the same John Milton Senior the messuage with its appurtenances against the same Anthony and Joan and the heirs of the same Anthony forever. And further the same Anthony and Joan have agreed for themselves and the heirs of the same Joan that they guarantee to the aforesaid John Milton Senior and John Milton Junior and the heirs of the same John Milton Senior the aforesaid messuage with its appurtenances against the same Anthony and Joan and the heirs of the same Joan forever. And in proof of this etc. Taken and acknowledged on the fourteenth day of June in the third year of King Charles before me, Thomas Richardson. Proclaimed in Trinity Term of the third year of Charles etc.]

JUNE 14. FATHER'S INDENTURE WITH RUDD ACKNOWLEDGED IN COURT.

Et memorand' qd' qvartodecimo die Junii anno supscript' prefat' Anthonius & Johēs Rudd venerunt coram dtō dnō Rege in Canc' sua & recognouerunt Jndentūr' predict' ac omia & singula in eadem content' & specificat' in forma sūpdtā./
From the indenture of May 25, 1627, *q.v.*

[And be it remembered that on the fourteenth day of June in the year above written the aforesaid Anthony and Joan Rudd came before the same Lord King in his Chancery and acknowledged the said indenture and all and singular contained and specified in the same in the form aforesaid.]

JUNE 23. FATHER BUYS LAND FROM ANN WESTRAWE.
Westrawe vid et Milton 19

To all to whome this p̄sent writing shall come I the said Ann Westrawe widowe send greeting knowe ye that I the said Ann westrawe for and in consideracōn of the sōme of one hundred and eight poundꝑ of lawfull money of England to me in hand at and before thensealing and delivery of theis p̄sentꝑ well and truly paid by John Milton Citizen and Scrivener of London whereof I doe acknowledge the receipt and thereof and of every part and pcell thereof doe clearely acquite and discharge the said John Milton his heires executors and administrators and every of them forevermore by theis p̄sentꝑ and for other good consideracōns me therevnto especially moving have granted bargained sold remised released enfeoffed and confirmed de-mised letten assigned and sett over and by theis p̄sentꝑ doe graunt bargaine sell remise release enfeoffe and confirme de-mise lett assigne and sett over vnto the said John Milton his heires executors administrators and assignes All that mesuage or teñte with thappᵉtenñcꝑ scituate lying and being in the parish of St Martins in the ffeildꝑ in the Countie of Midd now in the tenure or occupacōn of Mathew Lyster Doctor of Phisick or his assignes And all myne estate right title interest rent revercōn remainder ꝓpertie clayme and demaunde of in and to the same mesuage or teñte and p̄misses and of in and to every part and parcell thereof Together with all writingꝑ evidencꝑ escriptꝑ and munimentꝑ conc̄ning the same which mesuage or teñte and p̄misses lately were conveyed over vnto me the said Ann west-rawe by and from Anthony Rudd Citizen and Pewterer of London by his deed or writing indented bearing date the three and twentith day of June Anno dñi 1626 and in the second yere of his Maiesties raigne that now is of England To have and to hold the same mesuage or teñte and p̄misses with thappᵉtenñcꝑ and every part and parcell thereof to the said John Milton his

heires executors administrators and assignes to his and their
owne vse and vses forever and that in as large and ample manner
and sort to all intentȝ and purposes as I the said Ann Westraw
mine heires executors administrators or assignes or any of us
.may cann might should or ought to have and enioye the same
In witness whereof I the said Ann westrawe have herevnto
sett my hand and seale yeoven the three and twentith daye of
June 1627 and in the third yere of the raigne of our said soveraigne lord king Charles of England &c

Et memorand qd vicesimo quinto die Junii ann' suꝑscript
ꝑfat Anna westrawe vid venit coram dtō dnō Rege in cancellar'
sua et recogn' Script' ꝑdict ac om̄ia et singula in eadem contenta
et sꝓific in forma supradic̄t./ In^d vicesimo quinto die Junij Anno
ꝑdict

ex^{iij}

Public Record Office, C54/2715/19; Stevens, *Milton Papers*,
pp. 2, 40. There are photostatic facsimiles in the Harvard College Library (shelf-mark: 14495.58PF). The margin of the Latin endorsement bears the signature "Eden," undoubtedly Thomas Eden, Master
in Chancery 1625-1640.

[And note that on the twenty-fifth day of June in the year
above written the aforesaid Ann Westrawe, widow, came before
the said Lord King in his Chancery and acknowledged the aforesaid writing and all and singular contained and specified in the
same in the form above written. Indented on the twenty-fifth
day of June in the year aforesaid.]

JUNE 23. FATHER'S INDENTURE WITH RUDD IN-DENTED.

Jn^d vicesimo tc̄io die Junij Anno ꝑdict'.
From the indenture of May 25, 1627, *q.v.*
[Indented on the twenty-third day of June in the year afore-
said.]

JUNE 25. FATHER'S AGREEMENT WITH ANN WEST-RAWE ACKNOWLEDGED IN COURT.

Et memorand qd vicesimo quinto die Junii ann' suꝑscript

p̄fat Anna westrawe vid venit coram dtō dnō Rege in cancellar'
sua et recogn' Script' p̄dict ac om̄ia et singula in eadem contenta
et sp̄ific in forma supradict./ In^d vicesimo quinto die Junij
Anno p̄dict

ex^iij

From the agreement of June 23, 1627, *q.v.*

[And note that on the twenty-fifth day of June in the year
above written the aforesaid Ann Westrawe, widow, came before
the said Lord King in his Chancery and acknowledged the
aforesaid writing and all and singular contained and specified
in the same in the form above written. Indented on the twenty-
fifth day of June in the year aforesaid.]

JULY 5. FATHER ARRANGES HORSEY-COTTON BOND.

Sr Geo: Horsey & oth^rs p obl' Dat' v^to Julij 1627 . . . 100^li
Thomas Bower's schedule of Cotton's bonds made out by himself
and Milton's father; see below under date of November 25, 1630. ·

. . . Sr George Horsey & others by bond dated the ffift of
July One thowsand six hundred Twentie seven, One hundred
poundᵱ principall debt.
Sir Thomas Cotton's bill; see below under date of May 28, 1636.

OCTOBER 11. FATHER ARRANGES BLACKER-COTTON BOND.

Mr Blacker & oth^rs p obl' Dat' xj^o Octobr' 1627 . . . 100^li
Thomas Bower's schedule of Cotton's bonds made out by himself
and Milton's father; see below under date of November 25, 1630. The
original bond has not been found.

. . . Mr Blacker & others by bond dated the Eleventh day of
October One thowsand six hundred Twentie seven, One hun-
dred poundᵱ principall debt.
Sir Thomas Cotton's bill; see below under date of May 28, 1636.

NOVEMBER 7. FATHER ARRANGES WELBY-COTTON BOND.

Mr Welby & oth^rs by bond dated the vii^th of Novemb^r 1627
. . . 200^li

[145]

Thomas Bower's schedule of Cotton's bonds made out by himself and Milton's father; see below under date of November 25, 1630. The original bond has not been found.

... Mr Welby and others by bond dated 7 of Nouemb: 1627 200 principall debt ....

Sir Thomas Cotton's bill; see below under date of May 28, 1636.

NOVEMBER 21. MILTON-RUDD CONCORD OF FINE PROCLAIMED.

Scdā ꝓclam' fca' fuit vicesimo primo die Novembris tñnō sce' Michis Anno tcio Regis infrascrz.

Endorsement on final concord of June 10, 1627.

[The second proclamation was made on the twenty-first day of November in the term of St. Michael in the third year of the king written below (Charles I).]

NOVEMBER 30. FATHER ARRANGES VAUDRAY-COTTON BOND.

Mr Vaudray & oth^rs p obl' Dat' xxx° Novembr' 1627 ... 100^li

Thomas Bower's schedule of Cotton's bonds made out by himself and Milton's father; see below under date of November 25, 1630. The original bond has not been found.

... Mr Vaudray & others by bond [dated] the Thirtieth of November [One thousand six] hundred Twentie seven One hundred pound₽ principall debt ...

Sir Thomas Cotton's bill; see below under date of May 28, 1636.

DECEMBER 12. POWELL PAYS £12 INTEREST ON STATUTE STAPLE OF JUNE 11.

... the said Twelue pownds Jnterest was payd vpon the said Twelueth day of December Or soone after And that the growing Jnterest for the forbearance of the said Principall debt was for some yeares then following likewise payd And soe continued to bee paid vntill June Jn the yeare of our Lord One Thousand six hundred ffortie and ffower Att What time the said Richard Powell failed ... in the payment of the Jnterest then due and payable and from thence growing due and payable ....

Milton's answer to Elizabeth Ashworth, February 22, 1653/4, *q.v.* For the agreement by which the debt from Powell to Milton became due on this day, see the quotations given under date of June 11, 1627. On the authority of this quotation from Milton himself the payment of the interest will be noted on each succeeding December 12 until 1644. It must be understood that the probability is that the payments were not always made precisely on this date, and also that they were probably made twice a year rather than once; but this entry each year will serve as a reasonable approximation.

DECEMBER 17. FATHER ARRANGES DABRIDGECOURT-COTTON BOND.

M[r] Dabridgecourt & oth[rs] p obl' Dat' xvij° Decembr' 1627 ... 100[li]

Thomas Bower's schedule of Cotton's bonds made out by himself and Milton's father; see below under date of November 25, 1630. The original bond has not been found.

... M[r] Dabridgecourt & others by bond dated the seventeenth of December One thowsand six hundred Twentie seven One hundred pound∘ principall debt.

Sir Thomas Cotton's bill; see below under date of May 28, 1636.

DECEMBER 21. FATHER ARRANGES PREWET-COTTON BOND.

M[r] Prewet & oth[rs] p obl' Dat' xxj° Decembr' 1627 ... 100[li]

Thomas Bower's schedule of Cotton's bonds made out by himself and Milton's father; see below under date of November 25, 1630. The original bond has not been found.

... M[r] [Prewet] & others by bond dated the One & Twentieth of December One thowsand six hundred Twentie seven, One hundred [pound∘] principall debt.

Sir Thomas Cotton's bill; see below under date of May 28, 1636.

1628

SUPPOSED PORTRAIT BY JANSSEN.

[A portrait engraved by Pye and published in 1823 is labeled: "John Milton. Painted by C. Janssen. Engraved by Charles Pye. London.

Pub^d for the Proprietor, March, 1823." The subject of the portrait is said to be about twenty or twenty-five years old, or by another critic about eighteen. There is probably some confusion between this and other early portraits of Milton, though Dr. Williamson asserts that it bears no resemblance whatever to Milton. There is therefore no reason to believe it authentic. See his *Milton Tercentenary*, pp. 19, 86.]

PLANTS (ACCORDING TO TRADITION) MULBERRY TREE AT CAMBRIDGE.

The tradition that Milton planted a mulberry tree in the gardens of Christ's College while in attendance as a student is ubiquitous. The story appears, among other places, in the *Cambridge Portfolio*, 1 (1840), 207-210, together with an engraving; in the *Gentleman's Magazine*, New Series, XII (1839), 230-231; in an article by David Masson in *Good Words*, XXXIV (1893), 39 ff., with an illustration; and in most biographies. The tree in question, supported with props under the branches and by a mound of earth heaped up about the roots, was still standing and flourishing as late as 1936, when the present editor visited Cambridge. On the other hand, John Peile, in *Christ's College*, 1900, p. 119, makes it reasonably clear that this is one of a number of trees planted in 1608, the year of Milton's birth, by Troilus Atkinson, as a compliment to King James. Mr. Peile quotes the college records for the year 1608-09 to prove that the college paid 18s. 10d. for the planting of 300 of these trees. The tradition is recorded here, not because it is considered trustworthy, but because it seems desirable that all such gossip, however trivial or ill-founded, should receive fair treatment in such a collection.

FATHER RECEIVES NEW APPRENTICE.

1628 . . . John Hatton—of John Milton—1599

Bodleian Library, MS. Rawl. Misc. 51, f. 29v. The date 1599 at the end is that of Milton's own admission to the Scriveners' Company. Reprinted in *Athenaeum*, 1880, I, 565. Although "Hatton" seems to be the actual reading here, it should probably be "Hutton," since there are other references to his servant of that name.

FIRST PROLUSION—UNPOPULARITY AND DISTRUST OF CLASSMATES.

In Collegio, &c. *Utrum Dies an Nox præstantior sit?*

Scriptum post se reliquere passim Nobilissimi quiq; Rhetoricæ Magistri, quod nec vos præteriit, Academici, in unoquoq, dicendi genere, sive demonstrativo, sive deliberativo, sive judiciali, ab aucupanda Auditorum gratia exordium duci oportere;

alioqui nec permoveri posse Auditorum animos, nec causam ex sententia succedere. Quod si res ita est, quam sane, ne vera dissimulem, Eruditorum omnium consensu fixum ratumq; novi, miserum me! ad quantas ego hodie redactus sum Angustias! qui in ipso Orationis Limine vereor ne aliquid prolaturus sim minime Oratorium, & ab officio Oratoris primo & præcipuo necesse habeam abscedere. Etenim quî possim ego vestram sperare benevolentiam, cum in hoc tanto concursu, quot oculis intueor tot ferme aspiciam infesta in me capita; adeo ut Orator venisse videar ad non exorabiles. Tantum potest ad simultates etiam in Scholis æmulatio, vel diversa Studia, vel in eisdem studiis diversa judicia sequentium; ego vero solicitus non sum,

> Ne mihi *Polydamas* & *Troiades* Labeonem
> Prætulerint; Nugæ.

Veruntamen ne penitus despondeam animum, sparsim video, ni fallor, qui mihi ipso aspectu tacito, quam bene velint, haud obscure significant; à quibus etiam quantumvis paucis, equidem probari malo quam ab innumeris imperitorum Centuriis, in quibus nihil mentis, nihil rectæ rationis, nihil sani judicii inest, ebullienti quadam & plane ridendâ verborum spumâ sese venditantibus. . . . Si quis igitur est qui, spreta pacis conditione, ἄσπονδον πόλεμον mihi indixerit, eum ego quidem in præsentia non dedignabor orare & rogare, ut semotâ paulisper simultate, æquabilis adsit certaminis hujus arbiter; neve Oratoris culpa, si qua est, Causam quam optimam & præclarissimam in invidiam vocet. Quod si mordaciora paulo hæc & aceto perfusa nimio putaveritis, id ipsum de industria fecisse me profiteor: volo enim ut initium Orationis meæ primulum imitetur diluculum; ex quo subnubilo serenissima nascitur dies. . . .

Milton, *Epistolarum Familiarium Liber Unus*, 1674, pp. 67-82; CM, XII, 118 ff. The date of this prolusion, like that of several others, is most uncertain. It is assigned to 1628 simply as a likely possibility.

[Whether Day or Night is the more excellent?]

All the noblest masters of Rhetoric have left it everywhere written behind them, nor has the fact escaped yourselves, Fellow-Academics, that in every kind of speaking—whether the demonstrative, the deliberative, or the judicial—one ought to draw one's exordium from what will ensure the favour of his hearers; otherwise, neither can the minds of the hearers be moved, nor can the cause succeed according to purpose. But if this is the case,—and that so it is, not to conceal the truth, is, I know, fixed and ratified by the assent of all the learned,—alas for me! to what straits am I this day reduced, fearing as I do that, in the very outset of my oration, I may be going to bring forward something far from oratorical, and may have necessarily to deviate from the first and chief duty of an orator. For how can I hope for your good will, when, in this so great concourse, as many heads as I behold with my eyes, almost the same number do I see of visages bearing malice against me; so that I seem to have come as an *orator* to persons not *exorable*?* Of so much efficacy in producing private grudges is the rivalry even in schools of those who follow different studies or different methods in the same studies. But I care not that Polydamas and the women of Troy have preferred Labeo to me; a mere trifle.† Nevertheless, that I may not wholly despond, I do, unless I am mistaken, see here and there some, who, even by their silent aspect, signify to me not obscurely how well they wish me; by whom, very few though they be, I, for my part, prefer being approved than by numberless hundreds of unskilled ones, in whom there is no mind, no right reason, no sound judgment, priding themselves on a certain overboiling and truly laughable foam of words. . . . If, however, there is any one who, scorning terms of peace, has declared truceless war against me, him at present I will not disdain to beg and entreat, that, setting aside rivalry for a little, he be among us as a fair arbiter in this debate, and do not, for the fault of the orator, if there is any, bring into obloquy a cause the best and most illustrious possible. And, should you think what I have said a little too biting, and mixed with too much vinegar, I profess that I have done this purposely; for I wish that the beginning of my speech should re-

---

* The italics are Masson's.
† Masson omits this sentence, which is here translated by the present editor.

semble the first dawn of morning, out of which, when it is somewhat cloudy, there generally arises a very clear Day.]
    Masson, I, 242-243 (275-279).

PROLUSION III. HARD STUDY, DISLIKE OF SCHOLASTIC PHILOSOPHY, WEAK EYESIGHT.

In Scholis Publicis.
Contra Philosophiam Scholasticam.

. . . Sæpius ego, Auditores, cum mihi forte aliquoties imponeretur necessitas investigandi paulisper has argutiolas, post retusam diutinâ lectione & animi & oculorum aciem, sæpius inquam ad interspirandum restiti, & subinde pensum oculis emensus quæsivi miserum tædii solatium; cum vero plus semper viderem superesse, quàm quod legendo absolveram, equidem inculcatis hisce ineptiis quoties præoptavi mihi repurgandum *Augeæ* Bubile, fœlicemque prædicavi *Herculem,* cui facilis *Juno* hujusmodi ærumnam nunquam imperaverat exantlandam. . . .
    Milton, *Epistolarum Familiarium Liber Unus,* 1674, pp. 88-95; CM, XII, 158 ff. The date is uncertain.

[Delivered in the public schools. An attack
on the scholastic philosophy.

. . . Frequently, my hearers, when there chanced to be imposed upon me now and then the necessity of investigating these subtle trivialities, after blunting both my mind and my eyes with a day's reading, I have stopped to take breath, and thereupon, measuring the task with my eyes, I have sought a wretched relief from my fatigue; but, as I always saw more remaining than I got through in my reading, I as often wished that, instead of these vanities, there had been given me as a task the recleansing of the Augean cow-house, and I called Hercules a happy fellow, to whom Juno in her good nature had never commanded the endurance of this kind of toil. . . .]
    Masson, I, 248 ff. (281-282).

PUBLISHES A POEM NOW LOST?

At some time during this year Milton undoubtedly committed to type some scholastic exercise which he had written, and to which he refers in his letter to Gill on July 2, 1628. Whether it was one of his other works already known to us in other editions, or whether it was a different work, no longer extant or known, is problematical. See the comments under his *De Idea Platonica*, 1628; *Naturam non pati senium*, summer, 1628; and the letter to Gill, July 2, 1628. It is also possible that the sixth prolusion may have been the piece in question. See also CM, XVIII, 537.

DE IDEA PLATONICA.

De Idea Platonica quemadmodum Aristoteles intellexit.

Milton, *Poems*, 1645, part 2, pp. 62-63; Mackellar, pp. 140 ff.; CM, I, 266-269. It has been suggested (CM, XVIII, 537) that this may have been the poem separately printed in 1628 but now lost.

[On the Platonic idea as Aristotle understood it.]

JANUARY 22. NIECE ANNE PHILLIPS BURIED.

[Burials] Jan. [1627/8] . . . 22 Anna Phillips fa. Eduardi et Anne (Ch.).

The Register of St. Martin-in-the-Fields London 1619-1636, ed. J. V. Kitto, 1936 (Publications of the Harleian Society, Vol. LXVI), p. 233. I have not seen the original parish record.

[Anne Phillips, daughter of Edward and Anne, was buried on January 22, 1627/8, in the chancel.]

FEBRUARY 6. MILTON-RUDD CONCORD OF FINE PROCLAIMED.

Tcia pclam' fcā fuit sexto die ffebruarij tñno' sce' Hilarij Anno tc̄io Regis infrascrz.

Endorsement on final concord of June 10, 1627.

[The third proclamation was made on the sixth day of February in the term of St. Hilary in the third year of the king written below (Charles I).]

MARCH OR APRIL (?) LETTER FROM THOMAS YOUNG.

[Though this letter itself has not been found, the following phrases, taken from Milton's letter of July 21, 1628, to Young, indicate its principal contents and tone:]

... tardæ scriptionis excusationem attuleris. ... Te vero oblitum esse mei ut suspicer, tam multa tua de me recens merita nequaquam sinunt. ... Rus tuum accersitus, simul ac Ver adoleverit ... Stoam tuam Icenorum. ... Cæterùm qui tarditatis culpam deprecatus es. ...

See Milton's letter to Young, July 21, 1628. The reference to spring seems to point to a date in March or April for Young's letter, though Milton's reply would in this event seem very much delayed. See also CM, XVIII, 526.

[... you excused your slowness in writing. ... That I should suspect that you had forgotten me, however, your so many recent kindnesses to me by no means allow. ... Having been invited to your part of the country, as soon as spring is a little advanced ... to your Stoa of the Iceni. ... You have deprecated the blame of slowness. ...]

APRIL 9. NIECE ELIZABETH PHILLIPS BAPTIZED.

[Baptisms] Aprilis 1628 ... 9 Elizabetha Phillips fa. Edvardi et Anne.

The Register of St. Martin-in-the-Fields London 1619-1636, ed. J. V. Kitto, 1926 (Publications of the Harleian Society, Vol. LXVI), p. 54. I have not seen the original parish record.

[On April 9, 1628, Elizabeth Phillips, daughter of Edward and Anne, was baptized.]

MAY 1. SONG ON MAY MORNING.

SONG On *May* Morning.

Milton, *Poems*, 1645, pp. 26-27; CM, I, 31. It is impossible to date this poem with any accuracy. Grierson and Tillyard assign it to 1630, Hanford and Hughes to 1628, and Moody to 1632-33.

MAY? ELEGY 7. SUSCEPTIBILITY TO FEMININE BEAUTY, AND LOVE FOR A GIRL.

Elegia septima, Anno ætatis undevigesimo.

Nondum blanda tuas leges Amathusia norâm,
   Et Paphio vacuum pectus ab igne fuit.

Sæpe cupidineas, puerilia tela, sagittas,
    Atque tuum sprevi maxime, numen, Amor.
Tu puer imbelles dixi transfige columbas,
    Conveniunt tenero mollia bella duci.
Aut de passeribus tumidos age, parve, triumphos,
    Hæc sunt militiæ digna trophæa tuæ.
In genus humanum quid inania dirigis arma?
    Non valet in fortes ista pharetra viros.
Non tulit hoc Cyprius, (neque enim Deus ullus ad iras
    Promptior) & duplici jam ferus igne calet.
Ver erat, & summæ radians per culmina villæ
    Attulerat primam lux tibi Maie diem:
At mihi adhuc refugam quærebant lumina noctem
    Nec matutinum sustinuere jubar.
Astat Amor lecto, pictis Amor impiger alis,
    Prodidit astantem mota pharetra Deum:
Prodidit & facies, & dulce minantis ocelli,
    Et quicquid puero, dignum & Amore fuit.
Talis in ærerno juvenis Sigeius Olympo
    Miscet amatori pocula plena Jovi;
Aut qui formosas pellexit ad oscula nymphas
    Thiodamantæus Naiade raptus Hylas;
Addideratque iras, sed & has decuisse putares,
    Addideratque truces, nec sine felle minas.
Et miser exemplo sapuisses tutiùs inquit,
    Nunc mea quid possit dextera testis eris. . . .
Et modò quà nostri spatiantur in urbe Quirites
    Et modò villarum proxima rura placent.
Turba frequens, faciéque simillima turba dearum
    Splendida per medias itque reditque vias.
Auctaque luce dies gemino fulgore coruscat,
    Fallor? an & radios hinc quoque Phoebus habet.
Hæc ego non fugi spectacula grata severus,
    Impetus & quò me fert juvenilis, agor.
Lumina luminibus malè providus obvia misi,
    Neve oculos potui continuisse meos.

Unam forte aliis supereminuisse notabam,
    Principium nostri lux erat illa mali.

Sic Venus optaret mortalibus ipsa videri,
    Sic regina Deûm conspicienda fuit.

Hanc memor objecit nobis malus ille Cupido,
    Solus & hos nobis texuit antè dolos.

Nec procul ipse vafer latuit, multæque sagittæ
    Et facis a tergo grande pependit onus.

Nec mora, nunc ciliis hæsit, nunc virginis ori,
    Insilit hinc labiis, insidet inde genis:

Et quascunque agilis partes jaculator oberrat,
    Hei mihi, mille locis pectus inerme ferit.

Protinus insoliti subierunt corda furores,
    Uror amans intùs, flammaque totus eram.

Interea misero quæ jam mihi sola placebat,
    Ablata est oculis non reditura meis.

Ast ego progredior tacitè querebundus, & excors,
    Et dubius volui saepe referre pedem.

Findor, & hæc remanet, sequitur pars altera votum,
    Raptaque tàm subitò gaudia flere juvat.

Sic dolet amissum proles Junonia cœlum,
    Inter Lemniacos præcipitata focos.

Talis & abreptum solem respexit, ad Orcum
    Vectus ab attonitis Amphiaraus equis.

Quid faciam infelix, & luctu victus, amores
    Nec licet inceptos ponere, neve sequi.

O utinam spectare semel mihi detur amatos
    Vultus, & coràm tristia verba loqui;

Forsitan & duro non est adamante creata,
    Forte nec ad nostras surdeat illa preces.

Crede mihi nullus sic infeliciter arsit,
    Ponar in exemplo primus & unus ego.

Parce precor. . . .

Milton, *Poems*, 1645, part 2, pp. 35-39; Mackellar, pp. 100 ff.; CM, I, 214-223. The dates assigned to this piece by various editors and biographers vary, but 1628 is the year most widely favored. The time of year would seem to be May, since that month plays a prominent part in the poem. The degree of true autobiography in the poem, as opposed to poetic artifice, cannot be definitely determined. The erroneous "ærerno" in line 21 is corrected to "æterno" in the 1673 edition.

[Elegy the seventh. Written in his nineteenth year.

Not yet, O genial Amathusia, had I known thy laws, and my breast was free from the Paphian fire. Often I scorned the arrows of Cupid as but boyish darts, and derided thy deity, most great Love. "Do thou, child," I said, "pierce timid doves; such soft warfare befits so tender a warrior. Or win triumphs, young one, over sparrows; these are the worthy trophies of thy valour. Against brave men thou canst do nothing." The Cyprian boy could not bear this; nor is any god more prompt to anger than he. It was Spring, and the light, raying through the topmost roofs of the town, had brought to thee, O May, thy first day; but my eyes yet sought the flying night and could not endure the morning beam. Love stands by my bed, active Love with painted wings. The motion of his quiver betrayed the present god; his face also betrayed him, and his sweetly threatening eyes, and whatever else was comely in a boy and in Love. He looked like the Sigeian boy who on eternal Olympus mixes full goblets for amorous Jove, or like Hylas, son of Thiodamas, stolen by a Naiad, who coaxed the lovely nymphs to his kisses. He had added anger (but you would think this became him), and he had added ferocity, and threats not without animosity.* "Better," he said, "hadst thou been wise by the example of others; now thou shalt thyself be a witness what my right hand can do." ...

Anon I am taking my pleasure, now in those places in the city where our citizens walk, and now in the rural neighbourhood of the hamlets round. A frequent crowd—in appearance, as it might seem, a crowd of goddesses—is going and coming splendidly along the middle of the ways; and the growing day shines with twofold brightness. I do not austerely shun those agreeable sights, but am whirled along wherever my youthful impulse carries me. Too imprudent, I let *my* eyes meet *their*

---

* These two sentences, omitted in Masson's translation, are supplied by the present editor.

eyes, and am unable to master them. One by chance I beheld pre-eminent over the rest, and that glance was the beginning of my malady. Such as she would Venus wish herself to be seen by mortals; such as she was the queen of gods to be beheld of old. This fair one mischievous Cupid, remembering his threat, had thrown in my way; he alone wove the snare for me. Not far off was the sly god himself lurking, his many arrows and the great weight of his torch hanging from his back. And without delay he clings first to the maiden's eyebrows and then to her mouth; now he nestles in her lips and then he settles on her cheeks; and whatever parts the nimble archer wanders over, he wounds my unarmed heart, alas! in a thousand places. Immediately unaccustomed pains were felt in my heart. Being in love, I inly burn; I am all one flame. Meanwhile she who alone pleased me was snatched away from my eyes, never to return. I walk on silently, full of complaint and desponding, and often in hesitation I wish to retrace my steps. I am divided into two; one part remains, and the other follows the object of love; and it is my solace to weep for the joys so suddenly reft from me. What shall I, unfortunate, do? Overcome with grief, I can neither desist from my begun love, nor follow it out. O, would it were given me once to behold the beloved countenance, and to speak a sad word or two in her presence! Perchance she is not made of adamant; perchance she might not be deaf to my prayers! Believe me, no one ever burned so unhappily; I may be set up as the first and only instance of a chance so hard. Spare me, I pray. . . .]

Masson, I, 159-160 (189-190).

MAY? RECEIVES LETTER AND VERSES FROM ALEXANDER GILL.

Accepi Literas tuas, & quæ me mirifice oblectavêre, Carmina sane grandia. . . .

Milton's letter to Gill, May 20, 1628, *q.v.*

[I received your letter, and, what wonderfully delighted me, your truly great verses. . . .]

MAY 7. MILTON-RUDD CONCORD OF FINE PROCLAIMED.

Quarta ꝑclam' fca' fuit septimo die t̃no' Pasche Anno quarto Regis infrascrz.

Endorsement on final concord of June 10, 1627, *q.v.*

[The fourth proclamation was made on the seventh day of Easter term in the fourth year of the king written below (Charles I).]

The date is reached as follows. In 1628 Easter day was on April 13 (Old Style). The Easter term began seventeen days later, which would be April 30. The seventh day of the term was thus May 7.

MAY 20. LETTER TO ALEXANDER GILL.

Alexandro Gillio.

2. Accepi Literas tuas, & quæ me mirifice oblectavêre, Carmina sane grandia, & Majestatem vere Poeticam, Virgilianumq; ubiq; ingenium redolentia. Sciebam equidem quam tibi tuóq; genio impossibile futurum esset, à rebus Poeticis avocare animum, & furores illos cælitus instinctos, sacrúmq; & æthereum ignem intimo pectore eluere, cum tua (quod de seipso Claudianus)— *Totum spirent Præcordia Phœbum.* Itaq; si tua tibi ipse promissa fefelleris, laudo hîc tuam (quod ais) inconstantiam, laudo, siqua est, improbitatem; me autem tam præclari Poematis arbitrum à te factum esse, non minus glorior, & honori mihi duco, quam si certantes ipsi Dii Musici ad meum venissent judicium; quod Tmolo Lydii montis Deo populari olim contigisse fabulantur. Nescio sane an Henrico Nassovio plus gratuler de urbe capta, an de tuis Carminibus: nihil enim existimo victoriam hanc peperisse Poematio hoc tuo illustrius, aut celebrius. Te vero, cum prosperos sociorum successus tam sonorâ triumphaliq; tubâ canere audiamus, quantum vatem sperabimus, si forte res nostræ demum feliciores tuas Musas poscant Gratulatrices. Vale Vir Erudite, summasq; à me tibi gratias Carminum tuorum nomine haberi scias.

Londino, Maii 20. 1628.

Milton, *Epistolarum Familiarium Liber Unus,* 1674, pp. 9-10; CM, XII, 6 ff. Donald L. Clark (*John Milton at St. Paul's School,* Columbia, 1948, p. 68) considers "plausible" the suggestion of Eugenia Chifos

("Milton's Letter to Gill, May 20, 1628," in *Modern Language Notes*, XLI [1947], 37-39) that the correct date of this letter is 1630 rather than 1628. In the fifth line of the text "cælitus" seems to be a more correct reading than the CM's "cælius," since the 1674 edition shows a space between the "i" and the "u." In either case the meaning seems clear.

[I received your letter, and, what wonderfully delighted me, your truly great verses, breathing everywhere a genuine poetical majesty, and a Virgilian genius. I knew, indeed, how impossible it would be for you and your genius to keep away from poetry, and to discharge out of the depths of your breast those heaven-inspired furies and the sacred and ethereal fire, seeing that (as Claudian says of himself) "Let your heart breathe pure Phoebus."* Therefore, if you have broken the promises made to yourself, I here praise your (as you call it) inconstancy; I praise the sin, if there be any; and that I should have been made by you the judge of so excellent a poem, I no less glory in and regard as an honour than if the contending musical gods themselves came to me for judgment, as they fable happened of old to Timolus, the popular god of the Lydian mountain. I know not truly whether I should more congratulate Henry of Nassau on the capture of the city or on your verses; for I think the victory he has obtained nothing more illustrious or more celebrated than this poetical tribute of yours. But, as we hear you sing the prosperous successes of the Allies in so sonorous and triumphal a strain, how great a poet we shall hope to have in you, if by chance our own affairs, turning at last more fortunate, should demand your congratulatory muses! Farewell, learned Sir, and believe that you have my best thanks for your verses. *London, May* 20, 1628.]

Masson, I, 161 (190-191).

MAY 29. FATHER ARRANGES EWENS-COTTON BOND.

Mr Ewens & oth^rs p obl' Dat' xxix° Maij 1628 . . . 100^li

Thomas Bower's schedule of Cotton's bonds made out by himself and Milton's father; see below under date of November 25, 1630. The original bond has not been found.

---

* Masson leaves this quotation untranslated.

. . . [Mr Ewens & others] by bond dated the Nyne & Twentieth of May One thousand six hundred Twentie Eight One hundred pound℘ principall debt.

Sir Thomas Cotton's bill; see below under date of May 28, 1636. Without much doubt this Mr. Ewens is Matthew Ewens, for whom Milton arranged another loan from Rose Downer a few days later; see under date of June 10, 1628.

JUNE. FATHER CALLS IN ROSE DOWNER'S MONEY FOR CHANGE OF INVESTMENT.

. . . about the moneth of June one thousand six hundred twenty eight . . . the said John Milton according to the declaracōn and request of your said Oratrixe [Rose Downer] did call in the said money . . . and having gotten the same into his hand℘ did leaue the same as he nowe p'tend℘ in the possession of his then servant Thomas Bower. . . .

Public Record Office, Chancery Proceedings, C2 Charles I/D39/47 (Rose Downer's bill of April 26, 1631); French, *Milton in Chancery*, pp. 236-237.

JUNE. FATHER TERMINATES DOWNER-GREVILLE BOND.

. . . in or about the moneth of June one thousand six hundred twenty eight . . . your said Oratrixe repaired to [the] said John Milton and desired him to call in the said money . . . and the said John Milton . . . did call in the said money . . . And your said Oratrixe therevpon did deliuer vp the said obligacōn to the said John Milton . . . and therevpon the said John Milton receaved the said ffiftie pound℘ and interest and having gotten the same into his hand℘ did leaue the same as he nowe p'tend℘ in the possession of his then servant Thomas Bower to the end the same should be paid over to your said Oratrixe. . . .

Public Record Office, C2 Charles I/D39/47 (Rose Downer's bill of April 26, 1631); French, *Milton in Chancery*, p. 236.

. . . this Defendant saith that the said ffiftie pound℘ was paid in about the moneth of June One thowsand six hundred Twenty and Eight at this Defendant℘ shopp vnto the other Defendant Thomas Bower, for the Complaynant℘ vse. . . .

Public Record Office, C2 Charles I/D39/47 (Milton's answer to Downer, May 3, 1631); French, *Milton in Chancery*, p. 241.

. . . the said ffiftie poundꝑ was lent at Jnterest vnto Sʳ ffulke Grevill Knight vpon good securitie, where the same continued till about June One thowsand Six hundred Twenty and Eight, And then was voluntarily paid in with all Jnterest, therevpon due. . . .

Public Record Office, C2 Charles I/D39/47 (Bower's answer to Downer, May 3, 1631); French, *Milton in Chancery*, pp. 243-244. See also *ibid.*, pp. 247, 248, 251, 253.

JUNE. FATHER AND THOMAS BOWER ARRANGE LOAN AND BOND FROM BULTEELL TO EWENS AND KEYMER.

. . . about June One thowsand Six hundred Twenty and Eight . . . Master Ewens, and Mʳ Keymer in the bill named had occasion for a hundred poundꝑ, whereof ffiftie poundꝑ was then lent vpon their security by one Master Bulteell vpon Jnterest for Six moneths whoe liked them well. . . .

Public Record Office, C2 Charles I/D39/47 (Bower's answer to Downer, May 3, 1631); French, *Milton in Chancery*, pp. 243-244. The original bond has not been found. Though Bower does not specifically say that this bond was made at Milton's shop, such is the presumption from the familiar way in which he brings it into his story.

JUNE? FATHER AND THOMAS BOWER ARRANGE DOWNER-WARING LOAN AND BOND.

. . . about the same time, at this Defendantꝑ request she the said Complaynant Did lend vnto one Master Waring Thirtie poundꝑ at Jnterest for Six monethꝑ. . . .

Public Record Office, C2 Charles I/D39/47 (Bower's answer to Downer, May 3, 1631); French, *Milton in Chancery*, p. 244. The date is rather obscurely stated, but from the context one gathers that this transaction was at "about the same time" as the loan from Rose Downer to Ewens and Keymer, which was June 10, 1628.

JUNE? RECEIVES LETTER FROM ALEXANDER GILL, WHILE WORKING ON COLLEGE EXERCISE; SENDS GILL THE EXERCISE.

Negotium illud de quo scripsi subobscurius, ecce Tabellis

hisce involutum, in quo ego, cum tua ad me pervenit Epistola, districtus temporis angustiâ, magno tum primùm opere desudabam: quidam enim Ædium nostrarum Socius, qui Comitiis his Academicis in Disputatione Philosophicâ responsurus erat, Carmina super quæstionibus pro more annuo componenda, prætervectus ipse jamdiu leviculas illiusmodi nugas, & rebus seriis intentior, forte meæ Puerilitati commisit.

Milton, Letter to Alexander Gill, July 2, 1628. It is by no means clear to which of his writings Milton here refers. Hughes, in his edition of Milton's *Paradise Regained The Minor Poems and Samson Agonistes*, 1937, p. 104, identifies it as *Naturam non pati senium*. But it might equally well be Prolusion 6 or some other piece. CM, XVIII, 526.

[The matter respecting which I wrote to you rather obscurely, you will find contained in the accompanying sheets. When your letter reached me, I was (being hard put to by the shortness of the time) labouring upon it with all might: for a certain Fellow of our house who had to act as Respondent in the philosophical disputation in this Commencement chanced to entrust to my puerility the composition of the verses according to annual custom required to be written on the questions in dispute, being himself already long past the age for trifles of that sort, and more intent on serious things.]

JUNE? LATIN POEM ON IMMOVABLENESS OF NATURE.
Naturam non pati senium.

Milton, *Poems*, 1645, part 2, pp. 59-61; Mackellar, pp. 136 ff.; CM, I, 260-267. A. W. Pollard, in his bibliography of Milton in the *Library*, second series, X (1909), p. 1, thinks that this poem was separately published and that it was the work which Milton mentioned in his letter to Gill on July 2, 1628, as being included in that letter. Both Warton (1791, p. 513) and Todd (1826, VI, 323), it may be added, assume the separate printing of this poem without question: "[These verses] were printed, not for sale, and sent to his late schoolmaster at saint Paul's, Alexander Gill." No copy has yet been found, however, and the work in question may be some other writing of Milton's, such as a prolusion. See W. R. Parker, *Milton's Contemporary Reputation*, p. 8.

[That Nature is not affected by age.]

JUNE 9. FATHER'S AND THOMAS BOWER'S STORMY IN-
TERVIEW WITH ROSE DOWNER.

. . . the next day after the said ffiftie poundẹ was paid as aforesaid vnto the handẹ of the said John Milton or vnto the handẹ
of the said Thomas Bower or some other . . . your said Oratrixe
repaired to the dwelling house of the said John Milton in
Breadstreete . . . and there demaunded the said money . . . he
the said Bower refused soe to doe . . . whereat your said Oratrixe
being very much moved grew very angrie with the said Bower
and then the said Milton came in and bade his man pay the
money to your said Oratrixe . . . And your said Oratrixe . . .
was inforced to goe home without her money and the next
morning after your said Oratrixe had bene with the said Milton
and his man vīzt in or about the tenth day of June 1628. . . .

Public Record Office, C2 Charles I/D39/47 (Rose Downer's bill,
April 26, 1631); French, *Milton in Chancery*, p. 237. For further
details, see the complete text of the bill below and the depositions of
Olive Street (September 19, 1631) and Richard Sheratt (September 26,
1631), both given in full below. The story is reconstructed in some detail in *Milton in Chancery*, pp. 43-48.

JUNE 10. FATHER ARRANGES DOWNER-EWENS-KEY-
MER LOAN AND BOND.

. . . the next morning after your said Oratrixe had bene with
the said Milton and his man vīzt in or about the tenth day of
June 1628 the said Milton or Bower by the handẹ of one other
of his the said Miltons servantẹ sent to your said Oratrixe to
his house an obligacōn beareing date that day of the Penall
sumē of One hundred poundẹ wherein twoe persons were bound
to your said Oratrixe by the names of Mathew Ewen and William Keymer esquires condicōned for the payement to your said
Oratrixe of the sumē of ffiftie and twoe poundẹ the twelueth
day of December then next enseweing at the said Miltons house
in Breadstreete aforesaid, which bond was sealed by the said
supposed obligators as the said Milton and his servantẹ pretend
in the presence of the said John Milton Thomas Bower and
James ffisher . . . she refused to take it being taken without her

consent . . . whereto he said the securitie was good and he would
see her paid her money. . . .

Public Record Office, C2 Charles I/D39/47 (Rose Downer's bill,
April 26, 1631); French, *Milton in Chancery*, pp. 237-238. The
original bond has not been found.

. . . the said somē of ffiftie poundǫ was lent forth in the name
of the said Comp^lt. vpon the securitie of the said Mathewe
Ewenǫ and William Keymer in the bill named, and the bond
sealed at this Defendantǫ shopp.

Public Record Office, C2 Charles I/D39/47 (Milton's answer to
Downer, May 3, 1631); French, *Milton in Chancery*, p. 240. For
further details, see *ibid.*, pp. 239, 242, 247, 251, 254. In both proceedings and depositions in this case there is much discussion of the honesty
and solvency of the borrowers and of Milton's previous dealings with
them as it affected the use to which the new loan was put. See also
ibid., pp. 38-40, 158-159.

. . . Rose Downer late of [London] now deceased did in her
life tyme (vizt) in or about June one thousand six hundred
twenty eight at the earnest Jmportunitie of Mathewe Ewins of
Northcadburie in [the county of] Summersett Esqz now also
Deceased did lend vnto the said Mathewe Ewins the some of
ffiftie pounds of lawfull English mony to be repayd againe at
six Monthes followein[g And in] Consideration for forbearance
Thereof And for Assurance of Repayment of the same accordingly the said Mathewe Ewins together with William Keymer
of Pendower in the same County of Summersett Esqz as his
surtie became Joyntly and severally bound to the said Rose
Downer in one hundred poundǫ by obligation bearing date the
tenth day of June in the fowrth yeare of the Raigne of our now
Soueraigne Lord King Charles Conditioned for payment of the
said some of ffiftie pounds to the said Rose downer together
with Consideracōn according to the rate of eight poundǫ in the
hundred on the twelvth day of December then next ensueing
the date of the said obligacōn. . . .

From bill of Milton's father against Arthur Duck; see below under
date of February 16, 1636/7. Thomas Bower's answer to Rose Downer's bill (see May 3, 1631) adds the fact that Ewens and Keymer
needed altogether one hundred pounds, and that the other fifty was
borrowed from one Bulteell.

JULY? PROLUSION 6. VISIT TO LONDON, STUDY, HOS-
TILITY OF FELLOW-STUDENTS, STRICT LIFE, NICKNAME
OF "LADY," PLANS FOR GREAT POETRY.

In Feriis æstivis Collegii, sed concurrente, ut solet, tota
fere Academiæ juventute.
Oratio.
Exercitationes nonnunquam Ludicras Philosophi studiis
non obesse.

Cum ex ea Urbe quæ caput urbium est, huc nuper me recip-
erem, Academici, deliciarum omnium, quibus is locus supra
modum affluit, usque ad saginam, prope dixerim, satur, sper-
abam mihi iterum aliquando otium illud Literarium, quo ego
vitæ genere etiam cœlestes animas gaudere opinor; eratq;
penitus in animo jam tandem abdere me in Literas, & jucund-
issimæ Philosophiæ perdius & pernox assidere; ita semper asso-
let Laboris & Voluptatis vicissitudo amovere satietatis tædium,
& efficere, ut intermissa; repetantur alacrius. Cum his me incal-
entem studiis repente avocavit, atque abstraxit pervetusti moris
fere annua celebritas, jussusque ego cum eam operam quam
acquirendæ sapientiæ primo destinâram, ad nugas transferre, &
novas ineptias excogitandas: quasi jam nunc non essent omnia
stultorum plena, quasi egregia illa, & non minus *Argo* decantata
navis stultifera fecisset naufragium, plane denique ac si ipsi
Democrito materia jam ridendi deesset. . . . Tum nec mediocriter
me pellexit, & invitavit ad has partes subeundas vestra, vos qui
ejusdem estis mecum Collegii, in me nuperrime comperta
facilitas, cum enim ante præteritos menses aliquam multos
oratorio apud vos munere perfuncturus essem, putaremque lucu-
brationes meas qualescunque etiam ingratas propemodum fu-
turas, & mitiores habituras judices *Æacum* & *Minoa*, quam è
vobis fere quemlibet, sane præter opinionem meam, præter
meam si quid erat speculæ, non vulgari sicuti ego accepi, imo
ipse sensi, omnium plausu exceptæ sunt, immo eorum, qui in me
alias propter studiorum dissidia essent prorsus insenso & inimico
animo: generosum utique simultatis exercendæ genus, & regio
pectore non indignum; siquidem cum ipsa amicitia plerumque

multa inculpate facta detorquere soleat, tunc profecto acris & infesta inimicitia errata forsitan multa, & haud pauca sine dubio indiserte dicta, leniter & clementius quam meum erat meritum interpretari non gravabatur. Jam semel unico hoc exemplo vel ipsa demens ira mentis compos fuisse videbatur, & hoc facto furoris infamiam abluisse. . . . Ego tamen Festivitates & Sales, in quibus quoque perexiguam agnosco facultatem meam, non gravabor, ut potero, laudare; si prius hoc unum addidero, quod sane arduum videtur, & minime proclive, me jocos hodie seriò laudaturum. . . . Jam oratoriis soluti legibus prosiliemus in Comicam licentiam. In qua si forte morem meum, si rigidas verecundiæ leges transversum, quod aiunt, digitum egressus fuero, sciatis Academici, me in vestram gratiam exuisse antiquum meum, & parumper deposuisse: aut si quid solute, si quid luxurianter dictum erit, id quidē non mentem & indolem meam, sed temporis rationem & loci genium mihi suggesisse putetis. . . .

Prolusio. . . .

A quibusquam, audivi nuper Domina. At cur videor illis parum masculus? Ecquis *Prisciani* pudor? itane propria quæ maribus fœmineo generi tribuunt insulsi Grammaticastri! scilicet quia Scyphos capacissimos nunquam valui pancratice haurire; aut quia manus tenendâ stivâ non occaluit, aut quia nunquam ad meridianum Solem supinus jacui septennis bubulcus; fortasse demum quod nunquam me virum præstiti, eo modo quo illi Ganeones: verum utinam illi possint tam facile exuere asinos, quam ego quicquid est fœminæ. . . . Ego vero quicquid hoc Domini aut Dominæ est à me longe amolior atque rejicio, nisi in rostris atque subselliis vestris, Academici, dominari non cupio.

Milton, *Epistolarum Familiarium Liber Unus*, 1674, pp. 113 ff.; CM, XII, 204 ff. The date given here is that commonly accepted.

[In the summer meetings of the college, but, as is usual, with the presence of almost the whole student body of the academy. An Oration. That sportive exercises on occasion are not inconsistent with the studies of Philosophy.

When lately, Academicians, I returned hither from that city which is the head of cities (*i.e.*, London), filled, even to re-

pletion, with all the delights with which that place overflows, I
hoped to have again for some time that literary leisure, in which
as a mode of life I believe that even celestial souls rejoice; and
it was quite my intention to shut myself up in literature, and
study sweetest philosophy day and night. For the change from
work to pleasure always removes the fatigue of satiety, and
causes tasks left unfinished to be sought again with more
alacrity. But, just as I was getting into a glow, this almost
annual celebration of a very old custom has suddenly called me
and dragged me from these studies, and I am ordered to transfer to trifles and the excogitation of new frivolities those pains
which I had first destined for the acquisition of wisdom. As if,
forsooth, all things were not now full of follies; as if that illustrious Ship of Fools, no less celebrated in song than the Argo,
had gone to wreck; as if, finally, matter for laughter were now
wanting to Democritus himself! . . .

Then also there drew and invited me, in no ordinary degree,
to undertake this part, your very recently discovered gracious-
ness to me—you, I mean, who are of the same College with me.
For when, some few months ago, I was about to perform an
oratorical office before you, and was under the impression that
any lucubrations whatsoever of mine would be the reverse of
agreeable to you, and would have more merciful judges in
Æacus and Minos than almost any of you would prove, truly,
beyond my fancy, beyond my hope if I had any, they were, as I
heard, nay as I myself felt, received with the not ordinary applause of all—yea, of those who, at other times, were, on account
of disagreements in our studies, altogether of an angry and
unfriendly spirit towards me. A generous mode of exercising
rivalry this, and not unworthy of a royal breast, if, when friendship itself is wont often to misconstrue much that is blamelessly
done, yet then sharp and hostile enmity did not grudge to interpret much that was perchance erroneous, and not a little,
doubtless, that was unskilfully said, more clemently than I
merited. For once, in this one instance, that mad wrath seemed
to have been sane, and by this act to have escaped the disgrace

of wild fury. . . .* Yet I will not grudge to praise, to the extent of my power, festivities and jests, in which I do acknowledge my faculty to be very slight; premising only this, that it seems an arduous and far from easy task for me this day to praise jocularity in serious terms. . . . And, now, released from all oratorical laws, we are about to plunge into comic licence. In which, if by chance I shall outgo a finger's breadth, as they say, my proper character and the rigid laws of modesty, know, fellow-academicians, that I have thrown off and for a little while laid aside my proper self in your interest; or, if anything shall be said loosely or floridly, consider it suggested to me not by my own mind and disposition, but by the rule of the time and the genius of the place. . . .

The Prolusion. . . .

By some of you I used lately to be nicknamed "The Lady." Why seem I then too little of a man? Is there no regard for Priscian? Do pert grammaticasters thus attribute the "*propria quæ maribus*" to the feminine gender? Is it because I never was able to quaff huge tankards lustily, or because my hands never grew hard by holding the plough, or because I never, like a seven years' herdsman, laid myself down and snored at midday; in fine, perchance, because I never proved my manhood in the same way as those debauched blackguards? I would they could as easily doff the ass as I can whatever of the woman is in me. . . .

But I thrust far away and reject anything of "Lord" or "Lady." Except in your rostrums and tribunals, Students, I do not wish to be a lord.]

Masson, I, 252 ff. (285-297). Masson omits the last two sentences.

Anno Ætatis 19. *At a Vacation Exercise in the Colledge, part* Latin, *part* English. *The* Latin *speeches ended, the* English *thus began.*

> Hail native Language, that by sinews weak
> Didst move my first endeavouring tongue to speak,
> And mad'st imperfect words with childish tripps,

* This sentence, not translated by Masson, is supplied by the present editor.

Half unpronounc't, slide through my infant-lipps,
Driving dum silence from the portal dore,
Where he had mutely sate two years before:
Here I salute thee and thy pardon ask,
That now I use thee in my latter task:
Small loss it is that thence can come unto thee,
I know my tongue but little Grace can do thee:
Thou needst not be ambitious to be first,
Believe me I have thither packt the worst:
And, if it happen as I did forecast,
The daintiest dishes shall be serv'd up last.
I pray thee then deny me not thy aide
For this same small neglect that I have made:
But haste thee strait to do me once a Pleasure,
And from thy wardrope bring thy chiefest treasure;
Not those new fangled toys, and triming slight
Which takes our late fantasticks with delight,
But cull those richest Robes, and gay'st attire
Which deepest Spirits, and choicest Wits desire:
I have some naked thoughts that rove about
And loudly knock to have their passage out;
And wearie of their place do only stay
Till thou hast deck't them in thy best aray;
That so they may without suspect or fears
Fly swiftly to this fair Assembly's ears;
Yet I had rather, if I were to chuse,
Thy service in some graver subject use,
Such as may make thee search thy coffers round,
Before thou cloath my fancy in fit sound:
Such where the deep transported mind may soare
Above the wheeling poles, and at Heav'ns dore
Look in, and see each blissful Deitie
How he before the thunderous throne doth lie,
Listening to what unshorn *Apollo* sings
To th' touch of golden wires, while *Hebe* brings
Immortal Nectar to her Kingly Sire:

Then passing through the Spherse of watchful fire,
And mistie Regions of wide air next under,
And hills of Snow and lofts of piled Thunder,
May tell at length how green-ey'd *Neptune* raves,
In Heav'ns defiance mustering all his waves;
Then sing of secret things that came to pass
When Beldam Nature in her cradle was;
And last of Kings and Queens and *Hero's* old,
Such as the wise *Demodocus* once told
In solemn Songs at King *Alcinous* feast,
While sad *Vlisses* soul and all the rest
Are held with his melodious harmonie
In willing chains and sweet captivitie. . . .

Milton, *Poems*, 1673, pp. 64-68. Though properly part of the prolusion, this section of English verse was not included by Milton in the
1674 volume of these exercises, presumably because it was in English
whereas the rest of that volume was in Latin. cm, i, 19 ff. E. E. Kellet,
in the *Cambridge Review*, xxxvi (1915), 326-327, thinks that Edward King may have been one of the other students to take part in the
revels alluded to in the later part of Milton's verses. He points out that
Milton's poem is a perfect nest of puns, and that "War" may be Robert
Bell[um] (line 86), and the "King" (line 75) may be Edward King,
etc. In view of the accepted interpretation of Rivers (line 91) such in-
genuity would be entirely possible.

JULY 2. LETTER TO ALEXANDER GILL.

Eidem.

3. Priori illâ Epistola meâ non tam rescripsi tibi, quam rescri-
bendi vices deprecatus sum, alteram itaq; brevi secuturam tacite
promisi, in qua tibi me amicissime provocanti latius aliquanto
responderem; verum ut id non essem pollicitus, hanc utcunq;
summo jure deberi tibi fatendum est, quandoquidem singulas
ego literas tuas non nisi meis binis pensari posse existimem, aut
si exactius agatur, ne centenis quidem meis. Negotium illud de
quo scripsi subobscurius, ecce Tabellis hisce involutum, in quo
ego, cum tua ad me pervenit Epistola, districtus temporis
angustiâ, magno tum primùm opere desudabam: quidam enim
Ædium nostrarum Socius, qui Comitiis his Academicis in

Disputatione Philosophicâ responsurus erat, Carmina super quæstionibus pro more annuo componenda, prætervectus ipse jamdiu leviculas illiusmodi nugas, & rebus seriis intentior, forte meæ Puerilitati commisit. Hæc quidem Typis donata ad te misi, utpote quem nôrim rerum Poeticarum judicem acerrimum, & mearum candidissimum. Quod si tua mihi vicissim communicare dignaberis, certe non erit qui magis iis delectetur, erit, fateor, qui rectius pro eorum dignitate judicet. Equidem quoties recolo apud me tua mecum assidua pene colloquia (quæ vel ipsis Athenis, ipsâ in Academiâ, quæro, desideróq;) cogito statim nec sine dolore, quanto fructu me mea fraudârit absentia, qui nunquam à te discessi sine manifesta Literarum accessione, & ἐπιδόσει, plane quasi ad Emporium quoddam Eruditionis profectus. Sane apud nos, quod sciam, vix unus atq; alter est, qui non Philologiæ, pariter & Philosophiæ, prope rudis & profanus, ad Theologiam devolet implumis; eam quoq; leviter admodum attingere contentus, quantum forte sufficiat coniunculæ quoquo modo conglutinandæ, & tanquam tritis aliunde pannis consuendæ: adeo ut verendum sit ne sensim ingruat in Clerum nostrum sacerdotalis illa superioris sæculi Ignorantia. Atq; ego profecto cum nullos fere studiorum consortes hic reperiam, Londinum rectà respicerem, nisi per justitium hoc æstivum in otium alte Literarium recedere cogitarem, & quasi Claustris Musarum delitescere. Quod cum jam tu indies facias, nefas esse propemodum existimo diutius in præsentia tibi interstrepere. Vale.

Cantabrigia, July 2. 1628.

Milton, *Epistolarum Familiarium Liber Unus*, 1674, pp. 10-12; CM, XII, 8 ff. It is addressed "Eidem" because the previous letter is also to Alexander Gill (May 20, 1628). If Professor Donald L. Clark is correct in thinking that Milton's letter to Gill of May 20, 1628 (*q.v.*), should be dated 1630, then presumably the date of the present letter should be advanced similarly. The accompanying verses may have been *Naturam non pati senium* or some other early composition.

[To Alexander Gill.

In my former letter I did not so much reply to you as stave off my turn of replying; and I silently promised with myself that another letter should soon follow, in which I should answer somewhat more at large to your most friendly challenge; but even if I had not promised this, it must be confessed on the highest grounds of right to be your due, seeing that I think that each single letter of yours could not be balanced except by two of mine,—nay, if the account were more strict, not even by a hundred of mine. The matter respecting which I wrote to you rather obscurely, you will find contained in the accompanying sheets. When your letter reached me, I was (being hard put to by the shortness of the time) labouring upon it with all might: for a certain Fellow of our house who had to act as Respondent in the philosophical disputation in this Commencement chanced to entrust to my puerility the composition of the verses according to annual custom required to be written on the questions in dispute, being himself already long past the age for trifles of that sort, and more intent on serious things. The result, committed to type, I have sent to you, as knowing you to be a very severe judge in poetical matters, and a very candid judge of my productions. But if you in turn shall deign to communicate to me yours, there will assuredly be no one who will more delight in them, though there may be, I admit, who will more rightly judge of them according to their worth. Indeed, as often as I recollect your almost constant conversations with me (which even in this Athens, the University itself, I long after and miss), I straightway think, and not without grief, of how much benefit my absence from you has deprived me—me who never left your company without a manifest increase and ἐπίδοσις of literary knowledge, just as if I had been to some emporium of learning. Truly, amongst us here, as far as I know, there are hardly one or two here and there, who do not fly off unfeathered to Theology, while all but rude and uneducated in Philology as well as in Philosophy, content too lightly to pick up as much Theology as may suffice for anyhow sticking together a little sermon and stitching it over with worn rags from other quarters; insomuch that it is to be dreaded that by degrees there may spread among our clergy that priestly ignorance of a former age. And, finding as I do almost no companions in my studies here, I should certainly be looking to London, were I not thinking of retiring during this summer vacation into a deeply literary repose, and hiding myself, so to speak, in the bowers of the Muses. But, as this is what you do daily, I think it almost a crime longer to interrupt you with my din at present. Farewell.

Cambridge, July 2, 1628.]
Masson, I, 164-165 (193-194).

JULY 8. FRIEND CHARLES DIODATI RECEIVES M.A. AT OXFORD.

The original record of this event is not immediately available, but it is recorded in Andrew Clark's *Register of the University of Oxford*, Oxford, 1888, II, part iii, p. 444. See also Donald C. Dorian, "Charles Diodati at Geneva," *PMLA*, LIX (1944), 589-591.

JULY 21. LETTER TO THOMAS YOUNG.

Thomae Junio.

4. Inspectis Literis tuis (Præceptor optime) unicum hoc mihi supervacaneum occurrebat, quòd tardæ scriptionis excusationem attuleris; tametsi enim Literis tuis nihil mihi queat optabilius accidere, quî possim tamen, aut debeam sperare, otii tibi tantum à rebus seriis, & sanctioribus esse, ut mihi semper respondere vacet; præsertim cum illud humanitatis omnino sit, officii minime. Te vero oblitum esse mei ut suspicer, tam multa tua de me recens merita nequaquam sinunt. Neq; enim video quorsum tantis onustum beneficiis ad oblivionem dimitteres. Rus tuum accersitus, simul ac Ver adoleverit, libenter adveniam, ad capessendas anni, tuiq; non minus colloquii, delicias; & ab urbano strepitu subducam me paulisper, Stoam tuam Icenorum, tanquam ad celeberrimam illam Zenonis porticum, aut Ciceronis Tusculanum, ubi tu in re modica regio sane animo veluti Serranus aliquis aut Curius, in agello tuo placide regnas, deq; ipsis divitiis, ambitione, pompâ, luxuriâ, & quicquid vulgus hominum miratur & stupet, quasi triumphum agis fortunæ contemptor. Cæterùm qui tarditatis culpam deprecatus es, hanc mihi vicissim,

ut spero, præcipitantiam indulgebis; cum enim Epistolam hanc in extremum distulissem, malui pauca, eáq; rudiuscule scribere, quam nihil. Vale Vir Observande.

Cantabrigia, July 21. 1628.

Milton, *Epistolarum Familiarium Liber Unus,* 1674, pp. 12-13; CM, XII, 12 ff.; CM, XVIII, 526.

[To Thomas Young.

On looking at your letter, most excellent preceptor, this alone struck me as superfluous, that you excused your slowness in writing; for, though nothing could come to me more desirable than your letters, how could I or ought I to hope that you should have so much leisure from serious and more sacred affairs as to have time always to answer me—especially as that is a matter entirely of kindness, and not at all of duty? That, however, I should suspect that you had forgotten me, your so many recent kindnesses to me would by no means allow. I do not see how you could dismiss out of your memory one laden with so great benefits by you. Having been invited by you to your part of the country, as soon as Spring is a little advanced, I will gladly come to enjoy the delights of the year, and not less of your conversation; and will then withdraw myself from the din of town for a little to your Stoa of the Iceni,* as to that most celebrated porch of Zeno or the Tusculan Villa of Cicero—where you, with moderate means but regal spirit, like some Serranus or Curius, placidly reign in your little farm, and, contemning fortune, hold as it were a triumph over riches, ambition, pomp, luxury, and whatever the herd of men admire and are amazed by. But, as you have deprecated the blame of slowness, you will also, I hope, pardon me the fault of haste; for, having put off this letter to the last, I preferred writing little, and that in a rather slovenly manner, to not writing at all. Farewell, much to be respected Sir.

Cambridge, July 21, 1628.]

Masson, I, 172-173 (203-204).

* Masson points out that "Stoa" is a pun on "Stowmarket."

AFTER JULY 21 (?). VISITS THOMAS YOUNG AT STOW-MARKET (?).

In his letter of July 21, Milton promises to visit his old teacher soon. There is no documentary proof of his actually having fulfilled this promise. But tradition has preserved several details of his having gone. In *The History of Stowmarket*, 1844, pp. 188-189, A. G. H. Hollingsworth gives a somewhat full account of Young's connection with the locality, and assumes that Milton did accept the invitation. According to his testimony a room in the vicarage of St. Peter and St. Mary has since this time been known as Milton's room from the fact that he is supposed to have stayed in it, and the mulberry trees in the vicarage yard have been assumed to have been planted by the poet. On the validity of the latter tradition, compare the story of the so-called Milton mulberry tree at Cambridge. Hollingsworth gives pictures of the Stowmarket mulberry trees facing pp. 187 and 189, and says that in his own time one only remains standing, decayed but vigorous. A writer in *Notes and Queries*, v, i (1874), 465, notes that at this later date the tree was still extant; see earlier notes on it in the same periodical, II, v (1858), 250-251, 343. See also CM, XVIII, 548. On the tradition that he composed the epitaph on Young in the church at Stowmarket, see below under date of November 28, 1655.

SEPTEMBER 6. FATHER ARRANGES MORT-COTTON BOND.

Mr Mort & others by bond dated the vi^th of Septemb^r 1628 100^ll.

Thomas Bower's schedule of Cotton's bonds made out by himself and Milton's father; see below under date of November 25, 1630. The original bond has not been found.

. . . Mr Mort and others by bond dated the 6th of Sept: 1628 100^ll. principall debt. . . .

Sir Thomas Cotton's bill; see below under date of May 28, 1636.

OCTOBER 22. FATHER WITNESSES OAKELEY-MACIE BOND.

Noverint vniūsi per pñtes nos, Samuelem Oakeley Civem et Pannar' London', Ricardum Oakeley de Civitat Westm' Armiger', et Rōbtum Powell Civem et Clothworker London' teneri et firmiter obligari Johī Macie de Civitate Westm' p̄d Gener' in Ducentis libris leḡlis monet' Anglie solvend eidem Johī

Macie aut suo certo Attorn', executor', vel admīstrator' suis,
Ad qm̄ quidem solucōnem bene et fidelr' facieñd Obligamus
nos et quemlibet nr̄m per se pro toto et insolīd herēd, executor'
et admīstrator' nr̄os et cuiuslibet nr̄m firmiter per pñtes Sigillis
nr̄is sigillat' Dat Vicesimo Secundo die Octobris. 1628. Annoqz
Rꝑ dnī nrī Caroli Anglie &c Quarto.

Samuell Oakeley   M^r. Sa: Oakley 104

24 Apr 1629

Ri: Oakeley.   M^r. Ric Oakley

Robert Powell   M^r. Powell

Sigillat' et delibāt' in pñtia Jo: Milton: scr p dcū Robtū Powell William Prior Mr Richard Oakeleys man: Jo: Hutton p
quemlibet Henry Rothwell s^rvieñ p̄ Jo: Milton.

The Condic̄on of this obligac̄on is such, That if the wthin
bound Samuel Oakeley Richard Oakeley and Robtē Powell
theire heires, executo^{rs}, admīstrato^{rs}. or assignes, or anie of them
doe well and trulie paie, or cause to be paid to the wthin named
John Macie his executo^{rs}. admīstrato^{rs}. or assignes, the some
of One hundred and ffoure poundꝑ of lawfull money of Eng-
land. At the now dwelling house of John Milton Scrivener
scituate in Breadstreete London; On the ffoure and Twentith
daie of Aprill next ensueing the date wthin written, That then
this obligac̄on to be voyde; Or else to stand in force.

Westminster Abbey Muniments 28,515; *Athenaeum*, 1902, II,
722 (reproduced in full, modernized). The three signatures are written
on three ends near the bottom of the document. The reason for the
repetition of each name is probably that the second in each case was
written by a scribe to show the witness where to sign, and that the first
is his actual signature. The "condition," written in English, appears on
the back of the document. Robert Powell's relation to Richard Powell
of Forest Hill, if any, is unknown.

[Know all men by these presents that we, Samuel Oakeley,
citizen and clothworker of London, Richard Oakeley of the city
of Westminster, gentleman, and Robert Powell, citizen and
clothworker of London, are held and firmly bound to John
Macie of the city of Westminster aforesaid, gentleman, in two
hundred pounds of legal money of England, to be paid to the

said John Macie or his designated attorneys, executors, or administrators. To which payment, well and faithfully to be made, we oblige ourselves and each of us for himself completely and truly, our heirs, executors, and our administrators, and those of each of us firmly by these presents. Sealed with our seals. Given on the twenty-second day of October, 1628, and in the fourth year of the reign of our Lord Charles of England, etc. . . . Sealed and delivered in the presence of John Milton, scrivener, on behalf of the said Robert Powell; William Prior, Mr. Richard Oakeley's man; John Hutton for anyone whatsoever; Henry Rothwell, servant of the said John Milton.]

DECEMBER 12. RECEIVES INTEREST PAYMENT FROM RICHARD POWELL.

. . . the growing Jnterest for the forbearance of the said Principall debt was for some yeares then following likewise payd And soe continued to bee paid vntill June Jn the yeare of our Lord One Thousand six hundred ffortie and ffower. . . .

From Milton's answer to Elizabeth Ashworth, February 22, 1653/4, *q.v.*

DECEMBER 12. FATHER AND THOMAS BOWER CONTINUE DOWNER-EWENS AND KEYMER BOND.

. . . at the first six moneths end the said Bower being then the said Miltons man entreated yoʳ Oratrixe to forbear the said money one half Yeare more and promised her that his Master and he would paye in the said ffiftie poundꝑ & the interest to Your said Oratrixe at the end of the then next six moneths followeing. . . .

Public Record Office, C2 Charles I/D39/47 (Rose Downer's bill, April 26, 1631); French, *Milton in Chancery*, p. 238. The question of whether any interest was paid is vexing, since the accounts by the various parties bluntly disagree. See the following extracts.

. . . she received . . . the Jnterest as the same grewe dewe at severall dayes, and times afterwardꝑ. . . .

Public Record Office, C2 Charles I/D39/47 (Milton's answer to Downer, May 3, 1631); French, *Milton in Chancery*, p. 240.

. . . she the said Complaynant gave consent to and for the lending of the said ffiftie poundᵽ, vnto the said Ewens and Keymer, and a bond was then taken for the same, and afterwardᵽ by and with the consent, and good liking of the said Complaynant, was continued for Twoe, or three Six monethᵽ, and the Jnterest duly paid her for the same time, and by her accepted of, without any dislike at all. . . .

Public Record Office, C2 Charles I/D39/47 (Bower's answer to Downer, May 3, 1631); French, *Milton in Chancery*, p. 244.

. . . the sᵈ Ewens did confesse yt hee neu' pd any Jnterest for the sᵈ money & yᵗ if any interest were p'd to her the sᵈ widow Down' the same was pʸᵈ by the sᵈ deftᵽ or one of them out of their owne moneys And the sᵈ Ewens further sᵈ vnto this depᵗ yᵗ the sᵈ deftᵽ or one of them durst not but pay Jnterest for the sᵈ money at the first to theñd as hee confessed to bring the cōmpˡᵗ wᵗʰin compasse of accepting the sᵈ bond. or wordᵽ to the like effect.

Public Record Office, Chancery Depositions, C24/574/40 (George Broome's deposition in the Downer-Milton case); French, *Milton in Chancery*, p. 248.

1629

PORTRAIT BY UNKNOWN ARTIST (?).

Iohannes Milton, aetatis xxi, 1629.

Dr. Williamson (*Milton Tercentenary*, 1908, pp. 22, 34) gives what little is known of the history of this portrait. In the middle of the nineteenth century the Rev. J. Hildyard, Rector of Ingoldsby and at one time a fellow and tutor of Christ's College, bought it as a portrait of Milton as a young man. It bears the legend given above. It was exhibited at the tercentenary exhibition at Christ's College in 1908, and it now hangs in the hall of that college. It is reproduced in Williamson, facing p. 34. It bears a strong resemblance to the so-called Onslow portrait (see under December 9, 1629). A. E. S[hipley?], says (*Notes and Queries*, x, iii [1909], 127) that it bears the motto: "Nec ingratus nec inutilis videar vixisse" [Let me not appear to have lived ungrateful or useless].

SECOND PROLUSION.

In Scholis Publicis. *De Sphærarum Concentu.*
[Delivered in the Public Schools. On the Music of the Spheres.]

Milton, *Epistolarum Familiarium Liber Unus*, 1674, pp. 83-87; Masson, I, 246 (279-281); CM, XII, 148. The date is uncertain.

TRANSLATES FIFTH ODE OF HORACE.

The Fifth Ode of Horace. *Lib.* I.

Milton, *Poems*, 1673, p. 62; CM, I, 69. The date is highly uncertain. Fletcher (Milton's *Complete Poetical Works*, 1941, p. 137) considers it "a product of his full poetic maturity, and not an early exercise." Several commentators, however, put it at about 1629.

OWNS A BOOK ENTITLED "APOLOGIA PRO CONFESSIONE" (?).

A copy of a book entitled *Apologia pro Confessione*, dated 1629, containing the intitials "J M," was formerly in the library of Wynne Baxter, who described it in *Notes and Queries*, VI, vii (1883), 67-68. See French, "The Autographs of John Milton," no. 67; CM, XVIII, 577. The identity of the book and its later history are unknown, and there is no further proof, beyond Baxter's statement, that the initials were Milton's.

A RELATIVE APPRENTICED AS SCRIVENER (?).

1629 . . . James. Milton—of ffran. Strange—1596.

Bodleian Library, Rawl. MS. Misc. 51, f. 29; *Athenaeum*, 1880, I, 565. The relationship of James Milton to the poet is not known, but it seems likely that he was a relative, since the poet's father was a scrivener.

ITALIAN SONNETS WRITTEN (?).

II. *Donna leggiadra il cui bel nome honora . . .*
III. *Qual in colle aspro, al imbrunir di sera . . .*
Canzone. *Ridonsi donne e giovani amorosi . . .*
IV. *Diodati, e te'l dirò con maraviglia . . .*
V. *Per certo i bei vostr'occhi Donna mia . . .*
VI. *Giovani piano, e semplicetto amante. . . .*

Milton, *Poems*, 1645, pp. 45-48; CM, I, 48-59. The date of the writing of these poems is very uncertain. The tendency of most commentators, however, is to date them at about this period. John S. Smart (*The Sonnets of Milton*, Glasgow, 1921, pp. 133 ff.) considered them a commentary upon an early love affair with a girl named Emilia, which "took place before his Italian travels in 1638, and probably many years earlier."

[II. Graceful lady, thou whose beautiful name honours . . .
III. As on a rough hill, at the browning of even . . .
Canzone. The ladies and the amorous youths laugh . . .
IV. Diodati (and I tell it thee with wonder) . . .
V. Surely, my lady, it cannot be but that your fair eyes . . .
VI. Young, gentle, loving simply. . . .]

Masson, I, 772-774 (824-826). Masson dates them during or after Milton's Italian journey.

WRITES NIGHTINGALE SONNET.

O Nightingale, that on yon bloomy Spray. . . .

Milton, *Poems*, 1645, pp. 44-45; CM, I, 47. Like the Italian sonnets, this poem is of uncertain date. Stevens dates it "early," Smart thinks it was written at Cambridge, Hanford dates it 1629, and Tillyard assigns it to 1630. Smart calls it "one of Milton's earliest works," and thinks that "in its tone the poem resembles the Seventh Latin Elegy, which he composed at the age of twenty-one" (*The Sonnets of Milton*, Glasgow, 1921, p. 47).

FEBRUARY 9(?). MILTON "RESPONDS TO THE QUESTION" FOR HIS BACHELOR'S DEGREE.

Upon 12 Jan: being Pridie Termini,[1] the Lady Margaret's Professor doth make, or cause to be made, a Sermon ad Clerum at St. Mary's at 9 of the Clock in the Morning.

On Monday, Tuesday or Wednesday, either in the next or the next week save one after the said 12 day of Jan: the Quaestionists [Milton],[2] at the appointment of the V. C.[3] and Proctors,[4] do sit in the Regent House,[5] there to be examined by the Proctors, Posers,[6] & other Regents.[7]

[1] The day before the term.
[2] Candidates ready to answer the Aristotelian "question."
[3] The Vice-Chancellor.
[4] Officers charged with discipline and with various functions connected with examinations and the conferment of degrees.
[5] The upper of two houses into which the senate of the University of Cambridge was formerly divided.
[6] Examiners.
[7] Masters of Arts ruling or presiding over disputations in the schools.

The Posers Feast was antiently kept upon the Thursday at Night the Examination or Posing was ended. Unto which Supper the Proctors did invite Mr. V. C. the Heads of Houses,[8] Drs. Professors, the Caput Senatus,[9] & all the University Officers. Upon the said Thursday there must be a Congregation called against 8 of the Clock next morning.

Then the V. C. (after both Houses are called together) delivereth unto them, in a short speech, the cause of that meeting, & then sitteth down in his chair, whilst the senr. Poser (the other standing by him) on the left hand of the V. C. maketh a speech; which being ended, the V. C. goeth to his seat, where the Posers do deliver to him a Bill, wherein are written the names of all those Quaestionists [Milton] which they have approved of. Then a Bedel[10] desireth those of the Caput Senatus to come unto the V. C. for the passing of Graces[11] for the said Quaestionists [Milton]. The V. C. readeth all the graces, some one of the Head holding the Posers Bill to stay those whose names are not in the said Bill.

Mem.   That the name of the College be set in the margin of every Grace, & that the said Grace be subscribed by the Master, or Head Lecturer of the College, as is required Lib: Stat: Cap: 21.

If these Graces do pass the Head, the V. C. writeth "Ad:" being a note of approbation upon every Grace. Then they are carried down by one of the Bedels, unto the Non-Regent[12] House, & are there read by the Senior Scrutator,[13] his Brother standing by him.

After all of them are read, the Scrutators do go to every Non-

[8] I.e., the Regent House and the Non-Regent House.

[9] The ruling council of the university.

[10] An officer whose duty it was to walk before dignitaries in procession. The more common spelling, *beadle*, is not used at Cambridge.

[11] Originally a dispensation from statutable conditions required for the degree, the word later came to mean any decree of the governing body of the university or the permission which the candidate for a degree was required to obtain from his college or hall.

[12] A nonregent is a Master of Arts whose regency has ceased.

[13] An examiner or investigator, serving a purpose, for the Non-Regent House, similar to that discharged for the Regent House by the proctor.

Regent, to know his Pleasure concerning them; & if the greater part should approve of them all, then the Scrutators, looking towards the Regent House, the Senior saith, "Omnes placent."[14] But if any be disallowed & not liked, then the Senior Scrutator saith of A. B. C. D. &c. "Non placent," "Reliqui placent."

Then a Bedel carrieth all the Graces that passed, unto the Proctors, to be by them propounded unto the Regents, as they were unto the Non-Regents by the Scrutators: which order is always observed.

The Register is to write upon all Graces that are passed "Lect: & concess:" Jan: Ao. Domini ". . . ."[15] Mem: that the Proctors do ask their Graces "Ad intrandum."[16]

This Congregation is usually continued in Horam primam pomeridianam.[17] When the Houses are met, the Proctors, one of the Bedels & Register goe down to the Non-Regent House Door; & there the Proctors doe call for those of every several College, who have paid their Fees, & their Graces passed [Milton]. The Register is to search his Book of Subscription[18] to see that none go in at the Proctors call, but such only as have subscribed [Milton]. As the Quaestionists [Milton], having their Hoods on, pass into the Non-Regent House, the Schole-Keeper delivereth to every one of them a printed copy of that Oath, which they are to take before their admission. When every one of 3 or 4 Colleges have received the Copies of their Oaths [Milton], a Bedle holding up his Staffe, goeth before the Senior Father,[19] his sons following him into the Regent House;

---

[14] "All are in favor." The phrases in the next sentence may be translated: "they are not in favor," and "the remainder are in favor."

[15] "Read and granted, January, 16——." This entry is not found on Milton's supplicats, either because the treatment of graces differed slightly from that of supplicats, or because the rules were sometimes modified.

[16] "To be entered" (on the records).   [17] "Till one o'clock in the afternoon."

[18] The book in which every student subscribed to the rules and principles of the university.

[19] The appointment of a student as "father" and of others as his "sons" reminds one at once of Milton's sixth prolusion, in which he acted as "father" to ten "sons." This work, which has been variously dated, may have been delivered by Milton as his share in the responsion for which the supplicat of February 10 was a petition—which would date it in the spring of 1629. To venture still further into precarious guesses, may the seventh prolusion have been his offering in the examination for the master's degree in 1632?

whither all the Rest of the Fathers & Sons [Milton] do come in like manner. The Senr. Father first presenteth all his Sons (holding 4 or 5 of their right Hands in his own) unto the V.C. then sitting in his chair, & to the rest of the University, in these words, "Domine Procancellarie, & tota Universitas, praesento hosce Juvenes, quos scio tam Doctrina quam moribus idoneos esse ad respondendum Quaestioni: idque Tibi mea fide praesto totique Academiae."[20] In the like manner all the rest of the Fathers do present [Milton] according to their Seniority.

As the Quaestionists [Milton] are presented, they are directed to the lower part of the South Side of the Regent House by one of the Bedles, & there to stand whilst all the rest are presented.

Then the Senr. Proctor, standing with the Junior on the left hand of the V. C. (sitting still in his chair) doth read the Oaths, which they are to take, the Register holding the Book to one of the said Quaestionists [Milton]; unto whom only all the Oath is read; & when that Quaestionist hath Kissed the Book, about 5 or six of the rest do lay their hands upon it, whilst the Proctor saith: "Idem Juramentum quod praestitit A.B. in Persona sua, praestabitis et vos [Milton] in vestris Personis; sicut vos Deus adjuvet & Sancta ejus Evangelia."[21]

When all [Milton] are thus sworn, the V. C. doth admit every one of them [Milton] kneeling before him on the foot Pace, and holding their hands between his own, saith, "In Dei Nomine, Amen. Authoritate nobis commissa admittimus Te [Milton] ad respondendum Quaestioni; in nomine Patris, Filii, et Spiritus Sancti."[22]

When every one [Milton] is thus admitted, he riseth up, and after he hath done his obeisance to Mr. V. C. he [Milton] passeth between the Proctors unto the upper Table, & there

[20] "My Lord Vice-Chancellor, and all the University, I present these youths, whom I know to be fit in both doctrine and habits to reply to the question; and this I swear unto you and the whole University on my faith."

[21] "The same oath which A.B. swore in his own person you also will swear in your persons, so help you God and His Holy Gospel."

[22] "In the name of God, Amen. By authority committed to me I admit you to reply to the question; in the name of the Father, of the Son, and of the Holy Ghost."

kneeling down, giveth God Thanks in his [Milton] Private Prayers &c. When all [Milton] are admitted, a Bedel goes down with them into the lower House, & there leaveth them.

Then the V. C. if there be no after Business to be done, dissolveth the Congregation.

Mem. That all the Quaestionists [Milton], between the time of their Admission, & Ash Wednesday, are to enter their Priorums:[23] the manner of that Exercise, in Brief is thus.

One of the Bedels, having timely notice thereof from each Father, doth goe to the College about 8 or 9 of the clock in the Morning & cause the Butler to toll the Bell; which doth call all the Quaestionists [Milton] into the Hall; where the Bedle biddeth them to be in Readiness, with their Hoods on, to attend their Father to the Schools. When the Fellows come into the Hall, the Quaestionists [Milton] go out, & stand by the screen: then, after a little stay there, the junior Quaestionist goeth next unto the Bedle, & so all the rest [Milton] do goe in their Juniority, the Father cometh last after his eldest son; the Fellows, Fellow-Commoners, Bacrs. of Art, & the rest of the Students in that College, follow the Father into that School, in which he is to make his Speech.

The Bedle being entered a little way into the said School, saith with a loud voice, "Bona Nova Mater Academia, bona nova."[24] When he hath set up the Father, & Placed his sons [Milton] before him, then he saith, "Honorande Pater, filiorum nomine, Gratias tibi agimus, liceat tibi sedere, cooperiri, & filios tuos [Milton] affari, prout tibi visum fuerit."[25]

When the Father hath ended his speech, he doth then ask every one of his sons [Milton] a Question, beginning with the senior.[26] The Quaestions are out of Aristotles Priorums (as the name of this Exercise seemeth to import) which Quaestions being answered unto, he commendeth his sons [Milton] in a line

[23] Exercises based on Aristotle's *Prior Analytics.*

[24] "Good news, Mother University, good news."

[25] "Honored Father, in the name of your sons, I thank you; you may be seated, be covered, and speak to your sons, as it shall seem best to you."

[26] Was this by any chance the place in Milton's prolusion where Rivers was called on to rise?

or two & then cometh out of his Seat. The Bedle now goeth before him, & the sons [Milton] follow the Father in their Seniority, & all the company follow the Questionists [Milton] to the College.

Mem. That all the Quaestionists [Milton] are to goe bare headed, with their caps off, & to return Home in the like manner. It hath happened some time that 4 or 5 Colleges have kept their Priorums in the same morning: then all the 3 Bedles have employment enough to attend so many Priorums, & the Master of Arts Disses.[27]

Upon Ash-Wednesdy Morning between 7 and 8 of the Clock, the Bedles go to the several Colleges to bring the Quaestionists [Milton], or young Bachelors Commencers to St. Mary's. If they will go with the Bedle, they must go bare-headed, & in their Hoods, according to their Juniority. But in regard of the Cold Weather, Rain or Snow &c. they are unwilling to follow him bare-headed; & therefore they desire to come privately, when the Bell rings to the Clerum, or Supplications; which they never fail to do.

The Clerum is usually performed by one that intendeth to commence Bac: or Dr. in Divinity; but in case none will be persuaded to preach the said Sermon ad Clerum, then the Litany is there to be sung, either by the Proctors, or their Deputies: & then the V. C. doth end the Prayers. The School Bell doth ring to the Clerum, or Supplications at 9 of the Clock. Mem: that neither of them are to be called by the Bedles.

When the Clerum, or Supplications are ended, then all the Company [Milton] go from the Church to the School yard, the Junior Bedle going before the Commencers [Milton] & their Father; the 2d. Bedle before the Proctors; & the Senior Bedle before the V. C. Noblemen & Doctors. Now if there be no Business for a Congregation, then the V. C. Noblemen & Drs. the Proctors, Taxers,[28] & all that are Disputants [Milton] this Day goe into the Consistory, & fit themselves with gloves.

[27] I.e., dissertations.
[28] Officers who fixed the rents of students' lodgings, kept the standards of weights and measures, and punished offenders.

Then one of the Bedles carrieth the Proctors, Father, Disputants, Tripos[29] & the 2 Brothers unto their several Seats.

Then all Masters of Arts & fellow-Commoners, with the V. Crs. Leave, goe through the Doctors Seats, unto their own in the Philosophy Schools.

Now the V. C. Noblemen, Drs. & Strangers are brought up to their Seats without any crouding. Last of all the Door is opened for the Bachelors, Sophisters, & the rest of the Scholars to come in.

After a little Pause, the senior Proctor beginneth his Speech, & towards the end thereof, speaketh to the Father to make an Exhortation to his Sons [Milton] which, after the Father hath done, the Senior Proctor calleth up the Tripos, & exhorteth him to be witty, but modest withall.

Then the Tripos beginneth his Speech or Position, made for the Illustration & Confirmation of his 1st Question. He may, if he will, speak something of his 2d Question: but if he doth not, then the Senior Proctor commandeth the Senior Brother to reply upon the Tripos; & after him, the Junior Brother. Then the senior Proctor desireth the Father to urge his Sons [Milton] argument. The Father Propounding 2 or 3 Syllogisms in either Quaestion, Mr. Proctor dismisseth him, & calleth up the first Opponent, being a Mr. of Arts.

Now the Father may go out of the Schools, if he please, with a Bedle before him, & come in again when the 2d. opponent is disputing upon the 2d. Quaestion. Then presently after the Father is in his Seat, Mr. Proctor doth end the Tripos his Act, with a word or two in his commendation, if he deserves it.

Then Mr. Proctor speaketh unto the Father to begin his Position towards an ensuing Act in Philosophy; & whilst he is reading it, the Bedles do deliver his Verses to Mr. V. C. the Noblemen, Drs. Proctors, Taxers, Strangers, antient Bachelors in Divinity, & other grave men &c.

When the Position is ended, Mr. Proctor, or his Deputy,

[29] A Bachelor of Arts appointed to dispute, in humorous or satirical style, with the candidates for degrees at commencement.

being Moderator, doth call up the first opponent; who first makes a short Speech, & then disputeth upon the Father; he being taken off by the Moderator, the 2d. Opponent cometh up, & doth reply presently, without making any Speech or Oration; who, after he hath disputed a short Time upon both Quaestions, is taken of by the moderator, who doth briefly determine one, or both Quaestions, which Determination being ended, he concludeth with some thankfull expression to the company for their Patience &c.

Mem. That the senior Brother hath usually Leave to make a short Speech before he disputeth upon the Tripos, in which he thanketh the University for his Degree.

The Senior Mr of Arts, who is to dispute upon the Tripos, may likewise, if he please, make a Speech before he falls to his Disputation.

Mem. That the Bedels also are to deliver the Tripos's Verses to the V. C. Noblemen, Drs. &c. whilst the 2 Brothers are disputing upon him.

Presently after the Senior Proctor hath determined the Quaestions, & thanked the Auditory for the Patience (as mentioned before) a Bedel calleth the names of 10 or 12 Commencers, to whom the Father hath given Seniority, & if any presenteth himself to the Father, then Mr. Proctor saith, "Incipe: ad Oppositum."[30] And when the Father hath spoken to his son a word or two in his ear, Mr. Proctor saith unto him, "Exito." Then he goeth down, passing through the seat by his Father. And if any of them doth not appear, when he is called by the Bedel, Mr. Proctor saith, "Reservamus ei Senioritatem suam."[31]

When they [Milton] are all called whose names are in a Bill written by the Father, Mr. Proctor standing up in his Seat, saith with a loud voice, "Nos continuamus hanc Disputationem in Horam primam Diei Jovis Post 4tam Dominicam hujus Quadragesimae. . . ."[32]

[30] "Begin the opposition."   [31] "We keep his seniority for him."
[32] "We will continue this disputation at one o'clock on the Thursday after the fourth Sunday of this quadragesima [or Lent]."

The [latter] Act being ended, a Bedel calleth so many of the Sons [Milton] as are named & written in his Bill, the Proctor saying for every one that doth not appear, "Reservamus ei Senioritatem suam."

Then the Proctor saith, "Reliqui petant Senioritatem a Registro."[33] Last of all he saith, with a loud voice, "In Dei nomine, Amen. Authoritate qua fungimur, Decernimus, creamus & Pronuntiamus omnes hujus Anni Determinatores [Milton] finaliter determinasse et actualiter esse in Artibus Baccalaureos."[34]

Mem. That a little before the Senior Proctor beginneth his speech, one of the Bedels doth call a Congregation against 9 of the clock next morning. At which time the several Fathers doe deliver unto the Bedels all those Graces that are passed in their several Colleges for Inceptors in Arts[35] [Milton]. The V. C. Propoundeth these to the Caput Senatus, and writeth "ad" upon every one of them that is granted & approved [Milton].

These Graces are carried down into the Non-Regent House by one of the Bedels, there to be read by the Scrutators; & then into the Regent House to be read there by the Proctors. When they have been read in both Houses, the Register writeth on every Grace, Lect: Mart. Ao. Domini. . . .[36]

Though the above account of the proceedings in "responding to the question" was written about 1665, the man who wrote it had been bedel (or beadle) of the University of Cambridge for many years, and it may be assumed that the procedure was substantially what it had been in 1629. Since it is therefore almost an exact story of this event in Milton's life, it is printed here in full, with his name added in brackets wherever he is concerned. The source is John Buck's "Collections of some material Things which doe concern both the Corporations," dated 1665 (British Museum Add. MS. 5843), printed in George Peacock's *Observations on the Statutes of the University of Cambridge*, London, 1841, Appendix B, pp. lxv-lxxiii, and reprinted by the present editor in "Milton's Supplicats," *The Huntington Library Quarterly*, v (1942), 353 ff. Superior letters have been lowered.

[33] "Let the rest get their seniority from the Register."

[34] "In the name of God, Amen. By the authority with which I am invested, I decree, create, and pronounce all the determiners of this year to have finally determined and to be actually Bachelors of Arts."

[35] I.e., expectant Bachelors or Masters of Arts.

[36] "Read March, 16—." This entry, like that mentioned in note 15, does not occur on Milton's supplicats.

The date, February 9, has been determined as follows. Peacock states (*ibid.*, pp. 8 ff.): ". . . candidates for admission *ad respondendum quaestioni* . . . were called *quaestionists*, and on the Monday, Tuesday, Wednesday, and Thursday, of the week preceding Ash Wednesday, or at some earlier period in the same term, they were examined in the philosophy schools by the proctors, posers (subsequently called moderators), and other regent masters of arts. Those who were approved in this examination, were presented, with a proper *supplicat* from the authorities of their colleges, to the vice-chancellor and senate; and if the prayer of the petitioner was granted, he was admitted by the vice-chancellor *ad respondendum quaestioni*." Since Easter fell on April 5 in 1629, Ash Wednesday was February 18, and the period from Monday to Thursday preceding was February 9-12. Buck's date, between January 19 and January 28, is somewhat earlier, probably because Easter in 1665 fell on March 26, about ten days earlier than in 1629. February 9 is therefore a reasonably close approximation. The "supplicat" mentioned here is filed under the following day, February 10.

FEBRUARY 10(?). SUPPLICAT FOR DEGREE OF A.B.

ad   Coll: Chris:

Supplicat reverentiis vestris Joannes Milton, ut duodecim termini completi, in quibus lectiones ordinarias audiverit (licet non omninò secundùm formam statuti) unà cum omnibus oppositionibus, responsionib9, cæterisq̃z exercitiis p statuta regia requisitis, sufficiant ei ad respondendum quæstioni.

                    Joannes ffenwick præl: deput:

Original in the University Registry, Cambridge; reprinted by the present editor in "Milton's Supplicats," *The Huntington Library Quarterly*, v (1942), 349 ff., with facsimile on p. 351. I am indebted to the kindness of the University Registrary in furnishing me photostats of this and Milton's corresponding supplicat for the master's degree. The handwriting seems to be Milton's own except in the signature. For the discussion of the date see the note to the "response to the question," February 9.

[Approved. Christ's College. John Milton prays your reverences that twelve complete terms, in which he has listened to the ordinary lectures (though perhaps not entirely according to the letter of the statute), together with all oppositions, responses, and other exercises required by the royal statutes, may suffice him to answer the question. John Fenwick, constituted lecturer.]

MARCH 15. NEPHEW JOHN PHILLIPS BURIED.

[Burials] Mar. [1628/9] . . . 15 Johannes Phillipps fs. [blank] et [blank].

The Register of St. Martin-in-the-Fields London 1619-1636, ed. J. V. Kitto, 1936 (Publications of the Harleian Society, Vol. LXVI), p. 242. I have not seen the original parish record.

[On March 15, 1628/9, was buried John Phillips, son of (blank) and (blank).]

MARCH 26. SIGNS ARTICLES IN GRADUATION BOOK AND PROCEEDS A.B.

(1.) That the King's Majesty, under God, is the only supreme governor of this realm, and of all other his Highness's dominions and countries, as well in all spiritual or ecclesiastical things or causes, as temporal; and that no foreign prince, person, prelate, state, or potentate hath, or ought to have, any jurisdiction, power, superiority, pre-eminence, or authority, ecclesiastical or spiritual, within his Majesty's said realms, dominions, and countries.

(2.) That the Book of Common Prayer, and of ordering of bishops, priests, and deacons, containeth in it nothing contrary to the Word of God, and that it may lawfully so be used.

(3.) That we allow the Book of Articles of Religion agreed upon by the Archbishops and Bishops of both provinces, and the whole Clergy in the Convocation holden in London in the year of our Lord 1562; and acknowledge all and every the Articles therein contained, being in number Nine-and-Thirty, besides the ratification, to be agreeable to the Word of God.

We whose names are here underwritten do willingly and *ex animo* subscribe to the three Articles above-mentioned and to all things in them contained. . . .

Joannes Milton.

Christ's College, Cambridge, Graduation Book; Masson, I, 183-184 (217-218); Sotheby, *Ramblings*, facing p. 124; French, "The Autographs of John Milton," *ELH*, IV (1937), #99; CM, XVIII, 624. There are facsimiles of the signature in Sotheby and in Masson. According to Masson, the signing was done on March 26 and the degree conferred on that day, although the candidates had the privilege of dating it from the preceding January. The text of the articles is from Masson and not directly from the Graduation Book.

APRIL. ELEGY V. POETIC INSPIRATION.

Elegia quinta, Anno ætatis 20.
In adventum veris.

In se perpetuo Tempus revolubile gyro
Jam revocat Zephyros vere tepente novos.
Induiturque brevem Tellus reparata juventam,
Jamque soluta gelu dulce virescit humus.
Fallor? an & nobis redeunt in carmina vires,
Ingeniumque mihi munere veris adest?
Munere veris adest, iterumque vigescit ab illo
(Quis putet) atque aliquod jam sibi poscit opus.
Castalis ante oculos, bifidumque cacumen oberrat,
Et mihi Pyrenen somnia nocte ferunt.
Concitaque arcano fervent mihi pectora motu,
Et furor, & sonitus me sacer intùs agit.
Delius ipse venit, video Penëide lauro
Implicitos crines, Delius ipse venit.
Jam mihi mens liquidi raptatur in ardua cœli,
Perque vagas nubes corpore liber eo.
Perque umbras, perque antra feror penetralia vatum,
Et mihi fana patent interiora Deûm.
Intuiturque animus toto quid agatur Olympo,
Nec fugiunt oculos Tartara cæca meos.
Quid tam grande sonat distento spiritus ore?
Quid parit hæc rabies, quid sacer iste furor?
Ver mihi, quod dedit ingenium, cantabitur illo;
Profuerint isto reddita dona modo.
Jam Philomela tuos foliis adoperta novellis
Instituis modulos, dum silet omne nemus.
Urbe ego, tu sylvâ simul incipiamus utrique
Et simul adventum veris uterque canat. . . .

Milton, *Poems*, 1645, Part 2, pp. 25-30; Mackellar, pp. 88 ff.; CM, I, 194-207. There is fairly general agreement on 1629 as the date.

[Time, revolving in his ceaseless round, now again calls forth, by the warmth of Spring, the fresh Zephyrs; and the reinvigorated Earth puts on a short youth; and the ground, released from frost, grows sweetly green. Am I mistaken; or does strength also return to our verses, and is my genius with me by the gift of Spring? It *is* with me by the gift of Spring, and by this means (who would think it?) is reinforced, and already is demanding for itself some exercise. Castalia and the cleft hill flit before my eyes, and my nightly dreams bring Pyrene to my vision. My breast burns, stirred by secret commotion, and the sacred rage and tumult of sound possess me inwardly. Apollo himself comes! I see his locks enwreathed with Thessalian laurel; Apollo himself comes!

Now my mind is snatched up to the steeps of the serene heaven and, free of this body, is led through the wandering clouds. I am borne through the shades, through the sacred caves of the poet-prophets, and the inner sanctuaries of the gods lie open to me. My soul perceives what is being done on all Olympus, nor do the blind reaches of Tartarus escape my eyes.

What great utterance is my soul sounding through my open lips? What is this fury, this sacred madness, bringing forth? Spring will be sung by that inspiration which it gave me; the gifts given back in this way will bear fruit. Now, Philomela, wrapped in new leaves, you begin your songs, while all the grove is silent. Let us both begin together, I in the city and you in the wood; and let us both at once sing the coming of spring.]

Masson, I, 185 (219) (first paragraph only); the rest is by the present editor.

APRIL 1. LICENSE TO FATHER TO SELL LAND TO ALEXANDER DORINGTON.

p̄ licen' alien'   Rex Omĩbz ad quos &c sāltm./ Sciatis qd'
int' milton et   nos de grā nrā spīali ac p̄ triginta tribz
Dorington'./   solidis & quatuor denarijs solut' ffirmari
                   nrīs virtute lrar' Paten' Dnī Jacobi nup
Regis Anglie concessim⁹ & licentiam dedim⁹ ac p̄ nōb heredibz

& successoribz nr̄īs quantam in nōb est p p'sentes concedim⁹ &
licentiam dam⁹ Dīlco nōb Jōhi milton' qd' ipē vnū mesuagiū
cum gardin' eidem spectan' scituat' in Aldersgate Streete in
Parochia scī Bottolphi extʳ Aldersgate london', Que de nōb
tenentʳ in capite vt dicitʳ dare possit & concedere alienare aut
cognoscē p finem vel p recupacōem in Cur' nr̄ā coram Justici-
arijs nr̄īs de Banco aut aliquo alio modo quocunqz ad libitum
ipīus Johīs Dilcīs nōb Alexō Dorington genōso & marie vxī
eius. habendum & tenend' eisdem Alexō & marie ac heredibz
& assign' ipius Alexī imppm̄ de nōb heredibz & successoribz
nr̄īs p suic' inde debit' & de iure consuet'. Et eisdem Alexō &
marie qd' ipī p'dict' mesuag' & ceta p'missa cum ptin' a p'fat'
Johē recipe possint & tenere sibi ac heredibz & Assign' ipīus
Alexi de nōb heredibz & success' nr̄īs p suīcia p'dcā sicut p'dcm̄
est imppm̄ tenore p'sencm̄ similit' licentiam dedim⁹ ac p nōb
heredibz & successoribz nr̄īs p'dcīs dam⁹ spiālem. Nolentes qd'
p'dcūs Johēs vel heredes sui aut p'fat Alexūs & maria vel
heredes ipīus Alexī rōne p'missor' p nos heredes vel successores
nr̄ōs aut p Justiciar' Escaet' vicecom' Ballinos aut alios Offi-
ciarios seu ministros nr̄ōs aut dcōr' heredum vel successor' nr̄ōr'
quoscunqz inde occōnentʳ molestentʳ impetantʳ vexentʳ in aliquo
seu gñentʳ, nec eor' aliquis occōnetʳ molestatʳ impetatʳ vexetʳ
in aliquo seu granetʳ. In cuius rei &c. T R' apud Westm̄ primo
die Aprilis./

exʳ

Public Record Office, Patent Rolls, C66/2527/70. The superior 9
used here for the first personal plural endings of verbs represents the
manuscript abbreviation for -us, which looks like a 9. For the actual
indenture of sale see below under date of June 19, 1629.

[License patent to alienate, between Milton and Dorington.
The King to all to whom, etc., Greeting. Know that we of our
special grace and in consideration of 33 shillings and 4 pence
paid to our treasurers by virtue of Letters Patent of our Lord
James, formerly King of England, have granted and given
license and for us and our heirs and successors as much as in us
lies have granted by these presents and given license to our beloved John Milton that as for one messuage with its garden fac-

ing and situated in Aldersgate Street in the parish of St. Botolph without Aldersgate, London, which are held in chief, as it is said, from us, he may give, yield, alienate, or transfer this property by fine or recovery in our court before our justices of the bench or by any other method whatever at the pleasure of the said John, to our beloved Alexander Dorington, gentleman, and his wife Mary. To have and to hold to the said Alexander and Mary and the heirs and assigns of the same Alexander forever, from us, our heirs, and our successors by the service thence owed and according to established law. And to the same Alexander and Mary that they may receive and hold the aforesaid messuage etc. with its appurtenances from the said John, to themselves and the heirs and assigns of the said Alexander from us, our heirs, and our successors through the aforesaid service as has been rehearsed above, forever. By a copy of these presents similarly we have given, and for us, our heirs, and our successors aforesaid we give, special license, unwilling that the aforesaid John or his heirs or the said Alexander and Mary or the heirs of the said Alexander by reason of promises from us, our heirs or successors, or through justices of the Exchequer, sheriffs, bailiffs, or our other officers or ministers or those of our said heirs or successors whatsoever, should thence be disturbed, molested, bothered, vexed, or troubled in any way, or any of them be disturbed, molested, bothered, vexed, or troubled in any way. In which thing, etc. Witness the King at Westminster on the first day of April. Executed.]

JUNE 1 (?). FATHER LEASES PROPERTY TO CALEB RAWLINS.

[The Milton-Dorington deed of June 19, 1629, mentions] one lease thereof lately made and graunted by the said John Milton vnto one Caleb Rawlins for the tearme of eight yeres comencinge att the feast of the Nativitie of Saint John Baptist now next ensuinge.

See below under date of June 19, 1629. The day of the Nativity of St. John the Baptist was June 24, but the deed must have been drawn before June 19.

JUNE 12. FATHER AND THOMAS BOWER CONTINUE DOWNER-EWENS AND KEYMER LOAN.

... Your said Oratrixe ... was patient till that sixe monethes end [the second since the drawing of the bond on June 10, 1628] and then the money not coming in she addressed her-selfe to the said Milton for it whoe entreated her to sue the bond, yet promised neuertheless to be her paymaster him-selfe ... and paid not the same nor any pte thereof at the end of the said second sixe monethes nor at any time since nor any interest for the same but fedd her with faire wordɔ. ...

Public Record Office, C2 Charles I/D39/47 (Rose Downer's bill, April 26, 1631); French, *Milton in Chancery*, pp. 238-239. As to whether any interest was paid, see the following extracts and those given above under date of December 12, 1628.

... she received both the bond at the first and the Jnterest as the same grewe dewe at severall dayes, and times afterwardɔ, and that this Def^t. never knewe that she was vnwilling there-vnto, vntill now of late. ...

Public Record Office, C2 Charles I/D39/47 (Milton's answer to Downer, May 3, 1631); French, *Milton in Chancery*, p. 240.

... a bond was then taken for the same, and afterwardɔ by and with the consent, and good liking of the said Complaynant, was continued for Twoe, or three Six monethɔ, and the Jnterest duly paid her for the same time, and by her accepted of, with-out any dislike at all. ...

Public Record Office, C2 Charles I/D39/47 (Bower's answer to Downer's bill, May 3, 1631); French, *Milton in Chancery*, p. 244.

JUNE 19. INDENTURE BETWEEN FATHER AND ALEXANDER DORINGTON.

Mylton et
Dorington
18

This Indenture made the nyneteenth day of June in the yere of our Lord god one thousand six hundred twenty and nyne and in the fifte yere of the raigne of our soveraigne Lord Charles by the grace of god Kinge of England Scotland ffrance and Ireland defendor of faith &c Betweene John Milton Citti-zen and Scrivenor of London on thone party and Alexander

Dorington of Grayes Inne in the County of Midd gent and
Mary Dorington wife to the said Alexander Dorington and
late daughter to John Porter Late Cittizen and Cutler of London on thother party Witnesseth that the said John Milton for
and in consideracion of the sõme of three hundred poundₚ of
good and lawfull money of England vnto him the said John
Milton by the said Alexander Dorington att and before then-
sealinge and delivery of theis p̄sentₚ well and truly contented
and paid and thereof and of every part and parcell thereof he
the said John Milton doth by theis p̄sentₚ cleerely acquite
exonerate and discharge the said Alexander Dorington his heires
executors and administ^rs as alsoe for other good causes and con-
sideracions him the said John Milton therevnto movinge hath
bargained sold enfeoffed and confirmed and by theis p̄sentₚ doth
bargain seḻḻ infeoffe and confirme vnto the said Alexander Dorington and Mary Dorington and to the heires and assignes of
the said Alexander Dorington foreū All that mesuage or teñte
With the hereditam^ts or appᵣtenances therevnto belonging and
also one garden or garden plott on the backside of the said mesuage scituate and beinge in Aldersgate streete in the parishe of
Saint Buttolphe without Aldersgate London late in the tenure
or occupacion of Thomas Stuttvyle gent or his assignes and alsoe
the said John Milton for the consideracion aforesaid hath bargained and sold and by theis p̄sents doth fully and absolutely
bargaine and sell vnto the said Alexander Dorington and Mary
Dorington and the heires and assignes of the said Alexander
Dorington foreū aḻḻ the severall countp̄aines of Indentures of
Leases made demised and graunted of the foresaid mesuage or
tenem^t togeather with all and every the deedₚ evidencₚ chr̄es
or any other writingₚ whatsoever touchinge or in any wayes concerninge the p̄misses or any part or pcell thereof beinge in the
handₚ custody or possession of the said John Milton or of any
other to his vse To have and to hold aḻḻ the foresaid mesuage or
tenement togeather with the garden and other the appᵣtenancₚ
and every part and pcell thereof by theis p̄sentₚ graunted bargained and sold vnto the said Alexander Dorington and Mary

Dorington and the heires and assignes of the said Alexander
Dorington to the only and proper vse and behoofe of them the
said Alexander Dorington and Mary Dorington and the heires
and assignes of the said Alexander Dorington forever And the
said John Milton for him his heires executors and administrators
and for every of them doth covenant and graunt to and with
the said Alexander Dorington and Mary Dorington and to the
heires executors administrators and assignes of the said Alexander by theis p̄sentꝑ that all the said mesuage or tenem^t with
thappʳtenancꝑ and every part and p̄cell thereof by theis p̄sentꝑ
bargained and sold now remaine and be and att all and eūy tyme
and tymes hereafter shall remaine and contynue vnto the said
Alexander Dorington and Mary Dorington and to the heires
and assignes of the said Alexander Dorington foreū cleerely
acquitted discharged or otherwise sufficiently saved harmles by
the said John Milton his heires executors administrˢ or assignes
of and from all bargaines sales Joyntures dowers iudgmᵗꝑ exe-
cucions intrusions fynes alyenacions and other chargꝑ duties and
incombrancꝑ whatsoeū heretofor had made done or suffered by
the said John Milton or his assignes or by any other person or
persons by his meanes consent or ꝑcurement one lease thereof
lately made and graunted by the said John Milton vnto one
Calib Rawlins for the tearme of eight yeres comencinge att the
feast of the Nativitie of Saint John Baptist now next ensuinge
and the quit rentꝑ duties and paymentꝑ due unto the Kingꝑ
maiestie his heires and successors for and in respect of the
p̄misses only excepted and the said John Milton for him his
heires executors and administrators and for every of them doth
covenant and graunt to and with the said Alexander and Mary
Dorington and to the heires executors administrators and assignes of the said Alexander by theis p̄sentꝑ that he the said
John Milton att the makinge hereof standeth and is lawfull &
rightfull owner of the foresaid mesuage or teñte with thappʳtenancꝑ and every part & pcell thereof for any act or thing by him
done to the coñtry and that he is solely lawfully and rightly
seised of a good and perfect estate in fee simple or fee tayle

in his owne right and to his owne only vse of all the said mesuage
or tenem^t by theis p̄sentꝑ graunted bargained and sold for any
act or thinge by him done to the contrary and that he hath fułł
power ꝑfect lawfull and good authority for any act or thing by
him done to the contrary to bargaine sell and assure the same in
manner and forme aforesaid And further that he the said John
Milton and the heires of the said John Milton and ałł and
every other person or persons and their heires havinge or lawfully clayminge any lawfull estate or interest of or in the p̄misses
or any part or parcell thereof by from or vnder him the said
John Milton shall and will att the coste and charge of them
the said Alexander and Mary Dorington and the heires and
assignes of the said Alexander att ałł and every tyme and tymes
hereafter duringe the tearme of seaven yeres next ensuinge the
date hereof att the reasonable request of the said Alexander
Dorington and Mary Dorington and the heires or assignes of
the said Alexander Dorington doe suffer to be done ałł and every
such reasonable and further act and actꝑ thinge and thingꝑ devise and devises assurannce and assurannces whatsoever for the
further and better assurannce and sure makinge and for the
cleere and absolute havinge and enioyinge of ałł the foresaid
p̄misses with their appᵲtenancꝑ and every part and parcell thereof to be conveyed and assured to the said Alexander and Mary
Dorington and the heires and assignes of the said Alexander
Dorington be it by fyne feoffement recoverie deede or deedꝑ
inrolled inrollment of theis presentꝑ recovery with single or
double vouchers and with warranty only against the said John
Milton and his heires or without warranty or otherwayes as shall
be reasonably devised or advised by the said Alexander Dorington or by the Councell learned in the lawes of this Realme of
the said Alexander Dorington his heires or assignes In witness
whereof the said parties to theis p̄sent Indentures iñtchange-
ably have sett their handꝑ and seales yeoven the day and year
first above written./

Eden   Et memorand qd decano nono die Junij Ann sūpscript
p̄fat Johēs Milton venit coram dtō dnō Rege in Cancellār sua &

recogn Jndentur' p̄dict ac om̄ia & singula in eadem contenta & sp̄ificat in forma sup̄dta In decano octauo die Nouembr' anno p̄dict./
                 In^d   Ex^r

Public Record Office, Close Rolls, C54/2803/18; Stevens, *Milton Papers*, pp. 41-44; Brennecke, *John Milton the Elder and his Music*, p. 114 (brief mention only). Stevens omits the Latin note at the end. The Eden mentioned marginally near the end was probably Thomas Eden, Master in Chancery, 1618-1646.

[And be it remembered that on the nineteenth day of June in the year above written the aforesaid John Milton came before the said lord our King in his Chancery and acknowledged the aforesaid indenture and all and singular contained and specified in the same in the form above written. Executed and indented on the eighteenth day of November in the year aforesaid.]

June 26. Father arranges Sherfield- (or Cherfield-) Cotton bond.

Mr Sherfeild & oth^rs p obl' Dat' xxvj° Junij 1629 . . . 100^li

Thomas Bower's schedule of Cotton's bonds made out by himself and Milton's father; see below under date of November 25, 1630. The original bond has not been found.

. . . Mr Cherfeild & others by bond dated ye Six & Twentieth of June One thowsand six hundred Twentie Nyne One [hund]-red poundₚ principall [debt]. . . .

Sir Thomas Cotton's bill; see below under date of May 28, 1636.

July 7. Friend Charles Diodati receives M.A. at Cambridge.

The original record is not immediately available, but it is recorded in John and J. A. Venn's *Alumni Cantabrigienses*, Cambridge, 1922, II, part i, p. 44. See also Donald C. Dorian, "Charles Diodati at Geneva," *PMLA*, LIX (1944), 589-591.

July 18. Indenture between father and John Suckling.

Suckling et
Milton 7

This Jndenture made the Eighteenth day of July in the yeare of our lord god one thousand six hundred twenty and nyne and in the fiveth

yere of the reigne of our soveraigne lord Charles by the grace
of God king of England Scotland ffrance and Ireland defender
of the faith &c Betweene John Suckling of london Esquier sonne
and heire apparant of the honorable Sir John Suckling knight
deceased late Comptroller of his said maiesties houshold and
William Barrett of london gent' Executor of the last will and
Testament of the said Sir John Suckling on thone part And
John Milton Citizen and Scrivener of london on thother part
witnesseth that whereas the said Sir John Suckling by the name
of John Suckling by his last will and testament in writing bearing date the last day of September in the yere of our lord god
one thousand six hundred twenty and six and in the second yere
of the raigne of our said sovereigne lord king Charles did ex-
pressely will and authorize his executors in the same will men-
c̄oned within three yeres after the decease of him the said sir
John Suckling to grant bargaine and sell amongest other landꝑ
teñtꝑ and hereditamͭꝑ his house on Ludgate Hill London with
thapꝑtenñcꝑ in as large absolute and ample manner as the
same was conveyed vnto him and as he might graunt sell and
convey the same it being to rayse moneys for his daughters
porc̄ons and the payment of his debtꝑ requiring the said John
Suckling his sonne to ioyne with his Executors in the sale
thereof if it shalbe desired as he tendred the blessing of god
Almightie as by the same last will more playnly may appeare
which howse abovemenc̄oned to be on ludgate hill and by him
the said Sir John in and by his last will appointed intended and
authorized to be sould the said John Suckling and Wiłłm Barrett doe confesse and acknowledge to have beene heretofore
twoe mesuagꝑ or teñtꝑ one greater and one lesse and by him the
said Sir John were lately made and esteemed but one dwelling
house wherein he himselfe with his wife and famely sometymes
inhabited and dwelt and is scituate in the parish of Sͭ Martins
within ludgate london Now this Jndenture further witnesseth
that the said John Suckling and William Barrett in ꝑformance
of the said last will and testament of him the said Sir John
Suckling and alsoe for and in considerac̄on of the soḿe of five

hundred and threescore poundꝑ of good and lawfull money of
England by the said John Milton to the said William Barrett
at thensealing and delivery of theis p̄sentꝑ well and truely satisfied contented and paid whereof the said William Barrett doth
acknowledge the receipt and thereof and of every part and pcell
thereof doth fully and clearly acquite release and discharge the
said John Milton his heires executors and administrators and
every of them by theis p̄sentꝑ have granted bargained sould
aliened enfeoffed and confirmed and by theis p̄sentꝑ aswell by
vertue and authority of the said last will and testam^t of the said
sir John Suckling as by any other right title or interest whatsoeū
in them the said Sir John Suckling and William Barrett or either
of them being doe fully clearely and absolutely grant bargaine
sell alien enfeoffe and confirme vnto the said John Milton his
heires and assignes foreū All that the said house on ludgate hill
aforesaid or the said twoe mesuagꝑ or teñtꝑ scituate in the parish
of St Martins within ludgate london devised and appointed to
be sold as aforesaid with all shopps cellers sollers roomes entries
yardꝑ backsidꝑ leade and leaden pipes belonging to and pcell
of the said house mesuages or teñtꝑ or either of them with aɫɫ
and singuler their apptenñcꝑ except the branch or pipe of leade
conveying water into the kitchen of the greater of the said
mesuages And all the estate right title interest reverc̄on remainder inheritance ꝑperty clayme and demaund of them the
said John Suckling and William Barrett and either of them of
in and to the p̄misses and every part thereof except before excepted Together with all chr̄es writingꝑ and evidencꝑ touching
the same p̄misses or any part thereof which said greate mesuage
or teñte is scituate betweene the teñte now or late of Raphe
Brooke gent on the east and the teñte now or late of William
Smyth on the west and the said lesser teñte was sometymes in
the occupac̄on of Guy winyett gent or his assignes and is scituate in the lane or Alley com̄only called or knowne by the name
of Pañier Alley in the said parish of St Martin between part of
the yard of the mesuage or teñte hereby menc̄oned to be bargained and sould and the teñte of the said Raphe Brooke on

the east and the said lane or Alley on the west of which said
great mesuage or teñte one Diones Partridge widdowe deceased
late wife of John Hulson alsoe deceased was lately seized for
terme of her naturaƚƚ life To have and to hold the said house
mesuage or teñtꝑ above bargained and sold and by the said last
will of the said sir John Suckling menconed ment and intended
to be bargained and sold with their and every of their apꝑtenñcꝑ
and every part thereof vnto the said John Milton his heires
and assignes to the onely vse and behoofe of him the said John
Milton his heires and assignes forever And the said William
Barrett for him his heires executors and administrators doth
covenñt and grant to and with the said John Milton his heires
and assignes and to and with every of them by theis ꝑsentꝑ in
manner and forme following that is to say that he the said William Barrett at the tyme of thensealing and delivery of theis
ꝑsentꝑ for any act or thing by the said William Barrett done
to the contrary hath full power strength and lawfull authority
to grant bargaine and sell vnto the said John Milton his heires
and assignes foreū all that the said house mesuagꝑ or teñtꝑ and
ꝑmisses with thapꝑtenñcꝑ and every part thereof except before
excepted And alsoe except one demise or lease by the said William Barrett made or granted of the ꝑmisses vnto John Muraƚƚ
lynnendraper for the tenure of five yeares whereof there wilbe
remayning and vnexpired at the feast of the Nativitie of Sᵗ John
Baptist last past before the date of theis ꝑsentꝑ three yeeres and
three quarters of a yeare or thereaboutꝑ vpon which lease was
and is reserved during the contynuance of the said terme the
yearely rent of fortie poundꝑ of lawfull money of England
which said rent the said John Milton his heires and assignes by
the true intent and meaning of theis ꝑsentꝑ is and are from
henceforth to have and enioy during the said terme Jn witnes
whereof the said parties to theis ꝑsent Jndentures intchangeably
have set their handꝑ and seales yeoven the day and yeares first
above written Et memorand qd ꝑfat Johēs Suckling non sig-
nauit nec sigillauit neqz recognouit Jndentur' ꝑdict.'/ Et memorand qd die et anno suprascript' prefat' wiƚƚs Barrett Gener'

venit coram dtō dnō Rege in Cancellar' sua et recognouit Jndentur' predtām ac omnia et singula in eadem contenta et specificata
in forma supradtā. Jn^d vicesimo die July Anno p̄dict.'/ ex^r

Public Record Office, Close Rolls, C54/2800/7; Stevens, *Milton
Papers*, pp. 3, 44-46 (omitting the Latin note at the end); Brennecke,
John Milton the Elder and his Music, p. 114 (brief mention only).
The name Riche added in the margin of the Latin note probably refers
to Robert Rich, Master in Chancery, 1618-1646. There is a facsimile of the document in the Harvard College Library (shelf-mark
14495.58PF).

[And be it remembered that the aforesaid John Suckling
neither signed nor sealed nor acknowledged the aforesaid indenture. And be it remembered that on the day and year above
written the aforesaid William Barrett, gentleman, came before
the said Lord our King in his Chancery and acknowledged the
aforesaid indenture and all and singular in the same contained
and specified in the form above written. Indented on the twentieth day of July in the aforesaid year. Executed.]

JULY 20. FATHER'S INDENTURE WITH SUCKLING COM-
PLETED.

Jn^d vicesimo die July Anno p̄dict.'/
Final note on the indenture of July 18, 1629, *q.v.*

[Indented on the twentieth day of July in the aforesaid year.]

SEPTEMBER? ATTENDS UNIVERSITY PLAYS AND DISAP-
PROVES THEM.

But since there is such necessity to the hearsay of a Tire, a
Periwig, or a Vizard, that Playes must have bin seene, what difficulty was there in that? when in the Colleges so many of the
young Divines, and those in next aptitude to Divinity have bin
seene so oft upon the Stage writhing and unboning their Clergie
limnes to all the antick and dishonest gestures of Trinculo's,
Buffons, and Bawds; prostituting the shame of that ministery
which either they had, or were nigh having, to the eyes of
Courtiers and Court-Ladies, with their Groomes and *Made-
moisellaes*? There while they acted, and overacted, among other

young scholars, I was a spectator; they thought themselves gallant men, and I thought them fools, they made sport, and I
laught, they mispronounc't and I mislik't, and, to make up the
atticisme, they were out, and I hist.

Milton, *An Apology for Smectymnuus*, 1642, p. 14; CM, III, 300.
This passage, though of general import and incapable of exact dating,
is filed here because Masson (I, 187 ff. [221 ff.]) sees in it a reference
to the *Fraus Honesta* of Philip Stubbe, acted at Trinity College in September, 1629, in honor of the visit of the Chancellor, Lord Holland, and
the French Ambassador. Some details of the performance may be found
in Joseph Mead's letter to Sir Martin Stuteville, September 26, 1629,
printed in *The Court and Times of Charles the First*, II (1848), 29.

NOVEMBER. FATHER ARRANGES WELBY-COTTON BOND.

Mr Wm Welby & oth^rs p obl' Dat' [?] Novembr' 1629 . . .
100^li

Thomas Bower's schedule of Cotton's bonds made out by himself and
Milton's father; see below under date of November 25, 1630. The
original bond has not been found.

. . . [M^r] Will'm Welby & others [by bond dated y^e . . .] tieth
of November One thowsand six hundred Twentie Nyne One
hundred pound℈ principall debt.

Sir Thomas Cotton's bill; see below under date of May 28, 1636.
Unfortunately the exact date is missing from both this and the foregoing entries, though from the remnant of the word ". . . tieth" which is
visible in the present entry we are justified in assuming it was either the
twentieth or the thirtieth.

NOVEMBER 15. BUYS PINDAR'S POEMS.

ΠΙΝΔΑΡΟΥ ΠΕΡΙΟΔΟΣ, *Pindari Olympia, Pythia, Nemea,
Isthmia* [Saumur, 1620].

[Inscribed on a flyleaf, apparently in Milton's own hand, is
the note:] Novemb 15° 1629 pret:- 9^s - o.

[After the "finis" is written, also probably in Milton's hand:]
Δοξὰ τῳ δεῳ Jun: 17 1630 et Sept: 28. 1630.

This book, formerly the property of Charles Sumner, who bought it
at the sale of the library of J. B. Inglis, is now in the Harvard College
Library. It contains abundant marginal annotations and a manuscript
index at the end. See *Notes and Queries*, IV, viii (1871), 117; French,
"The Autographs of John Milton," #72; CM, XVIII, 276, 565. Many

of Milton's annotations are collected in the Columbia Milton. Though Milton's name does not appear, the tradition of his ownership seems well established, and the handwriting is like other known specimens. The dates seem to indicate that he bought the volume on November 15, 1629, for nine shillings and finished reading it through (twice?) on July 17, 1630, and September 28, 1630. But Harris Fletcher plausibly suggests to me that the dates may mean that Milton bought the book on November 15, 1629, and read it through in his next long vacation, between June 17, 1630, and September 28, 1630.

[November 15, 1629; price 9 shillings, no pence. . . . Glory to God! June 17, 1630, and September 28, 1630.]

NOVEMBER 18. FATHER'S AGREEMENT WITH DORINGTON INDENTED.

In decano octauo die Nouembr' anno p̄dict./
           Ex^r   In^d

Endorsement of the Milton-Dorington indenture of June 19, 1629, *q.v.*

[Executed and indented on the eighteenth day of November in the year aforesaid (1629)].

DECEMBER. BUYS DELLA CASA'S POETRY (AND OTHER WORK BY DANTE AND VARCHI?)

Rime et Prose di Giovanni della Casa [Venice, 1563].

[On the titlepage, in Milton's hand, is written:] Jo: Milton pre: 10^d. 1629. Dece[margin torn away].

This volume, bound with Dante's *L'Amoroso Convivio*, Venice, 1529, and *Sonetti de Benedetto Varchi*, Venice, 1555, is now in the New York Public Library. It had formerly belonged to Richard Heber, Sir William Tite, and others. There are some marginal comments, apparently by Milton, in both the della Casa and the Varchi sections, and numerous marks and textual corrections in all three sections. On some flyleaves near the back is a copy, perhaps in Milton's hand, of a letter from Varchi to Francesco de Medici. The precise day of Milton's buying the book cannot be discovered, because no transcription of the note before it was trimmed away has been found. See Sotheby, *Ramblings*, pp. 124-125 (with a facsimile of the note facing p. 124); French, "The Autographs of John Milton," #73; CM, XVIII, 345, 573.

[John Milton. Price ten pence. Dece(mber   ), 1629.]

DECEMBER 3. FATHER'S SHOP MENTIONED BY JOHN LENTHALL.

[Lenthall writes to a friend about two bonds:] . . . J owe none at miltons, nor neuer had to doe wth m^{r} Trotman . . .

Your trustye frende & louinge brother

Stoke 3° Dec: 1629   John Lenthall

From a letter among the Temple papers in the Huntington Library. Though unaddressed, it was probably sent to Sir Peter Temple or some relative. For previous connections between Milton and the Temples of Stowe, see above under date of July 4, 1623. For a story of these transactions with transcripts of the documents, see French, "John Milton, Scrivener, the Temples of Stowe, and Sir John Lenthall," *Huntington Library Quarterly*, IV (1941), 303 ff.

DECEMBER 9(?). SO-CALLED ONSLOW PORTRAIT MADE.

This original picture of Milton I bought in the year 1729 or 30 and paid 20 guineas for it of Mr Cumberbatch, a gentleman of very good consideration in Chester, who was a relation and executor of the will of Milton's last wife who died a little while before that time. He told me it hung up in her chamber till her death and she used to say that her husband gave it to her to show her what he was in his youth being drawn when he was about 21 years of age.

AR. ONSLOW.

Mr Hawkins Brown (author of the poem De Animi Immortalitate) told me (8 Oct. 1753) that he knew this Mrs Milton, visited her often and well remembered this picture hanging in her chamber which she said was her husband.

A. O.

Compare this picture with that of Milton in his old age or in the print of it by White.

N.B. The above I transcribed from the writings I found on the back of the original picture of Milton belonging to Lord Onslow when I made this copy for the Earl of Harcourt in November 1792.

BENJ. VAN DER GUCHT.

Inscriptions on the back of the Van der Gucht copy made in 1792 and exhibited at Christ's College in 1908; Williamson (*Milton Tercentenary*, 1908), p. 33; Darbishire, p. 334.

The original painting is now lost, and the identity of the painter is unknown. Speaker Onslow is rumored to have refused to sell the painting to Lord Harcourt, who wanted it, but to have agreed to let Benjamin Van der Gucht make a likeness of it in return for a copy of Kneller's portrait of Pope in Harcourt's possession. Onslow is also said to have become so annoyed by visitors wishing to see the original painting that he had it destroyed. On the other hand, Marsh intimated that he knew where it was and hinted that it might soon become known. It was evidently still in existence as late as 1792, when Van der Gucht copied it; and the copy seems still to be in the possession of the family of the Earl of Harcourt. Engravings and other reproductions by Vertue (1731), Houbraken (1741), Cipriani (1759), and others are well known. Copies appear in Masson, I, facing p. 1; Williamson, frontispiece; and CM, I, facing p. 18.

Information about the portrait may be found in *The London Magazine*, XXI (1752), 371-374, which reproduced the portrait in somewhat garbled form; F. Blackburne, *Memoirs of Thomas Hollis*, 1780, I, 85-86, 114; II, frontispiece, 619; Todd, 1826, I, 236; J. F. Marsh, *The Transactions of the Historic Society of Lancashire and Cheshire*, XII (1860), 135-188; Williamson, pp. 3 ff.; Darbishire, pp. 333-334; CM, XVIII, 388. A miniature owned by Arthur E. Shipley, exhibited at the Tercentenary exhibition in Cambridge in 1908, closely resembles the Houbraken engraving. Dr. Williamson considered it to be probably the original from which Houbraken worked, and thought it done by Bernard Lens the younger. See *Milton Tercentenary*, pp. 25, 31.

His widowe has his picture drawne very well & like when a Cambridge schollar . . . She has his picture when a Cambridge schollar, wch ought to be engraven: for the Pictures before his bookes are not *at all* like him.

Aubrey, fol. 63; Darbishire, p. 3.

DECEMBER 9(?). SELF-CONSECRATION TO HIGH CAREER.

And long it was not after, when I was confirm'd in this opinion, that he who would not be frustrate of his hope to write well hereafter in laudable things, ought him selfe to bee a true Poem, that is, a composition, and patterne of the best and honourablest things; not presuming to sing high praises of heroick men, or famous Cities, unlesse he have in himselfe the

experience and the practice of all that which is praise-worthy.
These reasonings, together with a certaine nicenesse of nature,
an honest haughtinesse, and self-esteem either of what I was,
or what I might be, (which let envie call pride) and lastly that
modesty, whereof though not in the Title page yet here I may
be excus'd to make some beseeming profession, all these uniting
the supply of their naturall aide together, kept me still above
those low descents of minde, beneath which he must deject
and plunge himself, that can agree to salable and unlawfull
prostitutions. Next, (for heare me out now Readers) that I may
tell ye whether my younger feet wander'd; I betook me among
those lofty Fables and Romances, which recount in solemne
canto's the deeds of Knighthood founded by our victorious
Kings; & from hence had in renowne over all Christendome.
There I read it in the oath of every Knight, that he should defend to the expence of his best blood, or of his life, if it so
befell him, the honour and chastity of Virgin or Matron. From
whence even then I learnt what a noble vertue chastity sure must
be, to the defence of which so many worthies by such a deare
adventure of themselves had sworne. And if I found in the
story afterward any of them by word or deed breaking that oath,
I judg'd it the same fault of the Poet, as that which is attributed to *Homer*; to have written undecent things of the
gods. Only this my minde gave me that every free and gentle
spirit without that oath ought to be borne a Knight, nor needed
to expect the guilt spurre, or the laying of a sword upon his
shoulder to stirre him up both by his counsell, and his arme to
secure and protect the weaknesse of any attempted chastity.
So that even those books which to many others have bin the
fuell of wantonnesse and loose living, I cannot thinke how
unlesse by divine indulgence prov'd to me so many incitements
as you have heard, to the love and stedfast observation of that
vertue which abhorres the society of Bordello's. Thus from the
Laureat fraternity of Poets, riper yeares, and the ceaselesse
round of study and reading led me to the shady spaces of
philosophy, but chiefly to the divine volumes of *Plato*, and his

equall *Xenophon*. Where if I should tell ye what I learnt, of chastity and love, I meane that which is truly so, whose charming cup is only vertue which she bears in her hand to those who are worthy. The rest are cheated with a thick intoxicating potion with a certaine Sorceresse the abuser of loves name carries about; and how the first and chiefest office of love, begins and ends in the soule, producing those happy twins of her divine generation knowledge and vertue, with such abstracted sublimities as these, it might be worth your listning, Readers, as I may one day hope to have ye in a still time, when there shall be no chiding; not in these noises, the adversary as ye know, barking at the doore; or searching for me at the Burdello's where it may be he has lost himselfe, and raps up without pitty the sage and rheumatick old *Prelatesse* with all her young *Corinthian Laity* to inquire for such a one. Last of all not in time, but as perfection is last, that care was ever had of me, with my earliest capacity not to be negligently train'd in the precepts of Christian Religion: This that I have hitherto related, hath bin to shew, that though Christianity had bin but slightly taught me, yet a certain reserv'dnesse of naturall disposition, and morall discipline learnt out of the noblest Philosophy was anough to keep me in disdain of farre lesse incontinences then this of the Burdello.

Milton, *An Apology against Smectymnuus*, 1642, p. 16; CM, III, 303-306. Though such an experience as Milton here describes cannot be dated precisely by month and day, it has been suggested by Hanford (*The Youth of Milton*, p. 123) that his twenty-first birthday was an appropriate date for such taking of stock. See below under December 25, 1629 (Elegy VI), for a passage in similar vein.

DECEMBER 12. RECEIVES INTEREST PAYMENT FROM RICHARD POWELL.

. . . the growing Jnterest for the forbearance of the said Principall debt was for some yeares then following likewise payd And soe continued to bee paid vntill June Jn the yeare of our Lord One Thousand six hundred ffortie and ffower. . . .

From Milton's answer to Elizabeth Ashworth, February 22, 1653/4, *q.v.*

DECEMBER 12. FATHER AND BOWER CONTINUE DOWNER-EWENS AND KEYMER BOND (?)

[The loan of fifty pounds from Rose Downer to Ewens and Keymer] was continued for Twoe, or three Six monethℓ, and the Jnterest duly paid her for the same time, and by her accepted of. . . .

Public Record Office, C2 Charles I/D39/47 (Bower's answer to Downer's bill, May 3, 1631); French, *Milton in Chancery*, p. 244. The first six months' period would be from June 10, 1628, to December 12, 1628; the second to June 12, 1629; the third to December 12, 1629. None of the other documents in the case mention this third period, except that Rose Downer denies steadily that she ever received any interest whatsoever at any time.

DECEMBER 13. LETTER FROM CHARLES DIODATI.

[Described in Milton's Sixth Elegy to Diodati:] *Ad Carolum Diodatum . . . Qui cum idibus Decemb. scripsisset, & sua carmina excusari postulasset si solito minus essent bona, quòd inter lautitias quibus erat ab amicis exceptus, haud satis felicem operam Musis dare se posse affirmabat, hunc habuit responsum.*

Milton, *Poems*, 1645, Part II, p. 31; CM, I, 206; XVIII, 527. The letter itself is lost, but it was evidently in Latin verse.

> . . . At tua quid nostram prolectat Musa camœnam . . .
> Quàm bene solennes epulas, hilaremque Decembrim
>   Festaque cœlifugam quæ coluere Deum,
> Deliciasque refers, hyberni gaudia ruris,
>   Haustaque per lepidos Gallica musta focos.
> Quid quereris refugam vino dapibusque poesin? . . .
> At tu siquid agam, scitabere (si modò saltem
>   Esse putas tanti noscere siquid agam) . . . .

Milton, *Poems*, 1645, Part II, pp. 31-35; CM, I, 206-212.

[To Charles Diodati. . . . When he had written on the Ides of December and asked that if his verses were less good than usual they should be excused, because amid the elegance in which he had been received by his friends he could not, he said, offer the Muses an adequately happy work. He received this answer. . . . But why does your Muse entice out my poetry? . . .

How well you describe the solemn feasts and the gay December and the feasts which greeted the god descending from the sky and the delights and joys of the country in winter and the French wines imbibed by the pleasant firesides! Why do you lament that poetry is absent from wine and feasts? . . . But if you wish to know what I am doing (if indeed you think it so important to know whether I am doing anything). . . .

A free translation is given in Masson, I, 193-194 (226-227). The present text is by the editor.

DECEMBER 25. ELEGY VI TO CHARLES DIODATI; MILTON'S IDEAL OF THE POET; HIS POETIC ACTIVITIES.

Elegia sexta. *Ad Carolum Diodatum ruri commorantem. Qui cum idibus Decemb. scripsisset, & sua carmina excusari postulasset si solito minus essent bona, quòd inter lautitias quibus erat ab amicis exceptus, haud satis felicem operam Musis dare se posse affirmabat, hunc habuit responsum.*

Mitto tibi sanam non pleno ventre salutem,
    Quâ tu distento forte carere potes.
At tua quid nostram prolectat Musa camœnam,
    Nec sinit optatas posse sequi tenebras?
Carmine scire velis quàm te redamémque colámque,
    Crede mihi vix hoc carmine scire queas.
Nam neque noster amor modulis includitur arctis,
    Nec venit ad claudos integer ipse pedes. . . .
At qui bella refert, & adulto sub Jove cælum,
    Heroasque pios, semideosque duces,
Et nunc sancta canit superum consulta deorum,
    Nunc latrata fero regna profunda cane,
Ille quidem parcè Samii pro more magistri
    Vivat, & innocuos præbeat herba cibos;
Stet prope fagineo pellucida lympha catillo,
    Sobriaque è puro pocula fonte bibat.
Additur huic scelerisque vacans, & casta juventus,
    Et rigidi mores, & sine labe manus.
Qualis veste nitens sacrâ, & lustralibus undis
    Surgis ad infensos augur iture Deos. . . .

At tu si quid agam, scitabere (si modò saltem
    Esse putas tanti noscere siquid agam)
Paciferum canimus cælesti semine regem,
    Faustaque sacratis sæcula pacta libris,
 Vagitumque Dei, & stabulantem paupere tecto
    Qui suprema suo cum patre regna colit.
Stelliparumque polum, modulantesque æthere turmas,
    Et subitò elisos ad sua fana Deos.
Dona quidem dedimus Christi natalibus illa,
    Illa sub auroram lux mihi prima tulit.
Te quoque pressa manent patriis meditata cicutis,
    Tu mihi, cui recitem, judicis instar eris.

Milton, *Poems*, 1645, Part II, pp. 31-35; Mackellar, pp. 96 ff.; CM, I, 206-215.

[To Charles Diodati staying in the country. When he had written on the Ides of December and asked that if his verses were less good than usual they should be excused, because amid the elegance in which he had been received by his friends he could not, he said, offer the Muses an adequately happy work, he received this answer.

I, with my stomach not full, send you sound health, which you, with distended stomach, may perhaps need. But why does your Muse entice out my poetry, and not allow it to seek the retirement it desires? If you wish to know in verse how I love and cherish you, believe me, you can hardly learn that from this song. For my love is not to be enclosed in rigid measures, nor does it come unimpaired to limping feet. . . .

But the man who speaks of wars and the heaven of the full-grown Jove, and pious heroes, and demi-god leaders of men; the man who now sings the holy counsels of the gods above, and now the subterranean realms guarded by the fierce dog—let *him* live sparely, after the manner of the Samian master, let herbs afford him his innocent diet, let clear water in a beechen cup stand near him, and let him drink sober draughts from a pure fountain! To this be there added a youth chaste and free from guilt, and rigid morals, and hands without stain. Being such, you rise up, glittering in sacred raiment and purified by lustral waters, an augur about to go into the presence of the angry gods. . . .

But if you will know what I am myself doing (if indeed you think it of so much consequence to know if I am doing anything), here is the fact:—We are engaged in singing the heavenly birth of the King of Peace, and the happy age promised by the holy books, and the infant cries and cradling in a manger under a poor roof of that God who rules, with his Father, the kingdom of Heaven, and the sky with the new-sprung star in it, and the ethereal choirs of hymning Angels, and the gods of heathen eld suddenly fleeing to their endangered fanes. This is the gift which we have presented to Christ's natal day. On that very morning, at daybreak, it was first conceived. The verses, which are composed in the vernacular, await your criticism; you shall be the judge to whom I shall recite them.]

Masson, I, 193-194 (226-228) (with additions and modifications by the present editor). The poem whose progress Milton here describes was pretty surely his "On the Morning of Christs Nativity," here filed under the same date.

DECEMBER 25. POEM ON THE NATIVITY.

On the morning of Christs Nativity. Compos'd 1629.
Milton, *Poems*, 1645, p. 1; CM, I, 1.

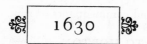

1630

PORTRAIT PAINTED BY DANIEL MYTENS (?).

Mr. Ivan Mavor, Librarian of St. Paul's School in London, kindly wrote to me in 1936, in response to my inquiry, that a picture, said to be a painting of Milton by Daniel Mytens, was bought at a sale at Christie's in 1933 and given to the Library. He had no further information about its authenticity.

A photograph and a description of it appear in the London *Times* for May 13, 1933, p. 16. A few additional details are furnished by C. W. B. in *Notes and Queries*, CLXIV (1944), 389. The picture is of a young man in his early twenties (hence my assignment of it to the year 1630). It had previously been in the collections of C. F. Huth and Frederick Seymour Clarke. It bears no signature.

LETTERS FROM FELLOWS AT CAMBRIDGE.

. . . that more then ordinary favour and respect which I found above any of my equals at the hands of those curteous and learned men, the Fellowes of that Colledge wherein I spent some yeares: who at my parting, after I had taken two degrees, as the manner is, signifi'd many wayes, how much better it would content them that I would stay; as by many Letters full of kindnesse and loving respect both before that time, and long after I was assur'd of their singuler good affection towards me.

Milton, *An Apology Against a Pamphlet*, 1642, p. 12; CM, III, 297; CM, XVIII, 526. This reference is put under 1630 because Milton mentions it as beginning "before that time" (i.e., his attaining the Master's degree in 1632). The correspondence appears to have extended for a number of years afterwards, probably up to and beyond the date of the *Apology*. Masson (II, 401) suggests that some of the writers may have been Thomas Bainbridge, Joseph Meade, Edward King, Nathaniel Tovey, and Henry More. No such letters have survived.

SKETCHES OUT A BOOK ON THE ART OF LOGIC (?).

Speaking of Milton's *Art of Logic*, Masson (VI, 685) suggests: "It may even have been sketched out in Milton's university days at Cambridge, between his taking his B.A. degree and his passing as M.A." This hypothesis is supported by G. C. Moore-Smith in the *Review of English Studies*, XIII (1937), 335-340. The book is based on the writings of Peter Ramus and commentators on him.

FATHER RETIRES TO HORTON.

[The elder Milton stated in 1637:] long since hee gave over his trade.

Milton's father's answer to the bill of Sir Thomas Cotton, dated April 13, 1637, *q.v.* The year 1630 is of course an approximation to the exact date, which cannot be determined without further evidence.

. . . out of a moderation, not usual with such as have tasted the sweets of gain, and perhaps naturally inclin'd rather to a retir'd life by his addiction to Music (for his skill in which hee stands registred among the Composers of his time) hee gave over his trade, and went to live in the Country.

The "earliest" biography, ff. 140-140v; Darbishire, p. 18.

MADRIGALS BY FATHER AND OTHERS.

Bernard Quaritch's *General Catalogue of Books*, London, 1877, p. 142, lists as No. 1427: "MADRIGALS, etc. by JOHN MILTON (father of the poet), Martin Pearson, Tho. Tompkins, Tho. Lupo, John Coprario, Richard Deering, William Simmes, George Kirby, John Ward, and others, 3 parts, obl. 8vo. (Cantus, Tenor, Bassus), *in the original calf, £5 about* 1630." Nothing further is known of this volume.

BEGINS TO KEEP A POETIC NOTEBOOK.

Although we cannot date it with any precision, the so-called Trinity or Cambridge Manuscript must have been begun somewhere near this year. Individually, the poems contained in it must have been composed over a period of at least twenty years, if not more, the latest being probably his sonnet to the memory of his second wife. The main entry for this book is given below under the year 1640.

COMPOSES POEM ON SHAKESPEARE.

An Epitaph on the admirable Dramaticke Poet, VV SHAKE-SPEARE.

Mr. William Shakespeares Comedies, Histories, and Tragedies, 1632 [The Second Folio], on the leaf following sig. A4; Milton, *Poems*, 1645, p. 27; CM, I, 31. On the bibliography of this poem, see Robert Metcalf Smith, *The Variant Issues of Shakespeare's Second Folio and Milton's First Published English Poem*, Lehigh University Publications, Volume II, 1928. There is some discussion of its sources in Heinrich Mutschmann, "Sources of Milton's *On Shakespeare*," *Further Studies Concerning the Origin of Paradise Lost*, 1934, pp. 47 ff., and in Theodore Spencer, "Shakespeare and Milton," *MLN*, LIII (1938), 366-367. The title given here is that used in the 1632 edition. The date comes from the title in Milton's *Poems* of 1645: "On Shakespear. 1630." Todd (1826, VI, 87) pointed out that there were many resemblances between Milton's poem and the epitaph to Sir Thomas Stanley sometimes attributed to Shakespeare.

ROSE DOWNER ENTREATS MILTON'S FATHER FOR HER MONEY.

[Milton's father and his partner Thomas Bower paid her none of the money due from her loan to Ewens and Keymer] nor any interest for the same but fedd her with faire wordǫ and promises albeit she in the interim called for her money of the said Milton and Bower diuers times . . . and your said Oratrixe finding herselfe deluded by them from time to time . . . .

Public Record Office, C2 Charles I/D39/47 (Rose Downer's bill, April 26, 1631); French, *Milton in Chancery*, p. 239. The date is hazy, but in the context it seems as if at least some of the visits here alluded to must have come later than 1629, when the regular process of the loan seems to have been going fairly smoothly. The reader would do well to read the whole bill (below under date of April 26, 1631) to fit this quotation into its setting. Probably Mrs. Downer was a frequent visitor both in this year and earlier.

[Richard Sheratt] well remembereth that some shorte tyme before this suite began in this hō^{ble}. Cor^t that he this dep^t had some conferrence wth the sd dēf^t Bowre in the p^{r}sence of the Cōmplt concerning the said money And saith that he this dep^t did charge the said Bowre with bad dealing and told him he offered but hard measure to the Cōmplt. . . .

Public Record Office, Chancery Depositions, C24/574/40 (deposition of Richard Sheratt, September 26, 1631); French, *Milton in Chancery*, p. 254.

EASTER TERM. FATHER AND HIS PARTNER BOWER ALLEGEDLY OFFER JOHN COTTON £2,000 FOR HIS INVESTMENTS.

. . . the sayd John Milton and Tho: Bower . . . did by ye practise & direcciō off one Thomas Holchar an attorney at law Who was vsed by ye s^d John Cotton in suing bonds forbeare to bring him in either the principall or most part of the interest of the said somes pretending that the partyes to whom the sayd somes were lett out were not sufficient By wch practice of deteyning ye s^d intrest money they did cause ye s^d John Cottō to beleeue that both principall & interest were desperate . . . & und^r these p^{r}tences so ǫswade ye s^d John Cottō to accept 2000^{li} fro ye s^d Miltō & Bow^r or one off them for ye s^d principal detǫ wch amounted to 3600^{li} . . . .

Sir Thomas Cotton's bill of May 28, 1636, *q.v.*

. . . the said John Milton from tyme to tyme calling the said debto^{rs} and sending after them to most of their habitacōns and not obteyning ether principall or interest the said Mr Milton did in Easter tearme one thousand six hundred and thirty acquaint John Cotton therewith wherevpon the said John Cotton as this defendant beleeueth did make enquiry after the said Debto^{rs} and did then offer to sell and assigne all the said debtǫ vnto the said John Milton for one thousand and ffyue hundred poundǫ . . . after such tyme as the said John Milton had refused the said bargayne . . . And att last the said John Cotton and your subiect by and with the consent of the now Compltē did mutually and reciprocally to and wth each other condiscend and come to an agreement by word of mouth to the effect followeing (that is to say) that this defend^t shou'ld Jmēdiately satisfy and pay two thousand poundǫ to the said John Cotton and that this defendant should haue the three thousand and six hundred powndes wth interest then due for the same . . . .

Thomas Bower's answer to Cotton's bill, April 8, 1637, *q.v.*

. . . the said John Cotton in his life tyme . . . did voluntarily make an offer to this defend^t. to accept of Two Thousand poundes in liew of all such monneys as were lent or mannaged for him at this defend^{te}. shopp . . . wch this defend^t. did vtterly refuse . . . this defend^t. hath heard that the said Thomas Bower did ioyne with one Thomas Holker an Attorney in the Common pleas whoe procured certaine moneys of S^r. Thomas Middleton late Alderman of London wch were paid to the said John Cotton . . . And this defend^t. sayeth although hee and the said other defend^t. Bower were Copartners in the Trade of a Scrivener yett they were never partners in or concerninge the said bargayne . . . .

Milton's answer to Bower's bill, April 13, 1637, *q.v.*

MARCH 28 (?) POEM ON CHRIST'S PASSION.

The Passion

Milton, *Poems*, 1645, p. 16; CM, 1, 23. Masson (1, 197 [230]) regards it as "the beginning of an anniversary ode intended for the Easter of 1630 (March 28) by way of sequel to the odes on the Nativity and the Circumcision."

[After 8 stanzas totaling 56 lines, Milton breaks off with the note:] *This Subject the Author finding to be above the yeers he had, when he wrote it, and nothing satisfi'd with what was begun, left it unfinisht.*

APRIL 9. FATHER DEPOSES IN PECK-RANDOLPH CHANCERY SUIT.

9: Aprilis 1630.	Ex pte Christopheri Pecke et Susannæ vxoris ejus q'tes, Cont' Edmudū Randolph
6. Caroli Reg'	Armī Defte testes exāte p RI. CHILD in Comettī exoñ.

John Milton. of the prish of All hallowes in Bredstreete London. scriuener of the age of 67. years or thereabouts sworne & exēd deposeth & s^th.

1. That hee doth know. Edmound Randolph. esq^r named for defend^t in the suite & hath: seene the Complt Christopher Pecke but hath little knowledge of him, but Susan his wife the other complt this dpon^t s^th hee Doth not know:

2. That hee doth know. that John Collins of Lincolnes Jnn in the Countye of midlesex. esq^r. did hertofore p^rtend to bee seised of certeine howses in Scroopes Courte in the prish of s^t Andrewes Holburne London; but what money hee pd for the same or what they were worth when the Defend^ts bought the same this dpon^t s^th hee knoweth not; nor doth he know what money or rent the s^d defend^t was to pay vnto the s^d John Collins for the same; howbeit hee s^th that hee doth remember that about 8 or 9 years. sithence hee this depōn^t did offer the s^d John Collins. money for the s^d houses, wch as hee taketh itt was about 12 years pchase. & soe much hee would then haue given for the same; & what the particular rents of the s^d howses. then were this dpon^t. s^th he now remembreth not, but as he taketh itt all the s^d houses. were letten for about 120^l p anñ; & this is as much as hee cann depose to the questions of this Jnt for he s^th hee doth not well remember how much rent S^r. Henrye Colt Knt pd for one of the s^d houses. but as he thinketh hee pd 45^l by yeare;

nor doth hee remember what money Docto^r Poe. & the rest of the creditors of the s^d Collins receiued;

[*Signed*] Jo: milton:

Public Record Office, Chancery Depositions, C24/566/73; French, *Milton in Chancery*, pp. 399-400.

[April 9, 1630, the sixth year of King Charles. On behalf of Christopher Peck and his wife Susanna, plaintiffs, against Edmund Randolph, gentleman, defendant, witnesses examined by Richard Child in Co. Exeter.]

APRIL 16. FRIEND CHARLES DIODATI MATRICULATES AT GENEVA.

Carolus Deodatus Anglus natu April. 16. 1630.

"Matricula Studiosorum S. Theologiæ in Geneuensi Academia ab Anno MDCXII," MS fr. 141c (Inv. 345) in the Bibliothèque Publique et Universitaire de Genève, fol. 9^v. I take this reference from the article in which it was first published: Donald C. Dorian, "Charles Diodati at Geneva," *PMLA*, LIX (1944), 589-591. Professor Dorian also gives several later entries from the same record, showing that Diodati remained in attendance at the Academy (later University) of Geneva until at least September, 1631. Professor Dorian therefore points out that we need to revise our previous notions that Diodati entered immediately after graduation into medicine, and that we should also perhaps reconsider the dating of Milton's Elegy VI and Sonnet IV and perhaps of all the Italian sonnets.

MAY 12. FATHER ARRANGES MARBURY-COTTON BOND.

Mr Marbury & oth^{rs} p obl' Dat' xij^o Maij 1630 . . . 100^{li}

Thomas Bower's schedule of Cotton's bonds made out by himself and Milton's father; see below under date of November 25, 1630. The original bond has not been found.

. . . Mr Marbury and others by bond dated the Twelueth [of] May one thousand six [hundred and thirty one hund]red pound$_e$ principall debt.

Sir Thomas Cotton's bill; see below under date of May 28, 1636.

MAY 20. FATHER ARRANGES REED-COTTON BOND.

Mr Reed & oth^{rs} p obl' Dat' xx^o Maij 1630 . . . 100^{li}

Thomas Bower's schedule of Cotton's bonds made out by himself and

Milton's father; see below under date of November 25, 1630. The original bond has not been found.

. . . M^r [Reed] & others by bond dated y^e [Twentieth of May] One thowsand six hundred & Thirtie One hundred pound℈ principall debt.

Sir Thomas Cotton's bill; see below under date of May 28, 1636.

JUNE. DOWNER-WARING BOND PAID, PRESUMABLY AT FATHER'S SHOP.

. . . she the said Complaynant Did lend vnto one Master Waring Thirtie pound℈ at Jnterest for Six moneth℈, and soe continued the same till about the moneth of June One thowsand Six hundred and Thirtie . . . .

Public Record Office, C2 Charles I/D39/47 (Bower's answer to Downer, May 3, 1631); French, *Milton in Chancery*, p. 244. Though not specifically so stated here, the place of settlement of the bond was probably Milton's shop, since it was probably originally drawn there, and since Bower speaks of it as a piece of business which he knows at first hand. We may also reasonably assume that interest had been regularly paid on this loan (*i.e.*, on December 10, 1628, June 10, 1629, December 10, 1629, and finally on the day of settlement); but since Bower does not mention such payments, they are not included in their proper places in this record.

JUNE 10. EDWARD KING IS GIVEN A FELLOWSHIP WHICH MILTON MAY HAVE DESIRED AND EXPECTED.

To our Trusty & well beloved Dr Bainbridge, Master of Christ's Coll: in our university of Cambr.
Charles R:

Trusty & well beloved, we greet you well. Whereas We are given to understand, that the Fellowship of M^r. Andrew Sandelandis of your Coll., is shortly to be made void & being well ascertained, both of ye present sufficiency & future hopes of a young scholer Edward King now B:A:, We out of our Princly care, that those hopeful part℈ in him, may receive cherishing & encouragement, are graciously pleas'd so far to express our Royal intention toward℈ him, as herby to will & require you, that when ye same Fellowship shall become void, you do presently admit the sd: Edw: King into yᵉ same, notwithstanding any Statute, Ordinance, or Constitution to yᵉ contrary. And for yᵉ doing thereof these shall be both a sufficient warrant unto you, & we shall account it an acceptable service. Given under our Signet at our manor of Sᵗ James Jun: 10ᵗʰ: Jn yᵉ sixth year of our Reign. 1630. /

Fato cessit, aquis submersus, 4: Jd: Sextil: an: 1637 V: Justa obsequies of Edw: King Latin & English, printed 1638.

[Marginal note:] Edw: King patriâ Hunting: consecratus Epūs: Elphinensis Dec: 1611: obiit Mar: 8: 1638. Edvardum hunc a sacro Fonte suscepit.

Baker's notes on Christ's College, British Museum, Harleian MS. 7036, p. 220; Masson, I, 205-206 (238-239). Masson assumes, as have numerous students of Milton, that Milton both desired and expected to receive this appointment instead of King. But there is no actual proof of such a feeling, any more than there is of his having been the logical candidate for the appointment.

[He yielded to fate, submerged in the waves, the fourth day before the Ides of the sixth month (August 10), in the year 1637. See *Justa*, etc.

Edward King, a native of Huntingdon, consecrated bishop of Elphin in December, 1611, deceased March 8, 1638, received this Edward at the sacred font (*i.e.*, was his godfather).]

JUNE 17. FINISHES (OR BEGINS) FIRST READING OF PINDAR'S POEMS.

[After the "finis" of Milton's copy of Pindar is written:] Δοξὰ τῳ δεῳ Jun: 17 1630 et Sept: 28. 1630.

See note on Milton's Pindar above under date of November 15, 1629.

[Glory to God! June 17, 1630, and September 28, 1630.]

AUGUST. NEPHEW EDWARD PHILLIPS BORN.

Edward Phillips was 15 year old August 1645.

Milton's note, in his own hand, among the entries in his family Bible, British Museum, Add. MS. 32,310; Darbishire, p. 336.

EDWARD PHILLIPS, son of a father of both his names by Anne his Wife, dau. of Joh. Milton, and Sister to Joh.

Milton the defender of the murder of k. Charles I. was born in the Strand near Charing Cross within the Liberty of Westminster in *Aug.* 1630.

Wood, *Athenae Oxonienses*, ed. Bliss, IV (1820), 759.

SEPTEMBER 28. FINISHES (SECOND?) READING OF PINDAR'S POEMS.

[After the "finis" of Milton's copy of Pindar is written:] Δοξὰ τῷ δεῳ Jun: 17 1630 et Sept: 28. 1630.

See note on Milton's Pindar above under date of November 15, 1629.

[Glory to God! June 17, 1630, and September 28, 1630.]

NOVEMBER. FATHER'S PARTNER BOWER AGREES TO BUY JOHN COTTON'S INVESTMENTS.

... the said John Cotton and especially the Cōmp^lt in Mayster Cottons behalfe in Michaellmas tearme one thousand six hundred and thirty ... did entertayne treaty and comunicacon to and wth this defendt about assigneing the said Dēbtȝ of three thousand and six hundred poundȝ for ready money, And att last the said John Cotton and your subiect by and with the consent of the now Compltē did mutually and reciprocally to and wth each other condiscend and come to an agreement by word of mouth to the effect followeing (that is to say) that this defend^t shou'ld Jmediately satisfy and pay two thousand poundȝ to the said John Cotton and that this defendant should haue the three thousand and six hundred powndes wth interest then due for the same to his vse. ...

Thomas Bower's answer to Sir Thomas Cotton's bill, April 8, 1637; French, *Milton in Chancery*, p. 267. Michaelmas term fell for the most part in the month of November.

NOVEMBER. FATHER'S PARTNER BOWER PAYS JOHN COTTON £2,000 FOR INVESTMENTS.

... this defendant in Michaellmas tearme one thousand six hundred and thirty did pay and satisfy vnto the said John Cotton or his assignes the full some of two Thousand poundȝ ... the said John Cotton did deliuer vnto this defendant all and euery the said Bondǫ for the payment of three thousand and six hundred poundǫ with interest . . . And the said John Milton was not present at the bargayne made or att the payment of all or any of the said two thousand powndǫ, or payd anye of the said two thousand powndǫ or had any thinge to doe therewith. . . .

Thomas Bower's answer to Cotton's bill, April 8, 1637, *q.v.* The receipt is dated November 25, 1630, *q.v.*

NOVEMBER 25. FATHER'S PARTNER THOMAS BOWER GIVES RECEIPT TO JOHN COTTON FOR NUMEROUS BONDS PREPARED FOR COTTON AT MILTON'S SHOP.

The Schedule of the Principall debtǫ

Mr Mort & others by bond dated the vith of Septemb^r 1628	100^{li}
Mr Welby & oth^{rs} by bond dated the viith of Novemb^r 1627	200^{li}
The Lord Strange & oth^{rs} p obl' Dat' vii° Novembr' 1626	300^{li}
Mr Marbury & oth^{rs} p obl' Dat' xij° Maij 1630	100^{li}
Mr Bold & oth^{rs} p obl^{con} Dat' xiiij^{to} April' 1625	100^{li}
Mr Lea & oth^{rs} p obl' Dat' xiij° Maij 1621	100^{li}
Sr Ric' Molineux & oth^{rs} p obl' Dat' xvij° Maij 1623	100^{li}
Sr Wm Norres & oth^{rs} p obl' Dat' xviij° Novembr' 1626..	100^{li}
Mr Wm Welby & oth^{rs} p obl' Dat' [?] Novembr' 1629	100^{li}
Mr Bannester & oth^{rs} p obl' Dat' xxj° Maij 1623	100^{li}
Mr Sherfeild & oth^{rs} p obl' Dat' xxvj° Junij 1629	100^{li}
Mr Ewens & oth^{rs} p obl' Dat' xxix° Maij 1628................	100^{li}
Mr Vaudray & oth^{rs} p obl' Dat' xxx° Novembr' 1627......	100^{li}
S^r ffrancis Leigh & oth^{rs} p obl' Dat' vltimo Novembr' 1624	100^{li}
Sr Robt Heath & oth^{rs} p obl' Dat' j Decembr' 1620	100^{li}
Mr Leigh & oth^{rs} p obl' Dat' xij Decembr' 1626	050^{li}
Sr Kenelme Digby & oth^{rs} p obl' Dat' vij° Augustj 1626	200^{li}
Mr Dabridgecourt & oth^{rs} p obl' Dat' xvij° Decembr' 1627	100^{li}

Mʳ Reed & othʳˢ p obl' Dat' xx° Maij 1630 .... 100ˡⁱ

Mʳ Prewet & othʳˢ p obl' Dat' xxj° Decembr' 1627 .... 100ˡⁱ

Bonds in suite

Mʳ Erdiswick & others p obl' xj° Maij 1624 .... 200ˡⁱ

Sʳ Wᵐ Sandys & othʳˢ p obl' Dat' xviij° Maij 1620 .... 100ˡⁱ

Mʳ Charnock & othʳˢ p obl' Dat' xix° Novembr' 1620 .... 200ˡⁱ

Mʳ Chetwode & othʳˢ p obl' Dat' xxvij° Novembr'
1623 .... 100ˡⁱ

Mʳ Clopton & othʳˢ p obl' Dat' xxj° Junij 1626 .... 100ˡⁱ

Sʳ Geo: Horsey & othʳˢ p obl' Dat' vᵗᵒ Julij 1627 .... 100ˡⁱ

Sʳ Geo: Horsey & othʳˢ p obl' Dat' xix° Decembr' 1626 .. 100ˡⁱ

Mʳ Veale & othʳˢ p obl' Dat' xxiiij ᵗᵒ Maij 1626 .... 100ˡⁱ

Mʳ Carrent & othʳˢ p obl' Dat' xxviij° Novembr' 1622 .... 100ˡⁱ

Mʳ Blacker & othʳˢ p obl' Dat' xj° Octobr' 1627 .... 100ˡⁱ

Mʳ Rodney & othʳˢ p obl' Dat' xij° Decembr' 1626 .... 050ˡⁱ

xxvᵗᵒ Die Novembr' 1630

Rec' the same day & yeare of John Cotton of Londoñ Esqʳᵉ all
the particular bondƷ above in this schedule mencõned wᶜʰ are all
that are due at Mʳ Miltons shop in Bread streete J say recᵈ all
the said seũall bondƷ

p Tho: Bower

British Museum, Cottonian Charters 1/5/4; French, *Milton in
Chancery*, pp. 257-258. Each item in this list has been entered in its
proper chronological place above as a part of the activity of Milton's
father or at least of his shop.

DECEMBER 12. RECEIVES INTEREST PAYMENT FROM
RICHARD POWELL.

. . . the growing Jnterest for the forbearance of the said
Principall debt was for some yeares then following likewise payd
And soe continued to bee paid vntill June Jn the yeare of our
Lord One Thousand six hundred ffortie and ffower. . . .

From Milton's answer to Elizabeth Ashworth, February 22, 1653/4,
q.v.

HAS A WATCH INSCRIBED WITH HIS NAME.

[This watch bears the inscription:] Ioanni Miltoni, 1631.

This watch is now in the British Museum, to which it was presented in 1862 from the collection of Sir Charles Fellowes by his son. It was for a time in America. The facts about it are given in E. J. Wood, *Curiosities of Clocks and Watches*, London, 1866, pp. 269-270. There is a note on it by Sir Charles's great-nephew Alfred Fellows in the London *Times*, September 3, 1936, p. 13e. It is mentioned in CM, XVIII, 583.

Edith C. Batho tells an amusing anecdote about it in her *The Later Wordsworth*, 1933, p. 106. Admitting that the story may be apocryphal, she tells how Milton's watch was once passed around an assembly in which Wordsworth was present; after it had made its rounds, Wordsworth quietly passed his own around after it.

Dr. Williamson (*Milton Tercentenary*, 1908, p. 160) says that a water color drawing of it was exhibited at Christ's College in 1908.

BUYS AND ANNOTATES ARATUS's "PHENOMENA."

[Title:] Αρατου Σολεως Φαινομενα [Paris, 1559].

[Inscribed on a flyleaf in Milton's hand:] Jo: Milton pre: 2ˢ - 6ᵈ. 1631.

British Museum, press-mark C.60.1.7; French, "The Autographs of John Milton," #74; CM, XVIII, 325, 568. There are facsimiles of some sections in Sotheby, facing p. 98. Milton wrote some marginal notes in this volume.

WRITES "L'ALLEGRO."
L'Allegro.

Milton, *Poems*, 1645, p. 30; CM, I, 34. The date of this poem is very uncertain, having been placed anywhere from 1630 to 1634. For further discussion see Hanford, *A Milton Handbook*, 1946, pp. 148 ff.

Mr. A. H. J. Baines ("The Topography of 'L'Allegro,'" *Notes and Queries*, CLXXXVIII, 1945, 68) attempts to show that the scenery described in the poem is that of the Chiltern summits, about two hours' ride from Horton, and that Milton spent the long vacation of 1631 there. He thinks this region is the "suburban home" of Prolusion 7. Fanny Byse (in *Milton on the Continent*, London and Lausanne, 1903, pp. xi-xiv and 15-77) attempts to demonstrate that Milton wrote this poem and "Il Penseroso" during his European travels, that the scenery "sound[s] like" the Tower of Duin near Bex in Dent du Midi, that the lady whose eyes rain bright influence was probably the Marquise de Rambouillet or Mlle. de Bourbon, and that other details are taken from the Simplon Pass. The argument is more romantic than convincing. Other students have located these twin poems in Cambridge, Horton, or London, or have thought them mere literary exercises without any actual scene. No confidence can be placed in any of these interpretations.

WRITES "IL PENSEROSO."

Il Penseroso.

Milton, *Poems*, 1645, p. 37; CM, I, 40. Probably written at about the same time as "L'Allegro," *q.v.* In addition to various other localities picked for this poem and "L'Allegro" (*q.v.*), Professor Donald L. Clark (*John Milton at St. Paul's School*, Columbia, 1948, p. 35) associates the "cloisters pale" of lines 156 ff. with St. Paul's School in Milton's early attendance there.

WRITES "ARCADES."

Arcades. Part of an Entertainment presented to the Countess Dowager of *Darby* at *Harefield*, by som Noble persons of her Family, who appear on the Scene in pastoral habit, moving toward the seat of State, with this Song. . . .

Milton, Cambridge Manuscript, p. 1; *Poems*, 1645, p. 51; CM, I, 72. The date is as uncertain as that of "L'Allegro" and "Il Penseroso." The poem and the family for which it was written are discussed at some length in Todd, 1826, v, 154 ff., and in Masson, I, 541 ff. (578 ff.) Willa M. Evans, in *Henry Lawes*, New York, 1941, p. 64, thinks it was presented before June 28, 1630, since King Charles began his summer progress on that day. She also thinks that Lawes planned, produced, and acted in it. Since he was probably concealed behind a terrace, she identifies him with the "unseen" "Genius of the Wood" in "Il Penseroso," therefore concluding that that poem was written after "Arcades." She conjectures too that Lady Alice Egerton sang Spenser's eighth sonnet after the performance of the masque, and that that is why this sonnet appears in Lawes's autographed manuscript, now in the possession of the Misses Church of Beaconsfield. She reproduces this poem in facsimile on p. 67.

JANUARY. VERSES ON HOBSON, CAMBRIDGE CARRIER.

[1] On the University Carrier who sickn'd in the time of his vacancy, being forbid to go to *London*, by reason of the Plague.

[2] Another on the same.

[3] *Vpon old* Hobson *the Carrier of* Cambridge.

Anon., *A Banquet of Jests*, 1640, pp. 129 ff.; Milton, *Poems*, 1645, pp. 28 ff.; CM, I, 32 ff.; CM, XVIII, 349, 359, 584, 590. All three poems are found in the *Banquet* and are reprinted in CM. Until recently only the first two have been thought of as Milton's compositions, but the evidence adduced by William R. Parker in *MLR*, XXXI (1936), 395-402, and summarized in CM, XVIII, 584, 590, makes it seem likely that the third also may be by Milton. In addition to the *Banquet* one or more of the poems appeared also in *Wit Restor'd*, 1658, and in several manuscript collections. Variant readings are given in CM, XVIII, 584, 590. As to the date, Hobson died on January 1, 1630/1; his will, proved February 1, 1630/1, is filed as 17 St. John in the Prerogative Court of Canterbury, London. See Masson, I, 207 ff. (240 ff.). All the Hobson verses which have been discovered are reprinted and discussed illuminatingly by G. Blakemore Evans in "Milton and the Hobson Poems," *Modern Language Quarterly*, IV (1943), 281 ff.

FEBRUARY 15. BROTHER CHRISTOPHER ADMITTED TO CHRIST'S COLLEGE.

Feb 15° 1630/31 Christopherus Milton Londinensis filius Johannis literis institutus sub M^{ro} Gillio publico gymnasio Paulino, admissus est pensionarius minor, aetatis suae 15° sub patrocinio M^{ri}. Tovey

Solvit p ingressm 10^s

Admission books, Christ's College, Cambridge; Masson, I, 210 (243).

[Feb. 15, 1630-31.—Christopher Milton, Londoner, son of John, grounded in letters under Mr. Gill in Paul's public school, was admitted a lesser pensioner, in the 15th year of his age, under the charge of Mr. Tovey. He paid ten shillings for admission.]

The translation is by Masson, except for the last sentence, which is omitted by him and supplied by the present editor.

FEBRUARY 19. NIECE ELIZABETH PHILLIPS BURIED.

[Burials] Feb. [1630/1] . . . 19 . . . Elizabetha Phillips fa. Edwardi et Annae (Ch.).

The Register of St. Martin-in-the-Fields London 1619-1636, ed. J. V. Kitto, 1936 (Publications of the Harleian Society, Vol. LXVI), p. 258. I have not seen the original parish record.

[On February 19, 1630/1, Elizabeth Phillips, daughter of Edward and Anne, was buried in the chancel.]

MARCH 25. FATHER (?) RENTS TWO TENEMENTS ON LONDON BRIDGE.

John Milton for two tenem^{te} demised for 21 yeares from our Ladye daye A°. 1631   x^{li}.

From a list of all the rentals of London Bridge made at Michaelmas, 1632, *q.v.* It is not certain that this John Milton is either the poet or his father, but he may easily be. Lady Day, or the Annunciation, is March 25.

APRIL (?). EPITAPH ON THE MARCHIONESS OF WINCHESTER.

An Epitaph on the Marchioness of *Winchester.*

Milton, *Poems*, 1645, p. 23; CM, I, 28. There is also a manuscript copy of the poem in the British Museum, Sloane MS. 1446, f. 37b; it is collated in CM, I, 425. According to William R. Parker (*Milton's Contemporary Reputation*, p. 9), it bears the contemporary manuscript note: "Jo Milton of Chr: Coll Cambr." The subject of the epitaph was Jane Savage, daughter of Thomas, Viscount of Rock-Savage. The nature and extent of Milton's acquaintance with her or her family is not known. She was the wife of John Paulet, fifth Marquis of Winchester; see Masson, I, 211 (244). See also Todd, 1826, VI, 64.

APRIL 26. FATHER SUED IN CHANCERY BY ROSE DOWNER.

xxvj° die Aprilis 1631/

To the right hō^{ble}. Thomas Lord Coventry Lord Keeper of the
    great Seale of England/

B Henley

Jn all humblenes complayning sheweth vnto yor. good Lo^p. yor. Daylie Oratrixe Rose Downer of London widdowe, That whereas yor. said Oratrixe about fiue Yeares since having in her hand℘ of her owne moneys the greatest pte of her estate being the sūme of ffiftie pound℘ and the same being come to the knowledge of John Milton of London Scrivener he repaired to yor. said Oratrixe about the said time and advised her to put out the said ffiftie pound℘ at interest rather then to imploye it any other wayes, and vsed diuers ℘swasions vnto yor. said Oratrixe that he might haue the putting of it forth telling her that shee should haue good securitie for the payement of the

[228]

same to hir againe, by meanes whereof yor. Oratrixe was drawne
to consent that hir said money should be put forth at interest
and that the said John Milton should haue the benefitt of the
brocage thereof, and of the making of the bondρ for the same,
but yet soe as your said Oratrixe would first know her securitie
and would haue time to consider of the same and to approue or
dissalowe thereof And the said Milton agreed and consented
therevnto, and afterwardρ within a very short time after the
said conference betweene the said John Milton and yor. Oratrixe, he the s[aid John] Milton did nominate vnto yor. said
Oratrixe a Principall and twoe suerties for the having and taking of the said ffiftie poundρ at interest, and your said Oratrixe
having taken advise and consideracōn of the same was willing
that hir said money should be sett forth vpon that securitie,
and willed the said John Milton to prepare the bondρ and take
the securitie and the money should be deliūed, All which was
done accordingly and yor. said Oratrixe was well pleased and
did acc[ept] of the same and afterwardρ. vīzt. in or about the
moneth of June one thousand sixe hundred twenty eight, (the
time being then expired and the said ffiftie poundρ growne due
and payeable) your said Oratrixe repaired to [the] said John
Milton and desired him to call in the said money declaring vnto
him hir urgent occasion to vse the same, and to imploye it otherwise, and the said John Milton according to the declaracōn and
request of your said Oratrixe did call in the said money out of
the said securities handρ, and did desire your said Oratrixe to
leaue the obligacōn in his handρ and he would receiue the money
for your said Oratrixe and deliuer vp the said obligacōn vpon
receipt of the said money and agreed to bee answereable for it,
And your said Oratrixe therevpon did deliuer vp the said obligacōn to the said John Milton and did entrust him to receiue
her money for her vpon his faithfull promise to pay it over
forthwith after vnto your said Oratrixe, and therevpon the said
John Milton receaved the said ffiftie poundρ and interest and
having gotten the same into his handρ did leaue the same as he
nowe p'tendρ in the possession of his then servant Thomas

Bower to the end the same should be paid over to your said
Oratrixe for supplie of hir occasions which was the mayne end
of calling in the said money. And yor. said Oratrixe further
sheweth vnto your good Lordshipp that ymediately vīzt the
next day after the said ffiftie poundɋ was paid as aforesaid vnto
the handɋ of the said John Milton or vnto the handɋ of the said
Thomas Bower or some other by his the said John Miltons appointment and direccōn, your said Oratrixe repaired to the
dwelling house of the said John Milton in Breadstreete in London to the end to have had and receaved the said money to furnish her occasions and there demaunded the said money but finding not the said John Milton then at home the said Thomas
Bower did signifie vnto yor. said Oratrixe that he had the money
in his the said Bowers owne possession and in his deske and your
said Oratrixe requiring him to pay the same vnto her, he the
said Bower refused soe to doe albeit he knewe her vse and neces-
sitie of the same, telling her that he thought she would put it
out againe, and soe deferred the payment thereof, whereat your
said Oratrixe being very much moved grew very angrie with
the said Bower and then the said Milton came in and bade his
man pay the money to your said Oratrixe bidding her doe with
it what she would and seemed in shewe to be much offended
that the said Bower should offer to withhold the said money
from your said Oratrixe, but yet with such gesture and subtile
cariage as your said Oratrixe did plainely perceiue that it was a
meere confederacie and a combinacōn betweene them to deteyne
her money from her, And your said Oratrixe being much discontented about this matter aswell for that she had not present
meanes to goe through with her busines, as also that she sus-
pected she was in danger to loose hir money and to be defrauded
betweene the Scrivener and his man was inforced to goe home
without her money and the next morning after your said Oratrixe had bene with the said Milton and his man vīzt in or about
the tenth day of June 1628 the said Milton or Bower by the
handɋ of one other of his the said Miltons servantɋ sent to your
said Oratrixe to his house an obligacōn beareing date that day

of the Penall sumē of One hundred poundӡ wherein twoe persons were bound to your said Oratrixe by the names of Mathew
Ewen and William Keymer esquires condicōned for the payement to your said Oratrixe of the sumē of ffiftie and twoe poundӡ
the twelueth day of December then next enseweing at the said
Miltons house in Breadstreete aforesaid, which bond was sealed
by the said supposed obligators as the said Milton and his servantӡ pretend in the presence of the said John Milton Thomas
Bower and James ffisher And the said ffisher or one other of the
said Miltons servantӡ presenting the said obligacōn to yor. said
Oratrixe at your said Oratrixes house she required of him what
it was and he answered her, a bond for her money meaning the
ffiftie poundӡ, that was in the said Milton or his man Bowers
hand as aforesaid, and she saying that she had occasion for her
money and would not haue it any longer at interest and therefore she had called it in, the said ffisher replied that she could
haue but good securitie for her money and there it was, and cast
the bond to your said Oratrixe and depted but she refused to
take it being taken without her consent, and your said Oratrixe
repaired to the said Milton and told him that she would not
accept of the said bond for that she was then to vse her money
and the suerties were men vnknowne to your Oratrixe, but must
haue her money in for present vse whereto he said the securitie
was good and he would see her paid her money and soe relyeing
therevpon she was driven to trie her frendӡ to borrowe moneys
for her owne buisines expecting payement of her money from
the said Milton and Bower and noe other and renouncing the
other pretended securitie noīated in the said Obligacōn for that
they were men not knowne to Your Oratrix and whom she yet
neuer sawe and dwelt farre remote in Somersetshire and were
vtterly disliked by yor. said Oratrixe, and at the first six moneths
end the said Bower being then the said Miltons man entreated
yor Oratrixe to forbeare the said money one halfe Yeare more
and promised her that his Master and he would paye in the said
ffiftie poundӡ & the interest to Your said Oratrixe at the end of
the then next six moneths followeing wherevpon she was pa-

tient till that sixe monethes end and then the money not coming
in she addressed herselfe to the said Milton for it whoe entreated her to sue the bond, yet promised neuertheless to be
her paymaster himselfe But soe it is right hō^{ble} that the said
Milton and Bower knewe and perceived that your poore Oratrixe was an ignorant poore old woeman and taking advantage
thereof, or in hope of her death combined togeather vtterly to
defraude your said Oratrixe of her money and paid not the
same nor any pte thereof at the end of the said second sixe
monethes nor at any time since nor any interest for the same but
fedd her with faire wordę and promises albeit she in the interim
called for her money of the said Milton and Bower diuers
times, insoemuch as the said money is still whollie oweing to
your said Oratrixe by the said Milton and Bower and your said
Oratrixe finding herselfe deluded by them from time to time
and pressing for satisfaccon they the said Milton and Bower in
conclusion declared that she must stick to her bond and get payement as she could, albeit she neuer assented to the said latter
putting of it forth nor was privie therevnto, nor accepted the
said bond for hir securitie. But relied whollie vpon the securitie
promises and agreementę of the said Milton and his man, and
therefore she hath long since offered and is still readie to make
over the said bond to them, But the said Milton and Bower haue
refused the same and doe nowe pretend that what promise so-
ever they made at the first to yor. Oratrixe yet since (she had the
bond which was cast to hir as aforesaid without her acceptance)
they hold themselues to be freed from the same against which
subtile and vniust practize she humblie praieth releife according to conscience Sheweing further that at that verie instant
when the said Ewen and Keymer became bound in the said
obligacōn the said Ewen and Keymer or one of them were or
was much indebted to the said Milton or some others which he
delt for, and that the said Ewen was then fallen into decay and
was vpon sale of his landę which were not competent to pay his
debtę as the said Milton and Bower then knewe, and that at that
time he the said Ewen did obscure himselfe, And that none or

very little of the said ffiftie poundꝑ came to the handꝑ of him
or the said Keymer, but was deteyned and defalked by the said
Milton to supplie and satisfie debtꝑ or interest to the said Milton
or others of his ffreindꝑ clientꝑ and acquaintance and that the
said ffiftie poundꝑ was enforced from your said Oratrixe without
M.ʳ Ewens privitie & consent or request but subtillie by the said
Milton to hedge in some despate debt or interest of the said
Ewens Jn tender consideracōn whereof and to the end the said
Milton and Bower may be compelled to satisfie the said ffiftie
poundꝑ and damages to your said Oratrixe, And forasmuch as
yo.ʳ said Oratrixe is vtterlie remediles by the strict rules of the
comōn lawes of this Realme to recouer her said money of the
said Milton and Bower or any other, and cañot make such precise
proofe of theire promises and agreement aforesaid as the said
lawes require but hopeth that the said Milton and Bower vpon
theyre Oathes will not denye the truth of the premisses, and to
the end, the same may be examined and that the said Milton and
Bower may sett downe and declare vpon theire answere to this
complaint whither Yo.ʳ Oratrixe did not call for her money in
from the form.ʳ securities, and whither they or either of them
received the same, and after put it forth againe to the said Ewen
and Keymer whither Yo.ʳ Oratrixe was privie or assenting thereto, whither she did not require her mony in, at what tyme the
said Milton or Bower had the same in their or one of their
handꝑ, and what promises and agreementꝑ they made to and
with Yo.ʳ said Oratrixe, and what disposicōn was made of the
said ffiftie poundꝑ vpon putting the same forth to the said Ewen
and Keymer, and what he the said Ewen then owed to the said
Milton or any of his ffrindꝑ and to the intent the said Milton and
Bower may pay Yo.ʳ said Oratrixe her said money with the interest & charges or shewe good cause to the contrary: May it
please Yo.ʳ hōᵇˡᵉ. good Loᵖᵖ. to grant vnto Yoʳ said Oratrixe his
Maᵗᵖ. most gracious writt of Subpena to be directed to the said
John Milton and Thomas Bower thereby comanding them and
either of them at a day certeyne and vnder a certeyne paine
therein to be limitted ꝑsonallie to be and appeare before yo.ʳ

good Lo^p in his Maiesties high and honorable Court of Chan-
cerye then and there to answere all and every the premisses vpon
their Corporall oathes, and to stand to and abide such further
order and direction therein as to your honorable good Lordshipp
in equitie and conscience shall seeme meete. And your said
Oratrixe shall daylie pray for your Lordshipp long to continue
in honor health and happines.

Goldsmythe

Public Record Office, C2 Charles I/D39/47; French, *Milton in
Chancery*, pp. 236 ff.

. . . Rose Downer . . . about the tearme of the holy Trinitie
in the Seaventh yeare of his Maties: Raigne that now is exhibited
her Bill of Complaynte into this Honō^ble Courte against your
Orators. . . .

From the bill of Milton's father and Bower against Arthur Duck
and William Child; see below under date of February 16, 1636/7.

MAY 3. FATHER ANSWERS ROSE DOWNER'S CHANCERY BILL.

Juratur 3° Maij 1631   The Severall answere of John Milton
Tho: Eden   one of the Defendantȝ to the Bill of
Maydwell   Rose Downer Widdowe Complaynant:/
The said Defendant saving to himselfe now and at all times
hereafter, all advantages of excepcōn, to the vncertainties, and
insufficiencies of the said Bill, for answere vnto soe much thereof,
as concerneth him this Defendant to make answere vnto, He
saith, That he knoweth it, to be true, That the said somē of
ffiftie poundȝ was lent forth in the name of the said Comp^lt.
vpon the securitie of the said Mathewe Ewenȝ and William
Keymer in the bill named, and the bond sealed at this Defendantȝ shopp. But this Defendant saith for any thing this Def^t.
knoweth to the Contrary the same was soe lent by the Comp^lt
willingly, for that she received both the bond at the first and
the Jnterest as the same grewe dewe at severall dayes, and times
afterwardȝ, and that this Def^t. never knewe that she was vnwilling therevnto, vntill now of late, And this Defendant, for

[234]

further satisfaccōn of this hō^ble. Court in the premises saith That one John Downer the Complaynantꝑ late husband, having beene this Defendantꝑ long acquaintance Did dispose of at this Def^tꝑ. shopp at Jnterest, vpon securitie, to the good liking of him the said John Downer some moneys, But this Def^t doth not well remember the particuler somē or somēs soe lent, And the said John Downer dying long since the said Complaynant hath sithence continued the said moneys or some ꝑt thereof at Jnterest voluntarily, and willingly till of late, and vntill this Defendant was desirous to have noe further dealingꝑ with her moneys, and to that end this Defendant perswaded the Complaynant to take in her moneys That this Defendant might be altogether quitt of her, and her moneys, And this Defendant denyeth that he ever repaired to the Complaynant, or did advise her to putt it forth at Jnterest, rather then to imploy it any other wayes, Or that this Defendant ever vsed, any ꝑswasions to the Complaynant to any such purpose, As in the said bill is vntruly surmised, for the reputting forth of any moneys at Jnterest, or that vpon any such perswasions the Complaynant was drawne to putt the same forth at Interest, But this Defendant saith that the said somē of ffiftie poundꝑ in the bill named, was putt forth at Jnterest to such men, and vpon such security as was to the good liking of the Complaynant and this Defendant saith that the said ffiftie poundꝑ was paid in about the moneth of June One thowsand six hundred Twenty and Eight at this Defendantꝑ shopp vnto the other Defendant Thomas Bower, for the Complaynantꝑ vse, and to be at her disposing, And this Defendant beleeveth that the Complaynant, Did afterwardꝑ require the said somē of ffiftie poundꝑ, of the said other Defendant Thomas Bower in the Bill named, But what satisfaccōn the said Thomas Bower, gave to the said Complaynant, Or why he did not p̄ntely deliver the same, vnto the Complaynant, he this Defendant doth not knowe but leaveth to the said Thomas Bower, to give answere therevnto, And this Defendant saith, That he the said Thomas Bower was then noe servant, of this Defendantꝑ, but a ffreeman of Londō and was then, and still is, Part-

ner with him this Defendant, in the benefitt wch. accreweth by
this Defendant̸ trade, and is sufficient, (as this Defendant verely
beleeveth) to answere the Complanyant if he hath done her any
wrong (as he verely beleeveth, he hath not done her any) And
this Defendant, absolutely denieth any confedracie, and Combinacōn between this Defendant, and the said other Defendant
Bower to deteyne the Complaynant̸ money from her, Or that
this Defendant Did vse any subtill gesture or Carriage, whereby
the Complaynant̸ said money might be deteyned from her, As
by the said bill is falsely and scandulously surmised, And this
Defendant beleeveth that the said bond was sealed by the said
Ewens and Keymer, and the said moneys lent to them, by the
privity and approbacōn of the said Complaynant, And this Defendant saith That he did knowe, that the said bond was after-
ward̸ sent vnto her the said Complaynant, But knewe not, that
the Comp^lt. did refuse to accept of the said bond, Or that this
Defendant̸ servant James ffisher Did deliver the bond in such
sorte as the Complaynant in her said Bill hath sett forth, ffor if
this Defendant had been informed thereof, he this Defendant
would have given him Due correccōn for the same, And this Defendant confesseth, That he this Defendant beleeving the said
moneys to be putt forth by the Complaynant̸ privitie, subscribed
his name as a Witnes therevnto, As he vsually doth in like cases,
And this Defendant saith that if the Complaynant, had then
made knowne her dislike of the lending of her moneys As in
the said Bill is alledged, and had p̃ntely brought back the bond
to this Defendant, He this Defendant would have seene that
the said Complaynant, Should have had her moneys forthwith
paid her, But this Defendant did, and doth verely beleeve and
conceive, that the same was fairely carried betweene the Complaynant and the said Bower, and that her consent was had to
and for the lending of the said ffiftie pound̸ vpon the security
aforesaid (for that the Plaintiffe to this Defendant̸ knowledge,) Did not shewe any dislike of the lending thereof, till
long time after the same was lent, But this Defendant denyeth
that he ever promised, or vndertooke to pay the Complaynant

her moneys or to become her Paymaster, either vpon the lending of the moneys or at any time before or afterwardꝑ, And
this Defendant denyeth that the said Ewens (to the knowledge
of this Defendant,) was fallen into decay at the time of the said
lending of the Complaynantꝑ money to the said Ewens and
Keymer, or that the said Ewens at that time did obscure himselfe, But this Defendant did beleeve the security to have beene
good and sufficient, and confesseth that the said Ewens Did then
owe some other moneys at this Defendantꝑ shopp, but to what
value this Defendant doth not well remember, And this Defendant further saith That he beleeveth that part of the said
somē of ffiftie poundꝑ was disposed, and paid over to Ewens his
vse, and by his appointment, and in such sorte as he did direct,
and that the remainder was paid into his own handꝑ, And this
Defendant conceiveth that the said Comp^{lt}. hath not p^rferred
the said bill against this Defendant of her owne disposicōn &
minde but by the instigacōn of some other ill disposed ꝑson for
that this Defendant saith that the said Comp^{lt}. hath oftentimes
in the hearing of this Defend^{tꝑ}. servant Cleared this Defendant
touching the lending of the said ffiftie poundꝑ:/Without that,
that there is any other matter or thing, Clawse, sentence, article,
or allegacōn in the said bill contenyed materiall, or effectuall, in
the Lawe, to be answered vnto, and not herein well & sufficiently answered vnto, or denied, traversed, or avoyded is true,
All wch. matters this Defendant is ready to Justefie, and avowe
as this hō^{ble}. Co^{rt}. shall award, and humbly prayeth to be dismissed out of the same, with his reasonable costꝑ, and damagꝑ
in that behalfe wrongfully susteined:./

W Greene

Public Record Office, C2 Charles I/D39/47; French, *Milton in Chancery*, pp. 240 ff.

. . . the said Rose downer to which said Bill of Complainte
your Orators answered. . . .

From the bill of Milton's father and Bower against Arthur Duck;
see below under date of February 16, 1636/7.

MAY 3. FATHER'S PARTNER, THOMAS BOWER, ANSWERS ROSE DOWNER'S CHANCERY BILL.

Jur' 3° Die Maij 1631 J Mychēll Maydwell

The severall answere of Thomas Bower one of the Def^{ts}. to the Bill of Complaint, of Rose Downer Widdowe Complaynant:/

The said Defendant saving to himselfe now & at all times hereafter all advantagǫ of excepcōn, to the vncertainties, & insufficiencies of the said Bill, for answere therevnto soe much thereof as concerneth him this Defendant, to make answere vnto, saith, That he verely beleeveth that the said bill of Complaint, against him this Defendant, into this Hō^{ble}. Court exhibited by the said Comp^{lt}. is of purpose, to vexe, molest, and troble this Defendant, and to putt him to vnnecessary charge, having thereby to drawe some moneys from him without any Just cause at all, Yett nevertheless for the satisfaccōn, of this most hō^{ble}. Court he this Defendant saith, That he was for the space of Eight yeares or thereaboutǫ now past servant to the said John Milton Scrivener, the other Defendant in the bill named, and hath beene for the space of Six yeares now past, or thereaboutǫ Partner with the said John Milton in the Profession which he now vseth, and hath within the said time beene a meanes of putting out many somēs of money at Jnterest, And that the husband of the Comp^{lt}. in his life time, had some moneys lent at Jnterest, at the shopp of the said Defendant John Milton, And further saith that true it is that the ffiftie poundǫ in the bill mencōned, was by the said John Milton and this Defendant, by and with the consent, and good liking of the said Complaynant, putt to Jnterest for the vse of the said Complaynant, into the handǫ of one Master Leigh vpon sufficient securitie by bond in November One thowsand six hundred Twenty & ffower And continued till about August One thowsand Six hundred Twenty & Six And then with all Jnterest paid in, And not long after by and with the privity and consent of the Plaintiffe, the said ffiftie poundǫ was lent at Jnterest vnto S^r. ffulke Grevill

Knight vpon good securitie, where the same continued till about
June One thowsand Six hundred Twenty and Eight, And then
was voluntarily paid in with all Jnterest, therevpon due, And
the said ffiftie poundꝑ remayning in the howse of the said John
Milton whereof the Complaynant had notice, At which time,
Master Ewens, and Mᣴ Keymer in the bill named had occasion
for a hundred poundꝑ, whereof ffiftie poundꝑ was then lent vpon
their security by one Master Bulteell vpon Jnterest for Six
moneths whoe liked them well, And the other ffiftie poundꝑ
was then lent by the Complaynant vpon Jnterest for the like
time, the said Ewens and Keymer being then reputed Gentleman of good worth, and sufficiency and the meaner of them to
have about ffive hundred poundꝑ p̄ Annū, And both of them
formerly having taken vp moneys at Jnterest, and delt fairely
and squarely therein from time to time, And vpon their request,
at that time there being such a some in the howse, This Defendant moved the Complaynant to lett them have the said ffiftie
poundꝑ informing her that their security was good, And this
Defendant was the rather induced soe to thinke, for that their
dealingꝑ had been formerly alwayes good and Currant, Vpon
which report and informacōn she the said Complaynant gave
consent to and for the lending of the said ffiftie poundꝑ, vnto
the said Ewens and Keymer, and a bond was then taken for the
same, and afterwardꝑ by and with the consent, and good liking
of the said Complaynant, was continued for Twoe, or three Six
monethꝑ, and the Jnterest duly paid her for the same time, and
by her accepted of, without any dislike at all, And this Defendant saith that the said Ewens vpon thenseling of the said bond
to the Complaynant for the said ffiftie poundꝑ Did appointe this
Defendant to pay pcell thereof vnto certaine psonꝑ to whome he
the said Ewens was then indebted, which was done, accordingly
and the remainder recd paid to the said Ewens himselfe, But
how much of the said ffiftie poundꝑ was paid by the said Ewens
his appointmᵗ. and how much came to his owne handꝑ this Defendant well remembreth not, And this Defendant further
saith, that this Complaynant was then soe farre from making

such Complaynt for want of money That about the same time, at this Defendantͼ request she the said Complaynant Did lend vnto one Master Waring Thirtie poundͼ at Jnterest for Six monethͼ, and soe continued the same till about the moneth of June One thowsand Six hundred and Thirtie, But the said Ewens, and Keymer, afterwardͼ failing in paying of the Jnterest of the said ffiftie poundͼ, the Plaintiffe tooke excepcōns & called in for her money And this Defendant hath divers times since very earnestly sollicitied and importuned the said Ewens, and Keymer for the payment of the same accordingly, whoe have divers times faithfully ͻmised the paym^t. thereof, And this Defendant verely beleeveth That the said ffiftie poundͼ, with all the Jnterest due for the same, wthin a while may be obteyned and he for his ͻt will doe his best endeavour to procure the payment thereof, And this Defendant doth vtterly denye the deteyning of the said ffiftie poundͼ, As in the said bill is falsely alledged, Neither that the bond was soe delivered as in the said bill is surmised Neither did this Defendant ever goe about to hinder or crosse her of the said ffiftie poundͼ. And doth vtterly deny that ever he vndertooke to secure the said ffiftie poundͼ or any part thereof Neither doth he or the other Defendant John Milton vse for to doe to any, having little reason for it, (in these evill times) But only doe their best endeavours to take good security for moneys lent, and afterwardͼ with much travell paines and care Doe seeke to gett such moneys in againe to give the lenders what content they may And denieth that he knewe or ever heard, (at the time of the lending of the said ffiftie poundͼ or of long time after) That the said Ewens and Keymer or either of them, were in any decay, in their estate, or did obscure themselves as in the said bill of Complaynt is alledged, And denieth any combinacōn with the other Defendant John Milton as is most scandalously sett downe;./ Without that That any other matter or thing in the said bill conteyned materiall to be answered vnto, and not herein sufficiently answered vnto, confessed, avoyded, traversed, or denied is true, All which this Defendant, is ready to averre, and prove as this hō^{ble}. Co^{rt}. shall award, and humbly prayeth to be dismissed out of the same, with his reasonable costȹ and damagȹ in that behalfe wrongfully susteined.:/

Steph: Atterbury/

Public Record Office, C2 Charles I/D39/47; French, *Milton in Chancery*, pp. 243 ff.

Summer (?). Enjoys vacation in the country.

. . . Testor ipse lucos, & flumina, & dilectas villarum ulmos, sub quibus æstate proxime præteritâ (si Dearum arcana eloqui liceat) summam cum Musis gratiam habuisse me jucundâ memoriâ recolo; ubi & ego inter rura & semotos saltus velut occulto ævo crescere mihi potuisse visus sum. . . .

Milton, seventh prolusion, *Epistolarum Familiarium Liber Unus*, 1674, pp. 136-137. Since the prolusion has here been dated tentatively 1632, the experience here described must have taken place in the summer of 1631. But both the date and the actuality of the experience are dubious.

[I call to witness for myself the groves, and rivers, and the beloved village-elms, under which in the last past summer, (if it is right to speak the secrets of goddesses,) I remember so pleasantly having had supreme delight with the Muses; where I too, among rural scenes and remote forests, seemed as if I could have grown and vegetated through a hidden eternity.]

Masson, I, 267 (297-302).

July 20. Mentioned in connection with a fellowship (?).

[Writing from Cambridge on July 20, 1631, to Dudley Carleton, Viscount Dorchester, Secretary of State, Thomas Bainbrigg, Master of Christ's College,] Excuses himself for not procuring a fellowship for Mr. Shute. The writer had been Shute's father's scholar, and his own and a brother's tutor, besides an uninterrupted series of mutual kind offices, but another holds so strong as the writer should conclude himself false to God, to the express will of their famous founders, and false to his country, if he should offer the least violence to his claim.

Public Record Office, abstracted in *Calendar of State Papers Domestic 1631-1633*, p. 116; J. O. Peile, *A Biographical Register of Christ's*

College, *1505-1905*, ed. J. A. Venn, 1 (1910), 363-364. Mr. Venn thinks that the "another" who "holds so strong" is Milton. There seems to be little real proof of such an identification.

AUGUST 12. FATHER WITNESSES WILL OF HIS SON-IN-LAW EDWARD PHILLIPS.

In the name of God Amen The twelueth Day of August one thousand six hundred thirty one And in the seauenth yeare of the raigne of our Soueraigne Lord King Charles of England &c I, Edward Phillips of London gentleman being weak in bodie but of good and perfect memory thankp bee to the Lord therfore, doe make this my last will and Testament in manner and forme following viz̄t ffirst J bequeath my soule into the hands of Allmightie God My bodie I Comītt vnto the earth from whence it Came when it shall please God to make a separaācon betweene my bodie and my soule hoping at the last day through the meritts of Christ myne onelie Sauyour it shall rise againe a glorious bodie and bee vnited vnto my soule to liue in heauen eternally And for such worldly estate as the Lord of his mercy hath giuen mee J bequeath as followeth Whereas there is an Jnuentory of such goods and Chattells as were left by my deceased father with my mother for her vse my Will is that these goods and chattells after my mothers decease shall bee devyded to and amongst my brothers and sisters then living And if such goods and Chattells shall not then come to the somē of ffourescore pounds being indifferently praysed Then J desire my louing wife Anne to make it vpp soe much that my said brothers and sisters being foure now lyuing may haue Twentie poundp apeece after my Mothers decease The rest and residue of all and singular my goodp Chattells Debts leases houshould stuffe and all other thingp J giue and bequeath vnto my said louing wife Anne whom J make Executrix of this my last Will Jn witnesse whereof J hereunto sett my hand and seale the day and yeare first aboue written Signed sealed deliuered and published by the said Edward Phillipps as and for his last will and Testament in the presence of Jo: Milton Henrie Rothwell seruant to the said Jo: Milton.

Prerogative Court of Canterbury, London, 99 St. John; Masson, II, 98. Phillips died within about ten days, and was buried on August 25. His will was proved on September 12.

AUGUST 25. BROTHER-IN-LAW EDWARD PHILLIPS BURIED.

Edus Phillipps gen,' in eccl'ia p'noctem.

Parish Register of St. Martin-in-the-Fields, London, as printed in *The Register of St. Martin-in-the-Fields, London, 1619-1636*, ed. J. V. Kitto, London, 1936 (Publications of the Harleian Society, Vol. LXVI), under date of August 25, 1631; W. R. Parker in *Times Literary Supplement*, 1938, p. 802. I have not seen the original register.

[Edward Phillips, gentleman, in the church at night.]

SEPTEMBER 12. WILL OF BROTHER-IN-LAW EDWARD PHILLIPS PROVED.

The will, which has been given above under date of August 12, was proved on September 12 before William Mericke, LL.D., Surrogate of Sir Henry Marten, by Anne Phillips, relict. Administration was granted. Edward Phillips is spoken of in the probate as of the parish of St. Martin-in-the-Fields. See *Abstracts of Probate Acts in the Prerogative Court of Canterbury*, ed. J. and G. F. Matthews, London, I (1902?), 107. The will is filed as 99 St. John in the Prerogative Court of Canterbury, London. Some of the details given here, which are not in the *Abstracts*, are taken from the original documents.

SEPTEMBER 19. DEPOSITION OF OLIVE STREET IN DOWNER-MILTON SUIT.

19. die Septembris. 1631.   Ex parte Rose Downer vīd quēr
Anº: R: Rp: Caroli. 7º./   versus Johēm Milton et āl dēftp
                               Testes examīᵗ: per Martinū Basill
                               in Cancellaria Examinatorem./

[September 19, 1631, in the seventh year of the reign of King Charles. On behalf of Rose Downer, widow, plaintiff, against John Milton and others, defendants, the witness examined by Martin Basil, Examiner in Chancery.]

Oliue Street of the parish of Sᵗ: Andrewes in the Wardorb London Embrowderer, aged Twenty Six yeares or thereaboutp sworne &c. and by direccōn examined vppon the 1.2.3.4.5.6.7. &.8ᵗʰ.

1. That he knoweth all the parties to this suite Cōmp^{lt}: and dēftꝑ, and hath knowne Rose Downer widdow named for Cōmp^{lt}:, for these Twenty yeares at the least., and John Milton and Thomas Bower named for dēftꝑ, for these Six yeares and vpwardes, And saieth that the Cōmp^{lt}: lives as A widow on the smale meanes she hath and keepes onely one Maide Seruant, and the Two dēftꝑ are by their ꝑfessions both Scriueno^{rs}, the dēft Bower, being heretofore the other dēft Miltons Seruant or Apprentice, and at this time writes vnder him in his Shopp, or did within these Three Monethes, And morever saieth, that the Cōmp^{lt}; liveth on Audlin Hill, in the s'd parish of S^t: Andrewes in the Wardorb, and the dēft Milton liues in Bredstreet London, But where the dēft Bower now lodgeth, this dept saieth hee knoweth not, but saieth that within these Six Monethes hee lodged in Long Lane, and did then write vnder the s'd Milton, in his Shopp in Bredstreet./

2. That as hee hath credibly heard and beleiueth, the dēft Milton, (haueing the report of an honest man in his ꝑfession) was heretofore trusted by the Cōmp^{lt}: wth puting forth at interest for her, the sūm of ffifty poundes, being (as was conceiued) the maine matter she had to liue on, for this dept saieth, that the s'd dēft Milton hath heretofore confessed to him this dept, that hee was soe trusted by the Cōmp^{lt} with puting forth of ffifty poundes for her, And more over saieth that as hee hath alsoe credibly heard, the Cōmp^{lt}, from time to time, was made acquainted with the security, and the names of the parties, to whome the s'd monie was lent, and that shee did vsually giue allowance or approue of such security, before her monie was soe lent./

3. That in or about the Moneth of Jun in the yeare. 1628. hee this dept, did goe along with the now Cōmp^{lt}, to the dēft Miltons house in Bredstreet, where this dept heard the s'd Cōmp^{lt}:, earnestly call in for, and desire of the s'd Milton, to haue her s'd monie, saying she could noe longer forbeare the same, in regard of her great occasions, and want, that

shee had thereof, and that therefore shee must have the same in, or to that effect./

4. That both before and after the Cōmp^{lt}: was wth the s'd dēft Milton to call in for her s'd monie, as is before deposed, hee this dept. (at the request and entreaty of her the s'd Cōmp^{lt}) was diuers and sundry times wth him the s'd deft, And did from her the s'd Cōmp^{lt}, and in her name, earnestly desire, and sollicitte the s'd dēft, to call in for the s'd monie when the same grew due, to thend the Cōmp^{lt}. might haue the same, to supplie her occasions withall, And this dept. further saieth, that at all the times, that this dept was with the s'd Milton to demaund the s'd monie as afores'd, he still ꝑmised this dept:, as hee did the Cōmp^{lt}: when shee was with him as afores'd, that shee should have in her s'd monie when the same was due, but the very time or times, or how often this dept was with the s'd deft Milton for the s'd monies, hee saieth hee is not now able to depose./

[*Signed*] Oliue Streete

5. That as the Cōmp^{lt} her self told him this dept: (at such time as hee this dept was with her when she called in for her s'd monies of the dēft Milton, and when this dept called in for the same, as is before deposed) that her s'd monie was in such securities handes, as shee very well liked of, shee further saying, that if shee had not had great occasion to haue vsed it, that shee would not have called for it in, shee liked the security soe well, or to that effect./

6. That as the dēft Milton himself told him this dept:, the s'd ffifty poundes and interest therefore (according to the desire and request of the Cōmp^{lt}), was (at or about the time the same was due) paid vnto him the s'd dēft in his Shopp in Bredstreet, by the principall or suerties whoe stood bound for the same, to the s'd Cōmp^{lt}.

7. That as hee hath credibly heard, (after such time as the Cōmp^{lt}. had notice that the s'd monie was paied in, to the dēft Milton, or the s'd Bower his seruant) shee the Cōmp^{lt} did ymediately repaire to the s'd Miltons house in Bred-

street afores'd, and there demaunded her monie of him,
wherevnto (as this dept hath likewise credibly heard) the
s'd dēft made answer, what A stirr is here about yoʳ monie,
and withall willed the other dēft. Bower, to pay her, her
monie, and saied hee would be ridd of her, and her monie,
and (in shew) seemed angrie with the s'd Bower that he
delayed to pay her the Cōmpˡᵗ, And moreover saieth, that
as hee hath alsoe credibly heard, the s'd Bower then answered, that hee had pmised to furnish A ffriend of his,
with soe much monie, and that hee must have that monie of
the Cōmpˡᵗᵉ hee further saying, that hee did knowe, that when
shee had it, shee would put it forth againe, and therefore
shee were, as good let his friend have it, as another man, and
soe would not let her have it, And further or otherwise to
the Interʳ hee saieth hee is not able to depose./

8. That not long after the s'd Cōmpˡᵗ: had bene with the s'd
dēftᵉ for her s'd monie, as before is deposed to the next
Interʳ precedent, the s'd Milton or Bower, or one of them
(as the Cōmpˡᵗᵉ then Seruant ffraunces Stacy told him this
dept.) sent A Seruant of theirs, to the Cōmpˡᵗᵉ, house, wᵗʰ
an Obligacōn in the names of Mathew Ewens, and Will'm
Keymer, for payment of ffifty poundes with Jnterest, at Six
Monethes, vnto her the s'd Cōmpˡᵗ: whereat (as the Cōmpˡᵗ:
s'd Seruant likewise told this dept) shee the Cōmpˡᵗ, was
very angrie, saying shee would not accept of the s'd Bond,
shee must have in her monie to serue her occasions, as shee
had oftentimes told them before, And that then the dēftᵉ
s'd seruant replied, and saied that the security was good,
and that his Mʳ (meaning the s'd Milton) would make it
good, as reason was hee should, and therevppon the dēftᵉ
s'd seruantᵉ, (against the Cōmpˡᵗ: will) did leaue the s'd
Obligacōn behinde him, saying shee could haue but good
security for her monie, and there it was, or to that effect./
And lastly saieth, that as the Cōmpˡᵗᵉ: s'd seruant likewise
told him this dept, the Cōmpˡᵗ was at that time sicke in her

Bedd, and not fitt to carry the s'd Obligacōn back againe./
And more &c./

[*Signed*] Oliue Streete

Public Record Office, C24/574/40; French, *Milton in Chancery*,
pp. 245-248.

SEPTEMBER 19. DEPOSITION OF GEORGE BROOME IN DOWNER-MILTON SUIT.

19° Sept Ao 1631   ꝑ Down'
Ao' Car Rꝑ. 7°

1   *George Broome* of the pʳcinct of Blackfriers London
scriuen' aged 51 yeares or thereaboutꝑ sworne & exañed
&c. To the ffirst Jnt saith That hee doth knowe the
widow Down' named for the cōmpˡᵗ & John Milton
named for one of the defᵗꝑ & hath knowne the cōmpˡᵗ
the space of seaven yeares or thereaboutꝑ & the defᵗ Milton some 27 or 28 yeares or thereaboutꝑ And doth know
yᵗ the sᵈ Milton is by ꝑfession a scriuenoʳ living in Breadstreet London But to his rēmbrance doth not knowe the
Defᵗ Thomas Bower, but hath heard & beleeueth yᵗ to
be true hee was svant sometymes to the sᵈ Milton & did
write vnder him in his the sᵈ Miltons shopp in Breadstreet aforesᵈ.

2   Hee hath credibly heard yᵗ the sᵈ Defᵗ Milton had the
reputacōn of a very honest man in the ꝑfession of a
scriuenoʳ And the sᵈ Defᵗ Milton hath confessed vnto this
Dept yᵗ the cōmpˡᵗ did trust him the sᵈ Milton with the
putting forth of ffifty poundꝑ at Jnterest of her estate &
hath also confessed yᵗ hee the sᵈ Milton did putt forth
the sʸᵈ 50ˡⁱ vnto & vppon such security as shee the sᵈ
cōmpˡᵗ did allow & apꝑue of And this is as much as hee
can depose to this Jnt hee this depᵗ. not knowing whether
the sʸᵈ cōmpˡᵗ from tyme to tyme were made acquainted
wᵗʰ the security & names of the pties to whom the same
money was lent as by the Jnt is demaunded./

6   That the sᵈ Defᵗ Milton hath confessed & acknowledged

vnto this dep^t that the s^d 50^{li} wth. the Jnterest was p'd
into the s^{,d} Miltons shopp in Breadstreet aforesd to the
vse of the now cōmp^{lt} into the handꝑ of the s^d Def^t Bower at or about the tyme in this Jnt meant & intended And
further to the Jnt hee cannot depose

7 That all y^t hee can depose to this Jnt is this vizt y^t the
s^d def^t Milton did acknowledge & confesse vnto this dep^t.
y^t the s^d Cōmp^{lt} not long after the s^d money wth the Jnterest therefore was p^d vnto the s^d Def^t Bower at the
s^d Miltons shopp in Breadstreet as afores^d did come &
repaire vnto the s^d Milton & demaund of him the s^d 50^{li}
wth Jnterest so p^d as afores^d vppon wch demaund as the
s^d Milton confessed vnto this dep^t. hee did will the s^d
Bower to pay the s^d money wth the Jnterest vnto the s^d
widow Down' & did by his owne confession seeme to bee
very angry saying y^t hee would bee ridd of her the
cōmp^{lt} & her money or wordꝑ to y^t effect And saith hee
hath heard the s^d cōmp^{lt} say and affirme y^t the said def^t
Bower did refuse at y^t tyme to pay the s^d money wth
the Jnterest therefore, & the s^d Cōmp^{lt} did then further
say y^t shee was very much greeued & discontented y^t
shee could not then haue the s^d money to furnish her
p̃nte necessities.

11.12 It is true y^t since the Comencing of this suite hee this
dep^t had speech & conference wth Mr Ewens in this Jnt
named about the lending of the s^d ffifty poundꝑ At w^{ch}
tyme this dep^t saith the s^d Ewens in this dep^{te}. opinion
seemed to bee very sorry y^t the s^d money was a widdowes
& did directly manifest & declare vnto this dep^t y^t it was
all one vnto him the s^d Ewens to whom hee was bound
for as hee then confessed it was to pay Debtꝑ owing by
him at the s^d Miltons shopp & did then confesse &
acknowledge y^t none or very little of the money (if any
at all thereof) came to his handꝑ & y^t at y^t tyme hee had
neu' seene the s^d widow And the s^d Ewens did further say
vnto this dep^t. y^t if the s^d def^{te} had not been p'd by his

the s^d Ewens entring into the s^d bond hee did not know wch way to haue p^d them, & did then further confesse vnto this dep^t. y^t the s^d def^{te} or one of them did moue & pswade him the s^d Ewens to enter into the s^d bond, say-ing vnto him y^t they hoped y^t they nor either of them should bee any loosers by him the s^d Ewens. And further saith y^t at the s^d conference the s^d Ewens did confesse y^t hee neu' pd any Jnterest for the s^d money & y^t if any interest were p'd to her the s^d widow Down' the same was p'^d by the s^d def^{te} or one of them out of their owne moneys And the s^d Ewens further s^d vnto this dep^t y^t the s^d def^{te} or one of them durst not but pay Jnterest for the s^d money at the first to theñd as hee confessed to bring the cōmp^{lt} wthin compasse of accepting the s^d bond. or word℘ to the like effect. And further saith y^t since the conferences afores^d wth the s^d Mr Ewens this dep^t. did at the request of the s^d cōmp^{lt} demaund the s^d money of the s^d Def^t Milton & did charge him the s'^d Milton wth a ℘mise y^t hee would see her p^d the s^d money, wherevnto hee answered y^t what ℘mise soeu' hee the s^d Milton made her at the first yet in regard y^t shee had accepted of interest for the s^d money hee held himselfe to bee discharged & s'^d y^t shee might gett her money where shee could or to y^t effect And more To the rest not exañed by direccōn

[*Signed*] Geo: Brome.

Public Record Office, C24/574/40; French, *Milton in Chancery*, pp. 248-250.

SEPTEMBER 19-26. FATHER STILL LIVES IN BREAD STREET.

[Olive Street deposes on September 19 that] the dēft Mil-ton liues in Bredstreet London.

[George Broome deposes on September 19 that] the s^d Mil-ton is by ℘fession a scriueno^r living in Breadstreet London.

[Frances Stacy deposes on September 23 that] the dēft℘ are

both of them by their ꝑfessions Scriueno͏ʳˢ, and liue (as this depᵗ taketh it) both togeather in one house in Bredstreet London.

[Richard Sheratt deposes on September 26 that] the said dēft Milton is by ꝑfession a Notarie and doeth now live in Breadstreet neere Cheap side London.

Public Record Office, Chancery depositions in Downer-Milton action, C24/574/40; French, *Milton in Chancery*, pp. 245-255. The second defendant mentioned in the third quotation is the elder Milton's partner Thomas Bower, about whose place of residence the deponents seem to be in disagreement. Olive Street deposed that six months previously Bower had lived in Long Lane; and Richard Sheratt deposed that in Hilary term he had lodged "at an vpholdsters house in the Strand London."

SEPTEMBER 23. DEPOSITION OF FRANCES STACY IN DOWNER-MILTON SUIT.

23. die Septembris. 1631.   ꝑ Downer vīd:./
Anᵒ: R: Rꝑ: Caroli 7ᵒ./
ffraunces Stacy of the parish of Sᵗ. Andrewes in the Wardorb London Spinster, aged Twenty Two yeares or thereaboutꝑ sworne &c./ and by direccōn examined vppon the 1.2.5.6. and 8. Interʳˢ./

1. That shee knoweth all the parties to this suite Cōmpˡᵗ: and dēftꝑ, And hath knowe Rose Downer widdow named for Compˡᵗ. euer since this deptꝑ rememberaunce, shee being this depᵗꝑ: Aunt, and hath bred, and educated this depᵗ from her Childhoode, And John Milton and Thomas Bower named for dēftꝑ, this depᵗ saieth shee hath knowne for these ffower yeares or thereaboutꝑ And moreover saieth that the Cōmpˡᵗ. is not of any ꝑfession but liues on Audlin Hill, in the s'd parishe of Sᵗ: Andrewes in the Wardorbb, on that smale meanes it hath pleased god to lend vnto her, And the dēftꝑ are both of them by their ꝑfessions Scriueno͏ʳˢ, and liue (as this depᵗ taketh it) both togeather in one house in Bredstreet London, the dēft Bower, being heretofore (to this dēptꝑ: knowledg) seruant to the other dēft Milton, and did write vnder him in his Shopp in Bredstreet afores'd./

2. That by her liueing wth the s'd Cōmp^lt: her Aunt, shee knoweth, that shee the s'd Cōmp^lt: (vppon the good report and oppinion that went, and was concieued, of the dēft Miltons honesty and vpright dealeing in his pfession) did trust him the s'd dēft, with the puting forth at Jnterest, of the sūm of ffifty poundes, for her the s'd Cōmp^lt:, being A great part of her the Cōmp^lte estate, And this dep^t. further saieth, shee alsoe knoweth, that the s'd Cōmp^lt, was from time to time, made acquainted with the securitie, and names of the parties, and their suerties, to whome the s'd monie was lent, and that she did vse to giue allowance and approue of such security before her s'd monie was disposed of, for this dep^t saieth, shee hath knowne the deft Milton send vnto the cōmp^lt to knowe if shee would let forth her monie, vppon such and such security wch shee did either allow, or disallow of as she pleased.

5. Shee alsoe knoweth that the Cōmp^lt: haueing earnest occasion to vse her s'd monie (soe put forth at interest as afores'd) did call in for the same to the s'd dēf^t Milton, when the same should grow due although it was then in such mens hands, or shee had such security for the same, as shee very well liked of, shee the Cōmp^lt: saying (that had not her owne earnest occasion for monies compelled her thereto), shee would not haue called for the same in, shee liked the security soe well, or to that effect./ And further or otherwise to the Jnter^r, shee saieth shee is not able to depose./

6. That as shee hath credibly heard, the s'd ffifty poundes, (according to the desire and request of the Cōmp^lt:) was, at or about the time the same grew due), paied in to the deftp, or one of them, at the dēft Miltons Shopp in Bredstreet afores'd, by the principall, or suerties whoe stood bound for the same to the Cōmp^lt And further therevnto shee saieth shee cannot depose./

8. That within A day or Two, or thereaboutp, after the Cōmp^lt: had bene at the dēft Miltons s'd Shopp for her monie, the

same being then due, the s'd dēftͻ, or one of them, sent one
of their Seruantͻ with an Obligacōn in the Names of one
Mathew Ewens, and Will'm Keymer, for payment of the
s'd ffifty poundes with Jnterest, at Six Monethes, vnto her
the Cōmp˪ᵗ And this dep˪ᵗ further saieth, that the Cōmp˪ᵗ:
was very angrie, wᵗʰ the s'd Seruant, that brought the s'd
Obligacōn and very much greiued, that shee could not haue
her monie to serue her occasions, and saied shee would not
accept of the s'd Obligacōn, for that shee must have her
monie, as shee had oftentimes told them the s'd dēftͻ wherevnto the s'd Seruant (in this deptͻ heareing) answered, that
the security was good, and that his Mʳ (meaneing as this
dept conceiued the dēft Milton) would make it good as
reason was hee should

[Deponent's mark?]

And therevppon the s'd Seruant (against the Cōmp˪ᵗͻ will)
did leaue the s'd Obligacōn behinde him vpon A Table in
the Roome saying vnto her that shee could haue but good
security for her monie, and there it was, or to that effect./
And this dept lastly saieth that the Cōmp˪ᵗ: was then ill at
ease and very aged and not able to stire forth of doores to
carrie back the s'd Obligacōn to the dēftͻ./ And more &c./
To the rest of the Jnter not to be examined

[Deponent's mark?]

Public Record Office, C24/574/40; French, *Milton in Chancery,*
pp. 250-251. The "deponent's mark" (if such it is) is a shapeless affair
vaguely resembling the letter W. There is no signature.

SEPTEMBER 26. DEPOSITION OF RICHARD SHERATT
IN DOWNER-MILTON SUIT.

26 Septemb': 1631 Ao   ͻ Downer
Rͻ Car' 7ᵐᵒ:

   Richard Sheratt Cittizen and Haberdasher of London
   dwelling within the p'cinct of bridwell aged 67 yeares or
1: therabouts sworne & examined &c To the 1 Jnt' saith
   That he doth know Rose Downer wid'. named for Cōmplt
   & soe hath done for the space of 20 yeares or theraboutͻ

and doeth likewise know John Milton and Thomas Bowre named for dēftℓ and hath knowne the sd Milton some twelue yeares or theraboutℓ and the said Bowre ten yeares or theraboutℓ And saith yᵗ the said dēft Milton is by pfession a Notarie and doeth now live in Breadstreet neere Cheape side London & yᵉ sd Bowre some 2 yeares since was a servant to the said dēft Milton & did writ vnder him in his shopp in Breadstreet beforesaid but of late (as this depᵗ hath credibly heard) the said Bowre is become an Attorney in his māᵗℓ Court of Comon pleas and did in Hillary Terme last past lodge at an vpholdsters house in the Strand London but whether he hath changed his Lodging since that tyme or noe this depᵗ knoweth not

2 : He doeth knowe it to be true yᵗ the Cōmplt did trust and imploye the sd dēfte Milton in the puting forth the sūme of ffifty poundℓ at Jnterest being a maine or great pte of her estate the said Milton being reputed and accompted to be a very honest and iust man in his pfession & dealing And saith that at the first putting forth of the said money the said Cōmplt was made acquainted with the names of the ptie & his suerties to whome yᵉ same was lente and did yeld her consent to the putting forth thereof And further he cannot depose to the Jnt'/.

3   He well remembereth that some short tyme before the end of six monthes or therābtℓ next after the first putting forth of the said money as aforesaid being in or aboute the yeare 1628 (but whether in the month of June or noe this depᵗ certainly remembereth not) the said Compˡᵗ did diuerse and sundry tymes goe vnto the said dēft Milton to haue in her said money to supplye her vrgent occasions and did earnestly importune & call vpon the said Milton for the same telling him in this depᵗℓ hearing that she would not haue the same to remaine any longer out of her owne handℓ she hauing as she said great want & vse thereof or vsed wordℓ to the same effecte/.

4 That about yᵉ tyme aforesd the sd Cōmplt did intreate this
depᵗ to repaire to the said Milton & earnestly to solicitte
him to call in the said money to yᵉ end that the same might
be paid vnto her the Cōmplt as the same should growe due
and this depᵗ according to her desire and sundry and often
tymes goe vnto him both with her the Cōmplt and alone and
did speake with the said Milton to the purpose aforesaid
And saith that the said Milton did allwayes answere this
depᵗ that he would calle in the said money Jnsoemuch that
at last he did seeme to be very angry with the Cōmplt for
coming and sending vnto him soe often for it saying that
she should not need to feare her money for ye security was
goode enough or wordꝑ to the like effecte but the p'cize
tymes when or how often this depᵗ went vnto the said dēft
Milton about it as aforesd he doeth not now remember/.

5 That as the Complt hath diverse tymes told this depᵗ she
had great and vrgent occasions to vse her said money when
she first did calle the same in otherwise it should not as shee
said haue bene taken out of theire handꝑ to whom it was first
lent And this depᵗ doeth vndoubtedly beleeue that if she
had bene minded to haue kept the same at Jnterest that she
would never haue called it in out of theire handꝑ whoe did
first borrow the same but this depᵗ saith that the said
Cōmpltꝑ occasions were such (as she did often tell this
depᵗ) that she was inforced to call in the said money & not
to dispose the same out againe at Jnterest

6 That as before he hath deposed the said dēftꝑ Milton and
Bowre haue confessed to this depᵗ that according to the request & desire of the Cōmplt the said money was called in
out of theire handꝑ to whome it was first lent and was paid
vnto them by ye principall or suerties or theire assignees
whoe stood first bounde for the same vnto the Cōmplt but
in what place the same was soe paid vnto them as by the
Jntᵗ is demanded this depᵗ knoweth not But verily beleeueth that the said money came to the handꝑ of the said

dēftꝑ by the Cōmpltꝑ calling the same in as aforesd & by noe other meanes/.

7   That he doeth not know whether the Cōmplt had any notice or noe that the said money was paid in vnto the said deftꝑ Howbeit saith that the Cōmplt supposing that the same was paid in at the tyme when it fell due did goe vnto the said Milton imeadiatly after it was due vnto his house in Breadstreet aforesd and did demande the same of him in this deptꝑ hearing And therevpon the said dēft Milton did will the other dēft Bowre he being then his servant to pay the same vnto her further saying what a stire is here J wilbe ridd of her & her money too seeming to be very angry with the said Bowre because he delayed to pay it vnto her whervnto the said Bowre then made answere that a freind of his had need of soe much money and he had put the same forth againe vnto him for her saying that he knewe that she would put the same forth againe to Jnterest and therefore he were as good haue the disposing thereof as another man or vsed wordꝑ to that effecte. And therevpon did in effecte vtterly deny to lett her haue her said money and sent her away much greved and discontented And moreover saith that he doeth verily beleeue that the said dēftꝑ when the Cōmplt demanded her money as aforesaid had the some in theire handꝑ & might haue payed it vnto her if they had pleased soe to doe And further he cannot depose to the Jnt'/.

9   That as this dep^t hath heard after the said dēftꝑ had received in the Cōmptꝑ money from them to whome it was first lent as aforesaid the said Bowre did put forth & lend the same vnto Ewen and Keymer in the Jnt' named whoe did therevpon enter into the bond in the Jnt' menconed to the Cōmplt at the Jnstance of the said dēftꝑ or one of them without the liking p'vity or knowledge of the Cōmplt as this dep^t vndoubtedly beleeueth but whether the said bond was entred into in leiwe of certaine desprate debtꝑ by

the said Ewen & Keymer then oweing & paiable to the said
Milton or Bowre or to some of those for whome they did
then put out money as by the Jnt' is questioned this dep^t
cannot say Howbeit saith y^t he hath heard y^t noe more
then the sūme of ffowreteene poundǫ of the Cōmpltǫ money
soe lent by the said dēftǫ as aforesaid did ever Come to the
handǫ of them the said Ewen and Keymer and this dep^t
hath likwise heard since the said money was lent vnto them
as aforesaid that they were men insolvent and Carles in
what & to whome they became bounde & indebted being
both of them farr more indebted then theire estates did
amounte vnto and were vnworthy of creditt for any such
sōme of money but what theire estates were at the tyme
when the said money was lent vnto them as aforesaid this
dep^t doeth not knowe Neither doe this dep^t know or can
tell what to beleeue touching the dēftǫ Jntencōns or either
of them to defeate the Cōmplt of her money as by the Jnt'
is demanded Nor can he otherwise depose for satisfacōn
thereof/.

10   That he well remembereth that some shorte tyme before
this suite began in this hō^{ble}. Co^{rt} that he this dep^t had some
conference wth the sd dēft Bowre in the p^rsence of the
Cōmplt concerning the said money And saith that he this
dep^t did charge the said Bowre with bad dealing and told
him he offered but hard measure to the Cōmplt she being
an Jgnorant & simple woman in putting forth her money
against her will and to men vnknown vnto her and withall
this dep^t told the said Bowre yt the dēft Milton laid all y^e
fault vpon him or wordǫ to that effecte Whervpon the said
Bowre seemed to be very angry with the said Milton saying that if he (meaning the Def^t: Milton) did tell he would
tell something also or to the same effecte And saith that he
this dep^t did moreover charge the said Bowre & told him
that all but a small ρte of the said money was to stopp &
pay debtǫ due vnto him & Milton by the said Ewans And
that but a small ρte of the said money came to the handǫ

of the said Ewens vnto wch the said Bowre made little answere but said that indeed he thought that the said Ewans
had but little pte thereof or that effecte And

[*Signed*] Rychard Shurratt

further saith that after the Conference & speeches aforesd
the said dēftp did advise the Cōmplt to put the said bonde
in suit against the said Ewans and Keymer But whether
the same were trickes between the said dēftp to pay themselues or others some weake debtp due to them by the said
Ewens & Keymer & so put the bond vpon her the pl't as
by the Jnt' is demanded this dep^t is not able to depose but
this dep^t beleeueth it was very hard measure & dealing
offered by them the s^d dēftp to the Cōmplt And more mat-
terially he saith he cannot depose for satisfacōn of any the
pticalar questions in this inter: ppounded Nor more To the
rest not to be examined by direccon

[*Signed*] Rychard Shurratt

Public Record Office, C24/574/40; French, *Milton in Chancery*,
pp. 252-255.

ABOUT OCTOBER. NEPHEW JOHN PHILLIPS BORN.

John Phillips is a year younger [than his brother Edward]
about Octob.

British Museum, Add. MS. 32,310, Milton's family Bible. The entry
is in Milton's hand. Edward Phillips was born in August, 1630.

NOVEMBER. BROTHER CHRISTOPHER ADMITTED TO THE INNER TEMPLE.

His admission as of this date is recorded in *Students Admitted to the
Inner Temple, 1547-1660*, n.d., p. 270, and in Edward Fosse, *A Biographical Dictionary of the Judges of England*, 1870, p. 446. Ernest
Brennecke, in his *John Milton the Elder and his Music*, 1938, p. 121,
offers a perplexing statement in this connection: ". . . Christopher, had determined to leave Christ's College, after only two years of residence
and without a degree, and to study law in the metropolis; he was duly
admitted to the Inner Temple on September 22." Since this entry comes
in a paragraph chronicling events in 1632, the author presumably dates
Christopher's admission into the Inner Temple on September 22, 1632.
He gives no authority for his statement, and even if his dates were correct, the interval since Christopher's admission to Christ's College would

be only one year and seven months instead of two years. Masson, how-ever (1, 525 [562]) supports the later date, *q.v.*

Christopher being principally designed for the Study of the Common-Law of *England*, was Entered Young a Student of the *Inner-Temple*, of which House he lived to be an Ancient Bencher, and keeping close to that Study and Profession all his Life-time, except in the time of the Civil Wars of *England*. . . .

Phillips, pp. v-vi; Darbishire, p. 52.

NOVEMBER 21. HENRY FISHER'S AFFIDAVIT IN DOWNER-MILTON SUIT.

Rosam Downer
vid q' Thomam
Bower et āl
Deftꝗ 469

Henry ffisher maketh oath that James ffisher this Def^t sonn is at this tyme resideinge in the kingdome of Ireland and that the said Deftꝗ doe informe this Dep^t that the said James ffisher is a very materiall witnesse to be examīed in this Cause on the s'd Deftꝗ

behalfes Jur' xxj° Novem 1631 Ro Riche

Public Record Office, C41/7, Michaelmas, 1631, #469; French, *Milton in Chancery*, p. 255. The word "Def^t" in the second line seems to be an error for "Dep^t," or deponent, since it must refer to the witness rather than to either of the defendants in the case.

NOVEMBER 28. JAMES FISHER ORDERED SUMMONED TO TESTIFY IN DOWNER-MILTON SUIT.

L xxviii No [1631] . . .

D Rosa Downer vid
q'Tho. Bower et al
r deft

fforasmuch as it appeareth by an Afft of one Henry ffisher that one James ffisher Who is A materiall witnesse for the Deft is at this tyme resideing in Jreland Jt is

therefore ordered vpon the mocōn of Mr Maundrell being of the Deftꝗ Councell that A Comī be awarded into Jreland to ex-amine the said James ffisher Retournable the Last Day of the next tearme, and in the meane tyme publicacō is staied but then to passe pemptorily./

ex' [Thomas?] R[oberts?].

Public Record Office, C33/161, f. 171; French, *Milton in Chancery*, p. 255.

December 9. Sonnet on reaching age of twenty-three.

How soone hath Time the suttle theefe of Youth
 Stolne on his wing my three, & twentith yeere
 my hasting days Fly on wth full careere
 but my late spring no bud or blossome shew'th
Perhapps my semblance might deceave ye truth
 that J to manhood am arriv'd so neere
 & inward ripenesse doth much lesse appeare
 that some more tymely-happie spirits indu'th
Yet be it lesse or more, or soone or slow
 it shall be still in strictest measure even
 to that same lot however meane or high
toward wch Tyme leads me, & the will of heaven
 all is if J have grace to use it so
 as ever in my great task-maisters eye.

Milton, The Trinity Manuscript, p. 6; *Poems*, 1645, p. 49; cm, I, 60. Collations are given in cm, I, 432. The manuscript version is used here as being closest to the version which Milton wrote at the time, though probably not the first version.

December 12. Receives interest payment from Richard Powell.

... the growing Jnterest for the forbearance of the said Principall debt was for some yeares then following likewise payd And soe continued to bee paid vntill June Jn the yeare of our Lord One Thousand six hundred ffortie and ffower. ...

From Milton's answer to Elizabeth Ashworth, February 22, 1653/4, *q.v.*

1632

Visits ireland (?).

In *Notes and Queries*, xi, iii (1911), 328 and 453, there is an account of letters which had recently appeared in newspapers in Belfast inquiring about Milton's supposed trip to Ireland during his Horton period.

No substantial proof of such a visit is offered, and nowhere in Milton's writings is there any mention of it.

FATHER'S MUSICAL COMPOSITIONS.

[1] Jf ye loue me.

Christ Church, Oxford, MS. 44, ff. 51v-53. This manuscript is a collection of works by Lupo, Ward, and others, including the present song by the elder Milton. The only words which appear in the manuscript are the four quoted, which are written in at the beginning. The song is set for four voices. At the top of f. 51v appears the name of the composer, "Jo: Milton." The manuscript is described in Brennecke, pp. 137 ff.; a modern transcription of the music, with words supplied, is given on pp. 198 ff. The music is mentioned, though not fully discussed, in Sigmund G. Spaeth, *Milton's Knowledge of Music*, 1913, p. 13n. This and the following compositions, though not dated, are placed here on the basis of Brennecke's hypothesis that they belong to "the Horton period or earlier" (p. 137).

[2] [a] Fantazia.

    [b] Fantazia.

    [c] Fantazia.

    [d] Jnomine.

    [e] Fantazia.

Christ Church, Oxford, MSS. 423, 424, 425, 426, 427, 428; these are the cantus, altus, tenor, quintus, sextus, and bassus parts, respectively, of a collection of songs by various composers, including John Milton Sr. Milton's four fantazias are for viols, and the "In nomine" for one male voice with viol accompaniment. The name of "Mr Milton" or "Mr Melton" appears at the top of each page. Brennecke discusses all five on pp. 139 ff., gives a facsimile of one page facing p. 142, and provides partial transcriptions on pp. 208 ff. Spaeth also refers to them in his *Milton's Knowledge of Music*, p. 13n.

Following are the words of the "In nomine," which appear only on the tenor part, MS. 425, f. 21:

If that a siner siges sent from a soule oprest
maye pearce the firmement the firmement, and mount the throane,
wheare greate Jehouah sittes, wheare great Jehouah sittes the god
    of rest,
then heare o Lord, the sad tone of my mone,
o gratious god, whoes goodnes gives mee light,
receaue my teares and prayers in thy sight, & prayeres in thy sight.

In the fourth line "tone" looks in the manuscript like "tane," but was probably written over. For some unaccountable reason, in transcribing these words on p. 141, Brennecke transcribes "teares" in the last line as "soul."

EPITAPH ON SHAKESPEARE PUBLISHED.

An Epitaph on the admirable Dramaticke Poet, VV SHAKE-SPEARE.

Mr. William Shakespeares Comedies, Histories, and Tragedies [the Second Folio], 1632, the page following sig. A4 but without pagination; Fletcher facsimile, 1, 366; CM, 1, 31, 429. See previous entry under 1630, the date of composition.

ANOTHER POEM ON SHAKESPEARE (?).

ON WORTHY MASTER SHAKESPEARE AND HIS POEMS.

Mr. William Shakespeares Comedies, Histories, and Tragedies [the Second Folio], 1632, prefatory pages. The poem is signed, *"I.M.S."* Those who attribute the poem to Milton at least tentatively (and these include Coleridge, Collier, and Sir Sidney Lee), interpret these initials as John Milton Student or John Milton Senior. Lee, in *A Life of William Shakespeare*, 1927, pp. 587-588, offers the further possibilities of Jasper Mayne Student and John Marston Student. *The Shakspere Allusion-Book*, edited by Ingleby-Smith-Furnivall and re-edited by John Munro, 1932, 1, 366-368, gives all these and also "In Memoriam Scriptoris." Disregarding the initials, it also proposes George Chapman and John Donne. Coleridge, as reported by J. P. Collier, in *Seven Lectures on Shakespeare and Milton by the late S. T. Coleridge*, 1856, pp. 105-107, says that Milton must have been the author, since "no other man, of that particular day, was capable of writing them."

It has even been suggested that Milton helped to edit the volume. Ludwig Tieck is reported to have told George Ticknor in 1836 that "he thinks Milton superintended the edition of Shakespeare to which his sonnet is prefixed, because the changes and emendations made in it, upon the first folio, are poetical and plainly made by a poet." This quotation is from Ticknor's *Life, Letters, and Journals*, London, 1876, 1, 472, quoted by Matthew W. Black and Matthias A. Shaaber in *Shakespeare's Seventeenth-Century Editors*, 1937, p. 97. The editors conclude, however, that the identity of the reviser is "doubtless lost beyond recovery."

JANUARY (?). TALKS WITH FRIEND [YOUNG?] ABOUT CAREER; FRIEND CAUTIONS HIM AGAINST TOO STUDIOUS AND RETIRED LIFE.

... you are often to me, & were yesterday especially, as a

good watchman to admonish that the howres of the night passe on (for so J call my life as yet obscure, & unserviceable to mankind) & that the day wth me is at hand wherin Christ comãnds all to labour while there is light. . . . But if you thinke, as you said, that too much love of Learning is in fault, & that J have given up my selfe to dreame away my yeares in the armes of studious retirement like Endymion wth the Moone as the tale of Latmus of goes. . . .

From Milton's letter to an unknown friend (Young?), filed below.

JANUARY (?). LETTER TO UNNAMED FRIEND; THOUGHTS ON FUTURE VOCATION; ANALYSIS OF OWN PERSONALITY; POEM ON AGE 23.

S^r, besides that in sundry other respects J must acknowledge me to proffit by you when ever wee meet, you are often to me, & were yesterday especially, as a good watchman to admonish that the howres of the night passe on (for so J call my life as yet obscure, & unserviceable to mankind) & that the day wth me is at hand wherin Christ comãnds all to labour while there is light. wch because J am psuaded you doe to no other purpose then out of a true desire that god should be honourd in every one; J therfore thinke my selfe bound though unask't, to give you account, as oft as occasion is, of this my tardie moving; according to the præcept of my conscience, wch J firmely trust is not wthout god. Yet now J will not streine for any set apologie, but only referre my selfe to what my mynd shall have at any tyme to declare her selfe at her bet ease But if you thinke, as you said, that too much love of Learning is in fault, & that J have given up my selfe to dreame away my yeares in the armes of studious retirement like Endymion wth the Moone as the tale of Latmus of goes, yet consider that if it were no more but the meere love of learning, whether it proceed from a principle bad, good, or naturall it could not have held out thus long against so strong opposition on the other side of every kind, for if it be bad why should not all the fond hopes that forward Youth & Vanitie are fledge with together wth Gaine,

pride, & ambition call me forward more powerfully, then a
poore regardlesse & unprofitable sin of curiosity should be able
to with hold me, wherby a man cutts himselfe off from all action & becomes the most helplesse, pusilanimous & unweapon'd
creature in the word, the most unfit & unable to doe that w^ch
all mortals most aspire to either to defend & be usefull to his
freinds, or to offend his enimies. Or if it be to be thought an
naturall pronenesse there is against y^t a much more potent in-
clination & inbred wch about this tyme of a mans life sollicits
most, the desire of house & family of his owne to wch nothing
is esteemed more helpefull then the early entring into credible
employment, & nothing more hindering then this affected soli-
tarinesse and though this were anough yet there is to this another act if not of pure yet of refined nature no lesse available
to dissuade prolonged obscurity, a desire of honour & repute, &
immortall fame seated in the brest of every true scholar wch all
make hast to by the readiest ways of publishing & divulging conceived merits as well those that shall as those that never shall
obtaine it, nature therfore would præsently worke the more
prævalent way if there were nothing but y^s inferiour bent of
her selfe to restraine her. Lastly the Love of Learning as it is
ye psuit of somthing good, it would sooner follow the more
excellent & supreme good knowne & præsented and so be
quickly diverted from the emptie & fantastick chase of shadows
& notions to the solid good flowing from due & tymely obedience to that comand in the gospell set out by the terrible seasing
of him that hid the talent. it is more probable therfore that
not the endlesse delight of speculation but this very consideration of that great comandement does not presse forward as soone as may be to underg[oe] but keeps off wth a
sacred reverence, & religious advisement how best to undergoe
not taking thought of beeing late so it give advantage to be
more fit for those that were latest lost nothing when the maister
of the vinyard came to give each one his hire. & heere J am come
to a streame head copious enough to disburden it selfe like
Nilus at seven mouthes into an ocean but then J should also

run into a reciprocall contradiction of ebbing & flowing at once
& doe that wch J excuse my selfe for not doing preach & not
preach. Yet that you may see that J am something suspicio[us]
of selfe, & doe take notice of a certaine belatednesse in me J am
the bolder to send you some of my nightward thoughts some
while since because they com in not altogether unfitly) made
up in a Petrarchian Stanza. wch J told you of

[How soone hath Time the suttle theefe of Youth
    Stolne on his wing my three, & twentith yeere
    my hasting days Fly on wth full careere
    but my late spring no bud or blossome shew'th
Perhapps my semblance might deceave ye truth
    that J to manhood am arriv'd so neere
    & inward ripenesse doth much lesse appeare
    that some more tymely-happie spirits indu'th
Yet be it lesse or more, or soone or slow
    it shall be still in strictest measure even
    to that same lot however meane or high
toward wch Tyme leads me, & the will of heaven
    all is if J have grace to use it so
    as ever in my great task-maisters eye]
           after ye stanza.

by this J beleeve you may well repent of having made mention at all of this matter, for if J have not all this while won
you to this, J have certainly wearied you to it. this therfore alone
may be a sufficient reason for me to keepe me as J am least
having thus tired you singly, J should deale worse wth a whole
congregation, & spoyle all the patience of a Parish. for J my
selfe doe not only see my owne tediousnesse but now grow
offended wth it that has hinderd [me] thus long from coming
to the last & best period of my letter, & that wch must now
cheifely worke my pardon that J am
         Yo^r true & unfained freind.

    Trinity or Cambridge Manuscript, p. 7; CM, XII, 322. This is the
second draft of the letter. The first, which directly precedes it in the
manuscript, is given in CM, XII, 320. The included poem, given here in
brackets, is not found in the second draft, but is taken from the first. We

may assume that when Milton wrote the letter which he finally sent to his friend, he copied the poem in the place here marked: "after ye stanza."

Both drafts show a great many alterations in the manuscript as well as a considerable change from the first to the second. The variants are carefully collected in CM, XII, 399-402. See also CM, XVIII, 527; Masson, I, 289 (323-325).

Both the date of the letter and the identity of the recipient are uncertain. Professor Mabbott places it in 1632, Professor Parker in 1633, and Professor Hanford in 1634. It is here dated January, 1632, because the language of the letter seems to indicate that it was written not long after the sonnet on arriving at the age of twenty-three. If that poem was written early in December, 1631, as we have assumed, and if we may put an ordinary interpretation on his reference to it here as "my nightward thoughts some while since," a month or so would be a reasonable interval to assume. It may, of course, have been somewhat longer. For recipient the favorite hypothesis has usually been Milton's former tutor, Thomas Young; but Hugh C. H. Candy, in a pencil note in John Diodati's *Piovs Annotations Vpon the Holy Bible*, London, 1643, front flyleaf (now in this editor's possession), proposes Charles Diodati: "The Author of these annotations was the uncle of Charles Diodati the intimate early friend to whom Milton addressed . . . the draft letter in English in the Trin. Coll. M.S. volume. . . ." The tone of the letter makes Young a far more likely guess than Diodati.

A few letters, no longer legible because of the wearing away of the edge of the sheet, are here printed in brackets because part of a stroke of one or more is still visible and because they are easily deducible from the context.

JANUARY (?). DISCARDS CHURCH CAREER.

. . . the Church, to whose service by the intentions of my parents and friends *I* was destin'd of a child, and in mine own resolutions, till comming to some maturity of yeers and perceaving what tyranny had invaded the Church, that he who would take Orders must subscribe slave, and take an oath withall, which unlesse he took with a conscience that would retch, he must either strait perjure, or split his faith, *I* thought it better to preferre a blamelesse silence before the sacred office of speaking bought, and begun with servitude and forswearing.

Milton, *The Reason of Church Government*, 1641, p. 41; CM, III, 242. There is nothing in the passage to offer a specific date; but the tone of it and the nature of the decision are so similar to that of the letter to an unknown friend given above that there seems to be every reason to assign this mental experience to the same time and to consider it identical.

FEBRUARY 7 (?). SUPPLICAT FOR DEGREE OF A.M.

Coꝶ xh: Ad

Supplicat Reverentijs vestris Johannes Milton vt novē termini completi post finalē eius determinationē in quibus lectiones ordinarias audiui[t] (licèt non omninò secundū formā statuti) v[na]* cū omnibus oppositionibus, responsionibus, disputationibus† declamatio[nibus]* cæterisque exercitijs per statuta Regia requisit [is]* sufficiant ei ad incipiendū in artibus.

Jo: Forster Præl: [deputat:]*

Original in the University Registry, Cambridge; reprinted by the present editor in "Milton's Supplicats," *The Huntington Library Quarterly*, V (1942), 349 ff., with facsimile on p. 352. On the method of ascertaining the approximate date, see the notes to the supplicat for the A.B., February 10, 1629, and the response to the question, February 9, 1629. The handwriting here is not Milton's.

[Christ's College. Approved. John Milton prays your reverences that nine complete terms after his final determination, in which he has listened to the ordinary lectures (though perhaps not entirely according to the form of the statute), together with all oppositions, responses, disputations, declamations, and other exercises required by the royal statutes, may suffice him to commence in arts. John Forster, constituted lecturer.]

APRIL 14. COPIES OF DEPOSITIONS MADE IN DOWNER-MILTON SUIT.

Downer vid' con Milton et al'

Rsē + Olive Street.

Rsē + ffrancꝑ Stacy.

Rsē + Richard Sherrat

Rsē + George Broomee

Copied the. 14. April. 1632. ffor Down' by Waad'

Michīms: An°: 7ᵐᵒ. Caroli Rꝑ.

---

* In the photographic copy provided me through the kindness of the University Registrary a few letters at the ends of some lines are missing. They are here supplied in brackets.

† Inserted above the line over a caret.

Public Record Office, C24/574/40 (endorsement of bundle); French, *Milton in Chancery*, p. 256. The original entries will be found under dates of September 19-26, 1631, to which the date at the end of this endorsement refers.

[Widow Downer against Milton and others. Responses of Olive Street, Frances Stacy, Richard Sheratt, and George Broome. Copied the 14th of April, 1632, for Mrs. Downer by Waad. Michaelmas in the 7th year of the reign of King Charles.]

APRIL (?) PROLUSION 7. PREVIOUS PROLUSIONS; HIGH INTELLECTUAL IDEALS; SENSE OF YOUTHFULNESS; RE-TIRING NATURE.

In Sacrario habita pro Arte.

Oratio.

Beatiores reddit Homines Ars quam Ignorantia.

Tametsi mihi, Auditores, nihil magis jucundum sit atque optabile aspectu vestro, assiduâque togatorum hominum frequentiâ, hoc etiam honorifico dicendi munere, quo ego vice unâ atque alterâ apud vos non ingratâ operâ perfunctus sum; tamen, si quod res est fateri liceat, semper ita fit, ut, cum neque meum ingenium, nec studiorum ratio ab hoc Oratorio genere multum abhorreat, ego vix unquam meâ voluntate, aut sponte ad dicendum accedam; mihi si fuisset integrum, vel huic vespertino labori haud illibenter equidem parsissem: nam quoniam ex Libris & Sententiis doctissimorum hominum sic accepi, nihil vulgare, aut mediocre in Oratore, ut nec in Poeta posse concedi, eumque oportere, qui Orator esse meritò & habere velit, omnium Artium, omnisque Scientiæ circulari quodam subsidio instructum & consummatum esse; id quando mea ætas non fert, malui jam prius ea mihi subsidia comparando, longo & acri studio ad illam laudem veram contendere, quam properato & præcoci stylo falsam præripere. Quâ animi cogitatione et consilio dum æstuo totus indies, & accendor, nullum unquam sensi gravius impedimentum & moram, hoc frequenti interpellationis damno; nihil vero magis aluisse ingenium, &, contra quam in corpore fit, bonam ei valetudinem conservâsse erudito & liberali otio. Hunc ego divinum *Hesiodi* somnum, hos nocturnos *Endymionis* cum Luna congressus esse crediderim; hunc illum duce *Mercurio Promethei* secessum in altissimas Montis *Caucasi* solitudines, ubi sapientissimus Deûm atque hominum evasit, utpote quem ipse *Jupiter* de Nuptiis *Thetidis* consultum isse dicatur. Testor ipse lucos, & flumina, & dilectas villarum ulmos, sub quibus æstate proxime præteritâ (si Dearum arcana eloqui liceat) summam cum Musis gratiam habuisse me jucundâ memoriâ recolo; ubi & ego inter rura & semotos saltus velut occulto ævo crescere mihi potuisse visus sum. . . .

Milton, *Epistolarum Familiarium Liber Unus*, 1674, pp. 135-155; CM, XII, 246 ff. The date, which is uncertain, is that suggested by Masson (I, 241 [275]) on the grounds that this piece was probably the final declamation required of Milton as candidate for the A.M. If so, it would logically come in the spring of 1632.

[Although nothing is more agreeable and desirable to me, my hearers, than the sight of you and the constant company of gowned gentlemen, and also this honourable office of speaking, which on more occasions than one I have with no unpleasant pains discharged among you; yet, to confess the actual truth, it always so happens that, though neither my genius nor the nature of my studies is at all out of keeping with the oratorical office, nevertheless I scarcely ever come to speak of my own free will and choice. Had it been in my power, I should not unwillingly have spared myself even this evening's labour; for, as I have learned this from the books and sayings of the most learned men, that, no more in the orator than in the poet, can anything common or mediocre be tolerated, and that it behoves him who would truly be and be considered an orator, to be instructed and thoroughly finished in a certain circular education of all the arts and all science, so, my age not permitting this, I would rather be working with severe study for that true reputation, by the preliminary practice of the necessary means, than hurrying on a false reputation by a forced and precocious style. In which thought and purpose of my mind while I am daily tossed and kindled more and more, I have never experienced any hindrance and delay more grievous than the frequent mischief of interruption, and nothing more nurturing to my genius and conservative of its good health, as contradistinguished from that of the body, than a learned and liberal leisure. This I would fain believe to be the divine sleep of Hesiod; these to be Endymion's nightly meetings with the Moon; this to be that retirement of Prometheus, under the guidance of Mercury, to the steepest solitudes of Mount Caucasus, where he became the wisest of gods and men, so that even Jupiter himself is said to have gone to consult him about the marriage of Thetis. I call to witness for myself the groves, and rivers, and the beloved village-elms, under which in the last past summer, (if it is right to speak the secrets of goddesses,) I remember so pleasantly having had supreme delight with the Muses; where I too, among rural scenes and remote forests, seemed as if I could have grown and vegetated through a hidden eternity.]

Masson, I, 266-267 (297-303).

JUNE 20. CHANCERY DECREE IN DOWNER-MILTON CASE.

Mer xx Junij [1632]/

D Rosa Downer vid q'   Whereby an order of the second of
  Johes Milton et Tho.   June instant taken vpon hearing of the
r Bower Deft   Cause. Jt was ordered and Decreed
                          that the Def^te should before thend of
this tearme paie vnto the p't 50^ll and therevpon the pl't should assigne over vnto the Dēft℘ the bond in question to help themselues ag^t the obligors Vpon opening of the matter this pñte Day vnto this Court by Mr Estcott being of the Deft Miltons Counsell Jt was alleadged that although it plainely appeared at the said hearing that the Deft Bower lent the said 50^l w^thout the Deft Miltons consent and that the Deft Milton comaunded the said Bower to pay the same vnto the pt', and although the intent of this Court (as was alleadged) then was that the said Dēft℘ should paie the said 50^ll equally and proporcōnably betweene them yet the said order being left geñall and not setting

downe in pticuler how much each of them shall paie the Deft Bower refuseth to pay the moiety of the said money although the said money miscarried thorough the fault and willfullnes of the said Bower. Jt is therevpon thought meete & soe ordered in case the said Milton shalbe charged wth the whole 50^ll that if the Deft Bowers shall not vpon the retourne of a spā shew good cause to the contrary then he shall pay A moiety of the said 50^ll vnto the said Milton./

ēx   R

Public Record Office, C33/161, f. 704; French, *Milton in Chancery*, p. 256. Though probably not the only decision pronounced in the case, this is the only one which has been found. The initial R at the end is probably that of Thomas Roberts.

. . . in the month of June in the eight yeare of his Ma^tieȝ Raigne and vpon hearing of the said Cause . . . it was thoughte meete ordered and decreed by this Honō^ble Courte that your Orators should pay vnto her the said Rose Downer the said ffiftie pounds and that therevpon the said Rose Downer should Assigne ouer vnto your Orators the said bond. . . .

From the bill of Milton's father and Bower against Arthur Duck and William Child; see below under date of February 16, 1636/7.

JUNE 20. FATHER PAYS FIFTY POUNDS TO ROSE DOWNER AS ORDERED BY COURT AND RECEIVES HER BOND.

. . . in obedience to the said decree your Orators vpon the twentith day of June in the said eight yeare of his Maties. said Raigne did pay vnto the said Rose Downer the said ffiftie poundȝ as by her receipt vnder her hand vpon the coppie of the said decree appeareth And shee the said Rose downer the said twentith day of June did Assigne ouer the said Bond to your Orators as was inioyned her by the said decree. . . .

From the bill of Milton's father and Bower against Duck and Child; see below under date of February 16, 1636/7.

SUMMER (?). FATHER RETIRES TO HORTON AND ACQUIRES HOUSE.

. . . Paterno rure, quo is transigendæ senectutis causâ concesserat. . . .

Milton, *Defensio Secunda,* 1654, pp. 82-83; CM, VIII, 120-121. Though the fact of the retirement is sufficiently clear, since the family remained there for a number of years, the exact date is open to question. However, we know that from September 19 to 26, 1631, the elder Milton was residing in London, since four deponents in a Chancery action so deposed. From the tone of Milton's statement here it seems reasonable to conclude that he went directly to Horton on receiving his A.M. at Cambridge in July. It may be reasonable, therefore, to assume that the move was made in the spring or summer of 1632.

Masson speculates on whether Milton's father bought or rented this house at Horton (I, 524 [561]). He rightly, I believe, considers the second alternative the more likely. As to the owner from whom he held it as tenant, Masson quotes Warton's note on "Epitaphium Damonis," line 149, that "Our author's father's house and lands at Horton near Colnbrook, were held under the Earl of Bridgewater." No authority for the statement is given by Warton, who, indeed, had stated in a note to Elegy I, line 50, that the poet's "father had *purchased* the estate at Colnebrook, before 1632" [italics mine]. Masson notes that "The Bulstrodes were the chief proprietors of land about Horton."

The house in which Milton lived at Horton no longer stands, having been torn down about 1798, though a number of traditions linger on about it in out-of-the-way articles and books. A careful study of it may be found in David Masson, "Local Memories of Milton," *Good Words,* XXXIV (1893), 41-44. Masson describes the neighborhood and gives illustrations of it from old pictures and contemporary sketches. Further material, much of it repetitious, occurs in the London *Times* for August 12, 1874, p. 7e; June 4, 1877, p. 12d; March 16, 1883, p. 3c; *Gentleman's Magazine,* NS XXIX (1848), 231; *Fraser's Magazine,* XXIII (1841), 519; Milton, *Works,* Pickering edition, I (1851), v; Todd, 1826, I, 23.

[. . . At my father's house in the country, to which he had gone to pass his old age. . . .]

JULY 3. SIGNS GRADUATION BOOK FOR DEGREE OF A.M.

[In the list of those who subscribe the three articles required of those who receive degrees:] Joannes Milton.

Christ's College, Cambridge, Graduation Book; Masson, I, 224-225 (258); French, "The Autographs of John Milton," *ELH,* IV (1937), #100; CM, XVIII, 624. The signature is reproduced in Masson, I, facing p. 780 (834); and in Sotheby, facing p. 124.

. . . Magistri, quem vocant, gradum, cum laude etiam adeptus. . . .

Milton, *Defensio Secunda,* 1654, p. 82; CM, VIII, 120. It seems unnecessary to furnish further proofs of his having received the degree, though several will be found under the subsequent entry concerning his removal to Horton.

[I received the degree of Master, as they call it, with honor.]

JULY. MOVES TO HORTON, FOR LIFE OF STUDY AND READING, WITH OCCASIONAL VISITS TO LONDON.

... Magistri, quem vocant, gradum, cum laude etiam adeptus, non in Italiam, quod impurus ille comminiscitur, profugi, sed sponte meâ domum me contuli, méique etiam desiderium, apud Collegii plerósque socios à quibus eram haud mediocriter cultus, reliqui. Paterno rure, quo is transigendæ senectutis causâ concesserat, evolvendis Græcis Latinísque scriptoribus summum per otium totus vacavi; ita tamen ut nonnunquam, rus urbe mutarem, aut coëmendorum gratia librorum, aut novum quidpiam in Mathematicis, vel in Musicis, quibus tum oblectabar, addiscendi. Exacto in hunc modum quinquennio, post matris obitum. . . .

Milton, *Defensio Secunda,* 1654, pp. 82-83; CM, VIII, 120-121.

[... Having also obtained the degree of Master, as they call it, with honor, I did not flee to Italy, as that wretch feigns, but voluntarily returned home; and I left with most of the fellows of the College, by whom I had been cultivated with more than indifference, a regretful desire for my presence. At my father's house in the country, to which he had gone to pass his old age, I gave myself up with the most complete leisure to reading through the Greek and Latin writers; with this proviso, however, that occasionally I exchanged the country for the town, for the sake of buying books or of learning something new in mathematics or in music, in which I then delighted. When five years had passed in this way, after the death of my mother. . . .]

Translation by the present editor.

After taking his degree of Master of Arts hee left the University, and, having no design to take upon him any of the particular learned Professions, apply'd himselfe for five yeers, at his Fathers house in the Country, to the diligent reading of the

best Classic Authors, both Divine & Humane; sometimes re-
pairing to London, from wch he was not farr distant, for learning
Music and the Mathematics.

The "earliest" biography, f. 140v; Darbishire, p. 19.

Soon after he had taken his Master's Degree, he thought fit
to leave the University: Not upon any disgust or discontent for
want of Preferment, as some Ill-willers have reported; nor
upon any cause whatsoever forc'd to flie, as his Detractors
maliciously feign; but from which aspersion he sufficiently clears
himself in his Second Answer to *Alexander Morus*, the Author
of a Book call'd, *Clamor Regii Sanguinis ad Cœlum*, the chief
of his Calumniators; in which he plainly makes it out, that after
his leaving the University, to the no small trouble of his Fellow-
Collegiates, who in general regretted his Absence, he for the
space of Five years lived for the most part with his Father and
Mother at their house at *Horton* near *Colebrook* in *Barkshire*;
whither his Father, having got an Estate to his content, and
left off all business, was retir'd from the Cares and Fatigues of
the world.

Phillips, pp. ix-x; Darbishire, pp. 54-55.

. . . after he had taken the degrees in Arts, he left the University of his own accord, and was not expelled for misdemean-
ours, as his Adversaries have said. Whereupon retiring to his
Fathers house in the Country, he spent some time in turning
over Latin and Greek Authors, and now and then made* excursions into the great City to buy books, to the end that he
might be instructed in Mathematicks and Musick, in which last
he became excellent, and by the help of his Mathematicks could
compose a Song or Lesson.

Wood, *Fasti Oxonienses*, I, 880; Darbishire, p. 36.

. . . some years I had spent in the stories of those Greek and
Roman exploits. . . .

Milton, *An Apology for Smectymnuus*, 1641, p. 52; CM, III, 357.
Although the time referred to is vague, this allusion is placed here because of its similarity to the others in this group.

* See in *Jo. Milton's* book intit. *Defensio secunda*: Edit. *Hag. Com.* 1654.
p. 61. &c. [Wood's note.]

JULY(?). LATIN POEM TO FATHER; RETIREMENT AND
STUDY; FATHER'S ENCOURAGEMENT.

Ad Patrem.

. . . Nec tu perge precor sacras contemnere Musas,
Nec vanas inopesque puta, quarum ipse peritus
Munere, mille sonos numeros componis ad aptos,
Millibus & vocem modulis variare canoram
Doctus, Arionii meritò sis nominis hæres.
Nunc tibi quid mirum, si me genuisse poëtam
Contigerit, charo si tam propè sanguine juncti
Cognatas artes, studiumque affine sequamur:
Ipse volens Phœbus se dispertire duobus,
Altera dona mihi, dedit altera dona parenti,
Dividuumque Deum genitorque puerque tenemus.

  Tu tamen ut simules teneras odisse comœnas,
Non odisse reor, neque enim, pater, ire jubebas
Quà via lata patet, qua pronior area lucri,
Certaque condendi fulget spes aurea nummi:
Nec rapis ad leges, malè custoditaque gentis
Jura, nec insulsis damnas clamoribus aures.
Sed magis excultam cupiens ditescere mentem,
Me procul urbano strepitu, secessibus altis
Abductum Aoniæ jucunda per otia ripæ
Phœbæo lateri comitem sinis ire beatum. . . .

Milton, *Poems,* 1645, Part ii, pp. 63-68; Mackellar, pp. 142 ff.;
CM, I, 268-279. This poem has been dated all the way from the summer of 1632 (Hanford, *Handbook,* p. 134) to 1640 (H. F. Fletcher,
Fred Newton Scott Anniversary Papers, 1929, pp. 199-205). It seems
to the present editor to be so closely related to the letter to a friend (also
filed under 1632) that it deserves to be placed here. In his recent edition of Milton's poems (*The Complete Poetical Works of John Milton,*
1941, p. 524) Harris Fletcher even suggests that the poem may have
been written as late as 1645, for a special compliment to his father, who
contributed to the cost of publication of the *Poems* of that year.

[To my father.

. . . And don't continue, I pray, to despise the holy Muses,
and don't think them vain or useless through whose aid you

yourself have become expert and set a thousand sounds to apt numbers, and, taught by them to vary your sweet voice by a thousand modulations, you may deservedly be the heir of Arion's name. Why now does it seem wonderful to you if it happens that you have been the father of me, a poet, if we, joined so closely by our dear blood, should follow related arts and closely connected studies? Phoebus himself, wishing to share himself among us two, gave one set of gifts to me and the other to my parent; and we, father and son, hold a divided god.

But though you yourself pretend to hate the tender Muses, I think you do not actually hate them, my father, for you did not order me to go by the road which lies wide open, where the area of gold lies all too inviting and the certain hope of making money gleams golden. Nor do you hale me to the law and the ill-kept statutes of the nation, nor condemn my ears to their insipid clamors. But desiring rather that my mind should be improved and enriched, you allow me, snatched far from the clamor of the city to deep seclusions, to wander through the pleasing leisure of the Aonian stream, a blessed comrade close beside Phoebus. . . .]

Translation by the present editor.

JULY (?). BEGINS COMMONPLACE BOOK.

Milton put himself through a wide course of reading, of which some notes remain in this book, now in the British Museum, Add. MS. 36,354. First discovered by A. J. Horwood among the papers of Sir Frederick Graham, Bart., it was published by him in facsimile in 1876 and (in transcription) in the same year in the publications of the Camden Society (also in revised form in 1877). It is given in full, with collation of the manuscript, in CM, XVIII, 128 ff. and 505 ff. For further details, see French, "The Autographs of John Milton," *ELH*, IV (1937), #9, where a substantial bibliography is given.

The Commonplace Book has been carefully studied by James Holly Hanford in "The Chronology of Milton's Private Studies," *PMLA*, XXXVI (1921), 251-314. He dates it (*Handbook*, p. 131) "from the Horton period to some time after Milton had become blind."

The notes are grouped under three headings: "Index Ethicus" (pp. 1-100), "Index OEconomicus" (pp. 101-176), and "Index Politicus" (pp. 177-250). There is an index on p. 251. Many pages remain blank, and there are entries in other hands than Milton's. The pages from 82 to 98 have been lost or torn out, leaving only strips half an inch wide, on which have been pasted new inserted leaves. One or two of these stubs show traces of writing, but too brief to decipher.

Either in this book on pages now lost or in a separate book Milton also kept jottings on other subjects. One of these is "Index Theologicus," the references to which are assembled in CM, XVIII, 226. An "Index Ethicus" is given at CM, XVIII, 221 ff. For further details about Milton's notebooks, see CM, XVIII, 505 ff.

SEPTEMBER 14. FATHER DEPOSES IN HUET-BARON SUIT.

14. Septembris 1632   p Huet.
A° Caroli Rp. 8°:

[September 14, 1632, in the 8th year of King Charles. On behalf of Huet.]

1   *John Milton* of Hammsmith in the County of Mĩdd gen'te of the age of 68 yeares or thereaboutp sworne & exaĩed &c' deposeth and saieth to the first Jnter' That he doth know Wᵐ Huet and Bersheba his wife named for Compltp and Sarah Baron widdow named for deft in this suite and did know xpofer Barron late hus'band of the deft Sarah. And did also know Raph Hamoʳ and Susan his wife in the aᵲcle named when they were liveing and hath knowne the Complt Huet these xx yeares or thereaboutp and Bersheba his wife from her Childhood and Sarah Baron from her childhood also And knew xpofer Baron above xxx yeares before he dyed and did know Raph Hamor and Susan his wife for many yeares before they dyed./

2   That he doth not rember what or how much the s̃d Raph Hamoʳ. did by his will bequeath to the Complt Bersheba but thinketh it was 300ˡⁱ and also beleeueth that Susan Hamoʳ his wife was executrix of the s̃d Raph. . . .

3   That he this dept did make Bondes for the s̃d xpōfer for monyes lent at interest and as he rembreth he did make three severall Bondes in the name of the s̃d Bersheba. for 300ˡⁱ vizt each bond for paymt of 100ˡⁱ wᵗʰ such interest as the Statute doth allow . . . but thinketh that Sʳ Richard Molineux now Lo:

[276]

Molineux was bound in one of the s̄d bondes and this he saieth
is the effect of that he can depose to thinter. . . .

Jo: Milton./

Public Record Office, Chancery Town Depositions, C24/587/46.
This document was found by Mr. Charles Bernau. The omitted portions
have no personal relation to Milton. It has not previously been published.

SEPTEMBER 22. BROTHER CHRISTOPHER ADMITTED TO
INNER TEMPLE (?).

Christopher Milton, second son of John Milton of London,
gentleman, admitted of the Inner Temple, 22d September,
1632.

Masson, I, 525 (562); Brennecke, p. 121. I have not seen this record,
which Masson says he took from the "books of the Inner Temple." The
printed records indicate rather that the admission was of November,
1631 (*q.v.*).

SEPTEMBER 29. FATHER (?) LISTED AMONG LESSEES
OF PROPERTY OF LONDON BRIDGE.

A rentall of all the landes, houses, and quit rentȝ belonginge
vnto London bridge, for one whole yeare endinge at Michās,
Anno Dnī, 1632, expressinge theire situacōns, and estates
thereof made, and granted./ . . .

Principall Weste parte of London bridge lately burned
downe./ . . .

John Milton for two tenemtȝ demised for ⎱
21 yeares from our Ladye daye A°. 1631 ⎰ x^{li}.

Bodleian Library, MS. Tanner 121, ff. 118, 121, 121v; photographic copy in Library of Congress. I am indebted to Dr. Leslie Hotson
for this reference. It is not certain, of course, that this John Milton was
either the poet or his father, but there is no reason why he should not
have been. In the same long list of persons holding London Bridge
property there are several names of interest in connection with Milton,
among them an Anne Powell and a Thomas Ellwood. Although neither
of these can well be the poet's friends, they may be their relatives. If this
John Milton is the poet or his father, moreover, any connection between
the properties named here and their other holdings in London remains
to be established.

DECEMBER 12. RECEIVES INTEREST PAYMENT FROM
RICHARD POWELL.

. . . the growing Jnterest for the forbearance of the said Prin-
cipall debt was for some yeares then following likewise payd
And soe continued to bee paid vntill June Jn the yeare of our
Lord One Thousand six hundred ffortie and ffower. . . .

From Milton's answer to Elizabeth Ashworth, February 22, 1653/4,
q.v.

ALLEGED PORTRAIT.

Iohannes Miltonus; circa annum aetatis XXV^m. Cedite Romani Scriptores, cedite Graii Propert. Viro ornatissimo Cuth-
berto Constable de Burton Constable in Com. Ebor, Tabulam
hanc merito votivam D.D.D. Francūs Peck, A.M.

Williamson (*Milton Tercentenary*, 1908, pp. 17, 83) describes this
portrait as an impudent attempt to foist off a pretended portrait of Mil-
ton on the public. Francis Peck, in his *Memoirs*, 1740, attributed it to
Milton because the subject of the picture held a copy of *Paradise Lost*.
Vertue, Warton, Marsh, and others have all rejected it indignantly.
The original being lost, it is known only through the prints made for
Peck.

[John Milton. About the 25th year of his age. Yield, you
Roman writers; yield, you Greek. Propertius. To the most illustrious man, Cuthbert Constable of Burton Constable in the
county of York, Francis Peck, A.M., gives as a well deserved
gift this votive tablet.]

POEM ON TIME.
On Time.

Milton, *Poems*, 1645, pp. 19-20; CM, I, 25-26. There is no means
of dating this poem with any accuracy. Neither in the *Poems* nor in the
Cambridge manuscript is there any evidence of the time when it was written. Like two other poems here placed beside it, "At a Solemn Music"
and "Upon the Circumcision," it has been dated all the way from
1631 to 1634. It may perhaps have been written on or near a birthday,

which would naturally lead the poet to think of the passing of time. In both the manuscript and the *Poems* the poems are placed together, though the order is somewhat varied.

POEM ON A SOLEMN MUSICAL SERVICE.

At a solemn Musick.

Milton, *Poems*, 1645, pp. 22-23; CM, I, 27-28. For discussion of date, which is most uncertain, see notes to "On Time," here grouped with it.

POEM ON THE CIRCUMCISION.

Upon the Circumcision.

Milton, *Poems*, 1645, pp. 20-22; CM, I, 26-27. For the date, see the notes to "On Time." It may or may not be relevant that the feast day of the Circumcision in the church calendar is January 1.

A RELATIVE IS A SCRIVENER (?).

1633 . . . John. Vnderwood—of Ric^d: Milton —1621.

Bodleian Library, Rawl. MS. Misc. 51, ff. 29-29v. The entry means that in 1633 John Underwood, an apprentice of Richard Milton, was admitted to the Scriveners' Company. What relation Richard was to John, if any, is uncertain.

FATHER'S CONTRIBUTIONS TO RAVENSCROFT'S "BOOK OF PSALMS" REPRINTED.

First published in 1621 (*q.v.*), this collection was reprinted in 1633. Warton (1791, p. 523, quoted in Todd, 1826, VI, 336) adds the interesting statement that the tenor part of his tune of York was "such a favourite, as to be used by nurses for a lullaby, and as a chime-tune for churches."

OCTOBER 9-NOVEMBER 28. FATHER AND ASSOCIATE BOWER BRING CHANCERY BILL AGAINST ARTHUR DUCK, WILLIAM CHILD, AND OTHERS.

. . . your Orators . . . did . . . in or about the tearme of St Michaell in the nineth yeare of his now Ma^tiee Raigne exhibite there bill of Comp^lt in this Courte against the said Docter Ducke and William Child Allexander Ewins Katherine and Barbara Ewins to be releeued of in vpon and Concerninge the p^rmisses.

. . .

From the bill of Milton's father and Bower against Duck and Child; see below under date of February 16, 1636/7. This earlier bill has not been found. It seems likely that Rose Downer was also one of the plaintiffs, and that her death soon after the bringing of the bill interfered with its regular progress through legal channels. The answer of Duck and Child (see below, March 16, 1636/7) states that the suit "is abated by the death of Rose Downer." But see various related entries under May, 1635.

. . . And these Defendantꝑ say that true it is that amongst others the said Rose Downer about the tyme in the Bill men-cõned Did exhibite a bill of Complaint into this Honble: Court against the sd Defendants [and the] others in the said Bill named. . . .

From the answer of Duck and Child to the suit of Milton and Bower; see below under date of March 16, 1636/7.

OCTOBER 9-NOVEMBER 28. DUCK AND CHILD AND OTHERS ANSWER BILL OF MILTON'S FATHER AND BOWER.

. . . vnto which bill the said Docter Ducke and William Child Answered and Confessed that there was moneyes left in theire handꝑ. . . .

From the bill of Milton's father and Bower against Duck and Child; see below under date of February 16, 1636/7. The original answer has not been found. See note to the bill, above, same date.

. . . to which these Defendantꝑ did make answere. . . .

From the answer of Duck and Child; see below under date of March 16, 1636/7.

OCTOBER 21. BUYS CRECCELIUS'S HISTORY.

[Title:] Collectanea Ex Historijs . . . Per Iohannem Crec-celium . . . Francofvrti Anno. MDCXIV.

[Milton's note:] pr 3^s. John Milton 1633 21st October.

The book is in the Huntington Library. Milton's note is written on the title page, perhaps in his own hand. Some of the letters are uncertain. See French, "The Autographs of John Milton," *ELH*, IV (1937), #75; CM, XVIII, 577.

DECEMBER 12. RECEIVES INTEREST PAYMENT FROM
RICHARD POWELL.

. . . the growing Jnterest for the forbearance of the said
Principall debt was for some yeares then following likewise
payd And soe continued to bee paid vntill June Jn the yeare
of our Lord One Thousand six hundred ffortie and ffower. . . .

From Milton's answer to Elizabeth Ashworth, February 22, 1653/4,
q.v.

1634

SISTER ANNE PHILLIPS REMARRIES.

. . . by a second Husband, Mr. *Thomas Agar*, who (upon
the Death of his Intimate Friend Mr. *Philips*) worthily Succeeded in the place, which except some time of Exclusion before and during the *Interregnum*, he held for many Years . . . .

Phillips, p. vii; Darbishire, p. 53; see Masson, II, 98-101, and VI,
770 ff. Anne's husband Edward Phillips had died in the fall of 1631
(*q.v.*); and Thomas Agar had had a child by his first wife, Mary
Rugeley, as late as 1633. This marriage must therefore not have taken
place until at least a decent interval after the death of the first Mrs.
Agar, the date of whose death is not known. It is here put under the
year 1634 arbitrarily.

BUYS A COPY OF LYCOPHRON'S "ALEXANDRA."

[Title:] ΛΥΚΟΦΡΟΝΟΣ ΤΟΥ ΧΑΛΚΙΔΕΩΣ ΑΛΕΞΑΝΔΡΑ
[Geneva, 1601.]

[Milton's inscription on a flyleaf reads:] Sum ex libris Jo:
Miltoni pre: 13ˢ. 1634.

This book is now in the possession of Mr. and Mrs. Adrian Van Sin-
deren of Brooklyn, New York. Milton also made many marginal annotations in the book as he read; they are published in CM, XVIII, 320 ff.
Further information may be found in French, "The Autographs of John
Milton," #77; CM, XVIII, 568.

BUYS AND ANNOTATES A COPY OF EURIPIDES' TRAGEDIES.

[Title:] ΕΥΡΙΠΙΔΟΥ ΤΡΑΓΩ-διων ὅσα σώζονται. Ἐvripidis *Tragœ-diœ quœ extant.* . . . *Excvdebat Pavlvs Stephanvs. Anno MDCII.*

[Milton's inscription on a flyleaf:] Jo. Milton pre: [12]s [6]d 1634.

Bodleian Library, Oxford, to which it was given in 1934 by W. W. Vaughan, Esq., M.V.O. There are numerous marginal annotations, which have been printed a number of times, the most complete text being that in CM, XVIII, 304. The price which Milton paid for the volume is no longer legible in his own inscription, but in another written by another hand and presumably copied from his, the figures given above may still be read. An outline of its history and other information about it may be found in French, "The Autographs of John Milton," #76, and in CM, XVIII, 566. Facsimiles of a number of entries are to be found in Sotheby, facing p. 108. See also Warton, 1791, pp. 568-9.

On a flyleaf is a note in the hand of an early owner, Thomas Birch, which reads as follows: "Liber hic olim fuit celeberrimi Johannis Miltoni, cujus nomen ab ipso suprà scriptum est, notæqz passim margini additæ. Ex Bibliothecâ Francisci Hare. Episcopi Cicestrensis transivit in Officinam Librariam Johannis Whistoni, à quo eum emebam die 12°. Aprilis 1754. Tho. Birch." [This was once the book of the illustrious John Milton, whose name has been written by himself above; his notes have been added here and there in the margin. From the library of Francis Hare, Bishop of Chichester, it passed to the bookshop of John Whiston, from whom I bought it on April 12, 1754. Thomas Birch.] Samuel Johnson consulted it in preparing his *Prefaces, Biographical and Critical, to the Works of the English Poets,* London, 1779. In this work, II, 138, he remarks: "His Euripides is, by Mr. Cradock's kindness, now in my hands: the margin is sometimes noted; but I have found nothing remarkable."

WRITES "COMUS."

Since this masque seems almost surely to have been written specifically for presentation at Ludlow Castle on September 29, 1634 (*q.v.*), and since under such circumstances an author would probably have only a fairly short time to work, we may reasonably assume that Milton wrote this masque in the early months of 1634.

There are several printed versions and several manuscripts. First published separately in 1637, *Comus* was included, with some changes, in the *Poems* of 1645 and 1673. It also occurs in the Cambridge or Trinity Manuscript; in the so-called Bridgewater Manuscript, now in the possession of the Bridgewater family (the Earl of Ellesmere); in British Museum Additional MS. 11,518; and in a manuscript now belonging to the Misses Church of Beaconsfield. With the exception of the last-named manuscript, all these versions are carefully collated in CM, I, 474 ff. The masque is printed in CM, I, 85 ff.

The Bridgewater Manuscript, formerly thought to be in the hand of Henry Lawes, who wrote the music and acted in the masque, is now considered to be the work of a professional scribe. It is said to be endorsed in the hand of the second Earl of Bridgewater: "Author Jo: Milton." The title is: "A Maske Represented before the right ho^ble: the Earle of Bridgewater Lord president of Wales and the right ho^ble: the Countesse of Bridgewater. At Ludlow Castle the 29th of September 1634." This is the actual stage copy which was used in the original presentation. It is reproduced in the Fletcher facsimile, I, 301 ff.

The British Museum Additional Manuscript comprises five songs written in a hand which might be seventeenth-century, signed with the name of Henry Lawes. The hand may be his. The songs bear the prefixed title: "Five Songs Set for a Mask presented at Ludlo Castle, before the Earl of Bridgewater Lord President of the Marches. October 1634." It is reproduced in the Fletcher facsimile, I, 341 ff.

The 1637 edition is entitled: "A Maske presented at Ludlow Castle, 1634: on Michaelmasse night, before the Right Honorable, Iohn Earle of Bridgewater, Vicount Brackly, Lord Præsident of Wales, And one of his Maiesties most honorable Privie Counsell."

The Trinity Manuscript is entitled simply: "A maske 1634."

The Church Manuscript, comprising the same five songs as the Additional Manuscript, is said to be in Lawes's hand. Other Lawes writing is also included. It is described in detail in Willa M. Evans, *Henry Lawes*, New York, 1941, pp. 235 ff. It was exhibited at Cambridge in 1908 (*Milton Tercentenary*, 1908, p. 160).

Comus has been edited numerous times. Among the most helpful recent editions are those by Lady Alix Egerton, 1910, and by E. H. Visiak and H. J. Foss in 1937. The former is from the Bridgewater Manuscript, with collations and facsimiles. The latter, which gives the music, has a foreword by the Earl of Ellesmere.

There were evidently many manuscripts prepared. In his dedication in the 1645 *Poems* Lawes says that *"the often Copying of it hath tir'd my Pen to give my severall friends satisfaction."*

On the Bridgewater family and *Comus*, see Warton, 1791, pp. 123 ff.; Todd, 1826, v, 204 ff.; Masson, I, 541-587 (587-623); Willa M. Evans, *Henry Lawes, passim* (especially the facsimile of "From ye Heav'ns" from the Church Manuscript on p. 103).

AFTER MARCH 27. FATHER APPOINTED MASTER OF
SCRIVENERS' COMPANY (?).

1634 . . . John Milton.*
   Charles Yeomans Master.
   W^m. Alexander ⎫
          ⎬ Wardens. . . .
   Steph. King ⎭

"An Annual Catalogue . . . of the Company of Scriveners," Bodleian
Library, MS. Rawl. Misc. 51, ff. 29v-30; *Athenaeum*, 1880, I, 565-
566. In the *Athenaeum* article Henry J. Sides dates the entry as above
and ventures the guess that the asterisk after Milton's name means that
he was appointed Master but paid a fine rather than to take office.

APRIL 17. FATHER DEPOSES IN ABDY-DUNSMORE
SUIT.

17°. Aprilis 1634.   ꝓ Abdye con' dunsmore
A° Caroli Rꝑ. 10./   dūn./

 [April 17, 1634, in the 10th year of King Charles. On behalf of Abdy against Dunsmore./]

1 *John Milton* of Hammersmith in the parrish of ffulham in
the County of Mīdd gent of the age of 71 yeares or thereabouᵗꝑ
sworne and exaїed &c' deposeth and saieth to the first Jntr'
That he doth know Anthony Abdy of London alderman named
for Complt and Frauncis Lo: dunsmore Sʳ Richard Grosvenoʳ
knᵗ & Barronett and Peter daniel Esqʳ named for defᵗꝑ in this
suite and hath knowne the Complt about these eight or nine
yeares and ffrauncis Lo: dunsmore these ten yeares or thereabouᵗꝑ and Sʳ Richard Grosenoʳ knᵗ & Barronet and Mʳ Peter
daniell a longe tyme./

2 That he doth find by a private note booke wᶜʰ he hath in his
owne Custodye that about the beginning of december *1624.*
That ffrauncis Leigh of Abskonet in the County of Surrey knᵗ
and Baronet Richard Grosvenoʳ of Eaton in the County of
Chester knᵗ and Baronett and Peter daniell of Talbey in the
County of Chester Esqʳ became bound vnto Humphrey Abdey
of Stretham in in [*sic*] the County of Surrey gent' in the sume
of 200ˡⁱ lawfull mony of England condiconed for the payment

of one hundred and five poundes at the then dwelling house of Humphrey Groveno^r scituate in Paternoster Row London on the third daye of June next ensueing the date of the s̄d Bond and this dept saieth that he verilie beleeveth that the bond bearing date the first daye of december 1624 and now shewed to him this dept at this the tyme of his examcon is the same bond for that he findeth the same to agree wth the note thereof wch he hath sett downe in his private book as afores̄d and saieth he is induced also to beleeve that it is the same bond because the bondℯ condicon is of the handwriting of one that was then his this dept ℯ servant and this dept doth also know the name of Thomas Bower thereto subscribed as a wittnes to be the s̄d Bowers hand writing who was then also his this dept ℯ servant, wch induceth this dept verilie to beleeve that the parties Oblig-ers did every of them respectively sett their hands and seales to the s̄d Bond and did deliver the same as their act ℯ and deedes to, or to the vse of the Obligee humfrey Abdey. And this he saieth is all he can depose to thintr'

Jo: Milton.

Public Record Office, Chancery Town Depositions, C24/591/2. This record was first discovered by Mr. Charles Bernau. It has not previously been published. Francis Lord Dunsmore, mentioned in the first paragraph, is probably the same person as the Sir Francis Leigh of the second paragraph, since Francis Leigh, later to be first Earl of Chichester (d. 1653), was created Baron Dunsmore in 1628 (*DNB*).

AUGUST 5. FATHER DEPOSES IN HUMPHREYS-DRABULL SUIT.

5° Augusti 1634   ℟ Drabūll con
An° Cariroli [*sic*] R℟ 10   Humfreys

[August 5, 1634, in the tenth year of King Charles. For Drabull against Humphreys.]

John Milton of Ham̄smith in the parrish of ffullham in the ₁ County of Mīdd gent of the age of 71 yeares or thereabout ℯ sworne and exaied &c' deposeth and saieth to the ffirst inter

That he doth not know John Drabull otherwise then of late he sawe him when he served him this dept wth a sub'pa to be exaied in this Cause and if he this dept did ever knowe or see Thomas Humfreys named for Complt he saieth he is now out of his rembrance But saieth he did know Wm Rogers Cittizen and Joyner of London deceased and knew him for many yeares before he died/

2   That he doth not well rember whether the deft drabull together wth the Complt and ffrauncis Michell Esqr did in or about the sixtenth daye of Aprill in the Tenth yeare of the reigne of o^r Late soeveraigne Lo: King James become bound by Obligacon vnto the s̄d Wm Rogers in the some of Twenty poundes or thereabout̢ for paymt of Ten poundes ten shilling̢ or thereabout̢ or no as by the arcle is questioned it is so long sithence howbeit he saieth it may well be that there is such a thing wch it if be he saieth the same is likely to be entred into a shopp Booke wch he this dept then kept, wch book he saieth was wth others left in the Custody of Thomas Bower a Scrivener now dwelling in ffleetstreet who was some tymes his this dept̢ servant vnto whome he this dept did give over his t̄rade togather wth his sd Shop booke. . . .

3   That he doth not rember that the s̄d Wm Rogers did make any Release vnder his hand and seale to the s̄d def^t drabull, but saieth that he beleeveth that the name of John Hutton who was late this dept̢ servant subscribed as a wittnes to the writing bearing date the 24 of June in the second yeare of the reigne of o^r now soeveraigne Lo: King Charles purporting to be such a release, is of the s̄d John Huttons owne handwriting. . . .

5   That he did know John Hutton named in the arcle for that he was his this dept̢ late servant and therefore did well know his handwriting and verilie beleeveth that the name of the s̄d John Hutton subscribed to the sd writing of release now shewed to him is of the s̄d John Huttons own ꝑpper handwriting./

Capt. co̅r Martino Basill/.   Jo: Milton

[Taken before Martin Basill]

Public Record Office, Chancery Town Depositions, C24/596/33.

[286]

This document, now first published, was first found by Mr. Charles Bernau.

AUGUST 21. RICHARD POWELL SUMMONED ABOUT COAT OF ARMS.

Memorandū that Ric powell of fforest hill in Com Oxfford Justice of ye peace in Com spdict being upon busines in that quallity when he should haue appered at Oxfford sent the kings of Armes ffees desiring respit to pffect these matters that concerne his Armes & descent at the heralds office in michelmes terme nex. wch was graunted at Thame. 21. August 1634.

George Ball.

Visitation of Oxfordshire in 1634, British Museum, Harl. MS. 1557, f. 111; Publications of the Harleian Society, v (1871), 334; Hunter, pp. 28-29; Masson, II, 497. At f. 111 v of the same manuscript (Publications, p. 335), is the further note: "Bollingdon hundr . . . M^r. Rich powell of fforest hill at Thame confformed."

SEPTEMBER 29. "COMUS" ACTED AT LUDLOW CASTLE; NAMES OF ACTORS.

A Maske presented at Ludlow Castle, 1634: on Michaelmasse night, before the Right Honorable, Iohn Earle of Bridgewater, Vicount Brackly, Lord Præsident of Wales, And one of his Maiesties most honorable Privie Counsell. . . .

Title of 1637 edition. According to the British Museum Additional Manuscript 11,518 version, it was presented in October. But the weight of evidence seems to be in favor of the earlier date.

A Maske Represented before the right ho^ble: the Earle of Bridgewater Lord president of Wales and the right ho^ble: the Countesse of Bridgewater. At Ludlow Castle the 29th of September 1634.

Title as given in the Bridgewater Manuscript.

The cheif persons which presented, were The Lord *Bracly,* Mr. *Thomas Egerton* his Brother, The Lady *Alice Egerton.*

Milton, *Poems,* 1645, p. 74 (preface to *Comus*).

To the Right Honourable, JOHN Lord Vicount BRACLY, Son and Heir apparent to the Earl of *Bridgewater, &c.* MY LORD, *This* Poem, *which receiv'd its first occasion of Birth from your*

Self, and others of your Noble Family, and much honour from your own Person in the performance, now returns again to make a finall Dedication of it self to you. . . . as in this representation your attendant Thyrsis, *so now in all reall expression Your faithfull, and most humble Servant* H. LAWES.

Dedication to *Comus* by Lawes, in Milton, *Poems,* 1645, pp. 69-70.

END OF NOVEMBER. TRANSLATES PSALM 114 INTO GREEK VERSE.

[Milton writes to Alexander Gill on December 4, 1634, enclosing a Greek composition:] Mitto itaq; quod non plane meum est, sed & vatis etiam illius vere divini, cuius hanc Oden alterâ ætatis septimanâ, nullo certe animi proposito, sed subito nescio quo impetu ante lucis exortum, ad Græci carminis Heroici legem in lectulo fere concinnabam . . . scias, ex quo ludum vestrum relinquerim hoc me unicum atq; primum græce composuisse. . . .

See below under date of December 4, 1634.

[I send, therefore, what is certainly not mine, but also belongs to that truly divine poet, this Ode of whom, only last week, with no deliberate intention certainly, but from I know not what sudden impulse before daybreak, I composed, almost in bed, to the rule of Greek heroic verse . . . understand that, since I left your school, this is the first and only thing I have composed in Greek. . . .]

Psalm 114.

Milton, *Poems,* 1645, Part ii, p. 69.

DECEMBER 2. LETTER FROM ALEXANDER GILL.

. . . Cum vero tam lepidum nobis, & venustum Hendecasyllabon nudiustertius donaveris . . . .

Milton, *Epistolarum Familiarium Liber Unus,* 1674, pp. 13-14; CM, XII, 14 ff. This quotation is from Milton's letter to Gill, dated December 4. Gill's letter is not known to be extant.

[Seeing, however, that you presented us the other day with a copy of Hendecasyllabics so sprightly and elegant . . . .]

Masson, I, 588 (623). Masson's translation of "nudiustertius" is inexact; it means three days ago according to Roman counting; in other words, the day before yesterday.

DECEMBER 4. LETTER TO ALEXANDER GILL; AC-
KNOWLEDGES RECEIPT OF GILL'S LETTER; SENDS GREEK
TRANSLATION OF VERSE; HINTS AT TROUBLE IN COL-
LEGE.

Alexandro Gillio.

5. Si mihi Aurum, aut cælata pretiose vasa, aut quicquid
istiusmodi mirantur Mortales, dono dedisses, puderet certe non
vicissim, quantum ex meis facultatibus suppeteret, te aliquando
remunerasse. Cum vero tam lepidum nobis, & venustum Hendecasyllabon nudiustertius donaveris, quanto charius quidem
Auro illud est merito, tanto nos reddidisti magis solicitos, quâ re
conquisitâ tam jucundi beneficii gratiam rependeremus; erant
quidem ad manum nostra hoc in genere nonnulla, sed quæ tuis
in certamen muneris æquale nullo modo mittenda censerem.
Mitto itaq; quod non plane meum est, sed & vatis etiam illius
vere divini, cujus hanc Oden alterâ ætatis septimanâ, nullo certe
animi proposito, sed subito nescio quo impetu ante lucis exortum,
ad Græci carminis Heroici legem in lectulo fere concinnabam:
ut hoc scilicet innixus adjutore qui te non minus argumento
superat, quam tu me artificio vincis, haberem aliquid, quod ad
æquilibrium compensationis accedere videatur; si quid occurrit,
quod tuæ de nostris, ut soles, opinioni minus satisfecerit, scias,
ex quo ludum vestrum relinquerim hoc me unicum atq; primum
græce composuisse, in Latinis, ut nosti, Anglicisq; libentius ver-
satum. Quandoquidem qui Græcis componendis hoc sæculo
studium atq; operam impendit, periculum est, ne plerumq;
surdo canat. Vale, meq; Die Lunæ Londini (si Deus voluerit)
inter Bibliopolas expecta. Interim si quid apud illum Doctorem,
annuum Collegii Præsidem, quâ vales amicitiâ, nostrum poteris
negotium promovere; cura quæso, ut meâ causâ quam cito adeas;
iterum Vale.

E nostro Suburbano, Decemb. 4. 1634.

Milton, *Epistolarum Familiarium Liber Unus,* 1674, pp. 13-14; CM,
XII, 14 ff.

[To Alexander Gill.

If you had presented to me a gift of gold, or of vases preciously embossed, or of whatever of that sort mortals admire, it were certainly to my shame not to have some time remunerated you, in as far as my faculties might serve. Seeing, however, that you presented us the other day with a copy of Hendecasyllabics so sprightly and elegant, by how much more dear than gold that gift is in value, by so much the more anxious have you made us as to the dainty device by which we should repay the kindness of so pleasant a benefit. We had, indeed, at hand some things of our own in this kind, but which I could nowise deem fit to be sent in trial of equality of gift with yours. I send, therefore, what is certainly not mine, but also belongs to that truly divine poet, this Ode of whom, only last week, with no deliberate intention certainly, but from I know not what sudden impulse before daybreak, I composed, almost in bed, to the rule of Greek heroic verse; in order that, relying on this coadjutor, who surpasses you no less in his subject than you surpass me in art, I should have something that might seem to approach a balancing of payments. Should anything occur to you in it not coming up to your usual opinion of our productions, understand that, since I left your school, this is the first and only thing I have composed in Greek,—employing myself, as you know, more willingly in Latin and English matters; inasmuch as whoever spends study and pains in this age on Greek composition runs a risk of singing generally to the deaf. Farewell, and expect me on Monday (if God will) in London among the booksellers. Meanwhile, if with such influence of friendship as you have with that Doctor, the annual president of the College, you can anything promote our business, take the trouble, I pray, to go to him as soon as possible on my account. Again, farewell.

From our suburban residence, Decemb. 4, 1634.]

Masson, I, 588 (623-624). Masson identifies the enclosed Greek composition with Milton's Greek version of the 114th Psalm. If he is correct, that piece of translation must have been done during the last few days of November, 1634. It may be noted that Milton here says categorically that this is the first Greek he has written since leaving St. Paul's School in 1625.

DECEMBER 12. RECEIVES INTEREST PAYMENT FROM
RICHARD POWELL.

... the growing Jnterest for the forbearance of the said Prin-
cipall debt was for some yeares then following likewise payd
And soe continued to bee paid vntill June Jn the yeare of our
Lord One Thousand six hundred ffortie and ffower. ...

From Milton's answer to Elizabeth Ashworth, February 22, 1653/4,
q.v.

1635

INCORPORATED A.M. AT OXFORD.

1635. ... This year was incorporated Master of Arts *John
Milton*, not that it appears so in the Register, for the reason I
have told you in the Incorporations 1629, but from his own
mouth to my friend, who was well acquainted with, and had
from him, and from his Relations after his death, most of this
account of his life and writings following.

Wood, *Fasti Oxonienses*, I, 880; Darbishire, p. 35. Under the
date of 1629, in *Fasti*, I, 865, Wood tells how John French was elected
Registrary this year and throughout all his time omitted to enter the incorporations of Cambridge graduates. Who Wood's friend was that
gave him this information we can not be sure, but John Aubrey would
be a likely guess.

BUYS COPY OF TERENCE'S COMEDIES.

[Title:] *Pvb. Terentii Comœdiæ Sex Ex recensione Hein-
siana. Lvgd. Batavorum, Ex Officina Elzeviriana. A°. 1635.*

[Milton's inscription on titlepage:] Jo Milton.

The book is now in the Harvard College Library. After Milton's
signature follow one or more words or figures no longer decipherable,
probably either the date or the price. The book contains some underlin-
ings and markings, but no marginalia of any importance. It is mentioned
in French, "The Autographs of John Milton," #61, and in CM, XVIII,
576.

BUYS A COPY OF WILLIAM AMES'S "CONSCIENTIA."

Gulielmi Amesij Conscientia, et eius jure, vel Casibus Libri Quinque [Amsterdam, 1635].

A copy of this book in the Princeton University Library contains a note which has been transcribed as "Ex libris Johannis Miltonii." Though this may not be actually Milton's copy, Edward Phillips mentions having read Ames with Milton. See "The Columbia 'Milton': Second Supplement," *Notes and Queries*, 179 (1940), 20-21.

JANUARY 8. FATHER DEPOSES IN CAMPION-TERRELL SUIT.

8° die Januarij 1634   p Campion sq coñ Terrell et
A° Caroli Rᵱ 10ᵐᵒ/   āl dēft

[January 8, 1634, in the 10th year of King Charles. On behalf of Campion, plaintiff, against Terrell and others, defendants.]

John Milton of Hamersmith in the County of Mĩdd gent' Aged 72 yeares or thereābtᵱ sworne and examined &c./

1   That hee doth well knowe Edward Campion named for Complt in this suite and did knowe John Terrell named for one of the dēftᵱ in the tytle to the Jnteῗrs now deceased but doth not knowe Willm̃ Hickes named for the other deft in this Cause but hath knowe the Complt Campion for diũse yeares and hath knowe Thomas Pittᵱ late heade Buttler of Lincolnes Jnne in the Jnteῗr enquired of and hath heretofore had some acquaintance wᵗʰ him but it is longe since he sawe the said Thomas Pittᵱ/

. . .

15   That he hath beene enformed and doth beleeve it to be true that the said Tho: Pittᵱ after hee went from Lincolnes Jnne and to his now best remembrance after he the said Pittᵱ the Complt Campion and Searle had sealed and deliũed the bond before menconed did sett vpp and keepe a Taverne in Holborne in the County of Mĩdd And saith that he this depont, beinge then a Scriuener did speake to the said Mʳ Terreˡˡ deceased to lend the said money that was lent and deliũed vppon the said bond entred into by the said Pittᵱ Campion and Searle and did

mediate wth the said Mr Terrell soe to doe, so he liked the securitie and this depont. after wardes did diūse tymes send to
the said Pittρ and alsoe to the Complt Campion for interest of
the said money due vppon the said bond and after wardρ for
the principall money when the said Mr Terrell desired to haue
the same payed in. . . . To the rest of the Jnterrs &c/

Jo: Milton

Public Record Office, Chancery Town Depositions, C24/600/37.
This document, now first published, was discovered by Mr. Charles
Bernau.

May. Father again tries to sue Duck and child (?).

Jn May. 1635. Rose Downer exhīted a bill for a debt of
50^{li}. wth Jnterest lent to Mathew the ffather in June. 4°. Cār. . . .

From a Chancery report and certificate of July 6, 1637, in a suit between Arthur Duck and William Child as plaintiffs and Alexander
Ewens and Mathew Ewens and others as defendants; see below under
date of July 6, 1637. Nothing is known of the original suit here referred
to, though it is likely that one existed. It is probable that Milton's father
was responsible for the action, because since her death in 1632 he had
frequently attempted to seek the recovery of the money he had paid for
her bond, and apparently he had used her name with his in legal actions
toward that end. Hence it is included here among the records of his
career. See the closely related entries under dates of October 9-Novem-
ber 28, 1633, and May 4-8, 1635.

May 4. Writ issued in Milton (?)-Duck action.

4 May [1635] . . .

D	Downer vid q̄	fforasmuch as the Deftρ appeared and
	Ducke, Child et	departed wthout aunswearing Jd Att vir
	Ewens Deftρ	mīdd r oct triñ./ Col R.

Public Record Office, London, Chancery Records, C33/167, f. 635v.
This is undoubtedly a document in the action mentioned under dates
of May, May 8, and June 13 of this year. For the connection with
Milton see the first of those entries. The abbreviation "vid q̄" means
"widow, plaintiff." Though the last part of the document indicates that
the case was scheduled to come up in Trinity term, no such appearance
has been found.

MAY 8. FATHER(?) BRINGS ACTION AGAINST SIR AR-THUR DUCK AND OTHERS.

Reference has already been made, under dates of May and May 4, to this action. On May 8 a Chancery bill (C8/39/39) was brought in the name of Rose Downer against Sir Arthur Duck and Matthew Ewens. The bill recounts the story of Rose Downer's investment of £50 with Ewens and Keymer and their failure to repay. See French, *Milton in Chancery*, pp. 63, 166. For Milton's connection with this affair, see entry under date of May, 1635. For the answer of Duck and others, see below under June 13.

JUNE (?). SUPPOSED PORTRAIT.

The *Illustrated London News*, cxv (1899), 13, reprints a number of portraits of past and present members of the Honourable Artillery Company, the muster-rolls of which go back to the time of Queen Eliza-beth. One is labeled. "JOHN MILTON, Admitted a Member of H.A.C. June 2, 1635." This is probably a picture of another John Milton. Al-though the date probably refers to the time of admission rather than of painting the portrait, it is mentioned here for lack of a more accurate date.

JUNE 13. DUCK AND OTHERS ANSWER FATHER'S (?) CHANCERY BILL.

On June 13, 1635, Sir Arthur Duck and William Child, two of the defendants in the bill brought against them in the name of Rose Downer on May 8 (actually by Milton's father?), presented their answer. The substance of their defense was that they were not liable for the debt men-tioned, and that they had no money with which to pay it anyhow. See French, *Milton in Chancery*, pp. 63-64.

SEPTEMBER 30. RELATIVE (?) BURIED.

1635, Sept. 30. [Buried] The daughter of Henry Milton, gent.

From the registers of St. Giles Cripplegate, London, quoted in J. P. Malcolm, *Londinum Redivivum*, III (1803), 299. I have not seen the original entry. Malcolm suggests that Henry Milton was "probably the uncle of the *Poet*; from whom he might have inherited his 'house situate on Bunhill.'"

DECEMBER 12. RECEIVES INTEREST PAYMENT FROM RICHARD POWELL.

. . . the growing Jnterest for the forbearance of the said

Principall debt was for some yeares then following likewise payd
And soe continued to bee paid vntill June Jn the yeare of our
Lord One Thousand six hundred ffortie and ffower. . . .

From Milton's answer to Elizabeth Ashworth, February 22, 1653/4,
q.v.

ATTRIBUTED VERSES ON PRINCE CHARLES, AND MANU-SCRIPT INSCRIPTION TO RICHARD BATEMAN.

Vivat io Vivat Princeps Carolinus, et Orbi.
Imperet, innumeris decorans sua sæcla Triumphis.

Flourish braue Prince, out shine thy Glorious Name,
Triumphant laurels ever crowne thy fame.   J. M.

Sir Walter Raleigh, *Tubus Historicus*, 1636; the verses are inscribed
under the frontispiece portrait of Prince Charles. Joseph Sabin (*Dictionary*, #67,591) ascribes them to Milton, partly because of the initials
J.M. and partly because of Milton's known interest in Raleigh's *Cabinet
Council*, 1658, *q.v.* See CM, XVIII, 357, 588.

A copy of this work in the Cambridge University Library contains a
manuscript inscription to Richard Bateman (given in the text immediately below this selection).

To the Reuerend & my Most Worthily Honord ffrend, M^r
Richard Bateman. Fellow & Bursar of the College-Royall at
Eton: J humbly consecrate these Affamiæ as a small Symbol of
my ever-vowed Observance. Meliora supersunt.   J. M.

Raleigh, *Tubus Historicus*, Cambridge University Library, shelf-
mark Syn. 7.63.246, blank page facing dedication to Prince Charles;
CM, XVIII, 588. The ascription of both this and the preceding item are
most doubtful, since the hand is decidedly not Milton's, and there is little
likelihood of his being so enthusiastic about Prince Charles at this time.
On the other hand, through his friend and future father-in-law, Richard
Powell, Milton may have been acquainted with and had some dealings
with Richard Bateman; see French, *Milton in Chancery*, pp. 80, 81,
83-85. The ascription to Milton was first made by C. Sayle in *Early
English Printed Books in the University Library, Cambridge*, III
(1903), 1739-1740. Another possible author is John Meredith, also

suggested by Sayle. See also French, "The Autographs of John Milton,"
#3.

PORTRAIT (?).

Robert Lemon, son of the discoverer of Milton's treatise *De Doctrina Christiana*, exhibited to the Society of Antiquaries on March 17,
1853, what he believed to be a portrait of Milton. Enclosed in an oval
border, it showed a young man, age 28-30, with curly hair, a high forehead, a plain falling band, and a cloak over his shoulder. Its present location being unknown and no copy being available, it is impossible to tell
whether it is authentic. See *Gentleman's Magazine*, xcvi (1826), ii,
61; *ibid.*, ns, xxxix (1853), 526.

BUYS COPY OF DION CHRYSOSTOM'S ORATIONS.

[Title:] ΔΙΩΝΩΣ ΤΟΤ ΧΡΤΣΟΣΤΟΜΟΤ ΛΟΓΟΙ Γ... Lu-
tetiæ. M.DCIV.

[Inscription:] Pre: 18ˢ. 1636. J. Milton./

This book is in the library of Ely Cathedral, to which it was presented by Simon Patrick, Bishop of Ely from 1691 to his death in 1707.
Within the front cover is a bookplate reading: "Eccles: Cathedr: Elyeus:
Donavit Reverendus in Christo Pater SYMON Episcopus Elyensis."
Milton's inscription is on a blank end-paper. There are no annotations
by him. See French, "The Autographs of John Milton," #79; CM.
xviii, 576.

APRIL 7. RELATIVE (?) RICHARD MILTON, SCRIVENER, WITNESSES WILL OF FRANCIS SPENCER.

Jn the name of God Amen, I Francis Spencer of the parrish
of St Giles wᵗʰout Criplegate London [marginal note: "Cittizen
and Brewer of London"] . . . doe make and declare this my
present last will and Testament. [Then follow legacies to various relatives.] . . . Yeoven the seaventh daye of Aprill Anno
Dnī. 1636 . . . ffraunces Spencer Signed sealed acknowledged
and published by the said ffrancis Spencer as and for his last will
and testamᵗ. the day of the date above written in the pʳsence of
Christopher Spight Richard Smith and of me Richard Milton
Scrʼ.

Prerogative Court of Canterbury, London, 106 Pile. I owe this
reference to the kindness of Dr. Leslie Hotson. This Richard Milton,
whose relation to John is not clear, is probably the same one mentioned

above under date of 1621. Spencer's will was proved on October 24, 1636, by Thomas Marler, Archdeacon of Sarum, because the testator's wife Margaret, named in the will as executrix, had died in the meantime ("ab hac luce etiam migravit").

MAY 12. FATHER DISCHARGED AS ASSISTANT TO COMPANY OF SCRIVENERS AT HIS OWN REQUEST.

Hyde Clarke, writing in the *Athenaeum*, 1880, 1, 760-761, quotes a passage from the records of the Company to show that the elder Milton petitioned to be allowed to resign from his position as assistant in the company on account of his "removal to inhabit in the country."

MAY 23. FATHER SERVED WITH ATTACHMENT IN COTTON SUIT (?).

Jt was ordered vpon the xxiijth of May last vpon p^{r}tence that the deft stood in contempt & living wthin 17 myles of Lond' That an Attach^t should be awarded agt him ret [*blank*] And that the deft for his delaye$\wp$ should pay the p^{lt} xx^s Cost$\wp$.

From the Court of Requests order of March 22, 1637, *q.v.* This reference is perplexing, not only because the original attachment has not been found, but because the date given here, May 23, 1636, even antedates Sir Thomas Cotton's bill against Milton. See French, *Milton in Chancery*, pp. 55-56. A date late in 1636 or early in 1637 would seem more logical. This may indeed be a garbled allusion to the order mentioned in the court record of February 18, 1637, *q.v.*

. . . in Easter tearme, we serued Bower by the messenger, & ffiled our bill the same tearme & tooke a P.S. vss Milton. . . .

Letter of Henry Perry to Sir Thomas Cotton, dated April 3, 1637, *q.v.* This may not refer to the same action as the preceding quotation, but the two are closely associated.

MAY 28. SIR THOMAS COTTON BRINGS ACTION AGAINST MILTON'S FATHER IN COURT OF REQUESTS.

To the kings most excellent Ma^{ty}.

Humbly sheweth vnto your gracious Ma^{ty} your loyall & dutifull subiect S^r. Tho: Cotton of Sawtry in Yo^r highnes county of Huntington Baronet, executor off ye last will & testam^t of John Cottō esqz deceased. That whereas ye s^d John Cotton vncle of yor s^d subiect being an old decripitt weake man of the age of fourscore yeares and vpwards did heretofore about five yeares

sithence put into the hands off one John Milton of Breadstreet
in yor ma^{ties} city of Londō scrivener and Tho: Bower seruant to
the sayd John Milton dīv great sumēs of money, in trust to be
lett out at interest aft^r ye rate of eight in the hundred by the sayd
John Milton and Tho: Bower which sayd somes were by seuerall
specialtyes put out by the sayd John Milton and Tho: Bower
viz Mr Mort and others by bond dated the 6th of Sept: 1628
100^{li}. principall debt, Mr Welby and others by bond dated 7
of Nouemb: 1627 200 principall debt The Lord Strang and
others, by bond dated 7 of Novemb 1626 300 principall debt
&^{c}. Mr Marbury and others by bond dated the Twelueth [of]
May one thousand six [hundred and thirty one hund]red
pound℘ principall debt. M^r. Bold & others by bond dated the
ffourteenth of Aprill One thousand six hundred Twentie & ffive
One hundred pound℘ [prin]cipall debt. M^r [Lea and others by
bond dated the thirteenth] of May One thousand Six hundred
Twentie & one One hundred pound℘ principall debt, Sr Richard
Molineux & others by bond dated the Seventeenth of May One
thousand [Six] hundred Twentie & three [one hundred pound℘]
principall debt. Sr Will'm Norris & others by bond dated ye the
Eighteenth of November One thousand six hundred Twentie &
Six One hundred pound℘ principall debt. [M^r] Will'm Welby
& others [by bond dated y^e (?)] tieth of November One thowsand six hundred Twentie Nyne One hundred pound℘ principall
debt. Mr Bannister & others by bond dated ye One & Twentieth
[of] May One thowsand Six [hundred twenty three] One hundred pound℘ principall debt, Mr Cherfeild & others by bond
dated ye Six & Twentieth of June One thowsand six hundred
Twentie Nyne One [hund]red pound℘ principall [debt M^r
Ewens & others] by bond dated the Nyne & Twentieth of May
One thousand six hundred Twentie Eight One hundred pound℘
principall debt. Mr Vaudray & others by bond [dated] the
Thirtieth of November [One thousand six] hundred Twentie
seven One hundred pound℘ principall debt, Sr Robert Heath &
others by bond dated the Tenth of December One thowsand six
hundred & Twentie One hundred pound℘ principall [debt. Sir

Francis] Leigh & others by bond dated the Last of November
One thowsand Six hundred Twentie ffoure One hundred pound℘
principall debt, Mr Leigh & others [by] bond dated ye Twelueth
of [December One thousand] six hundred Twentie six ffiftie
pound℘ principall debt. Sr Kenelm Digby & others by bond
dated the Seventh of August One thowsand six hundred Twentie six two hundred pound℘ [principall debt.] Mr Dabridgecourt & others by bond dated the seventeenth of December One
thowsand six hundred Twentie seven One hundred pound℘
principall debt. M^r [Reed] & others by bond dated y^e [Twen-
tieth of May] One thowsand six hundred & Thirtie One hundred
pound℘ principall debt. M^r [Prewet] & others by bond dated the
One & Twentieth of December One thowsand six hundred
Twentie seven, One hundred [pound℘] principall debt. M^r
Erdiswick & others by bond dated the Eleventh of May One
thowsand six hundred Twentie ffoure Two hundred pound℘
principall debt. Sr Willm Sandys and others by bond dated h^e
Eighteenth of [May One thousand] six hundred Twentie, One
hundred pound℘ principall debt, Mr Charnock & others by bond
dated the Nynteenth of November One thowsand six hundred
& Twentie Two hundred pound℘ principall debt. [Mr Chet-
wode] & others by bond dated the seven & Twentieth of November One thowand six hundred Twentie three One hundred
pound℘ principall debt. Mr Clopton & others by bond dated the
One & Twentieth day of June One thousand [six hundred]
Twentie six One hundred pound℘ principall debt. Sr George
Horsey & others by bond dated the ffift of July One thowsand
six hundred Twentie seven, One hundred pound℘ principall
debt. Sr George Ho[rsey & others by] bond dated the Nyneteenth day of December One thowsand six hundred Twentie
six One hundred pound℘ principall debt. Mr Veale & others by
bond dated the ffoure & Twentieth day of May One thowsand
six hundred Twentie six One hundred pound℘ principall debt.
Mr Carrent & others by bond dated the Eight & twentieth of
November One thowsand six hundred Twentie Two One hundred pound℘ principall debt. Mr Blacker & others by bond dated

the Eleventh day of October One thowsand six hundred Twentie seven, One hundred poundȝ principall debt. Mʳ Rodney
& others by bond dated the Twelueth of December [One tho]w-
sand six hundred Twentie six, ffiftie poundȝ principall debt.
All which somes togeather of principall debt amount to the
full some of 3600ˡˡ, for which sayd somes the sayd John Miltō
and Tho: Bowre did bring to the sayd John Cotton your subiects
said vncle halfe yearly the interest after the rate of 8 ᵽ cent
for some yeares and did often renew call in and put out the
sayd sumes as they thought best themselues euer pretending
to the sayd John Cotton that the sayd partyes to whom the
money was put out were very sufficient and able men, and as
in truth most of them were (as your subiect hath since learned)
But shortly after the sayd John Milton and Tho: Bower (finding the sayd John Cotton to be decripitt and vnable by reason
of his great yeares) any wayes to follow his occasions (being
constrained altogeather to keepe his chamber the sayd Milton
and Bower did by yᵉ practise & direcciō off one Thomas Holchar
an attorney at law Who was vsed by yᵉ sᵈ John Cotton in suing
bonds forbeare to bring him in either the principall or most
part of the interest of the said somes pretending that the partyes to whom the sayd somes were lett out were not sufficient
By wᶜʰ practice of deteyning yᵉ sᵈ intrest money they did cause
yᵉ sᵈ John Cottō to beleeue that both principall & interest were
desperate & that yᵉ debtors were ᵽsons non soluent. And hauing
so farre wrought vppō his conceit then they together wᵗʰ yᵉ sᵈ
Tho. Holchar vsed ᵽswasionȝ to the sayd John Cotton that it
would be more for his proffitt and ease if he toke some competent some of money and deliuer vp to them or one of them
his sayd bond. wherevppō they would endeuoʳ to get yᵉ principall money, and in consideration therof they or one of them
would giue him 2000ˡˡ in hand which the better to effect they
or one of them by yᵉ priuity & direcciō off yᵉ sᵈ Holchar did
combine & plot with one Tho: Collwell esq in whose house the
said John Cotton then lay & by reward of yᵉ sumē of 200ˡˡ giuē
to yᵉ sd Tho. Colwell by yᵉ sd Holchar Miltō & Bowʳ or some

of them they did draw yᵉ sᵈ Tho. Colwell to informe & often
to alledge to yᵉ sᵈ Jo: Cottō, that yᵉ sᵈ detρ were despate &
yᵉ ρties to be dead nonsoluant or beyond yᵉ seas. and resident
in the county Palatine of Chester and Lancaster where writtρ
could not easily be serued & undʳ these pʳtences so pswade yᵉ
sᵈ John Cottō to accept 2000ˡˡ fro yᵉ sᵈ Miltō & Bowʳ or one
off them for yᵉ sᵈ principal detρ wᶜʰ amounted to 3600ˡˡ. wᶜʰ
accordingly the sᵈ Tho: Colwel did By wʰ sᵈ practice & com-
binatiō they did draw yᵉ sᵈ John Cottō for the sayd some of
2000ˡˡ to deliuer vp in the handρ of the sayd Tho: Blower all
the sayd bondρ that they sayd Tho Blower might renew the
said bonds in his owne name or in the name of any other and
take the principall debt either to his owne vse or to the vse of
any other which sayd principall debt so referred to them to
gather vp is expressed in a scedule vnder the hand of the sayd
Tho: Bower, And the sayd Tho: Bower or he whose name the
sayd Thomas Bower did then vse wʰ was done by yᵉ priuity &
agreemᵗ of yᵉ sᵈ Holchar who vndʳhand was a sharʳ wᵗʰ yᵉ sᵈ
Bower in yᵉ sᵈ agreemᵗ & disbursed a great part of yᵉ sᵈ 2000ˡˡ.
(having the custody of the sayd bonds by yᵉ sᵈ Holchars meanes
& psecuciō at law did call in to his or their own vse or renew
most of yᵉ sᵈ bondρ for the said principall debt in his or their
owne name, And not contented with the sayd principall debt
(being a debt of their owne making, and being sixteene hundred poundρ more then the consideration they gaue for it) they
the said Thomas Bower & Tho. Holchar or they or hee whose
name hee or they vsed haue receaued off seūal psons dettors by
yᵉ sᵈ obligacions att least 500 for the interest due before the sayd
debt came to their vse; Shortly aftʳ wʰ time the sᵈ John Cotton
dyed, leauing yoʳ subiect his sole executor as aforesᵈ who did
vndʳtake yᵉ same And since that time yoʳ sᵈ subiect hath in
freindly mañʳ requested yᵉ sᵈ. John Milton & Tho Bowʳ to
accept their 2000ˡˡ, & to pay ouʳ to yoʳ sᵈ subiect yᵉ sᵈ monies
by thē receiued or secured vpon the sᵈ obligaciōns & to deliuʳ
ouer the new securities by them taken for any of yᵉ sᵈ detρ And
hath also requested thē & yᵉ sᵈ Holchar to expresse what sumēs

of money haue beene by them or any other to their vses received off any yᵉ psōs in yᵉ sᵈ obligatiō, obliged for intrest or
principall debt money or altered by new securities & whof yᵉ sᵈ
old obligaciōs remaine in their hands, & that they would account
to yoʳ sᵈ subiect for the sᵈ 3600ˡⁱ wᵗʰ yᵉ [interest] received or
secured It being noe reason that yᵉ sᵈ Holchar Miltō & Bowʳ
should by such practices & vndue cariage make so great ꝑfit to
thēselfes. But they haue hithʳto & stil doe refuse to entr into yᵉ
sᵈ accompt. Now forasmuch as yoʳ sᵈ subiect ought in equity
compel yᵉ sᵈ Holchar Miltō & Bowʳ to account wᵗʰ yoʳ sᵈ subiect
for yᵉ sᵈ principal detꝑ & [inte]rest monies off yᵉ sᵈ dettꝑ, but
is:, wthout remedy elswhere, for that he knoweth not yᵉ certaine sūms by them receiued altered or secured nor in whose
name yᵉ sᵈ bondꝑ are taken, nor who receiued yᵉ sᵈ sumēs. Jn
considʳaciō of all wᶜʰ pʳmises & for yoʳ subiects releife herein,
may it please yoʳ Maᵗʸ to grt to yoʳ sᵈ subiect yoʳ Maᵗʸᵉˢ ꝑces of
privy seale or othʳ comāund to be directed to yᵉ sᵈ Jo: Miltō &
Tho: Bower & Thomas Holchar &c. or such others as your sayd
subiect shall hereafter learne to be interested in the said money
& by the said [writt] thereby comānde[ing them . . . to] be
& appeare bef yoʳ Maᵗⁱᵉ & yoʳ Counsell of yoʳ highest Court of
Whitehall at Westminster then & there to ans[wer the premises
and also to] stand [to and abide such further ordēr and direction as to your Majesty and your Highness' Counsel shall seem
agreeable to] equity & good conscience [And] yoʳ subject [as in]
dutie bound shall ever praye for yoʳ Maᵗˢ long & happy [Reign
over us]

[*Signature illegible*]

[*Endorsed*:] Dat xxviij Die Maij Anno RRꝑ Caroli Duodecimo./   ꝑ Nunc./

There are two known texts of this action: British Museum Cottonian
Charters 1/5/5 and Public Record Office Req 2/630. The form given
here is a composite of both, with the latter as primary, supplemented by
the information in Thomas Bower's list of Cotton's bonds, November
25, 1630, *q.v.* There is an abstract of the bill in Cottonian Charters
1/5/5. See also Masson, I (1881), 627 ff.; *Academy*, VI (1874), 560;
Athenaeum, 1880, II, 15; French, *Milton in Chancery*, pp. 258 ff.

DECEMBER 12. RECEIVES INTEREST PAYMENT FROM
RICHARD POWELL.

... the growing Jnterest for the forbearance of the said Prin-
cipall debt was for some yeares then following likewise payd
And soe continued to bee paid vntill June Jn the yeare of our
Lord One Thousand six hundred ffortie and ffower. ...

From Milton's answer to Elizabeth Ashworth, February 22, 1653/4,
q.v.

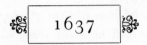

"COMUS" PRINTED.

*A Maske Presented At Ludlow Castle, 1634: On Michael-
masse night, before the Right Honorable, Iohn Earle of Bridgewater, Vicount Brackly, Lord Præsident of Wales, And one of
His Maiesties most honorable Privie Counsell. Eheu quid volui
misero mihi! floribus austrum Perditus*—London, Printed for
Hvmphrey Robinson, at the signe of the Three Pidgeons in
Pauls Church-yard. 1637.

Title of 1637 edition; reproduced in Fletcher facsimile, I, 263; CM,
I, 85 ff.; facsimile of title page in CM, I, facing p. 84.

PRESENTS COPY OF "COMUS" TO EARL OF BRIDGE-
WATER (?).

The Pforzheimer copy is said to "have been presented by either Milton or Lawes, more likely the latter, to Lord Brackly or his father, the
Earl of Bridgewater. Whether this is the dedication copy or not, there
can be no question but that its association with the family of the patron
in whose honor it was written outweighs any claim which might be adduced in favor of some other copy." It contains nine manuscript corrections in the text "which appear to be in Milton's hand." This copy,
formerly in the Huntington Library, from which it was sold in 1918, is
described in close detail in *The Carl H. Pforzheimer Library English
Literature 1475-1700* (ed. Emma Unger and W. A. Jackson), New
York, 1940, #714, and II, 1281-1282. Several pages are there reproduced in facsimile, including one with the manuscript corrections.
Though I have not seen the original volume, the writing in these looks

very much like that of Milton in the Cambridge Manuscript. Other details of the history of the volume appear in *American Book-Prices Current*, 1918, p. 496, and 1919, p. 535.

PRESENTS COPY OF "COMUS" TO KING CHARLES (?).

What was described as a dedication copy of *Comus* to Charles I was exhibited at Columbia University in 1908; its later history is not known, and there is no check on its authenticity. See *Athenaeum*, 1908, I, 354.

BUYS WORKS OF HERACLIDUS OF PONTUS.

[Title:] *Heraclidis Pontici . . . Allegoriæ in Homeri fabulas de dijs, Basiliæ* [1544].

[Inscription:] Jo. Milton p^d pre: 5^s 1637.

This volume, lost to sight for many years, was recently offered for sale in Maggs Brothers' *Mercurius Britannicus*, No. 100 (January, 1947), item 71, for £150. It had been in the libraries of Lord Rolle of Stevenstone and Lord Clinton at Bicton, Devonshire. It is described in Sotheby, p. 125 (facsimile of the inscription facing p. 124); French, "The Autographs of John Milton," No. 80; CM, XVIII, 577. It is now in the library of the University of Illinois.

JANUARY 23. WRIT ISSUED AGAINST FATHER BY COURT OF REQUESTS IN COTTON CASE.

1636 Termino scī Hillarij Anno Regni R$\wp$ Caroli xij°./ xxiij^{tio} die Januarij

A P. S^l. reñ to John Milton at the suite of ⎫
    Sr Thomas Cotton Barronett . . . . ⎬ 1° febr
                                ⎭

Public Record Office, Court of Requests Process Book, Hilary term, 12 Charles I, and Easter term, 13 Charles I, Req 1/186, f. IV; French, *Milton in Chancery*, p. 262. Opposite the main item in this entry stands a cancelled "1^s.8^d."

[1636, in the term of Saint Hilary, in the twelfth year of the reign of King Charles, the twenty-third day of January. A writ of Privy Seal rendered to John Milton at the suit of Sir Thomas Cotton, Bart., February 1.]

ABOUT JANUARY 23. FATHER PREPARES TO ANSWER COTTON'S BILL; ENGAGES COUNSEL.

Now forasmuch as it is alledged by the p$^{lt\wp}$ humble Peticõn exhīted to Sr Edward Powell Knt & barronett one of his Ma$^{t\wp}$ Councell of this Co^{r}t That the s̄d deft is an old man about fower-

skore yereꝑ of age and is infirme & vnfitt for Travell & that
he sent vp to his Atturnies to appeare in due time And for that
it appeares by the Certifficatt of George Miller gent one of the
Clarkꝑ or Atturneys of this Co^{rt} That about the beginning of
the last Terme he was reteyned to appeare for the s'd deft &
soone after having p^rpared a Coppy of the Bill vpon Affīft made
that the deft was aged & vnable to Travell made forth a ded.
Potestat for the taking of his Answere in the Countrey. . . .

From the Court of Requests order of March 22, 1637, *q.v.* The
last term previous to this date (*i.e.*, Hilary term) began on January 23.
Neither the certificate of George Miller nor the affidavit about Milton's
infirm condition nor the writ of dedimus potestatem has been found, but
there is no reason to doubt their genuineness.

JANUARY 27. FATHER SERVED WITH WRIT OF PRIVY
SEAL IN COTTON-MILTON SUIT.

Decimo Tertio die ffebruarij Anno RR^s duodecimo . . . William Witherington of the Cittye of Westm^r. señ maketh oath
that on the 27th. daye of Januarye last hee served John Milton
the elder with his Ma^{te}. Proces of P:S^l: issueinge forth of this
honō^{ble}. Court at the suite of Sr Thomas Cotton Barronett by
leavinge the same at his dwellinge house./

Public Record Office, Court of Requests Affidavit Book, Req 1/141,
f. 198v; French, *Milton in Chancery*, p. 262. This is probably the writ
issued on January 23, *q.v.* It is probably also the writ alluded to in the
Court of Requests order quoted by Masson, 1 (1881), 630; see French,
Milton in Chancery, p. 56. "P.S." stands for Privy Seal.

. . . in Easter tearme, we . . . tooke a P.S. vss Milton, and
after renewed it twice but only the laste was served. . . .

Letter of Henry Perry to Sir Thomas Cotton, April 3, 1637, *q.v.*
Probably the "last" writ mentioned here is that served on January 27.

ABOUT FEBRUARY 1 (?). FATHER AND PARTNER SERVED
WITH ATTACHMENTS AT SUIT OF SIR THOMAS COTTON.

. . . Laste tearme we tooke an attachm^t against Bower for
want of Aunswere and gott an order for his Comittm^t & encrease of Chardges for his delayes & Contemtꝑ, wth an other
order vss Milton allmost to the same effect. . . .

From Henry Perry's letter to Cotton, April 3, 1637; French, *Milton in Chancery*, p. 264. The last term before April 3 was Hilary term, which ran from January 23 to February 12. Since this passage follows, in Perry's letter, the mention of the serving of the writ on Milton the third time (January 27), a date near February 1 seems likely. Perry continues with news about Bower: "The warden of the ffleete hath that vss Bower who desires to be remembred vnto you, and hath vndertaken to bring in his body wth the Costes & Awnswere, and w^t else is requisite &c." See also the entry under date of February 18, 1637, which may be another version of this same action.

FEBRUARY 1. DATE SET FOR FATHER'S ANSWER TO COTTON'S BILL (?).

A P.S^l. reñ to John Milton at the suite
⎫
of Sr Thomas Cotton Barronett . . . ⎬ 1° febr
⎭

Public Record Office, Req 1/186, f. 1 verso; French, *Milton in Chancery*, p. 262. The complete text of this entry in the Process Book is given under date of January 23, 1637, above. The date at the right, February 1, is here interpreted as the date set for the elder Milton to appear in court to answer Sir Thomas Cotton. His actual answer did not come until April 13, *q.v.*

FEBRUARY 13. AFFIDAVIT OF WRIT SERVED ON FATHER IN COTTON CASE.

Decimo Tertio die ffebruarij Anno RR^s duodecimo . . .

Cotton. William Witherington of the Cittye of Westm^r. señ

Milton./ maketh oath that on the 27th. daye of Januarye last

hee served John Milton the elder with his Ma^te.

Proces of P: S^l: issueinge forth of this honō^ble. Court at the suite of S^r. Thomas Cotton Barronett by leavinge the same at his dwellinge house./

Public Record Office, Court of Requests Affidavit Book, Req 1/141, f. 198v; French, *Milton in Chancery*, p. 262.

FEBRUARY 16. FATHER AND ASSOCIATE BOWER SUE ARTHUR DUCK IN CHANCERY.

To the Right Honō^ble Thomas Lord Coventrey Lord
Keeper of the greate seale of England &c

Maydwell   xvj° Die ffebruarij 1636.

Humbly Complayneing sheweth vnto your Lordshipp your

Orators John Milton and Thomas Bower of London Scriveners
that whereas Rose Downer late of [London] now deceased in
her life tyme (vizt) in or about June one thousand six hundred
twenty eight at the earnest Jmportunitie of Mathewe Ewins of
Northcadburie in [the county of] Summersett Esqz now also
Deceased did lend vnto the said Mathewe Ewins the some of
ffiftie pounds of lawfull English mony to be repayd againe at
six Monthes followein[g And in] Consideration for forbearance
Thereof And for Assurance of Repayment of the same accordingly the said Mathewe Ewins together with William Keymer
of Pendower in the same County of Summersett Esqz as his
surtie became Joyntly and severally bound to the said Rose
Downer in one hundred poundϸ by obligation bearing date the
tenth day of June in the fowrth yeare of the Raigne of our now
Soueraigne Lord King Charles Conditioned for payment of the
said some of ffiftie pounds to the said Rose downer together
with Consideracōn according to the rate of eight poundϸ in the
hundred on the twelvth day of December then next ensueing
the date of the said obligacōn as named by the said obligacōn
and Condicōn doth and may more fully appeare and they
the said Mathewe Ewins and William Keymer not paye-
ing the said ffiftie poundϸ nor vse for the same at the tyme
limited by the Condicōn of the said Obligacōn shortly after
the said Mathew Ewins made his last will and testament
in writeinge and thereby Constituted and ordayned Mathew
Ewins his sonne and heire his Executo^r and shortly after
died leaueing a great estate behinde him both in landϸ and
goods after whose decease the said Mathewe Ewins the sonne
tooke vpon him the execucōn of his said fathers will and in
due forme of lawe paid the same and by virtue whereof he
possessed himselfe of all his said fathers goodϸ and personall
estate and entered into all and singuler the Mannors landϸ and
tenem^{ts} his said father died seized of being of very great value
as aforesaid and notwithstandinge did neglect to pay the said
ffiftie pounds and vse for the same to the said Rose Downer
wherevpon shee the said Rose in or about the tearme of the

holy Trinitie in the Seaventh yeare of his Ma[ties]: Raigne that
now is exhibited her Bill of Complaynte into this Hono[ble]
Courte against your Orators thereby alleadging That shee the
said Rose Downer did deliuer vnto your Orato[r] Milton ffiftie
pound℔ to be put out for her at Jnterest vpon ℘mise by him
made that he should ℘cure good securitie to be given vnto the
said Rose downer for the same which the said Milton did accordingly And that at the day of payment of the said money
the said Rose downer left the bond which was giuen for repayment of the said ffiftie pound℔ and vse with Your Orator Milton
who receiued the money and deliuered the same to your other
Orator Thomas Bower his then partner for the vse of her the
said Rose Downer And your Orators put forth the same at vse
for the said Rose Downer vnto the said Ewins and Keymer
who paid Jnterest for the same to your Orators for two six
monthes who payd the same to the said Rose Downer But shee
dislikeing her securitie required the money of your Orators who
not withstandinge Continued the same at Jnterest to the Obligors vpon that securitie for repayment thereof to the said Rose
and the said obligo[rs] became Jnsolvent the said Rose alleadginge
further by her said Bill that your Orators did refuse to pay the
said ffiftie pound℔ to the said Rose downer to which said Bill of
Complainte your Orators answered which Cause ℘ceeded to
hearing and in the month of June in the eight yeare of his
Ma[tie℔] Raigne and vpon hearing of the said Cause this Hono[ble]
Co[r]te was satisfied that your Orators did put forth the said
ffiftie pounds to the said Mathew Ewin℔ and William Keimer
themselues without the Consent of the said Rose Downer
wherevp̄o it was thoughte meete ordered and decreed by this
Hono[ble] Courte that your Orators should pay vnto her the said
Rose Downer the said ffiftie pounds and that therevpon the
said Rose Downer should Assigne ouer vnto your Orators the
said bond whereby they might be inabled at there owne Charges
to helpe themselues against the said persons to whome your
Orators had soe put forth the said ffiftie pounds as in and by
the said Bill and Answere, the said other ℘ceedings in the said

Cause and the decree therevpon remayneing vpon record in this
Honōᵇˡᵉ Courte more at large appeareth and in obedience to
the said decree your Orators vpon the twentith day of June in
the said eight yeare of his Maᵗⁱᵉˢ. said Raigne did pay vnto the
said Rose Downer the said ffiftie poundꝗ as by her receipt vnder
her hand vpon the coppie of the said decree appeareth And shee
the said Rose downer the said twentith day of June did Assigne
ouer the said Bond to your Orators as was inioyned her by the
said decree And shortly after your Orators haueing vnderstood
that the said Mathewe Ewins the sonne takeing vpon him the
discharge and payment of his said fathers debts was also willinge
to satisfie the said Debt of ffiftie pounds soe to him lent in the
name of the said Rose Downer and therevpon he the said
Mathew Ewins the sonne the better to inable him soe to doe
made sayle of some parte of the said Mannors landꝗ and pʳmisses
his said ffather died soe seized of as aforesaid vnto Arthur
Ducke Docter of the Civill lawe and William Child of London Scrivener or one of them and by sayle thereof raysed a
great some of Money sufficient to pay all his said fathers Debts
with a great surplusage a good parte whereof hee tooke into his
owne possession and two or three thousand poundꝗ residew
thereof he left in the handꝗ of the said Arthur Ducke and William Child or one of them for satisfaction of the said ffiftie
poundꝗ soe lent in the name of the said Rose and of the forbearance thereof and of other debts oweing by his said ffather
and for disingageing of the said Mannoʳˢ Landꝗ and tenements
of Jncumbrances wherewᵗʰ the same were lyable and shortly
after and before the said Debts satisfied he the said Mathewe
made his last will and testament and thereby made Constituted
and appoynted Alexander Ewins his brother and Cathrine
Ewins and Barbara Ewins his sisters his executoʳˢ and then died
leaueing diverse goodꝗ of his said ffather vnadministred and
did also leaue all the said monyes soe remayneing in the handꝗ
of the said Arthur Ducke and William Child or one of them
vndisposed of by them and after the decease of the said
Mathewe the said Alexander soly tooke vpon him the execucōn

of his said brothers will and in due form of Lawe pued the same (power being reserued to the said Cathrine and Barbara to ioyne with him in the probate thereof if they pleased) And the said Alexander Ewins by reason of the probate of the said will possessed himself of all the goodp of the said Mathew the father and of the said money wch did still remayne in the handp of the said Arthur Ducke and William Child for satisfaction of the said debte soe due to your Orators and others by the said Mathew the ffather as aforesaid all which your Orators Vnderstandinge did soone after the payment of the said ffiftie poundp to the said Rose Downer and assignem^t of the said Obligacōn to them by her (that is to say in or about the tearme of St Michaell in the nineth yeare of his now Ma^tiep Raigne exhibite there bill of Comp^lt in this Courte against the said Docter Ducke and William Child Allexander Ewins Katherine and Barbara Ewins to be releeued of in vpon and Concerninge the p^rmisses vnto which bill the said Docter Ducke and William Child Answered and Confessed that there was moneyes left in theire handp part of the monyes which should haue bene paid for the purchase of the said Mannors and p^rmisses or of some of them to the some of two thousand poundp or thereabouts and after the said Bill exhibited and before the said Cause came fitt for hearing she the said Rose Downer died farr remote from the Cittie of London soe that your orators Cannot learne how or to whom she disposed of her estate or what will shee made nor who hath taken Administration of her estate but humbly desire they may be admitted to make the said executo^r or admīstrato^rs pties to this bill when they shalbe discovered And for that by reason of the death of her the said Rose the said bond soe entered into to her the said Rose for payment of ye sayd fifty powndp & vse Cannot be put in suite at lawe against the said Allexander Ewins but in the name of the said Executor or admīstrator of the said Rose and for that that the said Executor or admīstrator is vnknowne to your Orators so that yor Orators cannot pcure any assignem^t of the said bond or warrant to sue [at the Common Lawe] and for that it will as your Orators hope stand with the equitie of this Honō^{ble} courte that sithence by the decree thereof your Orators were inioyned to pay the said ffiftie pound℘ vnto the said Rose downer and shee to Assigne the said bond to your Orators both which were done accordingly as aforesaid and after the said Assignem^t became defective by the strict Course of the Common lawe therin that your Orator should take the full beniffitt of the intention of the said decree by haueing the said money paid vnto them and a full Assignem^t of the said debt whereby to recouer the same against the said Allexander Ewins who hath so possessed himselfe of the personall estate of his said father and brother as aforesaid And the said Arthur Ducke and William Child or one of them are possessed of the said monyes left in there or one of theire hand℘ as aforesaid for payment of the said Mathew Ewins the fathers debts and Clearing the said mannors land℘ and p^rmisses of Jncumbrances and yet doe not nor any of them doth make payment to your Orators of the said some of ffiftie pound℘ soe before lent in the name of the saide Rose by reason whereof your Orators are likely to loose the said debt of ffiftie pounds and the forbearance thereof haueing noe meane℘ for recouery thereof but by the order of this Honō^{ble} Courte Jn tender Consideracōn whereof and for that your Orators Cannot discouer the perticuler personall estate of the said Ewins the father left behind him nor where the same is neither the perticuler land℘ the said Ewins the father died seized of nor what estate he had therein at the time of his death nor what estate did Discend vnto the said Mathew the sonne nor Doe your Orators knowe what parte of the monyes soe left vpon the purchase of the sayd land℘ doe remaine as aforesaid in the hand℘ of the said Arthur Ducke and William Child or one of them for payment of the said debt due vpon the obligacōn entered into to the said Rose Downer and for that your Orators were inforced to pay her the said Rose in readie money and your Orators have bene from the said twentith day of June in the said eight yeare of his Maties Raigne out of purse the said ffiftie pound℘ and noe parte of principall or Jnterest payd to your

Orators [and] for [that] the said Mathew Ewins the sonne knowinge the Justnes of the said debt due by the said Bond entered into to the said Rose Downer and other debts of his said ffather [in] order for payment and satisfaction of the same as aforesaid and Disingageing the said Landꝑ of Jncumbranceꝑ the same discendinge to the said Mathew Ewins the sonne [al]soe he [as] heire to his said ffather being lyable and Chargable to satisfie the said Debt to the said Rose downer And to the end that the said Arthur Ducke and William Child may accordinge to the trust reposed in them and accordinge to theire Agreem^t with the said Mathew Ewins vpon the purchase of the said land pay the said Debt due by the said obligacōn entered into to the said Rose Downer as aforesaid with damages for the same And that the said Allexander Ewins Barbara and Kathrine Ewins may discouer and sett forth the perticulers of the personall estate and the true value thereof whereby it may be made lyable to the payment of the said debt due by the said obligacon as aforesaid, and for that your Orators bee remediles herein at the Comon Lawe Jt may therefore please yor Lo^{pp} to graunt vnto your Orators his Maties most gratious writt or writts of Subpena to be directed to the said Arthur Ducke William Child Allexander Ewins Barbara Ewins and Katherine Ewins & to ye Executor or admīstrator of ye s^d Rose when they shalbe discouered and euery of them Commanding them and every of them at a certaine day and vnder a Certaine payne in the said writt to be lymitted personally to appeare before your Lo^{pp} in his Mat^{ieꝑ}: High Court of Chauncry then and there to Answere the p^{r}emisses and to shew Cause why they or some of them should not forth with make payment of the s^d Just and due debt by the said obligacōn with theire reasonable forbearance and Costs which they have bene putt vnto for recouery thereof and to stand to and abide such order in the p^{r}misses as to your Lo^{ppꝑ} graue wisdome shall seeme meete & agreeable to your Conscience and your Orators as in al dutie bound shall ever pray &c./

R[oberts?]

[312]

Public Record Office, C2 Charles I/M78/26; French, *Milton in Chancery*, pp. 280 ff. Illegible and torn passages have been conjecturally restored in square brackets. Near the beginning there is a marginal note, "Pxiij°," which is presumably a page reference to another record.

FEBRUARY 18. FATHER AND HIS ASSOCIATE BOWER PENALIZED BY COURT OF REQUESTS IN COTTON CASE.

On the 18th of February 1636-7 the Court took up the case rather effectively:—The serving of the process on Milton three weeks before having been duly proved, and Milton not having appeared nor sent in his answer, he was treated, according to the usual form in such cases, as "standing out in contempt," and it was ordered, on the motion of Mr. Bernard, counsel for the complainant, that an attachment, *i.e.* a writ for seizing certain of his goods in gage, should be forthwith awarded against him, and also that he should forfeit a sum of 20*s.* to the complainant by way of costs for the delay. The procedure the same day against Bower was more severe. An attachment having already been awarded against him for his contempt, or non-appearance to answer, and he having subsequently appeared personally, but having since "in further contempt of this Court departed away without the leave of this Court and without putting in answer," the order now was that he should be taken into custody and committed to the Fleet prison, "there to remain until upon his submission further order shall be taken in this Court for his enlargement," forfeiting, moreover, a sum of money for additional costs of delay.

Records of the Court of Requests, London; Masson, 1 (1881), 630; French, *Milton in Chancery*, p. 56; Brennecke, p. 131. I have been unable to find the original record, and the text here quoted is Masson's account. See also the note filed under February 1(?), 1637, which may be another version of this same action.

MARCH 10. WRIT ISSUED FOR FATHER IN COTTON CASE.

By the Kinge:/

Trustie and w[ell beloved] wee greete you well: And send vnto you here inclosed a Bill of Cōmpt. vnto vs exhibited by Sʳ Thomas Cotton knight pl't against John Milton defendant

Wherevppon wee trusting in your approued wisdomes learningͣ
and indifferencies [do command] you that by authority hereof
calling afore you in our name the said Defendant yee then do
receaue his answeres vnto the contentͣ of the said Bill by his
[oa]the in due forme of lawe sworne, and of the same his answeres soe by you receaued in forme aforesaid, Duely to cer-
tifie vs and our Councell by your Writeings with the said Bill
vnder your Seales in our Court of Whitehall att Westm': in
the tresmaines of Easter: next To th'intent that wee by thadvise
of our said Councell [may] further doe therein as the case
rightfully shall require, Nott fayling hereof as yee tender our
displeasure and th'advance^{mt}. of Justice. Given vnder our Privy
[S]eale att our Pallace of West[minster the] tenth Daye of
Marche in the xij^{th}. [ye]are of our Raigne./

Willm. Parker dep^{t}: Tho Parker

[*Endorsed:*] Executio istius Comīssionis patet in quadam
Responsione huic annex'

Tho Agar
John Agar

Public Record Office, Req 2/630; *Academy*, VI (1874), 560;
French, *Milton in Chancery*, p. 262.

[The performance of this order appears in a certain answer attached hereto.]

MARCH 16. ARTHUR DUCK AND WILLIAM CHILD AN-SWER FATHER'S SUIT.

Arthurus Duck iur.	The Joint and severall answeres and de-
16°. Martij. 1636.	murrer of Arthur Ducke Docto^{r}. of lawes
John Page.	and William Childe Two of the Defend-
Robinsonn	ants to the bill of Complaint of John Milton and Thomas Bower Complayn-antͣ./.

The said Defend^{tͣ} saveing to themselues now and at all tymes
hereafter all manner of advantage and benefitt of excepcõn to
the incerteyntyes insufficiency and manyfold imperfeccons of
the said Complaynants Bill of Complaynt [for answer] vnto
soe much thereof as concerneth them these Defend^{tͣ}: to make

answere vnto They these Defend^{te}. say and each of them saith
That they doe not know that Rose Downer in the bill named
did lend vnto Mathew Ewins [the] ffather [in the bill] named
the somē of ffifty Poundꝑ in the bill mencōned or any somē of
money at all nor for what tyme the same was lent if any such
were nor what obligacōn or security shee tooke for repaym^t:
thereof wth Jnterest for the vse [of the same] when the same
was payable neither doe these Defend^{te}: know of any of the
passages orders proceedingꝑ or decrees in the said Bill of Complaint mencōned to be had or made betweene the said Rose
Downer and the Complaynants either in this Court or elsewhere about the said debt if any such were, Neither doe these
Defend^{te}: know of any assignem^t: of the said debt p^r.tended by
the Complaynantꝑ to be to them made by the said Rose Downer
[and these] Defend^{te}. say if any such were they were mere
strangers to them And therefore these Defend^{te}: therein leave
the said Complaynantꝑ to such proofe thereof as they shalbe
able to make And these Defend^{te} say that th[ey believe it] to
be true that the said Mathew Ewens the ffather in his life tyme
made his last will and Testam^t: and thereof constituted Mathew
Ewens his sonne and heire in the Bill named Executo^r: and
about the tyme [in the bill] named dyed But what estate the
said Mathew the father left behind him or what he was indebted at his death they these Defend^{te}. know not, And they
beleiue it also to be true that the said Mathew the sonne p[roved
the] said will And that after the decease of his said ffather he
the said Mathew the sonne as heire to his said ffather entred
into the Manno^{rs}: landꝑ and tenem^{te}: Whereof his said ffather
dyed seised as was [lawful for] him to doe, But of what par-
sonall estate belonging to his said ffather he possessed himselfe
these Defend^{te}. know not nor whether he neglected to pay the
said ffifty poundꝑ wth: Jnterest to the said Rose Downer [as the
same] were due as by the said Bill of Complaint is supposed
And these Defend^{te}. further say true it is That this Defend^t:
Docto^r. Duck for valuable consideracōns did about the moneth
of December in the ffift yeare of his Ma^{ts} [reign] that now is

purchase and buy of the said Mathew Ewens the sonne the Manno^{rs}. of North Cadbury and South Cadbury in the bill mencōned And this Defendant Docto^r. Duck did truely satisfie and pay vnto the said Mathew [Ewens the son] or to others by his appointm^t: All the money agreed vpon for the purchase thereof saveing the somē of Two Thousand Poundꝑ which by agreem^t: betweene the said Mathewe and this Defend^t. Docto^r. Duck was deliūed to the [other defendant] William Childe to lye deposited in his handꝑ for the space of Seaven yeares as a security against such incombrances as might rise vp or happen to be discovered against the said purchased landꝑ and to defray and beare such [expenses and] charges as these Defend^{te}. might susteyne or be put vnto about cleering and discharging such incombrances as within the tyme aforesaid might rise vpp against the said purchased landꝑ Which Two Thousand Pounds or [as much] thereof as should remayne in the handꝑ of the said Defend^t: William Childe at the end of the said Seaven yeares the incombrances Jn the meane tyme appearing and the aforesaid Costꝑ and charges to be expended there[from being] thereout deducted and allowed true it is was by the said agreement to be paid vnto the said Mathew the sonne his executo^{rs}. admīstrators or assignes, Out of which said somē of Two Thousand Poundꝑ this Defend[ant William] Childe saith That the said Mathew Ewens the sonne in his life tyme did receave for supplie of his occasions the somē of five hundred Poundꝑ or thereaboutꝑ And these Defendantꝑ doe absolutely denie That the said somē of Two Thousand Poundꝑ or any parte thereof was left in the handꝑ of either of these Defendantꝑ vpon any trust reposed in th[em or either] of the[m] for satisfaction of the debt p^r:tended to be owing to the said Rose Downer and the forbearance thereof or for satisfaction of any other debtꝑ owing by the said Mathew Ewens the ffather and Mathew E[wens the] sonne or any other wayes then is expressed or that the said Mathew the sonne tooke any order with these Defendantꝑ or either of them for satisfyeing the same out of the said money as by the [bill] is vniustly surmised And these Defendantꝑ fur-

ther say that they beleive it to be true that the said Mathew
the sonne alsoe made his last will and Testament in writing
and thereof did [appoint the] Defendantꝑ Alexander Ewens
Katherine Ewens and Barbara Ewens Executors and dyed After
whose decease these Defendnantꝑ beleive the said Alexander and
Barbara did prove the said [will and took] vppon them the
execution thereof but what goodꝑ either of the said Mathew
the father vnadministred by the said Mathew the sonne or of
the said Mathew the sonne came to his handꝑ thereby or [of
what value] the same were these Defendantꝑ know not nor
either of them knoweth And these Defendantꝑ further say that
divers persons pʳtending themselves to be Creditors to the said
Mathew the ffa[ther and] Mathew the sonne for divers somēs
of money farr surmounting in all the aforesaid sumē of Two
Thousand Poundꝑ divers of them alsoe as they alleadge haveing
obteyned seuāll [judgments against the] said Mathew the
ffather and Mathew the sonne and against the said other Defendant Alexander as executoʳ. to the said Mathew the sonne
have exhibited their Bills of Complaint into this Honᵇˡᵉ Co[urt
against these] Defendantꝑ and against the said Alexander
Ewens and Barbara to be releiued for their said pʳ.tended debtꝑ
and demaundꝑ out of the Remainder of the said money soe
deposited as aforesaid which suitꝑ[?] And these Defendantꝑ
say that true it is that amongst others the said Rose Downer
about the tyme in the Bill mencōned Did exhibite a bill of Complaint into this Honᵇˡᵉ: Court against the sd Defendants [and
the] others in the said Bill named to such or the like purposes
as in the said Bill of Complaint now exhibited are sett forth
for certeinety wherein these Defendantꝑ referr themselves to
the said Bill made [of] Record in this Honᵇˡᵉ: Court to which
these Defendantꝑ did make answere Which suite as these Defendantꝑ are informed by their Councell is abated by the death
of the said Rose Downer And the said assignemᵗ [of the] said
debt pʳ:tended by the Complainantꝑ to be to them made by the
said Rose Downer if any such were as these Defendantꝑ are
informed is become also Defective and void And as to the Re-

mainder of the said sume of [Two] Thousand Poundp and the
satisfaction which the said Complainantp by their bill of Complaint p^r.tend in equity ought to be made vnto them by these
Defendantp for the aforesaid debt by them pretended to be
[owing unto the] said Rose Downer out of the aforesaid somē
of Two Thousand Poundp deposited in the handp of this Defendant William Childe or out of the Remainder thereof if
any should be, for that it appeareth by the Com[plainants]
owne shewing in and by their said Bill of Complaint That the
said Alexander Ewens one other of the Defendantp in the said
bill of Complaint named was by the said Mathew Ewens the
sonne nōmted and [appointed to be] one of the executo^rs. of
his last will and Testament and that he the said Alexander
proved the said will and tooke vppon him the execucōn thereof
And by reason thereof as by the said Compla[inant by his own]
shewing appeareth he the said Alexander possessed himselfe
of the aforesaid money which remained in the handp of these
Defendantp whereby these Defendantp by the Complainantp
owne shewing are acquited of an[y money] remaining in their
handp wherewith to make the Complainantp satisfaction if their
should be any reason or cause therefore And the Complainantp
are wholly to resort to the said Defendant Alexander Ewens
for [satisfaction And] These Defendantp doe demurr in Law
and humbly craue the Judgement of this hon^ble. Court whether
they shalbe compelled to make any further or other answere
therevnto. Without that that any other matter or [thing] whatsoever in these Complaynantp bill sett forth and herein not sufficiently answered vnto confessed or avoided traversed or denyed is true in such manner and forme as in and by the said bill
of Complaint [is set] forth or in any other manner whatsoeuer
All which matters these Defendantp are and wilbe ready to averr
mainteyne and prove as this Honorable Court shall award and
humbly prayeth to be dismissed out [of this Court with] their
reasonable Costp and Charges in this behalfe wrongfully and
without iust cause susteyned./././

Maie Hil ter

Tho[mas Roberts?]

Public Record Office, C2 Charles I/M78/26; French, *Milton in Chancery*, pp. 285 ff. Illegible spots have been conjecturally restored in square brackets.

MARCH 22. FATHER ORDERED SERVED WITH WRIT OF DEDIMUS POTESTATEM IN COTTON CASE.

xxij^{do} die Martij

Cotton.   Whereas in the Cause at the suite of Sr Thomas Cot-
Milton   ton barrt p^{lt} ag^t John Milton th'elder deft Jt was or-
dered vpon the xxiijth of May last vpon p^rtence that
the deft stood in contempt & living wthin 17 myles of Lond'
That an Attach^t should be awarded agt him ret [*undated?*]
And that the deft for his delayeρ should pay the p^{lt} xx^s Costρ
Now forasmuch as it is alledged by the p^{ltρ} humble Peticōn
exhīted to Sr Edward Powell Knt & barronett one of his Ma^{tρ}
Councell of this Co^{rt} That the s'd deft is an old man about
fowerskore yereρ of age and is infirme & vnfitt for Travell &
that he sent vp to his Atturnies to appeare in due time And for
that it appeares by the Certifficatt of George Miller gent one
of the Clarkρ or Atturneys of this Co^{rt} That about the beginning of the last Terme he was reteyned to appeare for the s'd
deft & soone after having p^rpared a Coppy of the Bill vpon Affīft
made that the deft was aged & vnable to Travell made forth a
ded. Potestat for the taking of his Answere in the Countrey Jt
is therefore ordered That the s'd Attacht shalbe hereby staid
And that the xx^s Costρ awarded by the s'd former order shalbe
suspended And the Dedimus Potestatem so made as aforesaid
shall issue forth for taking the s'd Deftρ Answere to the p^{ltρ}
said Bill accordingly./

Public Record Office, Court of Requests Order Book, Req 1/71, p. 227; Masson, 1 (1881), 630; French, *Milton in Chancery*, p. 263.

. . . Milton since the tearme hath obtayned an order that o^r Costes shall for the p^rsent be suspended, and that in regard of his age he maye haue a dedimus potestat to take his Awn-swere in the Countrey. . . .

Letter of Henry Perry to Sir Thomas Cotton, April 3, 1637, *q.v.* The last term, Hilary, would have ended on February 12; so March 22 is well after the end of the term.

APRIL 1. BROTHER CHRISTOPHER MAKES AFFIDAVIT THAT FATHER IS TOO INFIRM TO ATTEND COURT IN LONDON IN ANSWER TO COTTON'S BILL; FATHER NOW LIVING IN HORTON.

Primo die Aprilis 1637 . . .

Milton./ Whereas John Milton geñ hath bin served with
Cotton./ his Ma^te. Poces of P:S^1; issueinge forth of this
honō^ble. Court to answere to a bill of Comp[laint ag]ainst him exhibited by Sr Thomas Cotton Barronet plt, Christopher Milton sonne of the said defendant maketh oath, that his said father beinge aged about 74 yeares is not by reason of his said aige and infirmitye able to trauell to the Cittye of westm^r. to make his perfect answere to the said bill without much p^riudice to his health hee livinge at Horton in the Countye of Buck about 17 miles distant from the Cittye of westm^r./

Public Record Office, Court of Requests Affidavit Book, Req 1/141, f. 218; *Athenaeum*, 1880, II, 15-16; Masson, I (1881), 631; French, *Milton in Chancery*, p. 264.

APRIL 3. COTTON-MILTON LAW-SUIT DESCRIBED IN LETTER TO SIR THOMAS COTTON FROM HIS ATTORNEY.

(Noble S^r.) for yor businesses vss/ Bower & Milton they stande thus., in Easter tearme, we serued Bower by the messenger, & ffiled our bill the same tearme & tooke a P.S. vss Milton, and after renewed it twice but only the laste was served; Laste tearme we tooke an attachm^t against Bower for want of Aunswere and gott an order for his Comittm^t & encrease of Chardges for his delayes & Contemptp, wth an other order vss Milton allmost to the same effect, The warden of the ffleete hath that vss Bower who desires to be remembred vnto you, and hath vndertaken to bring in his body wth the Costes & Awnswere, and w^t else is requisite &c./ Milton since the tearme hath obtayned an order that o^r Costes shall for the p^rsent be suspended, and that in regard of his age he maye haue a dedimus potestat to take his Awnswere in the Countrey, as soone as ever J heard of it J sent the name, of a gent that liues thereaboutp who to be putt into the dēd for you: who J hope will be pʳsent when the Ansʳ is taken., att the beginninge of next tearme you need not feare but to haue both there Awnsweres, and the Cause to stand in a right & ready way for further ᵱceedings as shall then be advised./ J have here sent you newse of the chardges and Copyes of all the orders, whereby you may be further satisfyed [that], when yoʳ other bill comes J shalbe as carefull in yt as [I] maye be/ And thus with my humblest service & respects vnto you first

[?]ves 3 April 1637   Yoʳ Worˢʰ ever to be Comāunded
Hen: Perry:

[*Endorsed:*] The right Worpᶠᵘˡˡ Sʳ Thomas Cotton Baronett oʳ sent these: [*In another hand:*] Tho Bower expresse in his answer what interest was r[ecei]ued.

British Museum, Cottonian Charters 1/5/5; *Athenaeum*, 1880, II, 15; Masson, I (1881), 632-633; French, *Milton in Chancery*, p. 264.

APRIL 3. MOTHER DIES.

Heare lyeth the Body of Sara Milton the wife of John Milton who Died the 3ʳᵈ. of April 1637.

Inscription on her gravestone in Horton church, where she was buried on April 6, *q.v.*; Masson, I, 595 (632).

1637 . . . 3 Sara uxor Johīs Milton generosi Aprilis 6° . . . obijt 3°.

Horton parish register; Masson, I, 593 (639).

APRIL 6. MOTHER BURIED.

1637 . . . 3 Sara uxor Johīs Milton generosi Aprilis 6° . . . obijt: 3°.

Horton parish register; Masson, I, 593 (639). The "6°" after "Aprilis" is followed by what appear to be the astronomical symbols for Jupiter and Mars, with the figure 9 between them.

[1637: Sara, wife of John Milton, gentleman, buried April 6; died the 3rd.]

Heare lyeth the Body of Sara Milton the wife of John Milton who Died the 3ʳᵈ. of April 1637.

Inscription on her gravestone in Horton church; Masson, I, 595 (632).

APRIL 6(?). ACQUIRES HIS MOTHER'S BIBLE(?); WRITES PRAYER IN IT(?).

A Bible of 1599, bound with the Psalms of 1639, was described in the Los Angeles *Examiner* for January 20, 1929. It was said to have been for generations in the possession of the Jeffrey family, which was that of the poet's mother. In addition to some genealogical notes about a family of Miltons shortly after 1700, it contained a manuscript prayer, written on a page between the two Testaments, which was thought by Professor J. T. Armstrong of the University of Southern California to be in the hand of the poet. With it were a French prayer-book and a volume of sermons, also said to have been Milton's. No further trace of these books has been found. See French, "The Autographs of John Milton," #69; CM, XVIII, 564-565. If Milton did actually acquire this Bible from his mother, he would naturally do so just after her death, for which reason this entry is placed here. There is, however, no certainty of the genuineness of the book.

APRIL 8. AFFIDAVIT OF FATHER'S PARTNER, THOMAS BOWER, IN COTTON-MILTON SUIT.

8°. Aprilis 1637.

Bower./ Thomas Bower sworne &c saith that hee this de-
Cotton./ ponent about the end of Easter Tearme last tooke
out A Coppye of a bill exhibited against him and one Milton in this honō[ble] Court by S[r] Thomas Cotton Barronet and forthwith carried the same to his Councell to drawe vpp an answere therevnto who shortlye after went out of towne and by reason of the sicknes and the adiourninge of Midsumēr and Michaelmas tearme came not to towne againe as this Deponent could by any meanes learne vntill the beginninge of Hillarie tearme last who at his Cominge had lost the Coppye of the said bill wherevppon this deponent about Candlemas last was inforced to take out a new Coppye of the said bill wherevnto this deponent by reason of sickness and his extraordinarye occasions in his other buisines could not till of late make answere./

Public Record Office, Court of Requests Affidavit Book, Req 1/141, f. 220; Masson, 1 (1881), 633; French, *Milton in Chancery*, p. 265.

APRIL 8. FATHER'S PARTNER, THOMAS BOWER, AN-SWERS COTTON BILL.

viij° die Aprilis Anno R Rᵖ Caroli xiij°./.	The seuerall Aunsweare of Thomas Bower one of the defendantᵖ to the Bill of Complaynt of Sʳ Thomas Cotton Baronett Cōmpˡᵗ./
Perry ꝑ Quer/ Exaīatʳ./.	All advauntages of excepcōns. to the vntruthes incertentyes and manifest imperfeccōns vnto the said Bill of Complaint vnto him this de-

fendant now and att all tymes hereafter saved and reserved for a full perfect & direct Answeare vnto the said Bill of Complaint and to soe much of the materiall Contentᵖ as anie way Concerneth him this defᵗ to aunsweare vnto hee saith as followeth That he beleeveth that the Complayntᵗ is executor of the last will and testament of the said John Cotton in the Byll named and that the said John Cotton was decrepite weake and about the age of eightye yeares; And this defᵗ saith hee was servant to John Milton in the Bill named And doth beleeve and hath beene enformed by the said Mʳ Milton that the said John Cotton for thirty yeares or thereaboutᵖ did ymploye the said John Milton to lett out att interest diurse great somēs of money after the rate of Tenne and eight in the hundred & accordingly the said John Milton by the direccōn and assent of the said John Cotton did lett out the said somēs to sundry persons But this defendant denyes that the said John Milton and this defᵗ or this defendant onely hadd wᵗʰin five or six yeares last past putt into the handᵖ of them or this defendant by the said John Cotton or his assignes any somē or somēs of money whatsoeū to be lett out att interest, Jt is true during such tyme as this defᵗ did serve the said John Milton which was vntill or about seaven yeares last past this defᵗ as servaunt to the said John Milton and together wᵗʰ him the said John Milton did by the advice and Consent of the said John Cotton and John Milton and each of them putt out all the said seuerall somēs in the Bill mencōned to the seuerall persons in the bill named in and

by the seuerall specialtyes about the seuerall tymes and dates
in the bill sett forth, All which somēs togeather of principall
money amounted to three thousand and six hundred poundes
or thereaboutꝑ And the defendant saith that the said John Milton and this defendant or one of them did bring the said John
Cotton halfe yearly the interest after the Rate of eight poundes
per Centum for some yeares of all or most parte of the moneyes
they or eyther of them were imployed to putt out for the said
John Cotton, And this defendant togeather wᵗʰ the said John
Milton or one of them with the approbacōn & direccōn of the
said John Cotton did call in and putt out the said somēs as
they and the said Cotton thought best and not as this defendant
and the said John Milton or eyther of them thought best, But
this defendant sayth that the three Thousand and Six hundredd poundꝑ being in the handꝑ of the said persons aforenamed
many of them did much decline in their estates and liued pri-
uately and obscurely and did neglect to pay the principall or
interest for two or three yeares togeather to the said John Cotton or to this defendant for his vse, the said debtoʳˢ being the
Remaynder and worst in estate of twice or three tymes soe
many debtoʳˢ as the said John Cotton had caused the said John
Milton and this defendant or one of them to put forth his
money at interest vnto, by Reason whereof the said John Cotton
finding that many of the said Debtoʳˢ were likely to proue
desperate, and not to be brought in without great trauayle and
large expence and almost halfe the said three thousand and
six hundredd poundꝑ being due by seuerall persons whoe in-
habitted in the Counties Palatyne of Lancaster and Chester
and would occasion an increase of trouble and expence for the
recouering thereof, wherevpon the said John Milton from
tyme to tyme calling the said debtoʳˢ and sending after them
to most of their habitacōns and not obteyning ether principall
or interest the said Mʳ Milton did in Easter tearme one thousand six hundred and thirty accquaint John Cotton therewith
wherevpon the said John Cotton as this defendant beleeueth
did make enquiry after the said Debtoʳˢ and did then offer to

sell and assigne all the said debtǫ vnto the said John Milton
for one thousand and ffyue hundred poundǫ But the said John
Milton as this defend^t beleeueth did soe much mistrust the
seuerall abilityes of the said Debto^rs that hee would by noe
meanes condiscend to compound agree or giue him the said
John Cotton one thousand ffyue hundred poundǫ ready money
for the said debtǫ of three thousand and six hundredd poundǫ,
Butt did diswade him the said John Cotton from makeing any
such Bargayne and after such tyme as the said John Milton
had refused the said bargayne the said John Cotton and especially the Cōmp^lt in Mayster Cottons behalfe in Michaellmas
tearme one thousand six hundred and thirty did make further
enquiry both by friendǫ & also strangers after the said debto^rs
and found the same desperate as this def^t conceiues, and therevpon the Cōmp^lt togeather with the said John Cotton did entertayne treaty and comunicacōn to and wth this defendt about
assigneing the said Dēbtǫ of three thousand and six hundred poundǫ for ready money, And att last the said John Cotton
and your subiect by and with the consent of the now Compltē
did mutually and reciprocally to and wth each other condiscend
and come to an agreement by word of mouth to the effect followeing (that is to say) that this defend^t shou'ld Jmēdiately
satisfy and pay two thousand poundǫ to the said John Cotton
and that this defendant should haue the three thousand and six
hundred powndes wth interest then due for the same to his vse
in Manner followeing (that is to say) he should haue power
to renew any of the said bondǫ for the said three thousand and
six hundred powndes wth interest in this defend^tǫ name or in
the name or names of any person or persons to his vse but should
not haue power to sue any bond in the name of the said John
Cotton, But if there were Judgmentǫ vpon any of the said bondǫ
he this defend^t might to his owne vse, cause execucōn therevpon to be made and executed, accordingly this defendant in
Michaellmas tearme one thousand six hundred and thirty did
pay and satisfy vnto the said John Cotton or his assignes the
full some of two Thousand poundǫ (whereof one thousand

poundꝑ the said John Cotton forthw^th gaue and deliuered the p^lt in Consideracōn thereof the said John Cotton did deliuer vnto this defendant all and euery the said Bondꝑ for the payment of three thousand and six hundred poundꝑ with interest, And further the said John Cotton did then and thereby giue graunt and assigne power to this def^t to sue execucōn vpon Judgmentꝑ vpon the bondꝑ and to renew all and euery the said bondꝑ to his owne vse, but nott to sue any bondꝑ in the name of the said John Cotton, other then such as Judgementꝑ were then had therevpon All which two thousand poundꝑ this defendant borrowed and paid interest for the greatest parte thereof after the rate of Eight poundꝑ per Centū with other great gratuytyes for ꝑcureing of parte thereof, frōm seūall parties, And the said John Milton was not present at the bargayne made or att the payment of all or any of the said two thousand powndꝑ, or payd anye of the said two thousand powndꝑ or had any thinge to doe therewith or any parte thereof neyther did euer receiue any benefitt by the said bargayne makeing And this defendant att such tyme as he bargained with the said John Cotton by the assent of the said Complaynant would not haue payd soe great a Somē, but that hee was in hope to gett something thereby but this defendant had noe sooner paid his two thousand poundꝑ and concluded the said bargaine, but his feare was greater then his hopes for he was exposed to such travayle and trouble into seūall counteyes and to soe great chardges and Expences in soliciteing seūall persons and for such long tyme putt in soe little hope of recouery against many of the said Debto^rs for three thousand and six hundred poundꝑ that this defendt was doubtfull he should haue been a great looser in makeing the said bargaine. But att last after infinite expence and great trauayle and much losse of tyme in his other busines this defendant did gett all the three thousand and six hundred poundꝑ (saueing one hundred Markes debt due by one Charnocke and others, and an hundred poundꝑ debt due by Sr William Sandys and one hundred poundꝑ due by the Lord Mollineux and some other debtꝑ amounting

[326]

with interest and Charges as this defendant beleeueth to the
value of ffyue hundredd pound℘ the perticulers whereof this
defendant now remembreth nott, And this defendt denyes that
the said John Milton to this defendt℘ knowledge or this defendant did euer dispose of the said somes amounting to three
thousand and six hundred pound℘ or any of them but by and
wth the Consent of the said John Cotton Jt is true the said
John Cotton was alsoe decreped and kept his chamber, And
the defendant confesseth that he of himselfe & togeather w^{th}
the said Milton Neyther did nor could bring to the said John
Cotton eyther the principall or most part of the intrest in respect the partyes to whom the said moneyes were lett were
then insufficient as this defendant then feared and belieued
they haueing not paid the same, Butt this defendant denyes it
was vpon any pretence or practice to deteyne the principall and
the said Jnterest money or any parte thereof neyther did this
defendant of himselfe or togeather With the said Milton euer
cause or procure the said John Cotton to belieue that the principall & Jnterest of the said somēs were desperate neyther did
the defendant of himselfe or togeather with the said John Milton euer worke vpon him or vse perswatiōn to the said John
Cotton that it would be more for his proffitt and ease if hee
tooke some Competent somē of money and deliuer vpp to this
defendant and the said John Milton or one of them the said
Bond℘ But it is true at such tyme as this def^t agreed wth the
said John Cotton hee did say hee would do his indeauour to
gett in the principall and interest but it was not his offer but
the offer of the Cōmp^{lt} and the said John Cotton to this def^t:
that hee this def^t should haue the said bargayne of three thousand and six hundred powndes wth interest for two thousand
powndes And this def^t denyeth that hee of himself or together
wth the said John Milton did ever Combyne or plott wth Thomas
Collwell esquier in the bill named in whose house the said
John Cotton then lay, or did this def^t of himselfe or together
with the said Milton ever giue reward or sumē of Two hundred pownd℘ or any money or somē whatsoeuer to the said

Collwell or anie other person or persons whatsoeū, neither did
this def^t of himself or together wth the said Milton ever drawe
or perswade the said Collwell to informe the said Cotton that
the said Debtọ or any of them were desperate or that the partyes
obligors or any of them were dead and non soluant or beyond
the seas, Jt is true this def^t hath often said to the said Cotton
that a great parte of the said debtọ were due in the Countyes
palatyne of Lancaster and Chester where wryttọ could not
easily be served but this def^t of himself or together with the
said Milton never said soe vppon any pretence to perswade the
said John Cotton to accept of the said two thowsand powndes
from the said Milton and this def^t or eyther of them for the
said principall Debtọ wch amovnte to three thowsand & six
hundred powndọ Nor did this def^t ever wish or require the
said Mr Collwell to effect anie such buisines or was the said
agreem^t and bargaine aforesaid between the said John Cotton
and this def^t to this defendantọ knowledge done by the advice
or meanes of the said Collwell, And this def^t deyes all practise
& Combynacōn to drawe the said John Cotton for the said somē
of two thowsand powndes to deliuer vpp into the handes of this
def^t all or any of the said Bondes that this def^t might renewe
the same in his owne name or in the name of any other but
whether there be any schedule vnder the hand of this defendant hee knoweth not neither Can this defend^t now remember
whose names were vsed for the renewing of the said Bondes
it being above six yeares since the agreem^t making And this
def^t denyeth that the said debt was a debt of this def^tọ making
but this def^t saith he beleeveth he gave ffive hundred powndes
ready money more then any would haue given for the same it
being before that tyme offered to and refused by others neither
did this def^t or any one whose name this def^t ever vsed receive
of all or any the seuerall debtors by the said obligacōns five
hundred powndes or any sumē of money whatsoeuer due before the said debt Came to this def^t or to their vse or vses, Jt is
true this def^t beleeveth the said John Cotton about a yeare
since dyed & did make the Cōmp^lt his sole executo^r and the

Cōmp^lt did vndertake the same But this def^t denieth that the
Cōmp^lt did ever request this def^t by himself or together wth the
said Milton to accept of Two thowsand powndes and to pay
the Cōmp^lt all the moneys by them received or secured vpon
the said Obligacōns or to deliuer over the new securytyes by
them taken for any of the said debtℯ neyther did this Cōmp^lt
euer request this defendant to expresse what somēs of money
hath been by this defendt of himselfe or togeather wth any
other to his vse receiued of any the persons in the said obligacōns
obliged for interest money or principall debt or renewed or
altered by new securyty, this defendant saith he hath onely in
his handℯ one bond for payment of one hundredd poundℯ principall money which is vnsatisfyed And this defendt denyes to
accompt wth the Cōmp^lt, for the said three thousand and six
hundred powndℯ, for that this defend^t did vndergoe such a
hazard as he did to disburse two thousand poundℯ without any
any practise or vndue carriage, which somē of two thousand
poundℯ might haue been all or most parte of itt lost, therefore
if this defendt after his trauell Charge and long expence and
adventure hath altered & compounded for all the three thousand and six hundredd poundℯ, but three or ffower hundred
powndℯ or thereaboutℯ, he hopeth to make appeare, that it
was iustly gayned and therefore this defendt hopeth he ought
not vnder fauo^r of this honorable Courte to giue accompt to
the Cōmp^lt for the same and the rather for that the Cōmp^lt
in the life tyme of the said Cotton was the partye that allured
and perswaded the said Cotton and this def^t to Come to the
said agreem^t and was the Agent actor and procurer of this def^t
to condiscend thereunto the said Cōmp^lt having offered the same
to others who refused to deale therein and if there had beene
any iust cause why this def^t should make any such accompt as
in and by the said Bill is required the said bargayne being made
by and with the advice consent & approbacōn of the Cōmp^lt
this defendant Conceives hee ought to haue bin questioned for the
same in the life tyme of the said John Cotton who lived as this
def^t hath beene enformed aboue five yeares after the said bar-

gaine making in the house of the now Cōmp^lt and there aboutᵽ a yeare sithence dyed so that the now Cōmp^lt had tyme sufficient in the life tyme of the said Cotton to haue perswaded the said Cotton to Call this def^t to an accompt if there had beene any iust Cause for the doeing thereof And this def^t denyes all Combynacōn and practise laid to his Chardge and Without that that any other matter thing Article or allegacōn in the said bill of Cōmp^lte Materiall or effectuall in Lawe for this defendant to answere vnto and not herein or hereby sufficiently answered confessed [and] avoyded trauersed or denyed is true All which matters and chargᵽ this defendt is ready to averr and proue as this honorable Court shall award and therefore humbly prayeth to bee hence dismissed [with his] costᵽ in this behalfe most wrongfully [susteyned]

> fran: Walsted:
>
> Pedaell: Harlowe

British Museum, Cottonian Charters 1/5/2; Masson, 1 (1881), 633-635; French, *Milton in Chancery*, pp. 265 ff.; Brennecke, pp. 131-132. An abstract of this answer is in Cottonian Charters 1/5/5.

APRIL 13. FATHER ANSWERS SIR THOMAS COTTON'S BILL.

The Answere of John Milton one of the defendtᵽ. to the Bill of Complaynt of S^r. Thomas Cotton Baronett Executor of the last Will and Testam^t of John Cotton Esquyer deceased Complaynant

The said defend^t. saving to himselfe now and at all tymes hereafter all advantages of Excepcon to the incertainty and insufficiency of the said Byll of Complaynt ffor answere therevnto saith That it is true that the said John Cotton in the Bill named was a man of good yeares but certeynly what age hee was of the defend^t. knoweth not but this defend^t. saith that hee was of good vnderstanding and memory at the tyme of the defendtᵽ. knowledge of him and able to walke abroad and did soe oftentymes to this defendtᵽ. shopp in London And was then noe wayes decreipte in bodye or defective in myndе to his this defendtᵽ. knowledge And this defend^t. denyeth that about ffive yeares sithence the said John Cotton did putt into his handꝑ or to this defend^te. knowledge into the handꝑ of the said Thomas Bower then this defend^te. partner and not his servant as in the Bill is alleadged any such sōme or sōmes as in the Bill is pretended in trust to be lett out at interest after the rate of Eight poundꝑ p centum, by this defend^t. or the said Thomas Bower but this defend^t. sayth that before this defend^t. became partner wth the other defend^t. Thomas Bower and after their Copartnership vizt, in all, for the space of neere fforty yeares the said John Cotton did dispose of and lend at the shopp of this defend^t scituate in Bredstreete in London divers somes of money vnto a good value about Three Thousand poundꝑ sometyme more sometymes lesse, before the loane whereof this defend^t. as hee was moved by such person and persons as desyred to borrowe the same did alwayes acquaint the said John Cotton of the security offered therefore, Whereof the said John Cotton did take notice And by inquiry otherwayes then by this defend^t. (as he supposeth), and as hee told this Defend^t, would be and was satisfied of the sufficiency thereof, before hee would or did at any time dispose of the same or any some or somēs of money at his this Defendauntꝑ shopp before and after the Copartnershipp, Between this defend^t. and the said Thomas Bower, And the bondꝑ and other assurances therefore taken ffor the most part were made at his this Defendaunts shopp either by him or his servants before the said Copartnershipp or by them or their ioynt servants wch manner of Dealinge betwixt this defend^t and the said John Cotton did Continue before the Copartnershipp Betwixt this Deffendaunt and the said Thomas Bower about the space of thirty and ffive yeares, as this Defendaunt taketh it, and after this Copartnershipp for the space of Two yeares or thereaboutꝑ Jn all which tyme the said John Cotton sustayned noe losse at all of any of the moneys, hee soe disposed of there or at least very little if any at all And this Defendaunt saith that what sōme and sōmes of money of his the said John Cotton were lent and disposed of at any tyme at this Defendaunts said shopp were disposed of by him this Defend^t before his Copartnershipp wth the other deffendaunt and afterwards by them both for ought hee knoweth as aforesaid and not otherwayes And this Deffendaunt denyeth that the said John Cotton reposed any such trust in him this defend^t as in the Bill is alleadged or that this Deffendaunt did take the same upon him, butt the said John Cotton from tyme to tyme acquainted this defend^t what moneys he had in his hands, and wch hee desired to dispose of during the tyme aforesaid, and of his desire to dispose of the same at interest at the rate aforesaid, And desired this defend^t. to help him to good security therefore, wch hee as occasion was offered from tyme to tyme, did informe him of And vppon the approbacōn of the said John Cotton, the moneys desired vpon such security as this def^t. informed him of were disposed of from tyme to tyme by the said John Cotton and not otherwayes, Soe that this defend^t had not the trust of Disposinge thereof comītted vnto him as in the bill is vntruely alleadged, And soe, and in such sort as aforesaid the said John Cotton Did lend and putt out divers somes of money at his this defend^tρ shopp, but the perticuler somes lent the tymes when, and the perticuler persons that borrowed the same and to whome they were bound this defend^t. doth not now remember (his imploym^t. beinge greate that way and longe since he gave over his trade but this defend^t. confesseth hee thincketh it may be true that the same somēs in the Bill mencōned or most of them were by the said John Cotton lent out uppon interest to the said ρsons therein alsoe named and thincketh that they or the most of them are able men in estate but sayeth, that the said moneys were not putt into the hands of this defend^t. or the other defend^t. Thomas Bower about ffive yeares sithence it manifestly appeares by the pl'tρ owne Bill for that by the same it appeares the bondρ therefore taken beare date before that tyme and divers of them about ffiftene yeares sithence And this defend^t. doth not remember that the said John Cotton did dispose of any more moneys at the tymes in the said Bill mencōned at his this Defend^tρ. said shopp then the somē of Three

Thousand and Three Hundreth pounds or thereaboutꝑ And
this defend^t. saith that as the interest for the said moneys was
received by him soone after it was paid alwayes by him or his
appointment to the said John Cotton sometymes at the said
shopp of this defend^t. and sometymes it was sent home to the
said John Cotton And this defend^t. denyeth that he did ever
receive call in or putt out the said somes or any of them or tooke
the securityes for them or any of them in the byll mencōned
wthout the approbacōn consent and good liking of the said John
Cotton first had But this defend^t. confesseth that it is true he
did at several tymes informe the said John Cotton that the
partyes he tendred him for security were very sufficient and
able men in estate as they were as he then conceaved and as the
Complaynant by his owne Bill setts forth they were Whereby
it manifestly appeares this defend^t. had respect to the satisfaccōn
of the said John Cotton and care that he should be duely repayd
his money againe together with the Consideracōn for the forbearance thereof And this defend^t. doth deny that he found the
said John Cotton to be decreipte or vnable by reason of his
greate yeares to follow his occasions beinge constrayned altogether to keepe his Chamber or that it was soe wth the said John
Cotton or that in that reguarde he did forbeare to bring him the
said John Cotton the principall or part of the interest of the
said somes as in the said Bill mencōned pretending the partyes
to whome the said moneys were lent were not sufficient or that
by deteyning the same or by practize wth the other defend^t.
Thomas Bower hee did cause the said John Cotton to beleeve
that both principall or interest were desperate or that the debtors
were non solvant or that having soe wrought vppon the said
John Cottons Conceipt hee wthout or with the said Thomas
Bower the other defend^t. perswaded the said John Cotton that
it would be more for proffitt and ease if hee the said John Cotton would take some competent some of money and deliver
vpp the said bonds to him or to him and the other defend^t.
Thomas Bower or that they in Consideracōn thereof would
give him the said John Cotton Two Thousand pounds in hand

or that the better to worke the same hee and the said Thomas
Bower the other defend^t. did combyne and plott wth the said
Thomas Collwell in the Bill named or that by reward or for
a sōme of Two Hundred poundɋ or any other sōme given to
the said Collwell by this defend^t. and the saide Thomas Bower
or either of them to this defend^{te}. knowledge this defend^t. did
by himselfe or wth the said Thomas Bower drawe the said Collwell to informe or alleadge to the said John Cotton that the
said debts were desperate or the partyes that borrowed the
same or any of them dead or non solvant or beyond the seas
or resident in the Countyes Palatine of Chester and Lancaster
or that this defend^t. vnder such or any other pretences perswaded the said John Cotton to accept Two Thousand poundɋ
from this and the other defend^t. or one of them for the debt
in the Byll mencōned or any other the debts of the said John
Cotton or that the said Thomas Colwell did to the knowledge
of this defend^t. moove or perswade the said John Cotton as
by the said Bill is pretended or that by any practize or Combynacōn this defend^t. by himselfe or any other did drawe the
said John Cotton for Two Thousand poundɋ to deliver vpp
into the handɋ of the said Thomas Bower the other defend^t.
all or any the bondɋ in the Byll mencōned that the said Thomas
Bower might renew the said bondɋ in his owne name or in the
name of any other or take the principall debt to his owne vse
or that the said principall debt or any other was referred to
this defend^t. and the said Thomas Bower to gather vpp and
expressed in a Schedule vnder the hand of the said Thomas
Bower to this defend^{te}. knowledge But this defend^t. confesseth
that the said John Cotton in his life tyme out of what reason
this defend^t. knoweth not but conceaveth it to be out of timorous-
nes and feare that he might loose some of his said Debts did
voluntarily make an offer to this defend^t. to accept of Two
Thousand poundes in liew of all such monneys as were lent or
mannaged for him at this defend^{te}. shopp being as this de-
fend^t. conceaveth Three Thousand and Three Hundred poundɋ

or thereabouts And vrged this defend^t. to agree wth him to that purpose wch this defend^t. did vtterly refuse And was much greeved at the same And tooke it very ill of the said John Cotton that he should make such an offer as well in reguard that he would not that the said John Cotton should susteyne any losse at all by non payment of the moneys by him soe lent As alsoe that it was a greate disparagement to this defend^t. and his said Trade and shopp And this defend^t. thought himselfe much iniured thereby And told the said John Cotton that hee did very much wronge him this defend^t. and himselfe thereby ffor that the obligors and debtors were very sufficient men in estate and there was noe cause whie hee should doe soe or feare the losse of any part of his moneys then disposed of at his this defend^{te}. shopp and soe hee departed from this defend^t. And what hee did therein afterwardρ this defend^t. knoweth not But it should seeme the said John Cotton persisted in his feare and doubt of losse of all or parte of the said moneys disposed of att this defend^{te}. shopp as aforesaid ffor this defend^t. hath heard (but doth not knowe the same of his owne knowledge) that after the Defend^t. refused the said offer of the said John Cotton hee dealte wth the other defend^t. Thomas Bower wthout the privity or consent of this defend^t but the perticulers of what they did agree vppon this defend^t. certainely knoweth not nor ever had any benefitt or proffitt thereby neither doth hee knowe whether ever any such thing were don or not but by the reporte of others And this defend^t. saith hee hath heard that the said John Cotton made the like offer to the said Thomas Bower for the better performance whereof this defend^t. hath heard that the said Thomas Bower did ioyne with one Thomas Holker an Attorney in the Comon pleas whoe procured certaine moneys of S^r. Thomas Middleton late Alderman of London wch were paid to the said John Cotton vppon a bargaine for the said bondρ but what and how much this defend^t. knoweth not neither doth this defend^t. knowe that the said Thomas Bower the other defend^t. or any other whose name the said Thomas Bower vsed having the cus-

tody of the said bondℓ did call in to his or their owne vse or
renewe most part of the said bondℓ for the principall debt in his
or their owne name neither doth this defend^t. knowe that the
said Bower or any other whose name hee vsed, or might use
received ffive hundred poundes for the interest due before the
said debts came to their handℓ or any other some therefore
neither doth this defend^t. knowe that the said Complaynant
is Executor to the said John Cotton but referrs himselfe to the
Will and Probate of the Will of the said John Cotton in that
behalfe if any such be And this defend^t. denyeth that the Complaynant ever requested this defend^t. to accept of the said Two
Thousand poundes and to pay over to him the moneys received
vppon the said bondℓ or to deliver over any new security taken
for the said debts or to expresse what somēs of money had bin
receaved of any of the persons bound in the said obligacōns in
the byll menconed for interest or principall or renewed or
altered by new security or wch of the said obligacōns remayne
in this defendtℓ. handℓ or that this defend^t. would accompte
to the Complaynant for the said Three Thousand and sixe
Hundred poundℓ with the interest received or secured neither
did this defend^t. ever refuse to enter into any such accompt
And this defend^t. denyeth all practize and Combynacon whatsoever with the said Bower or any other in about or conceringe
any the matters in the Byll mencōned And this defend^t. sayeth
although hee and the said other defend^t. Bower were Copartners
in the Trade of a Scrivener yett they were never partners in or
concerninge the said bargayne or agreem^t. pretended by the
said Byll to be made by theis defēndtℓ. with the said John Cotton if any such bargayne or agreement were made nor had this
defendant ever any benefitt by any such bargaine or agreem^t.
if any such were Without that that any other matter or thing
in the said Byll of Complaynt materiall for this defendant to
make answere vnto And herein not sufficiently answered confessed and avoyded traversed or denyed is true All wch this
defend^t. is ready to averr and proove as this honorable Court
shall award And humbly prayeth to be dismissed from forth

the same wth his reasonable costs and charges in this behalfe wrongfully susteyned.

Whitfelde

Jūr xiij° die Aprilis 1637 coram nōb

Tho Agar

John Agar

British Museum, Cottonian Charters 1/5/1; Public Record Office, Req 2/630; *Academy*, VI (1874), 560; *Notes and Queries*, II, x (1860), 34; Masson, I (1881), 635; French, *Milton in Chancery*, pp. 271 ff. The text is from the Requests copy, supplemented by the Cottonian. See also the entry below under date of May 6, 1637. Brennecke, pp. 132-133, summarizes this document but calls it a "deposition."

[The note at the end reads: Sworn on the thirteenth day of April before us.]

MAY 6. FATHER'S ANSWER TO COTTON'S BILL RECEIVED IN LONDON (?).

Respons Milton ad sectā Cotton v'. j°. Maij p Johem Agar geñ . . . . Com.

Endorsement on Requests copy of Milton's answer of April 13. Why there should have been so long an interval between the swearing of the answer and its receipt in London (if indeed this is the proper interpretation of the endorsement) is not clear; perhaps the plague was the chief cause. See French, *Milton in Chancery*, p. 60.

[The answer of Milton to the suit of Cotton, May 6, by John Agar, gentleman, Commissioner.]

v j°. Maij 1637 p Joh Agar gen. . . . Com.

Endorsement on the British Museum copy of Milton's answer of April 13.

JUNE 9. FATHER'S OPPONENTS IN CHANCERY, ARTHUR DUCK AND WILLIAM CHILD, ARE OBJECTS OF COURT DECREE.

V. 9 Junij [1637]

D   Arthur Ducke Legū   Vpon opening of the Matter this pñte
L   Doctor et Ws Child   daie vnto this Court by Mr Edward
    q' Alex' Ewens Deft   Hide of Councell wth the Deft Alex-
                           ander Ewens Jt was informed that

Mathew Ewens the deft Alexanders Late brother in his life time conveyed divers Manno^{rs} & Land$\wp$ in the bill menc̄oned to the Deft Doctor Ducke in consideracon of 11300^{li} and by agreem^t 2000^{li} of the purchase money was Deposited in the hand$\wp$ of the said Mr Child for 7. yeares after the sd purchase for discharging such Jncumbranc$\wp$ as might be in that time Discovered and for bearing such charg$\wp$ as should arise thereabout$\wp$ and if in that time none should appeare then the said 2000^{li} wth Damag$\wp$ should be repaid vnto the said Mathew Ewens and it was further informed that there being A suite here in this Court betweene one Thomas ffarewell p't and Doctor Ducke and others Deft$\wp$ concerning severall som̄es of money for wch the said Mathewe Ewens stood bound in severall bondes vnto the pl't ffarewell vpon wch the pl't had Judgmtz and Demaunded satisfaccōn out of the 2000^{li} Deposited as aforesaid, and the Cause coming to hearing Jt was ordered that M^r Dr Ducke and Mr Child should paie vnto the said pl't his said principall monies and Damages to be cast vpp and ascertained by Mr Page &c Now forasmuch as the said tearme of 7 yeares is expired and the said Deft Alexand^r Ewens being willing to satisfie all Jncombrances incident to the said Lands and all his brothers the said Mathew Ewens his iust debt$\wp$ soe as he may haue the Remaind^r of the 2000^{li} soe deposited wch he Claimes as Executor to his said brother Jt was humblie moved that the said Alexand^r may haue the Jnterrest of the sd Rem^r of the 2000^{li} vntill this Cause come to hearing, but vpon hearing M^r ffountayne being of Councell wth the Creditors of the said Mathewe Ewens who alleadged that the greatest part of the said Deposited money will be taken away by the said Doctor Ducke for discharge of Jncombrances, and that there are diuers other Judgm$^{t\wp}$ and debt$\wp$ to be satisfied out of the said money Jt is nevertheles ordered that the said M^r doe forthwth expedite his Certifft according to the said recited order and the M^r. is to expedite his report by thend of this tearme, and in the meane tyme the said Mr Child in respect of the Deft$\wp$ present necessities is to paie

and deliver vnto the said Alexander Ewens the some of xx^li.
and the said M^r. Child is hereby discharged for the same/
　　ex'　　　　　　　　　　　　　[John] Ch[urchill?]

Public Record Office, C33/171, ff. 414-414v; French, *Milton in Chancery*, pp. 288-289.

[The introductory note reads: Arthur Ducke, LL.D., and William Child, plaintiffs; Alexander Ewens, defendant.]

SUMMER (?). STAYS IN LONDON (?).

Nuper etiam cum mihi temere Londini perlatum esset . . . jam cras sumus rus illud nostrum redituri, urgetq; iter, ut vix hæc propere in chartam conjecerim. Vale. *Londino*, Septemb. 2. 1637.

From Milton's letter to Charles Diodati, September 2, 1637, *q.v.* From the tone of this reference we may assume that Milton had been in London for some time and was anxious to return to Horton; but there is no way of being sure when he went to London. He had evidently made several visits to Diodati's house and to his brother in London. In view of the fact that, in his letter of September 23 to Diodati, he was again in London and was thinking of taking rooms in one of the Inns of Court, it seems highly possible that he alternated between Horton and London, spending considerable stretches of time first in one place and then in the other.

[Lately, also, when it had been fallaciously reported to me in London . . . and now to-morrow we are about to return to that country residence of ours, and the journey so presses that I have hardly had time to put these things on the paper. Farewell. London: Septemb. 2, 1637.]

Masson, I, 598 (643). Masson unfortunately omits the phrase "in London" from the first sentence.

SUMMER (?). VISITS DIODATI'S HOUSE AND BROTHER.

. . . habeto me ineunte autumno ex itinere ad fratrem tuum eo consilio deflexisse, ut quid ageres, scirem. Nuper etiam cum mihi temere Londini perlatum esset à nescio quo te in urbe esse, confestim & quasi αὐτοβοεὶ proripui me ad cellam tuam, at illud σκίας ὄναρ, nusquam enim compares.

Milton's letter to Diodati, September 2, 1637, *q.v.* The date is not quite certain, but approximate.

[... understand that, in the beginning of the autumn, I turned aside from a journey to see your brother with the design of knowing what you were doing. Lately also, when it had been fallaciously reported to me in London by I know not whom that you were in town, straightway and as if with a shout I rushed to your crib; but, 'twas the vision of a shadow! for nowhere did you appear.]

Masson, I, 598 (643). Masson unfortunately omits the important phrases, "to see your brother," and "in London."

JULY 6. FATHER'S SUIT AGAINST DUCK AND CHILD MENTIONED.

Jnter Arthurū Ducke legū Doctor et Willm' Child q^{tes} Alexandr' Ewens executor' Mathew Ewens et al' Creditor' dict Mathei defend^{tes}.

6° Julii 1637 ...

Jn May. 1635. Rose Downer exhīted a bill for a debt of 50^{li.} wth Jnterest lent to Mathew the ffather in June. 4°. Cār & is since dead, since whose death in ffebr'. 1636. Milton & Bowers Scriveners that putt forth that money & by Decree of this C^{rt} had paid Downer have exhīted a bill for the same debt ...

John Page.

Public Record Office, Chancery Reports and Certificates, C38/86; French, *Milton in Chancery*, p. 289. The section quoted is part of several pages of items concerning Duck and Child, the purport of which is that the claims against Child are greater than his assets which can be used for this purpose.

[Between Arthur Ducke, LL.D., and William Child, plaintiffs, and Alexander Ewens, executor of Mathew Ewens, and other creditors of the said Mathew, defendants.]

AUGUST 10. FRIEND EDWARD KING, SUBJECT OF "LYCIDAS," DROWNED.

P.M.S. Edovardus King ... invisens, haud procul a littore Britannico, navi in scopulum allisa, et rimis ex ictu fatiscente, dum alii vectores vitæ mortalis frustra satagerent, immortalem anhelans, in genua provolutus oransque, una cum navigio ab aquis absorptus, animam Deo reddidit; IIII. eid. sextileis; anno salutis MDCXXXVII; ætatis XXV.

Justa Edovardo King Naufrago, 1638, sig. [A2]; CM, XVIII, 655. Though sometimes ascribed to Milton, this tribute seems unlikely to have been written by him.

[P.M.S. Edward King . . . the ship in which he was having struck on a rock not far from the British shore, and being stove in by the shock, he, while the other passengers were fruitlessly busy about their mortal lives, having fallen forward upon his knees, and breathing a life which was immortal, in the act of prayer going down with the vessel, rendered up his soul to God, Aug. 10, 1637, aged 25.]

Masson, I, 606 (651).

SEPTEMBER 2. LETTER TO CHARLES DIODATI; WRITES SELDOM; STUDIES HARD; VISITS DIODATI'S BROTHER; ABOUT TO LEAVE LONDON FOR COUNTRY.

Carolo Diodato.

6. Jam istuc demum plane video te agere, ut obstinato silentio nos aliquando pervincas; quod si ita est, euge habe tibi istam gloriolam, en scribimus priores: quanquam certe si unquam hæc res in contentionem veniret, cur neuter alteri οὕτω δία χρόνου scripserit, cave putes quin sim ego multis partibus excusatior futurus: δηλον ὅτι ὡς βραδὺς καὶ ὀκνηρός τις ὢν φύσει πρὸς τὸ γράφειν, ut probe nôsti, cum tu contra sive naturâ, sive consuetudine, ad hujusmodi Literarias προσφωνήσις haud ægre perduci soleas. Simul & illud pro me facit, quod tuam studendi rationem ita institutam cognovi, ut crebro interspires, ad amicos visas, multa scribas, nonnunquam iter facias; meum sic est ingenium, nulla ut mora, nulla quies, nulla ferme ullius rei cura, aut cogitatio distineat, quoad pervadam quo feror, & grandem aliquam studiorum meorum quasi periodum conficiam. Atq; hinc omnino, nec aliunde, sodes, est factum, uti ad officia quidem ultro deferenda spissius accedam, ad respondendum tamen, O noster Theodote non sum adeo cessator; neq; enim commisi ut tuam Epistolam unquam ullam debitâ vice nostra alia ne clauserit. Quid! quod tu, ut audio, Literas ad Biblio-

polam, ad Fratrem etiam sæpiuscule; quorum utervis propter vicinitatem satis commode præstitisset, mihi, si quæ essent, reddendas. Illud vero queror, te, cum esses pollicitus, ad nos fore ut diverteres cum ex urbe discederes, promissis non stetisse: quæ promissa abs te præterita si vel semel cogitasses, non defuisset prope necessarium scribendi argumentum. Atq; hæc habui quæ in te merito, ut mihi videor, declamitarem. Tu quæ ad hæc contra parabis ipse videris. Verum interim quid est quæso? rectène vales? ecquinam iis in locis erudituli sunt quibuscum libenter esse, et garrire possis, ut nos consuevimus? quando redis? quamdiu tibi in animo est apud istos ὑπερβορείους commorari? tu velim ad hæc mihi singula respondeas: sed enim ne nescias non nunc demum res tuæ cordi mihi sunt, nam sic habeto me ineunte autumno ex itinere ad fratrem tuum eo consilio deflexisse, ut quid ageres, scirem. Nuper etiam cum mihi temere Londini perlatum esset à nescio quo te in urbe esse, confestim & quasi αὐτοβοεὶ proripui me ad cellam tuam, at illud σκίας ὄναρ, nusquam enim compares. Quare quod sine tuo incommodo fiat, advola ocyus & aliquo in loco te siste, qui locus mitiorem spem præbeat, posse quoquo modo fieri ut aliquoties inter nos saltem visamus, quod utinam nobis non aliter esses vicinus, rusticanus atq; es urbicus, ἀλλὰ τοῦτο ὥσπερ θεῶ φίλον. Plura vellem & de nobis, & de studiis nostris, sed mallem coram; & jam cras sumus rus illud nostrum redituri, urgetq; iter, ut vix hæc propere in chartam conjecerim. Vale.

Londino, Septemb. 2. 1637.

Milton, *Epistolarum Familiarium Liber Unus*, 1674, pp. 14-16; CM, XII, 18 ff.

[To Charles Diodati.

Now at length I plainly see that what you are driving at is sometimes to vanquish us completely by an obstinate silence; and, if it is so, bravo! have that little glory over us, for lo! we write first; although certainly, if ever that matter were to come into contention, why neither has written to the other for so long, it is for you to beware of thinking but that I shall be by many degrees the more excused—manifestly so indeed, as being one by nature slow and reluctant to write, as you well know; while you, on the other hand, whether by nature or habit, are wont without difficulty to be drawn into epistolary correspondence of this sort. It makes also for my favour that I know your method of studying to be so arranged that you frequently take breath in the middle, visit your friends, write much, sometimes make a journey: my genius, however, is such that no delay, no rest, no care or thought almost of anything holds me aside until I reach the end I am making for, and round off, as it were, some great period of my studies. And hence wholly, nor from any other cause, believe me, has it happened that I am slower in approaching the voluntary discharge of my good offices; but in replying to such, O our Theodotus, I am not such a putter-off; nor have I ever been guilty of not meeting any letter of yours by one of mine in due turn. What! that you, as I hear, should have sent letters to the bookseller, to your brother too not unfrequently, either of whom would, conveniently enough, on account of their nearness, have caused letters to have been delivered to us, if there had been any! This, however, I complain of, that, whereas you promised that it would be with us that you would take up your quarters on your departure from the city, you did not keep your promises; the neglect of which promises by you if you had but once thought of, there would not have been wanting an almost necessary occasion for writing. All this I had, as I imagine, wherewith to lecture you deservedly. What you will prepare in answer, see yourself. But, meanwhile, how is it with you, pray? Are you rightly in health? Are there in those parts any learned folks or so with whom you can willingly associate and chat, as we were wont together? When do you return? How long do you intend to dwell among those hyperboreans? I would have you answer me these questions one by one; but (don't mistake) not now only are your affairs at my heart,—for understand that, in the beginning of the autumn, I turned aside from a journey to see your brother* with the

---

* Masson omits the last phrase, which is important; as also the phrase "in London" in the next sentence.

design of knowing what you were doing. Lately also, when it had been fallaciously reported to me in London by I know not whom that you were in town, straightway and as if with a shout I rushed to your crib; but, 'twas the vision of a shadow! for no-where did you appear. Wherefore, as far as may be without inconvenience to you, fly hither all the sooner, and fix yourself in some place which may give me a more pleasant hope that somehow or other we may at least sometimes exchange visits; for I would that you were no otherwise our neighbour, being in the country, than you are, being in the town. But this is as it pleases God! I would say more both about ourselves and about our studies; but would rather do so in your presence; and now to-morrow we are about to return to that country residence of ours, and the journey so presses that I have hardly had time to put these things on the paper. Farewell.

London: Septemb. 2, 1637.]

Masson, I, 597-598 (642-643).

ABOUT SEPTEMBER 15(?). LETTER FROM CHARLES DIODATI.

. . . ad ea enim quæ tute prius, & alii adhuc sola afferre possunt vota, jam nunc artem insuper tuam, vimq; omnem medicam quasi cumulum accedere vis me scilicet intelligere. Jubes enim salvere sexcenties, quantum volo, quantum possum, vel etiam amplius. . . . immo vero quâ tarditatis excusatione usus Literarum initio es . . . Multa solicite quæris, etiam quid cogitem. . . .

Though the original letter has not been found, these phrases from Milton's reply of September 23, 1637, give some idea of the contents. The date must be very close, because Diodati's letter must have been provoked by Milton's of September 2; thus a date part way between September 2 and September 23 is certain.

[. . . for to those mere wishes which were all that you formerly could and that others hitherto can bring, you wish me, I suppose, to understand that there is now added, as in a heap, your art and all your medical force. For you bid me be well six hundred times, as well as I wish to be, as well as I can

be, or even better. . . . nay truly, that very excuse for your delay
which you have employed in the beginning of your letter. . . .
You make many anxious inquiries . . . even as to what I am
thinking of. . . .]

Masson, I, 599-601 (643-645).

September 23. letter to charles diodati; again
in london; meditating great work and fame;
living in cramped quarters; has been reading
much greek and roman history.

Eidem.

7 Quod cæteri in Literis suis plerunq; faciunt amici, ut unicam
tantum salutem dicere sat habeant, tu illud jam video quid sit
quod toties impertias; ad ea enim quæ tute prius, & alii adhuc
sola afferre possunt vota, jam nunc artem insuper tuam, vimq;
omnem medicam quasi cumulum accedere vis me scilicet intelligere. Jubes enim salvere sexcenties, quantum volo, quantum
possum, vel etiam amplius. Næ ipsum te nuper Salutis condum
promum esse factum oportet, ita totum salubritatis penum dilap-
idas, aut ipsa proculdubio sanitas jam tua Parasita esse debet, sic
pro Rege te geris atq; imperas ut dicto sit audiens; itaq;
gratulor tibi, & duplici proinde nomine gratias tibi agam necesse
est, cum amicitiæ tum artis eximiæ. Literas quidem tuas, quoniam ita convenerat, diu expectabam; verum acceptis neq; dum
ullis, si quid mihi credis, non idcirco veterem meam erga te
benevolentiam tantillum refrigescere sum passus; immo vero
quâ tarditatis excusatione usus Literarum initio es, ipsam illam
te allaturum esse jam animo præsenseram, idq; recte, nostræq;
necessitudini convenienter. Non enim in Epistolarum ac Saluta-
tionum momentis veram verti amicitiam volo, quæ omnia ficta
esse possunt; sed altis animi radicibus niti utrinq; & sustinere se;
cœptamq; sinceris, & sanctis rationibus, etiamsi mutua cessarent
officia, per omnem tamen vitam suspicione & culpâ vacare: ad
quam fovendam non tam scripto sit opus, quam vivâ invicem
virtutum recordatione. Nec continuò, ut tu non scripseris, non
erit quo illud suppleri officium possit, scribit vicem tuam apud

me tua probitas, verasque literas intimis sensibus meis exarat, scribit morum simplicitas, & recti amor; scribit ingenium etiam tuum, haudquaquam quotidianum, & majorem in modum te mihi commendat. Quare noli mihi, arcem illam Medicinæ tyrannicam nactus, terrores istos ostentare, ac si salutes tuas sexcentas velles, subductâ minutim ratiunculâ, ad unam omnes à me reposcere, si forte ego, quod ne siverit unquam Deus, amicitiæ desertor fierem; atq; amove terribile illud ἐπιτείχισμα quod cervicibus nostris videris imposuisse, ut sine tua bona venia ne liceat ægrotare. Ego enim ne nimis minitêre, tui similes impossibile est quin amem, nam de cætero quidem quid de me statuerit Deus nescio, illud certe; δεινόν μοι ἔρωτα, εἰπέρ τω ἄλλω, τοῦ καλοῦ ἐνέταξε. Nec tanto Ceres labore, ut in Fabulis est, Liberam fertur quæsivisse filiam, quanto ego hanc τοῦ καλοῦ ἰδέαν, veluti pulcherrimam quandam imaginem, per omnes rerum formas & facies: (πολλαὶ γὰρ μορφαὶ τῶν Δαιμονίων) dies noctesq; indagare soleo, & quasi certis quibusdam vestigiis ducentem sector. Unde fit, ut qui, spretis quæ vulgus pravâ rerum æstimatione opinatur, id sentire & loqui & esse audet; quod summa per omne ævum sapientia optimum esse docuit, illi me protinus, sicubi reperiam, necessitate quâdam adjungam. Quod si ego sive naturâ, sive meo fato ita sum comparatus, ut nullâ contentione, & laboribus meis ad tale decus & fastigium laudis ipse valeam emergere; tamen quo minus qui eam gloriam assecuti sunt, aut eo feliciter aspirant, illos semper colam, & suspiciam, nec Dii puto, nec homines prohibuerint. Cæterum jam curiositati tuæ vis esse satisfactum scio. Multa solicite quæris, etiam quid cogitem. Audi, Theodote, verum in aurem ut ne rubeam, & sinito paulisper apud te grandia loquar; quid cogitem quæris; ita me bonus Deus, immortalitatem. Quid agam vero? πτεροφυῶ, & volare meditor: sed tenellis admodum adhuc pennis evehit se noster Pegasus, humile sapiamus. Dicam jam nunc serio quid cogitem, in hospitium Juridicorum aliquod immigrare, sicubi amœna & umbrosa ambulatio est, quod & inter aliquot sodales, commodior illic habitatio, si domi manere, & ὁρμητήριον εὐπρεπέστερον quocunq; libitum erit excurrere; ubi nunc sum, ut nosti, obscure, & anguste sum; de studiis etiam nostris fies certior. Græcorum res continuatâ lectione deduximus usquequo illi Græci esse sunt desiti: Italorum in obscura re diu versati sumus sub Longobardis, & Francis, & Germanis, ad illud tempus quo illis ab Rodolpho Germaniæ Rege concessa libertas est; exinde quid quæque Civitas suo Marte gesserit, separatim legere præstabit. Tu vero quid? quousq; rebus domesticis filius-familias imminebis urbanarum sodalitatum oblitus? quod, nisi bellum hoc novercale, vel Dacico, vel Sarmatico infestius sit, debebis profecto maturare, ut ad nos saltem in hyberna concedas. Interim, quod sine tua molestia fiat, Justinianum mihi Venetorum Historicum rogo mittas; ego meâ fide aut in adventum tuum probe asservatum curabo; aut, si mavis, haud ita multo post ad te remissum. Vale.

Londino, Septemb. 23, 1637.

Milton, *Epistolarum Familiarium Liber Unus*, 1674, pp. 17-20; CM, XII, 22 ff. The *"Eidem"* at the top refers to Diodati, to whom the preceding letter had been addressed.

[To Charles Diodati.

What other friends generally do in their letters, thinking it enough to express one single wish for one's health, I see now how it is that you do the same so many times; for to those mere wishes which were all that you formerly could and that others hitherto can bring, you wish me, I suppose, to understand that there is now added, as in a heap, your art and all your medical force. For you bid me be well six hundred times, as well as I wish to be, as well as I can be, or even better. Verily you must have lately been made the very steward of the larder, the clerk of the kitchen to Health, you make such havoc of the whole store of salubrity; or, doubtless, Health ought now to be your parasite, you so act the king and command it to be obedient. I therefore congratulate you, and it is consequently necessary that I should return you thanks on a double account—both of your friendship and your excellent art. I did indeed, as it happened so to be, long expect your letters; but, having never received any, I did not, believe me, on that account suffer my old good-will to you in the least degree to grow cold; nay truly, that very excuse for your delay which you have employed in the beginning of your letter, I had anticipated in my own mind you would offer. And rightly so and agreeably to our requirement! For I would not that true friendship turned on balances of letters and salutations, all which may be false; but that it should depend on both sides on the deep roots of the mind and sustain itself there, and that, once begun on sincere and sacred grounds, it should, though mutual good offices should cease, yet be free from suspicion and blame during the whole of life— for the fostering of which friendship there is not need so much of writing, as of a loving recollection of virtues on one side and on the other. Nor even now, should you not have written, would there be a lack of means of supplying that good office. Your probity writes with me in your stead, and indites true letters on my inmost feelings; your innocence of morals writes to me, and your love of the good; your genius also, by no means an every-day one, writes to me and commends you to me more and more. Wherefore, don't, having attained that tyrannic citadel of Medicine, wave those terms before me, as if you meant, abating a little bit by bit, to demand back from me your six hundred healths down to one, if by chance (which may God never permit!) I should become a traitor to friendship; and remove that terrible embargo which you seem to have hung on our neck, to the effect that it should not be lawful for us to be sick without your good leave. For, lest you should threaten too much, know it is impossible for me not to love men like you. What besides God has resolved concerning me I know not, but this at least: He has instilled into me, at all events, a vehement love of the beautiful. Not with so much labour, as the fables have it, is Ceres said to have sought her daughter Proserpine, as I am wont day and night to seek for this idea of the beautiful through all the forms and faces of things (for many are the shapes of things divine), and to follow it leading me on as with certain assured traces. Whence it happens that, whoso, scorning what the vulgar opine in their depraved estimation of things,

dares to feel and speak and be that which the highest wisdom
through every age has taught to be best, to that man I attach
myself forthwith by a real necessity, wherever I find him. And
if, either by nature or by my fate, I am so circumstanced that,
by no effort and labour of mine, I can myself rise to such an
honour and elevation, yet that I should always worship and
look up to those who have attained that glory, or happily aspire to it, neither gods nor men, I think, have bidden nay.

But now I know you wish to have your curiosity satisfied.
You make many anxious inquiries—even as to what I am thinking of. Hearken, Theodotus, but let it be in your private ear,
lest I blush; and allow me for a little to speak big words to you!
You ask what I am thinking of? So may the good Deity help me,
of Immortality! But what am I doing? I am pluming my wings
and meditating flight; but as yet our Pegasus raises himself on
very tender pinions. Let us be lowly wise!

I will now tell you seriously what I am thinking of:—of
migrating into some Inn of the Lawyers, wherever there is a
pleasant and shady walk, because there I shall have both a more
convenient habitation among some companions, if I wish to
remain at home, and more suitable head-quarters if I choose to
make excursions anywhere. Where I am now, as you know, I
live obscurely and in a cramped manner. You shall also be
made more certain respecting our studies. We have by continued
reading brought down the affairs of the Greeks as far as the
time when they ceased to be Greeks; we were long engaged on
the obscure business of the Italians under Longobards, Franks,
and Germans to the time when liberty was given them by Ro-
dolph, King of Germany; from that period it will be better to
read separately what each state (in Italy) did by its own wars.
But what are *you* doing? How long will you hang over domestic
matters as a *filius familias*, forgetting your town companion-
ships? But, unless this step-motherly war be worse than the
Dacian or the Sarmatian, you will certainly require to make
haste, so as at least to come with us into winter-quarters. Meanwhile, if it can be done without trouble to you, I beg you to send

me Justinian, the historian of the Venetians. I will, on my word, see that it is well kept against your arrival, or, if you prefer it, that it is sent back to you not so very long after receipt. Farewell.

London: Septemb. 23, 1637.]

Masson, I, 599-601 (643-646).

NOVEMBER (?). SIR THOMAS COTTON OFFERS EXCEPTIONS TO THE ANSWER OF MILTON'S FATHER'S PARTNER, THOMAS BOWER, IN COTTON-MILTON SUIT.

Jntᵽ Thōm Cottō [versus] Thōm Bower

Exceptions to yᵉ deftᵽ answeare.

The bill chargeth. That yᵉ deft by practice did ᵽswade John Cotton deceased to accept 2000ˡⁱ, frō yᵉ deft or one Miltō for yᵉ sᵈ principal detᵽ, naming thē in ᵽticulᵽ, wᶜʰ amounted to 3600ˡⁱ. By wᶜʰ practice they drew him to deliuʳ yᵉ bondᵽ, wᶜʰ were expʳssed in a schedule. & hau[e since that time] receiued yᵉ monies therevppō. And not only yᵉ [principal money, but] hath receiued of seuʳal ᵽsonᵽ dettorᵽ by yᵉ sᵈ obligaciōᵽ, at least [500]ˡⁱ for yᵉ interest due before yᵉ sᵈ det came to his vse.

They haue beene requested to expʳᵽ what monies they haue receiued for intrest mony or principal money.

Resp. That yᵉ principal mony was 3600ˡⁱ [fol.] 4. That miltō offred but 15[00ˡⁱ for these] detᵽ off 3600ˡⁱ. 8. He did get [bonds for] 3600 [pounds principal money,] amounting wᵗʰ intrest & chargeᵽ to [over 4100.ˡⁱ] He denieth to haue receiued off all or any yᵉ dettorᵽ 500ˡⁱ. or any sumē of money whatsoeuʳ due before yᵉ sᵈ det came to this deft. fol. 22.

Except. He hath not set forth what intrest he hath receiued frō euʳy of yᵉ sᵈ dettorᵽ, due before the sayd principall dett came to his vse wᶜʰ he ought to doe, Jt being [a pl]aine questiō iff yᵉ bondᵽ be wel granted and yet [he sh]al not haue such intrests as were due before the bondᵽ were [granted], Jt being no ᵽte of yᵉ [360]0ˡⁱ put ouʳ.

2ˡʸ. Jn this point, yᵉ answeare is cautelous, That he did not receiue 500ˡⁱ or any sumē due, before yᵉ sᵈ det cāe to him. Whereas he should haue shewed what intrest he hath receiued since the sayd dettꝑ came to his vse which were due before, Jt is not likely that he should receiue any before yᵉ det came to him. The Court must Judge whethʳ Jt belongꝑ to him, or not.

British Museum, Cottonian Charters 1/5/5; French, *Milton in Chancery*, p. 276. Bracketed portions are the editor's conjectural readings in passages which are torn or otherwise illegible. The folio references are to pages in Bower's answer of April 8, 1637. Though not dated, this paper must have been prepared after that answer and before Bower's "further answer" of December 5, 1637, probably shortly before the latter. It has therefore been tentatively dated in November.

NOVEMBER. WRITES "LYCIDAS."

Lycidas Novemb: 1637.

Jn this Monodie the author bewails a lerned freind unfortunatly drownd in his passage from Chester on the Jrish Seas 1637.

Milton, Cambridge Manuscript, p. 31; CM, I, 460. The date, "Novemb: 1637," was later cancelled. In the printed versions there is no indication of the date of composition.

. . . there was a Young Gentleman, one Mr. *King*, with whom, for his great Learning and Parts, he had contracted a particular Friendship and Intimacy; whose death (for he was drown'd on the *Irish* Seas in his passage from *Chester* to *Ireland*) he bewails in that most excellent Monody in his forementioned Poems) Intituled *Lycidas*. Never was the loss of Friend so Elegantly lamented.

Phillips, p. ix; Darbishire, p. 54.

NOVEMBER 26. BROTHER CHRISTOPHER "RESTORED TO COMMONS."

[At a Parliament in the Inner Temple on November 26, 1637, it was voted] that Milton be restored into commons.

Records of the Inner Temple, ed. Inderwick, II, 239. The published records shed no light on this note, though it is virtually certain that the Milton concerned was Christopher, brother of the poet, who figures rather frequently in these pages.

NOVEMBER 30. FATHER'S PARTNER, THOMAS BOWER, ARRANGES TO MAKE FURTHER ANSWER TO SIR THOMAS COTTON'S BILL IN COTTON-MILTON SUIT.

xxx° Die Noüebris. . . .

Thomas Bower psonal' compet corā Coño Rꝓ virtute ordinis adꝓ Thomæ Cotton [*an illegible word*] quer' postea viz': quinto Die Decembris anno predto admiss est compere ꝑ Noel Boteler geñ atturñ suū cū coño Mrī Walsted.

Public Record Office, Court of Requests Appearance Book, 13-14 Charles I, Req 2/117, p. 124; French, *Milton in Chancery*, p. 277. The illegible word may be "militis" (knight) or "barronetti" (baronet).

[November 30. . . . Thomas Bower is to appear personally before the King's Council by virtue of an order at the suit of Thomas Cotton (baronet?) hereafter as follows: on the fifth day of December in the aforesaid year he is allowed to appear through Noel Boteler, gentleman, his attorney, with the help of Master Walsted.]

DECEMBER 5. FURTHER ANSWER OF FATHER'S PART-NER, THOMAS BOWER, IN COTTON-MILTON SUIT.

Quinto die decembris   The further Answere of Thomas
Anno R Rꝓ Caroli xiij°   Bower defend' to the bill of comp'' of
                         S' Thomas Cotton Baronet./

The sayd defend' for a full Answer to the sayd Bill and to the exceptions taken to this defendꞇ former Answere hee this defend' sayth that in and by his this defendꞇ agreement to and wᵗʰ John Cotton esquire in the Bill named the sayd John Cotton did Assigne & put ouer to this defend' all & euerie the seuerall principall sūmes of money and also all and euȳe the seuerall vse & Interest money then due & owing to the sayd John Cotton by vertue of all and every the seũall Obligacōns in the Bill mencōned for the considerations in this defendꞇ former Answere set forth And this defend' was in and by the sayd agreement to haue all & euerie the Jnterest money then due & owing at the Tyme of the said Assignemᵗ and putting over of the said Bondꝓ Obligacōns and specealties but how much vse or Jnterest

money was then due vpon all and every or any of the sayd
Bondɒ and Obligations at the Time of the sayd Assignement &
putting ouer to this Defend^t of all and every the sayd Bondɒ
in the Bill mencōned hee this defend^t knowes not but beleeues
hee hath receiued since the sayd John Cottons Assignement &
putting over of of the sayd Bondɒ to this defend^t of all & euery
the sayd seuerall debtors by vertue of the sayd Bondɒ for Jnterest and of money due vpon the sayd Bondɒ before the sayd
Assignement and putting over the sayd Bondɒ the sumē of an
Hundred and Three score poundɒ or thereaboutɒ & noe more
but of wch of the sayd Creditors or debtors in perticuler by
vertue of all or any the sayd Obligations or how much vse or
Jnterest money in pticuler was then due or oweing before or att
the tyme of the sayd Assignement of the sayd bondɒ for or by
reason of all or any the sayd Bondɒ or how much thereof this
Defend^t or any person or persons to his vse receiued since the
sayd Assignem^t: or putting over of the same this defendt knoweth not it being seauen Yeares since or thereaboutɒ but this de-
fend^t nor any person or persons to his vse did ever receiue before the sayd Assignement or putting ouer the sayd bondɒ
any Jnterest or Vse money due vpon all or any the sayd bondɒ
in the bill menconed & this defendant conceiueth the Jnterest
money due vppon all and every the sayd bondɒ vntill the sayd
Assignement and putting ouer of the same to this defend^t. did
not belong to the sayd John Cotton & the complaynant or
either of them but to this defend^t by the agreem^t & Assignement
of ye sayd bondɒ by the sayd John Cotton as aforesayd therefore not materiall to the comp^{lt} to know how much thereof this
defend^t receiued or of whome

ff. Weelsted

[Endorsed:] Respons:
Bower
adv^s
Sr Tho: Cotton Bar:
S

Public Record Office, Req 2/630; British Museum, Cottonian Charters 1/5/3; *Academy*, VI (1874), 560-561; *Athenaeum*, 1880, II, 15; French, *Milton in Chancery*, p. 277. The text given here is a composite of the Requests and Cottonian manuscripts.

[December 5, 13 Charles I . . . Bower's answer at the suit of Sir Thomas Cotton, Bart.]

DECEMBER 12. RECEIVES INTEREST PAYMENT FROM RICHARD POWELL.

. . . the growing Jnterest for the forbearance of the said Principall debt was for some yeares then following likewise payd And soe continued to bee paid vntill June Jn the yeare of our Lord One Thousand six hundred ffortie and ffower. . . .

From Milton's answer to Elizabeth Ashworth, February 22, 1653/4, *q.v.*

1638

ALLEGED PORTRAIT.

John Milton. From an Original Picture in the Collection of Lord Orford, at Strawberry Hill . . . 1796.

Inscription on an engraving published in 1796 by E. and S. Harding; Williamson (*Milton Tercentenary*, 1908), pp. 19, 84-85. The original is said (in the *British Museum Catalogue of Engraved British Portraits*, II [1910], 695) to be a portrait of Sir William Killigrew by A. van Dyck, formerly at Strawberry Hill and now at Clumber. Williamson notes that the same plate was published by Evans of Great Queen Street as of Killigrew. There is therefore no reason to consider it a portrait of Milton, but it is mentioned here because of these former ascriptions. The reason for putting it under this year is that Williamson says that the original portrait, in the possession of the Duke of Newcastle, is so dated.

A RELATIVE (?) TAXED FOR BUILDINGS IN LONDON.

[A list of persons who have compounded for buildings erected in London contrary to proclamation includes:] Henry Milton for nine houses enlarged by Limehouse.

John Milton · 1638

Calendars of State Papers, Domestic, 1638-1639, p. 262. I have not checked the original documents.

Epitaph on Lady Talbot in the Parish Church at Stowmarket (?).

According to a note in *Notes and Queries*, ii, v (1858), 343, "an inscription on a lady of the Talbot family in the parish church, 1638, has been thought to be Milton's composition." The writer gives a reference to Hollingsworth's *Stowmarket*, but no confirmation of the claim is available. This report is probably an offshoot, by the well-known process of growing rumors, of Milton's later associations with Thomas Young of Stowmarket.

"Lycidas" printed.

Lycidas

Justa Edovardo King naufrago, 1638, part ii (*Obsequies to the memorie of M*^r *Edward King*, 1638), pp. 20-25; reproduced in Fletcher facsimile, I, 347 ff.; a fragment of what appears to be Milton's corrected proof, now in the Cambridge University library, is reproduced *ibid.*, I, 346; CM, I, 76. Reproductions of both the English and the Latin title pages are given in CM, I, between pp. 458 and 459.

Corrects several copies of "Lycidas" for presentation (?).

Four copies of this poem, one fragmentary and the others containing the whole volume of *Justa Edovardo King naufrago*, all of which have manuscript corrections in a hand resembling Milton's, are known. One is in the British Museum, two (including the fragment) are in the Cambridge University Library, and the fourth was offered for sale in William H. Robinson's 65th catalogue, 1938, item 80. They are described in detail, with further references, in French, "The Autographs of John Milton," #4-6 (not including the Robinson copy), and in CM, XVIII, 550, 640, 655. Collations are given in CM, I, 459 (the Cambridge copies only) and in CM, XVIII, 640 and 655. It seems quite likely, as the authors of the Pforzheimer Catalogue suggest (II, 724), that these copies were corrected, probably by the author or the printer, for presentation. Miss Helen Darbishire ("The Chronology of Milton's Handwriting," *The Library*, Fourth Series, XIV [Transactions of the Bibliographical Society, Second Series, XIV, 1934], 229-235) asserts that there is "no room for doubt that the corrections in the British Museum copy of *Lycidas* (C.21.c.42) are in Milton's hand."

In this connection it might simply be mentioned that the copy of *Justa* now owned by the Elizabethan Club at Yale University formerly belonged to Isaac Walton and bears his autograph. See Luther S. Livingston, *Auction Prices of Books*, III (1905), 222. The most likely date for Walton to have bought this volume is shortly after its publication.

EDWARD KING'S FAMILY'S COPY OF THE MEMORIAL VOLUME ?

Justa Edovardo King naufrago.

Bernard Quaritch's Catalogue #446, 1931, item 438, describes a copy of this volume which the editor believes was a presentation to the King family by one of the contributors. It contains the bookplate of Edward King, first Earl of Kingston (1726-1797). The advertised price was £1350. Item 439 in the same catalogue is a copy of Nicholas Monarder's *Joyfull News out of the New-found World*, London, 1580, with the signature of Edward King himself on the title page.

READS AND ANNOTATES GILDAS'S HISTORY.

[Title:] *De Excidio et Conqvestv Britanniæ Epistola,* [which forms one section of] *Rervm Britannicarvm, id est Angliae, Scotiae, Vicinarvmqve Insvlarvm ac Regionvm* [edited by Hieronymus Commelinus, Heidelberg, 1587].

The copy of this work in the Harvard College Library contains annotations which seem without much doubt to have been written by Milton. A full description of the book, together with the text and facsimiles of the annotations, is given by J. Milton French in "Milton's Annotated Copy of Gildas," *Harvard Studies and Notes in Philology and Literature*, XX (1938), 75-80. See also CM, XVIII, 327, 569. The date of Milton's reading is highly uncertain, but there is some reason for setting it at 1638 because of similarities between Milton's annotations and the English translation of Gildas published in that year.

BUYS A VOLUME BY PEACHAM (?).

[Title:] *The Valley of Varietie, or, A Discovrse fitting for the Times* [London, 1638].

This work by Henry Peacham the younger was offered for sale in G. H. Last's catalogue #217, 1936, item 36. It contains the initials "J M" and the name Catherine Clark on the title page; and the catalogue describes the signature as "undoubtedly that of John Milton," and his autograph. But as in other similar instances it is most difficult to be sure of mere initials. Our skepticism is not lessened by the fact that Peacham is nowhere mentioned in Milton's writings. For further details, see CM, XVIII, 578.

FEBRUARY 1. COURT OF REQUESTS DISMISSES COTTON-MILTON SUIT.

Primo die ffebruarii Anno RRꝑ Caroli decimo tertio./ Whereas S͏ʳ Thomas Cotton K͏ᵗ. long since exhibited his bill of Cōmplt vnto the Kingꝑ Ma͏ᵗⁱᵉ before his highnes Councell in his ho͏ᵇˡᵉ Court of Whitehall att Westm' ag͏ᵗ John Milton Defend͏ᵗ Vnto w͏ᶜʰ bill the s̄d Def͏ᵗ the same Tearme answered w͏ᵗʰ w͏ᶜʰ as it seemeth the s̄d Cōmplt resteth satisfyed for that hee hath by the space of two whole Tearmes last past and vpwardꝑ fayled to replye or otherwise to ꝑceede in the said cause whereby to bring the same to hearinge as by the ordinary Course of this Court hee ought to have done, Therefore it is by his Ma͏ᵗʸˢ said Councell of this Court ordered that the same matter shalbe from henceforth out of this Court Cleerely and absolutely dismissed for ever (for want of ꝑsecucōn) and the said Defend͏ᵗ as concerninge the same is discharged of any further attendance in this behalfe and lycensed to depart att his lībtie (sine die) and that the said Cōmplt S͏ʳ Thomas Cotton shall p'sentlie vppon sight or knowledge hereof Content and pay vnto the s'd Defend͏ᵗ Milton or to his assignes demaundinge the same the full somē of Twentie shillingꝑ of Currant English money for his costꝑ herein wrongfully susteyned

Concordat' cū Regr̄o et exam̄
ꝑ W. lane dep Regr̄.

[February 1, 13 Charles I. . . . Agreed with the Registrar and examined by W. Lane, Deputy Registrar.]

British Museum, Cottonian Charters 1/5/5; *Athenaeum*, 1880, II, 15; Masson, I (1881), 660-661; French, *Milton in Chancery*, pp. 278-279. Though there should be a copy among the records of the Court of Requests, none has been found. A facsimile is given in Brennecke, facing p. 132; but the accompanying partial transcription contains numerous inaccuracies. A few errors in my transcription in *Milton in Chancery* are also corrected here.

FEBRUARY 1. LENDS SIR JOHN COPE AND OTHERS £150 AND TAKES BOND FOR REPAYMENT.

. . . S͏ʳ John Cope late of Hanwell in the County of Oxōn

deceased togeather with Robert Lee of Bilseley in ye County of [Warwick?] Esqz and Thomas Ofley of greate Doulby in ye County of Leicester alsoe Esqz by their Obligacōn or writinge Obligatory bearinge date ye first day of ffebruary in ye thirteenth yeare of ye late Kinge Charles and in ye yeare of our Lord god *1637* became ioyntly & severally bound to yor Orato^r in ye penall sumē of 300^{li}. of lawfull English money Condicōned for ye paym^t. of 150^{li} principall money lent & 3^{li} Jnterest for ye same vpon ye third day of May then next ensueinge . . . .

From Milton's bill against the Copes, June 16, 1654; French, *Milton in Chancery*, p. 325. The original bond has not been found.

MARCH (?). BROTHER CHRISTOPHER MARRIES THOMASINE WEBBER AND SETTLES IN HORTON.

Though there is no documentary proof of this event, it seems likely that it must have taken place about this time. By March 26, 1639 (*q.v.*), the newly married couple had had a child which died as an infant. They would be unlikely to postpone the marriage until after John's departure for the Continent. Brennecke, to be sure, states that in 1637 they "had already married" (p. 135), but he gives no proof whatsoever. See Phillips, p. xxvii; Masson, I, 685 (735).

Thomasine Webber was the daughter of John Webber of St. Clement Danes, a tailor, who was buried in the church there on June 5, 1632, and whose will (67 Audley) was proved on July 11, 1632. Among legacies amounting to well over £1,200 is a residuary legacy to Thomasine of a half share in a lease of lands in Devonshire. The will was proved by the relict Isabel. He was evidently reasonably well-to-do. A careful study of Christopher Milton's family was made by Perceval Lucas in *Notes and Queries*, XI, vii (1913), 21.

There is again no certainty about the time when Christopher moved to Horton. But since his infant child was buried there, it seems a reasonable guess that he moved there at the time of his marriage.

MARCH (?). ASKS HENRY LAWES TO PROCURE HIM A PASSPORT (?).

Though there is no absolute proof of this fact, Lawes's letter to Milton of about April, 1638 (*q.v.*), seems to imply a preceding request from Milton. There is no reason to suppose that Lawes would have asked the Warden of the Cinque Ports for a passport unless Milton had so requested him. This note is therefore put in here as almost a certainty.

On the procedure involved in securing this passport, see Willa M. Evans, *Henry Lawes*, New York, 1941, p. 148.

APRIL (?). OBTAINS LETTERS OF RECOMMENDATION FROM INFLUENTIAL FRIENDS FOR FOREIGN JOURNEY.

. . . At *Paris*, being Recommended by the said Sir *Henry* and other Persons of Quality . . . .

Phillips, p. xi; Darbishire, p. 56. The date given is of course only an approximation.

. . . Commendatum ab aliis . . . .

Milton, *Defensio Secunda*, 1654, p. 83; CM, VIII, 120.

[Recommended by others]

APRIL (?). HENRY LAWES SENDS MILTON LETTER AND PASSPORT.

S^r

I haue sent you wth. this A letter from my Lord Warden of the Cinque Portes vnder his hand & seale, wch wilbe A sufficient warrant, to Justify yor goinge out of the Kings Dominions. if you intend to wryte yor selfe you cañot haue a safer convoy for both than from Suffolke House, but that J leaue to yor Owne Consideration & remaine

yor faithfull friend & servant
Henry Lawes.

[Endorsed:] . . . any waies Aprooved,
Mr John Milton
haste these.

British Museum, Add. MS. 36,354 (Milton's Commonplace Book), front flyleaf; CM, XII, 325-326. The Warden of the Cinque Ports, who issued the passport enclosed in this letter, must have been Theophilus Howard, Earl of Suffolk. The passport itself is no longer extant.

Written on the back of this letter, in what seems undoubtedly Milton's hand but at a date unknown, is a couplet:

Fixe heere yee overdaled sphears
that wing the restlesse foote of time.

See CM, XII, 402, and XVIII, 266, 536, 604.

APRIL 1(?). MEETS SIR HENRY WOTTON; PLEASANT
EVENING AND CONVERSATION; ASKS ADVICE ABOUT
EUROPEAN JOURNEY; ACCOMPANIED BY FRIEND.

It was a special favour, when you lately bestowed upon me
here, the first taste of your acquaintance, though no longer then
to make me know that I wanted more time to value it, and to
enjoy it rightly . . . you left me with an extreme thirst . . . that
we might have banded together som good Authors of the antient time: Among which, I observed you to have been familiar.

Sir Henry Wotton's letter to Milton, April 13, 1638, *q.v.* The date,
though not quite certain, must be almost so, since Wotton speaks of the
visit as having been made "lately," and speaks in the subsequent paragraph of Milton's letter to him dated April 6. It is barely possible that
the first connection between the Milton and Wotton families may have
come at Stanton St. John, the elder Milton's native village. Wotton was
granted the lease of a farm there in 1599; see Logan P. Smith,
The Life and Letters of Sir Henry Wotton, Oxford, 1907, I, 301-302.
Milton's visit to Wotton is described at I, 220.

Abeuntem, vir clarissimus Henricus Woottonus, qui ad Vene-
tos Orator Jacobi regis diu fuerat, & votis & præceptis . . . me
amicissimè prosequutus est.

Milton, *Defensio Secunda*, 1654, p. 83; CM, VIII, 120-121.

[When I left, that most distinguished man, Henry Wotton,
who had long been King James's ambassador to the Venetians,
followed me in most friendly fashion with good wishes and good
advice.]

He was acquainted with Sr Henry Wotton Ambassador at
Venice who delighted in his company.

Aubrey, f. 63; Darbishire, p. 2. Aubrey originally wrote after "acquainted," "beyond sea," but later erased it.

Sir *Hen. Wotton* . . . delighted in his company.

Wood, I, 880; Darbishire, p. 36. In Wood's original book the
"Hen." is misprinted as "Htn."

APRIL 6. WRITES LETTER TO SIR HENRY WOTTON, EN-
CLOSING A POEM.

Since your going, you have charg'd me with new Obligations,
both for a very kinde Letter from you dated the sixth of this

Month, and for a dainty peece of entertainment which came therwith.

From Wotton's letter of April 13 to Milton, *q.v.* The poem may well have been a copy of "Comus."

APRIL 13. LETTER FROM SIR HENRY WOTTON.

From the Colledge, this 13. *of April,* 1638.

SIR, It was a special favour, when you lately bestowed upon me here, the first taste of your acquaintance, though no longer then to make me know that I wanted more time to value it, and to enjoy it rightly; and in truth, if I could then have imagined your farther stay in these parts, which I understood afterwards by Mr. *H.,* I would have been bold in our vulgar phrase to mend my draught (for you left me with an extreme thirst) and to have begged your conversation again, joyntly with your said learned Friend, at a poor meal or two, that we might have banded together som good Authors of the antient time: Among which, I observed you to have been familiar.

Since your going, you have charg'd me with new Obligations, both for a very kinde Letter from you dated the sixth of this Month, and for a dainty peece of entertainment which came therwith. Wherin I should much commend the Tragical part, if the Lyrical did not ravish me with a certain Dorique delicacy in your Songs and Odes, whereunto I must plainly confess to have seen yet nothing parallel in our Language: *Ipsa mollities.* But I must not omit to tell you, that I now onely owe you thanks for intimating unto me (how modestly soever) the true Artificer. For the work it self, I had view'd som good while before, with singular delight, having receiv'd it from our common friend Mr. *R.* in the very close of the late *R*'s Poems, Printed at *Oxford,* wherunto it was added (as I now suppose) that the Accessory might help out the Principal, according to the Art of *Stationers,* and to leave the Reader *Con la bocca dolce.*

Now Sir, concerning your travels, wherin I may chalenge a little more priviledge of Discours with you; I suppose you will not blanch *Paris* in your way; therfor I have been bold to trouble you with a few lines to Mr. *M. B.* whom you shall easily find attending the young Lord *S.* as his Governour, and you may surely receive from him good directions for the shaping of your farther journey into *Italy*, where he did reside by my choice som time for the King, after mine own recess from *Venice*.

I should think that your best Line will be thorow the whole length of *France* to *Marseilles*, and thence by sea to *Genoa*, whence the passage into *Tuscany* is as Diurnal as a *Gravesend* Barge: I hasten as you do to *Florence*, or *Siena*, the rather to tell you a short story from the interest you have given me in your safety.

At *Siena* I was tabled in the house of one *Alberto Scipioni* an old *Roman* Courtier in dangerous times, having bin Steward to the *Duca di Pagliano*, who with all his Family were strangled, save this onely man that escap'd by foresight of the Tempest: With him I had often much chat of those affairs; Into which he took pleasure to look back from his Native Harbour; and at my departure toward *Rome* (which had been the center of his experience) I had wonn confidence enough to beg his advice, how I might carry my self securely there, without offence of others, or of mine own conscience. *Signor Arrigo mio* (sayes he) *I pensieri stretti, & il viso sciolto* will go safely over the whole World: Of which *Delphian* Oracle (for so I have found it) your judgement doth need no commentary; and therfore (Sir) I will commit you with it to the best of all securities, Gods dear love, remaining

Your Friend as much at command
as any of longer date
Henry Wootton.

Postscript

SIR, *I have expresly sent this my Foot-boy to prevent your departure without som acknowledgement from me of the receipt of your obliging Letter, having my self through som busines, I know not how, neglected the ordinary conveyance. In any part where I shall understand you fixed, I shall be glad,*

*and diligent to entertain you with Home-Novelties; even for
som fomentation of our friendship, too soon interrupted in the
Cradle.*

British Museum, Add. MS 28,637, fol. 1; Milton, *Poems*, 1645, pp.
71-73; Masson, I, 683-684 (737-738); CM, I, 476-477. The Addi-
tional MS. is probably an eighteenth-century copy of the lost original.
The initials are identified in Verity's edition of *Comus and Lycidas* as fol-
lows: Mr. R: John Rouse; Mr. H: John Hales; the late R: Thomas
Randolph; Mr. M. B.: Michael Branthwaite; Lord S.: Lord Scudamore.
The foreign phrases may be translated as follows: "Ipsa mollities":
sweetness itself; "Con la bocca dolce": with a sweet taste in the mouth;
"Signor Arrigo mio . . . I pensieri stretti, & il viso sciolto": My Lord
Harry, thoughts concealed and countenance open. This letter is men-
tioned in Phillips, p. x; Wood, I, 880; Milton, *Defensio Secunda*, p. 83.
Wotton's letter is printed in Logan P. Smith's *The Life and Letters of
Sir Henry Wotton*, Oxford, 1907, II, 381-383. Smith discusses Wotton's fondness for Scipione's aphorism ("thoughts concealed and countenance open") at I, 22, and shows the real dangers of travel in Italy
at I, 17-21. The text used above is that of 1645.

APRIL 15. COMPLETES SALE OF LAND IN ST. MARTIN-
IN-THE-FIELDS TO SIR MATHEW LYSTER.

hec est finalis Concordia fat' in Cur' dni' Regis apud Westm'
a die pasche in tres septiman' Anno regnor' Caroli' Dei' gra'
Anglz Scotie ffranc' & hibñie Regis fidei' defens' &c' a conqu'
quartodecimo coram Johē ffinch Rico' Hutton' Georgio Vernon' & ffrancisco Crawley Justic' & alijs dni' Regis fidelibz
tunc ibi' p̄sentibz Jnt' Matheum lyster' Militem quer' et Johēm
Milton' seniorem gen'osum & Johēm Milton' Juniorem gen'-
osum deforc' de vno mesuagio vno gardino & vno pomario cum
ptin' in parochia sci' Martini' in Campis vnde plitm' convenco'is
sum' fuit int' eos in eadem Cur' Scilt' qd' p̄dci' Johēs & Johēs
recogn' p̄dca' ten' cum ptin' esse ius ipīus Mathei' vt iłł que
idem Matheus hēt de dono p̄dcor' Johīs & Johīs Et iłł remiser'
& quiet'clam' de ipis' Johē & Johē & hered' suis p̄dco' Matheo
& hered' suis imp̄p̄m' Et p̄t'ea idem Johēs Milton senior concessit p̄ se & hered' suis qd' ipi' Warant' p̄dco' Matheo & hered'
suis p̄dca' ten' cum ptin' cont' p̄dcm' Johēm & hered' suos
imp̄p̄m' Et ult'ius idem Johēs Milton' Junior concessit p̄ se

& hered' suis qd' ipi' Warant' p̄dco' Matheo & hered' suis p̄dca' ten' cum p̄tin' cont' p̄dcm Johēm & hered' suos impp̄m' Et p̄ hac recogn' remissione quiet'clam' Warant' fine & Concordia idem Matheus dedit p̄dcīs Johī & Johī centum libras sterlingor:./

Midd':./   ex'

[Endorsed:] Scdm̄ formam statuti'

Prima p̄clam' fca' fuit septimo die Maij t'nno' pasche Anno quartodecimo Regis infrascr' Scda' p̄clam' fca' fuit sexto Junij t'nno' eod' Trinitatie Anno quartodecimo Regis infrascr' T'cia' p̄clam' fca' fuit nono die Novembr' t'nno' eod' Michī Anno quartodecimo Regis infrascr' Quarta p̄clam' fca' fuit Vicesimo quinto die Januarij t'nno' eod' hillerij Anno quartodecimo Regis infrascr:/

ex'

Public Record Office, CP 25/2/458, 14 Charles I E; typed copies in Harvard College Library. Though never previously published, this document was mentioned in French, *Milton in Chancery*, p. 13.

[This is a final concord made in the court of our Lord the King at Westminster within three weeks from Easter Day in the fourteenth year of the reign of Charles by the grace of God King of England, Scotland, France, and Ireland, Defender of the Faith, etc., before John Finch, Richard Hutton, George Vernon, and Francis Crawley, Justices, and other faithful servants of our Lord the King then present in the same place, between Mathew Lyster, Knight, plaintiff, and John Milton Senior, gentleman, and John Milton Junior, gentleman, deforcients, concerning one messuage, one garden, and one orchard with appurtenances in the parish of St. Martin-in-the-Fields, from which the suit arose between them in this same court. Know that the said John and John admit the said tenement with appurtenances to be the property of the said Mathew as that which the said Mathew holds by gift of the said John and John. And they have given and quit claim from the said John and John and their heirs to the said Mathew and his heirs forever. And furthermore the said John Milton Senior has conceded for himself and his heirs that they have guaranteed to the said Mathew and his heirs the said tenements with appurtenances against the said John and his heirs forever. And furthermore the said John Milton Junior has conceded for himself and his heirs that they have guaranteed to the said Mathew and his heirs the said tenements with appurtenances against the said John and his heirs forever. And in return for this recognizance, remission, quitclaim, guarantee, fine, and concord the said Mathew has given the said John and John one hundred pounds sterling.

Middlesex   Entered

Endorsed: According to the form of the statute. The first proclamation was made on the seventh day of May in Easter term in the fourteenth year of the king written below. The second proclamation was made on the sixth day of June in Trinity term in the said fourteenth year of the king written below. The third proclamation was made on the ninth day of November in Michaelmas term in the said fourteenth year of the king written below. The fourth proclamation was made on the twenty-fifth day of January in Hilary term of the said fourteenth year of the king written below.]

MAY 3. RECEIVES INTEREST ON COPE BOND (?).

... neyther ye s'd principall debt of 150^{li} nor any pte thereof nor any Jnterest due for ye forbearance of the same since November 1641 hath been paid or satisfied. ...

Milton's bill against Lady Elizabeth Cope and Sir Anthony Cope, June 16, 1654, *q.v.*; French, *Milton in Chancery*, p. 328. From the wording, which is admittedly negative rather than positive, it would seem that interest on this bond *was* paid until November, 1641, since Milton asserts that it was *not* paid after that date. The amount is not quite certain, though the inference seems to be that interest payments were to be made at the rate of £12 a year, since the payment of £3 specified in the bond covers the period from February 1 to May 3, which is three months. This would mean a yearly interest rate of eight per cent.

MAY 7. FIRST PROCLAMATION OF SALE OF LONDON TENEMENT MADE.

Prima ℔clam' fca' fuit septimo die Maij t'nno' pasche Anno quartodecimo Regis infrascr'.

From the Milton-Lyster concord of fine, April 15, 1638, *q.v.*

[The first proclamation was made on the seventh day of May in Easter term in the fourteenth year of the king written below.]

MAY (?). LEAVES ENGLAND FOR CONTINENTAL TOUR.

Ajunt hominem Cantabrigiensi Academia ob flagitia pulsum dedecus & patriam fugisse, & in Italiam commigrasse.

Moulin, *Regii Sanguinis Clamor*, Hague, 1652, p. 8. Moulin is of course less concerned with the facts than with discrediting Milton.

[They say that the man, having been expelled from the University of Cambridge for his profligacy, fled from the disgrace and from his native country, and migrated to Italy.]

Masson, IV, 456.

Verùm ego Italiam, non, ut tu putas, facinorosorum latibulum aut asylum, sed humanitatis potiùs, & civilium doctrinarum omnium hospitium & noveram antea, & expertus sum. . . . Exacto in hunc modum quinquennio, post matris obitum, regiones exteras, & Italiam potissimùm, videndi cupidus, exorato patre, uno cum famulo profectus sum.

Milton, *Defensio Secunda*, 1654, pp. 78, 83; CM, VIII, 114, 120.

[But I went to Italy, not, as you think, as to a den of thieves or a place of refuge, but rather because I knew before and have now found out that it is the home of humane studies and of all civilized teachings. . . . After five years spent in this way and after the death of my mother I desired to see foreign countries and especially Italy. Having gained my father's consent, I set out with one servant.]

Translation by the present editor.

Beeing now become Master of what useful knowlege was to bee had in Books; and competently skill'd, amongst others, in the Italian language, hee made choice of that Country to travel into; in order to polish his Conversation, & learn to know Men. And having receiv'd instructions how to demean himselfe with that wise observing Nation, as well as how to shape his Journy, from Sr Henry Wotton, whose esteem of him appeers in an elegant letter to him upon that Subject, hee took his way thorough France.

The "earliest" biography, fol. 140v; Darbishire, p. 19.

After the said term of Five years, his Mother then dying, he was willing to add to his acquired Learning the observation of Foreign Customs, Manners, and Institutions; and thereupon took a resolution to Travel, more especially designing for *Italy*; and accordingly, with his Father's Consent and Assistance, he put himself into an Equipage suitable to such a Design; and so intending to go by the way of *France*, he set out for *Paris* accompanied onely with one Man, who attended him through all his Travels; for his Prudence was his Guide, and his Learning his Introduction and Presentation to Persons of most Eminent Quality.

Phillips, p. x; Darbishire, p. 55.

. . . then he travelled into Franc & Italie. . . . He went to travell about ye year 1638 & was abroad about a years space cheifly in Italy.

Aubrey, ff. 63, 64v; Darbishire, pp. 2, 12.

(6) That after five years being thus spent, and his Mother (who was very charitable to the poor) dead, he did design to travel, so that obtaining the rudiments of the Ital. Tongue, and Instructions how to demean himself from *Sir Htn. Wotton* who delighted in his company, and gave him Letters of commendation to certain persons living at *Venice*, he travelled into *Italy*, an. 1638.

Wood, 1, 880.

MAY OR JUNE(?). MEETS JOHN, VISCOUNT SCUDAMORE, IN PARIS.

. . . nobilissimus vir Thomas Scudamorus vicecomes Slegonensis, Caroli regis Legatus, Parisiis humanissimè accepit.

Milton, *Defensio Secunda*, 1654, p. 83; CM, I, 120-122. Milton's "Thomas" is an error for "John."

[The most noble man Thomas Scudamore, Viscount Sligo, ambassador of King Charles, received me most politely in Paris.]

Translation by the present editor.

[He made no stay at Paris] save that, with the recommendation of the Lord Scudamore, our Kings Ambassador at Paris, hee waited on Hugo Grotius.

The "earliest" biography, fol. 140v; Darbishire, pp. 19-20. Before "our Kings" the writer first penned "hee waited," which he later cancelled.

At *Paris* being Recommended by the said Sir *Henry* and other Persons of Quality, he went first to wait upon my Lord *Scudamore*, then Embassador in *France* from King *Charles* the First. My Lord receiv'd him with wonderful Civility; and understanding he had a desire to make a Visit to the great *Hugo Grotius*, he sent several of his Attendants to wait upon him, and to present him in his Name to that Renowned Doctor. . . .

Phillips, p. xi; Darbishire, p. 56.

. . . he touched at *Paris*, where *Joh. Scudamoure*, Vicount *Slego*, Embassador from K. *Ch.* I. to the French King, received him kindly, and by his means became kuown to *Hugo Grotius*.

Wood, I, 880; Darbishire, pp. 36-37.

MAY OR JUNE(?). VISITS HUGO GROTIUS AT PARIS.

. . . méque Hugoni Grotio viro eruditissimo, ab Regina Suecorum tunc temporis ad Galliæ regem legato, quem invisere cupiebam, suo nomine, & suorum uno atque altero deducente, commendavit.

Milton, *Defensio Secunda*, 1654, pp. 83-84; CM, VIII, 122.

[Viscount Scudamore gave me letters of recommendation under his own name, and several of his retainers to accompany me, to Hugo Grotius, a most learned man, the ambassador at that time from the Queen of the Swedes to the king of France, whom I wished to see.]

Translation by the present editor.

. . . hee waited on Hugo Grotius, who was there under that Character [*i.e.*, ambassador] from the Crown of Sweden.

The "earliest" biography, fol. 140v; Darbishire, p. 19.

. . . he had a desire to make a Visit to the great *Hugo Grotius* . . . that Renowned Doctor and Statesman, who was at that time Embassador from *Christina*, Queen of *Sweden*, to the *French* King. *Grotius* took the Visit kindly, and gave him Entertainment suitable to his Worth, and the high Commendations he had heard of him.

Phillips, p. xi; Darbishire, p. 56.

. . . [he] became kuown to *Hugo Grotius*, then and there Embassador from the Qu. of *Sweden*.

Wood, 1, 880; Darbishire, p. 37.

MAY OR JUNE(?). RECEIVES RECOMMENDATORY LETTERS FROM VISCOUNT SCUDAMORE.

. . . discedenti post dies aliquot Italiam versùs, literas ad mercatores Anglos, quà iter eram facturus, dedit, ut quibus possent officiis mihi præstò essent.

Milton, *Defensio Secunda*, 1654, p. 84; CM, VIII, 122.

[When I left for Italy some days later, he (*i.e.*, Viscount Scudamore) gave me letters to English merchants where I was going, that they might be ready to help me in any way they could.]

Translation by the present editor.

. . . my Lord *Scudamore* . . . at his departure from *Paris*, gave him Letters to the *English* Merchants residing in any part through which he was to Travel, in which they were requested to shew him all the Kindness, and do him all the Good Offices that lay in their Power.

Phillips, p. xi; Darbishire, p. 56.

MAY OR JUNE (?). LEAVES FRANCE.

In this Kingdom, the manners & Genius of which hee had had in no admiration, hee made small stay, nor contracted any Acquaintance. . . .

The "earliest" biography, fol. 140v; Darbishire, p. 19. The author originally wrote "hee made no stay, having" after "In this Kingdom," but later cancelled it for the present reading.

... he touched at *Paris* ... but the manners and genius of that place being not agreeable to his mind, he soon left it.

Wood, I, 880; Darbishire, pp. 36-37.

JUNE 6. SECOND PROCLAMATION OF SALE OF LONDON TENEMENT MADE.

Scda' pclam' fca' fuit sexto Junij t'nno' eod' Trinitatie Anno quartodecimo Regis infrascr'.

From the Milton-Lyster concord of fine, April 15, 1638, *q.v.*

[The second proclamation was made on the sixth day of June in Trinity term in the said fourteenth year of the king written below.]

JUNE OR JULY (?). PASSES THROUGH NICE.
... Nicææâ solvens ....

Milton, *Defensio Secunda*, 1654, p. 84; CM, VIII, 122.

[leaving Nice]
Hasting to Italy by the way of Nice. ...

The "earliest" biography, fol. 140v; Darbishire, p. 19.

From *Paris* he hastened on his Journey to *Nicæa*. ...

Phillips, p. xii; Darbishire, p. 56.

JUNE OR JULY (?). PASSES THROUGH GENOA.

... Genuam perveni ....

Milton, *Defensio Secunda*, 1654, p. 84; CM, VIII, 122.

[I reached Genoa.]
... passing through Genua ....

The "earliest" biography, fol. 140v; Darbishire, p. 19.

... *Nicæa*, where he took Shipping, and in a short space arrived at *Genoa*.

Phillips, p. xii; Darbishire, p. 56.

... by *Geneva* and other places of note ....

Wood, I, 880; Darbishire, p. 37. The name appears thus in Wood.

JULY (?). VISITS LEGHORN.

. . . mox Liburnum . . . .
Milton, *Defensio Secunda*, 1654, p. 84; CM, VIII, 122.

[I soon came to Leghorn.]
. . . passing through . . . Ligorn . . . .
The "earliest" biography, fol. 140v; Darbishire, p. 19.

. . . from whence he went to *Leghorn* . . . .
Phillips, p. xii; Darbishire, p. 56.

. . . thro *Legorne* . . . .
Wood, I, 880; Darbishire, p. 37.

JULY (?). COMES TO PISA.
. . . & Pisas . . . .
Milton, *Defensio Secunda*, 1654, p. 84; CM, VIII, 122.

[and to Pisa.]
. . . passing through . . . Pisa . . . .
The "earliest" biography, fol. 140v; Darbishire, p. 19.

. . . thence to *Pisa* . . . .
Phillips, p. xii; Darbishire, p. 56.

. . . he went . . . thro . . . *Pisa* . . . .
Wood, I, 880; Darbishire, p. 37.

AUGUST 27. FRIEND CHARLES DIODATI BURIED.

[Burials, August 27, 1638:] Mr. Charles Deodate, from Mr.
Dollam's.

Parish Registers, St. Anne Blackfriars, London, as quoted in Masson,
II (1894), 80. I have not seen the original entry. Charles Diodati was
of course the friend to whom Milton's *Epitaphium Damonis* was addressed later. Other events in the life of the Diodati family during this
same year were the burial of Charles's sister Philadelphia on August 10,
the burial of Isabell, wife of John, on June 23, and the baptism of
Richard, son of John and Isabell, on June 29.

AUGUST AND SEPTEMBER (?). ARRIVES IN FLORENCE;
MAKES MANY FRIENDS, ATTENDS ACADEMIES; IS HIGH-
LY HONORED.

. . . inde Florentiam. Illa in urbe, quam præ cæteris propter
elegantiam cum linguæ tum ingeniorum semper colui, ad duos

circiter menses substiti; illic multorum & nobilium sanè & doctorum hominum familiaritatem statim contraxi; quorum etiam privatas academias, (qui mos illic, cum ad literas humaniores, tum ad amicitias conservandas laudatissimus est) assiduè frequentavi. Tui enim Jacobe Gaddi, Carole Dati, Frescobalde, Cultelline, Bonmatthæi, Clementille, Francine, aliorúmque plurium memoriam, apud me semper gratam atque jucundam, nulla dies delebit.

Milton, *Defensio Secunda*, 1654, p. 84; CM, VIII, 122.

[Thence to Florence. In that city, which I have always cherished more than the others for its elegance of speech and manners, I stayed about two months. There I quickly contracted intimacy with many truly noble and learned men. I also assiduously attended their private academies, an institution which is most highly to be praised there, not only for preserving the arts but also for cementing friendships. Time shall never efface the memory, forever grateful and pleasing to me, of you, James Gaddi, Charles Dati, Frescobaldi, Cultellino, Bonmatthei, Clementillo, Francini, and numerous others.]

Translation by the present editor.

. . . hee arriv'd at Florence. Here hee liv'd two moneths in familiar & elegant conversation with the choice Witts of that Citty, and was admitted by them to thir private Academies; an Oeconomy much practis'd among the virtuosi of those parts, for the communication of Polite literature, as well as for the cementing of friendships. The reputation hee had with them they express'd in several Commendatory Verses, wch are extant in his book of Poems.

The "earliest" biography, fol. 140v; Darbishire, pp. 19-20.

. . . so to *Florence*: In this City he met with many charming Objects, which Invited him to stay a longer time then he intended; the pleasant Scituation of the Place, the Nobleness of the Structures, the exact Humanity and Civility of the Inhabitants, the more Polite and Refined sort of Language there, than elsewhere. During the time of his stay here, which was about Two Months, he Visited all the private Academies of the

City, which are Places establish'd for the improvement of Wit
and Learning, and maintained a Correspondence and perpetual
Friendship among Gentlemen fitly qualified for such an Institution: and such sort of Academies there are in all or most of the
most noted Cities in *Italy*. Visiting these Places, he was soon
taken notice of by the most Learned and Ingenious of the Nobility, and the Grand Wits of *Florence*, who caress'd him with all
the Honours and Civilities imaginable, particularly *Jacobo
Gaddi, Carolo Dati, Antonio Francini, Frescobaldo, Cultellino,
Banmatthei* and *Clementillo*: Whereof *Gaddi* hath a large
Elegant *Italian Canzonet* in his Praise: *Dati*, a Latin Epistle,
both Printed before his Latin Poems, together with a Latin
Distich of the Marquess of *Villa*, and another of *Selvaggi*, and a
Latin *Tetrastick* of *Giovanni Salsilli* a *Roman*.

Phillips, pp. xii-xiii; Darbishire, pp. 56-57.

. . . he went to *Florence*, where continuing two months, he
became acquainted with several learned men, and familiar with
the choicest Wits of that great City, who introduced and admitted him into their private Academies, whereby he saw and
learn'd their fashions of literature.

Wood, 1, 880; Darbishire, p. 37.

AUGUST AND SEPTEMBER (?). WARM RECEPTION IN
ITALIAN ACADEMIES, ESPECIALLY IN FLORENCE.

But much latelier in the privat Academies of *Italy*, whither
I was favor'd to resort, perceiving that some trifles which I had
in memory, compos'd at under twenty or thereabout (for the
manner is that every one must give some proof of his wit and
reading there) met with some acceptance above what was lookt
for, and other things which I had shifted in scarsity of books and
conveniences to patch up amongst them, were receiv'd with
written Encomiums, which the Italian is not forward to bestow
on men of this side the *Alps*. . . .

Milton, *The Reason of Church Government*, 1641, p. 37; CM,
III, 235-236. One would hesitate to venture to identify the early poems
which Milton read to his Italian acquaintances. If they were any which

still survive, the likeliest possibilities are some of his college Latin poems on the deaths of officials, his Greek translations, or possibly his Italian verses. It is, however, not impossible that his "under twenty" may be slightly exaggerated. See also the preceding section.

So remarkable was he for his Knowledge in the *Italian* Tongue that the *Crusca* (an Academy Set up for the Reducing, and keeping the *Florentine* Language to its First Purity) made no Scruple to Consult Him, Whom they had receiv'd an Academician, on Difficult and Controverted Points.

Richardson, p. viii; Darbishire, p. 210.

O ego quantus eram, gelidi cum stratus ad Arni
Murmura, populeumque nemus, quà mollior herba,
Carpere nunc violas, nunc summas carpere myrtos,
Et potui Lycidæ certantem audire Menalcam.
Ipse etiam tentare ausus sum, nec puto multùm
Displicui, nam sunt & apud me munera vestra
Fiscellæ, calathique & cerea vincla cicutæ,
Quin & nostra suas docuerunt nomina fagos
Et Datis, & Francinus, erant & vocibus ambo
Et studiis noti, Lydorum sanguinis ambo.

Milton, "Epitaphium Damonis," *Poems*, 1645, part ii, pp. 83-84; CM, I, 308-309.

[O how great I was when, lying beside the murmurs of the cool Arno and its poplar grove, where the grass was soft, I could pick first violets and then myrtle-tips and could hear Menalcas vying with Lycidas. I too dared to contend, and I think I did not much displease, for I still have your gifts of small baskets (two kinds) and waxen fastenings of hemlock. Indeed, Dati and Francini taught our names to their beeches; both were noted for their voices and their studies, both of the blood of the Lydians.

Translation by the present editor.

Nunc abs te peto, ut quam veniam, non dico Aligerio, & Petrarchæ vestro eadem in causa, sed meæ, ut scis, olim apud vos loquendi libertati, singulari cum humanitate, dare consuevistis.

Milton, letter to Charles Dati, April 21, 1647, *q.v.*; CM, XII, 50.

[Now I beg you to give me, not the forbearance that you would to Dante or Petrarch in such case, but what you used to show me, as you know, with remarkable kindness in my freedom of speech with you.]

Translation by the present editor.

September. Poetic tribute from Antonio Malatesti.

La Tina Equivoci Rusticali in Cinquanta Sonetti di Antonio Malatesti Fiorentino composti nella sua Villa di Tajano il Settembre dell' anno 1637 e da lui regalati al grande poeta inghilese Giovanni Milton Londra, A spese dell' editore.

The story of this volume is still somewhat obscure. Masson (1, 735n. [786]) summarizes it as follows. A Mr. Brand found the original manuscript of these poems on a bookstall in London about 1750 and presented it to his friend Thomas Hollis. Hollis made a copy of it, which he sent in 1758, together with other Miltoniana, to the Della Crusca Academy in Florence. In 1757 Brand presented either the original or another copy to Giovanni Marsili, of the University of Padua, then in London. From one or the other of these sources a Venetian editor printed about fifty copies in or about 1837. The poems are full of equivocal lines. See also cm, xviii, 554.

The title as given above is that of the printed volume, of which copies may be found in the British Museum and at Harvard. The dates assigned to it vary fantastically, since none is printed on the title page. The Harvard Library copy bears the date 1757 in pencil; the British Museum catalogue gives [1860?]. Masson, drawing on information published in 1850 and 1853 in *Notes and Queries,* shows that since the volume is mentioned in the fourth volume of the Italian bibliographer Gamba's *Serie dei Testi di Lingua e di altre opere importanti nella Italiana Letteratura,* 1837, it must have been printed before that date, but that since it does not appear in the earlier editions, the date must be not long before.

The title given by Masson and the catalogue of the library of Thomas Hollis differs considerably from that of the printed book, a difference which it seems must have been introduced by Hollis in his copying of the manuscript. The title as given in Masson, which with some variations of spelling is substantially that in the Hollis catalogue and elsewhere, is: *La Tina: Equivoci Rusticali di Antonio Malatesti, cōposti nella sua Villa di Taiano il Settembre dell anno 1637: Sonetti Cinquanta: Dedicati all' Illmo. Signore et Padrone Oss^{mo} Signor Giovanni Milton, nobile Inghlese.*

No trace of the manuscript has been found in recent years.

[La Tina: Rustic Equivocations in Fifty Sonnets of Antonio Malatesti, Florentine, Composed at his Country-house at Taiano in September of the year 1637, and by him presented to the great English poet John Milton of London at the Cost of the Editor.]

SEPTEMBER (?). POEM TO SALSILLI.

Ad Salsillum poetam Romanum ægrotantem. SCAZONTES.

> ... Hæc ergo alumnus ille Londini Milto,
> Diebus hisce qui suum linquens nidum
> Polique tractum, (pessimus ubi ventorum,
> Insanientis impotensque pulmonis
> Pernix anhela sub Jove exercet flabra)
> Venit feraces Itali soli ad glebas,
> Visum superbâ cognitas urbes famâ
> Virosque doctæque indolem juventutis,
> Tibi optat idem hic fausta multa Salsille,
> Habitumque fesso corpori penitùs sanum. ...

Milton, *Poems*, 1645, part ii, pp. 70-72; CM, I, 282-285. The date of writing is of course uncertain, but it seems most appropriate to put it here beside the entry concerning the poetic tributes of Italian poets to Milton.

[To Salsillus, a Roman poet, when he was sick, scazons. These come to you from that London-bred Milton, who in these days leaving his nest and his own tract of sky, where the worst of winds, unable to control its mad lungs, swiftly panting, blows blasts beneath the sky, came to the fruitful soil of Italy to see its cities, known by proud fame, and its men and its learned and ingenious youths. He wishes you many blessings, Salsilli, and a completely healthy condition for your exhausted body.]

Translation by the present editor.

AUGUST AND SEPTEMBER (?). POETIC TRIBUTES FROM ITALIAN FRIENDS.

Hæc quæ sequuntur de Authore testimonia, tametsi ipse intelligebat non tam de se quàm supra se esse dicta ... judicium

interim hominum cordatorum atque illustrium quin summo sibi
honori ducat, negare non potest.

*Joannes Baptista Mansus, Marchio Villensis Neapolitanus ad
Joannem Miltonium Anglum.* . . .

*Ad Joannem Miltonem Anglum triplici poeseos laureâ coron-
andum Græcâ nimirum, Latinâ, atque Hetruscâ, Epigramma
Joannis Salsilli Romani.* . . .

Ad Joannem Miltonum . . . Selvaggi. . . .

Al Signor Gio. Miltoni Nobile Inglese. Ode. . . . Del sig.
Antonio Francini gentilhuomo Fiorentino.

Joanni Miltoni Londinensi. . . . *offert Carolus Datus Patri-
cius Florentinus.*

Milton, *Poems*, 1645, part ii, pp. 3-10; cm, i, 154-166. Though
these poems were most likely composed and given to Milton during
his Italian journey, it is impossible to date them exactly. Some may
very well have been written to him during his stay in Florence, however, and they are therefore grouped together under the time of his
visit there. They contain no significant biographical facts, so that the
texts of the individual poems need not be quoted.

In this connection may be quoted the notice of these poems in the
writing of an early Italian writer. Todd (i, 1826, 33) quotes Rolli's
Vita di Milton, 1735, as follows: "Osservissi nelle lodi dagl' Italiani date
a questo grand Uomo; com' essi fin d'allora scorvevano in lui l'alta forza
d'Ingegno che lo portava al primo Auge di gloria letteraria nel suo
Secolo e nella sua Nazione; e gliene facevano gli avverati Prognostici."
(One observes in the praises of Italians given to this great man, how they
since then saw in him the high power of genius which was leading him
to the highest zenith of literary glory in his century and in his nation, and
how they made prophecies which have since been fulfilled.)

[These testimonials about the author which follow, although
he was aware that they were spoken not so much about him as
over him . . . in the mean time he cannot deny that the judgment of wise and famous men confer on him the greatest honor.

John Baptista Manso, Marquis of Villa, of Naples, to the
Englishman John Milton. . . .

An epigram of John Salsilli, a Roman, on the Englishman
John Milton, who surely ought to be crowned with a triple
laurel of poetry—Greek, Latin, and Italian. . . .

To John Milton . . . Selvaggi. . . .

To Mr. John Milton, the noble Englishman, an ode. . . . From Mr. Antonio Francini, a gentleman of Florence.

To John Milton of London . . . offered by Charles Dati, a nobleman of Florence.]

Translated by the present editor.

AUGUST-SEPTEMBER (?). LOST SONNETS TO CHIMEN-TELLI AND OTHER WRITINGS (?).

Warton (1791, p. 333n.) mentions the following attempt to trace some supposedly lost writings of Milton: "In 1762, the late Mr. Thomas Hollis examined the Laurentian library at Florence, for six Italian Sonnets of Milton, addressed to his friend Chimentelli; and, for other Italian and Latin compositions and various original letters, said to be remaining in manuscript at Florence. . . . But he was unsuccessful in his curious enquiries." Nothing further is known of these poems and other writings. See CM, XVIII, 538, 597. William Hazlitt repeated the conjecture about the existence of such poems in his *Notes of a Journey through France and Italy*; see his *Collected Works*, ed. A. R. Waller and Arnold Glover, IX (1903), 218.

SEPTEMBER. SEES ANDREINI'S "ADAMO" PERFORMED (?).

Milton, as he was travelling through *Italy* in his Youth, saw at *Florence* a Comedy call'd *Adamo*, writ by one *Andreino* a Player, and dedicated to *Mary de Medicis* Queen of *France*. The Subject of the Play was the *Fall of Man*; the Actors, God, the Devils, the Angels, *Adam*, *Eve*, the Serpent, Death, and the Seven mortal Sins. That Topick so improper for a Drama, but so suitable to the absurd Genius of the *Italian* Stage, (as it was at that Time) was handled in a Manner intirely conformable to the Extravagance of the Design. The Scene opens with a Chorus of Angels, and a Cherubim thus speaks for the Rest. "Let the Rainbow be the Fiddlestick of the Fiddle of the Heavens, let the Planets be the Notes of our Musick, let Time beat carefully the Measure, and the Winds make the Sharps, *&c.*" Thus the Play begins, and every Scene rises above the last in Profusion of Impertinence.

Milton pierc'd through the Absurdity of that Performance to the hidden Majesty of the Subject, which being altogether unfit for the Stage, yet might be (for the Genius of *Milton*, and for his only) the Foundation of an *Epick* Poem.

Voltaire, *An Essay upon the Civil Wars of France, Extracted from curious Manuscripts. And also upon the Epick Poetry of the European Nations from Homer down to Milton*, London, 1727, p. 103. Frequently quoted by Johnson and other critics. Todd (i, 1826, appendix iv) gives a lengthy analysis of the piece by Hayley. Later editions of Voltaire's account show considerable variations from the one given above.

On trouvera ici, touchant Milton, quelques particularités omises dans l'abrégé de sa vie qui est au-devant de la traduction française de son Paradis perdu. Il n'est pas étonnant qu'ayant recherché avec soin en Angleterre tout ce qui regarde ce grand homme, j'aie découvert des circonstances de sa vie que le public ignore.

Milton, voyageant en Italie dans sa jeunesse, vit représenter à Milan une comédie intitulée Adam ou le Péché originel, écrite par un certain Andreino, et dédiée à Marie de Médicis, reine de France. Le sujet de cette comédie était la chute de l'homme. Les acteurs étaient Dieu le Père, les Diables, les Anges, Adam, Ève, le Serpent, la Mort et les sept Péchés Mortels. Ce sujet, digne du génie absurde du théâtre de ce temps-là, était écrit d'une manière qui répondait au dessin.

La scène s'ouvre par un chœur d'Anges, et Michel parle ainsi au nom de ses confrères: "Que l'arc-in-ciel soit l'archet du violon du firmament; que les sept planètes soient les sept notes de notre musique, que le temps batte exactement la mesure...."

Milton, qui assista à cette représentation, découvrit à travers l'absurdité de l'ouvrage, la sublimité cachée du sujet. . . .

Milton conçut le dessein de faire une tragédie de la farce d'Andreino: il en composa même un acte et demi. Ce fait m'a été assuré par des gens de lettres qui le tenaient de sa fille, laquelle est morte lorsque j'étais à Londres.

Voltaire, *Oeuvres Complètes*, Paris, VII (1817), 263, 317, 318. It will be noticed that Voltaire has changed the name of the city from Florence (in the first version) to Milan, and the indefinite "a cherubim" to Michel. None of the details about Milton's daughter are in the earlier version.

[There will be found here several particulars about Milton omitted from the account of his life which is prefixed to the French translation of his *Paradise Lost*. It is not astonishing that, having searched carefully in England for everything which concerns this great man, I should have discovered some circumstances of his life of which the public is not aware.

Milton, traveling in Italy in his youth, saw exhibited at Milan a comedy entitled *Adam, or Original Sin*, written by a certain Andreino, and dedicated to Mary de Medici, Queen of France. The subject of this comedy was the fall of man. The actors were God the Father, the devils, the angels, Adam, Eve, the serpent, Death, and the Seven Deadly Sins. This subject, worthy of the absurd genius of the theater of that time, was written in a manner which matched the design.

The scene opens with a chorus of angels, and Michael speaks thus in the name of his associates: "Let the rainbow be the bow of the violin of the heavens; let the seven planets be the seven notes of our music; let the time beat exactly the measure. . . ."

Milton, who was present at this representation, discovered through the absurdity of the work the hidden sublimity of the subject. . . .

Milton conceived the design of making a tragedy of Andreino's farce; he even composed one act and a half. I was assured of this fact by some men of letters who had it from his daughter, who died while I was in London.]

SEPTEMBER (?). VISITS GALILEO.

. . . I could recount what I have seen and heard in other Countries . . . when I have sat among their lerned men, for that honor I had. . . . There it was that I found and visited the famous *Galileo* grown old, a prisner to Inquisition, for thinking in Astronomy otherwise then the Franciscan and Dominican licencers thought.

Milton, *Areopagitica*, 1644, p. 24; CM, IV, 329-330. Though Liljegren and others have seriously questioned the truth of Milton's statement, there seems to be no good ground for skepticism. Stern (I, i, 276) accepts Milton's statement and conjectures that the meeting took place at Arcetri, not far from Florence. Masson (I, 737 [788]) points out the references to Galileo in *Paradise Lost*, I, 287-291, and V, 262, which suggest a meeting; and the Columbia *Milton* (XVIII, 612) calls attention to the fact that Charles Dati, in his letter to Milton on December 4, 1648, includes the younger Galileo as one of a group who send affectionate greetings to Milton.

In this connection may be mentioned an extensive series of letters purporting to have been written between Milton and Galileo and among them and other contemporaries, about which a considerable controversy raged in 1869. M. Chasles, a member of the Académie des Sciences, Paris, wrote an article for *Comptes Rendus Hebdomaires des Séances de l'Académie des Sciences*, LXVIII (1869), 31 ff., describing this find. After several controversial articles he gave the texts of many of these letters at pp. 740 ff.; these included letters between Milton and Louis XIV, Voiture, and Molière. They were reprinted with a summary of the discussion in *Fraser's Magazine*, LXXIX (1869), 678 ff. There is no further trace of any such letters, and it would seem justifiable to conclude with the editor of Milton's letters (CM, XVIII, 535) that they were nineteenth-century forgeries.

SEPTEMBER (?). VISITS VALLOMBROSA (?).

Nel 1638 / Qui dimorò / il sommo poeta inglese / Giovanni Milton / studioso dei nostri classici / devoto alla nostra civiltà / innamorato / di questa foresta e di questo cielo / 30 Agosto 1925.

A memorial to Milton's supposed visit in Vallombrosa, bearing the above inscription, was unveiled in 1925; the inscription was composed by Ugo Ojetti and carved by the English sculptor Anderson. The ceremony is described in the London *Times*, August 28, 1925, p. 15e; September 1, 1925, p. 12c; and September 3, 1925, p. 14 (with a photograph of the unveiling); *Notes and Queries*, CLXIX (1925), 163. I have not seen the monument. There is no positive evidence of his actual visit to Vallombrosa, though the famous simile of the "Autumnal Leaves that strow the Brooks / In *Vallombrosa*" (*Paradise Lost*, I, 303-304) has the vividness of a personal experience.

There are traditions of other connections between Milton and Vallombrosa. The organ there used to be shown as one on which Milton played (CM, XVIII, 584). Letters from him to the fathers at Vallombrosa were reported in existence in the 1870's, but no trace of them can now be found (CM, XII, 413).

[In 1638 the great English poet John Milton stayed here; studious of our classics; devoted to our civilization; in love with these trees and this sky; August 30, 1925.]

ABOUT SEPTEMBER 1. MEETS AND TALKS WITH BENE-
DETTO BONMATTEI.

Jam vide, obsecro, numquid satis causæ fuerat, quæ me vobis ultimum ab Oceano hospitem per hosce aliquot dies dederit, vestræq; Nationis ita amantem, ut non alius, opinor, magis. Quo magis merito potes meminisse, quid ego tanto opere abs te contendere soleam. . . . Atq; hæc ego tametsi videor mihi abs te (nisi me animus fallit) jam primo impetrasse, quoties in istius rei mentionem incidimus, quæ tua comitas est, & benignum ingenium. . . .

From Milton's letter to Bonmattei, September 10, 1638, *q.v.* From the wording of this passage, Milton must have met Bonmattei and discussed the latter's work warmly and for some time before the letter was written.

[See now, I entreat, whether the reason has been sufficient that has given me to you, for these some days your latest guest from the ocean, and so great a lover of your nation that, as I think, there is no other more so. On which account you may, with more reason, remember what I am wont so earnestly to request of you. . . . And, although I seem already (unless my memory deceive me) to have made this demand of you as often as we have fallen on the mention of that affair, (such is your politeness and kindly disposition!). . . .]

Masson, I, 739-740 (791).

SEPTEMBER 10. LETTER TO BENEDETTO BONMATTEI.
Benedicto Bonmatthæo Florentino.

8. Quod novas patriæ linguæ Institutiones adornas (Benedicte Bonmatthæe) jam jam operi fastigium impositurus, & commune tu quidem cum summis quibusdam ingeniis iter ad laudem ingrederis, & eam spem, quod video, eamq; de te opinionem apud Cives tuos concitâsti, ut qui ab aliis quæ tradita jam sunt, iis aut lucem, aut copiam, aut certe limam, atq; ordinem

tuo marte facile sis allaturus. Quo nomine profecto populares tuos quam non vulgarem in modum tibi devinxeris, ingrati nempe sint ipsi, si non perspexerint. Nam qui in civitate mores hominum sapienter nôrit formare, domiq; & belli præclaris institutis regere, illum ego præ cæteris omni honore apprime dignum esse existimem. Proximum huic tamen, qui loquendi scribendiq; rationem & normam probo gentis sæculo receptam, præceptis regulisq; sancire adnititur, & veluti quodam vallo circummunire; quod quidem ne quis transire ausit, tantum non Romuleâ lege sit cautum. Utriusq; enim horum utilitatem conferre si libet, justum utiq; & sanctum Civium convictum alter ille solus efficere potest; hic vero solus liberalem, & splendidum, & luculentum, quod proxime in votis est. Ille in hostem fines invadentem, ardorem credo excelsum, & intrepida consilia suppeditat; Hic Barbariem animos hominum late incursantem, fœdam & intestinam ingeniorum perduellem, doctâ aurium censurâ, Authorúmq; bonorum expeditâ manu, explodendam sibi, & debellandam suscipit. Neq; enim qui sermo, purúsne an corruptus, quæve loquendi proprietas quotidiana populo sit, parvi interesse arbitrandum est, quæ res Athenis non semel saluti fuit: immo vero, quod Platonis sententia est, immutato vestiendi more habituq; graves in Republica motus, mutationésq; portendi, equidem potius collabente in vitium atq; errorem loquendi usu, occasum ejus Urbis, remq; humilem & obscuram subsequi crediderim: verba enim partim inscita & putida, partim mendosa, & perperam prolata; quid nisi ignavos, & oscitantes, & ad servile quidvis jam olim paratos incolarum animos haud levi indicio declarant? Contra, nullum unquam audivimus imperium, nullam Civitatem non mediocriter saltem floruisse, quamdiu Linguæ sua gratia, suusq; cultus constitit. Tu itaque, Benedicte, hanc operam Reipublicæ tuæ navare modo ut pergas, quam pulchram, quamq; solidam civibus tuis necessario gratiam initurus sis, vel hinc liquido specta. Quæ à me eo dicta sunt, non quod ego te quidquam horum ignorare censeam, sed quod mihi persuadeam, in hoc te magis multo intentum esse, quid tute patriæ tuæ possis persolvere, quam quid illa tibi jure optimo sit debitura. De exteris jam nunc dicam, quorum demerendi, si tibi id cordi est, persane ampla in præsens oblata est occasio; ut enim est apud eos ingenio quis forte floridior, aut moribus amœnis et elegantibus, Linguam Hetruscam in deliciis habet præcipuis, quin & in solida etiam parte eruditionis esse sibi ponendam ducit, præsertim si Græca aut Latina, vel nullo, vel modico tinctu imbiberit. Ego certe istis utrisque Linguis non extremis tantummodo labris madidus; sed siquis alius, quantum per annos licuit, poculis majoribus prolutus, possum tamen non-nunquam ad illum dantem, & Petrarcham aliosq; vestros com-plusculos, libenter & cupide commessatum ire: nec me tam ipsæ Athenæ Atticæ cum illo suo pelludico Ilisso, nec illa vetus Roma suâ Tiberis ripâ retinere valuêrunt; quin sæpe Arnum vestrum, et Fæsulanos illos colles invisere amem. Jam vide, obsecro, numquid satis causæ fuerat, quæ me vobis ultimum ab Oceano hospitem per hosce aliquot dies dederit, vestræq: Na-tionis ita amantem, ut non alius, opinor, magis. Quo magis merito potes meminisse, quid ego tanto opere abs te contendere soleam; uti jam inchoatis, majori etiam ex parte absolutis, velles, quantâ maximâ facilitate res ipsa tulerit, in nostram ex-terorum gratiam, de recta linguae pronuntiatione adhuc paulu-lum quiddam adjicere. Cæteris enim sermonis vestri consultis in hanc usq diem id animi videtur fuisse, suis tantum ut satis-facerent, de nobis nihil soliciti. Quanquam ille meo quidem judicio, & famæ suæ, & Italici sermonis gloriæ, haud paulo cer-tius consuluissent, si præcepta ita tradidissent, ac si omnium mortalium referret ejus linguæ scientiam appetere: verum per illos non stetit quo minus nobis videremini vos Itali, intra Al-pium duntaxat pomœria sapere voluisse. Hæc igitur laus præ-libata nemini, tota erit tua, tibi intactam & integram hucusq; se servat; nec illa minus, si in tanta Scriptorum turba common-strare separatim non gravabere, quis post illos decantatos Floren-tinæ linguæ auctores poterit secundas haud injuriâ sibi asser-ere: quis Tragœdia insignis, quis in Comœdia festivus & lepi-dus; quis scriptis Epistolis aut Dialogis, argutus aut gravis; quis in Historia nobilis: ita & studioso potiorem quemq; eligere volenti non erit difficile, & erit, quoties vagari latius libebit, ubi pedem intrepide possit figere. Quâ quidem in re, inter Antiquos Ciceronem & Fabium habebis, quos imiteris; vestrorum autem hominum haud scio an ullum. Atq; hæc ego tametsi videor mihi abs te (nisi me animus fallit) jam primo impetrasse, quoties in istius rei mentionem incidimus, quæ tua comitas est, & benignum ingenium; nolo tamen id tibi fraudi sit, quo minus exquisite, ut ita dicam, atq; elaborate exorandum te mihi esse putem. Nam quod tua virtus, tuusq; candor, minimum rebus tuis pretium, minimamq; æstimationem addicit; iis ego, justam volo, & exactam, cum rei dignitas, tum adeo mea observantia imponat; & certe hoc æquum est ubique, quanto quis petenti faciliorem se præbet, tanto minus concedentis honori deesse oportebit. De cætero, si forte cur in hoc argumento, Latinâ potius quam vestrâ Linguâ utar, miraris; id factum eâ gratiâ est, ut intelligas quam ego Linguam abs te mihi præceptis exornandam cupio, ejus me plane meam imperitiam, & inopiam Latine confiteri; & hâc ipsâ ratione plus me valiturum apud te speravi simul & illud, si canam; & venerandam è Latio matrem, in filiæ causâ suæ mecum adjutricem adduxissem, credidi fore ejus authoritati, & reverentiæ, augustæque per tot sæcula Majestati, nihil ut denegares. Vale.

Florentiæ, Septemb. 10. 1638.

Milton, *Epistolarum Familiarium Liber Unus,* 1674, pp. 20-25; CM, XII, 30 ff.

[To Benedetto Bonmattei of Florence. In adorning afresh, as you are doing, Benedetto Bonmattei, the institutes of your native tongue, now also about to place the keystone on your work, you are both entering on a path to glory common to some intellects of the highest order, and have also, as I see, raised a hope and an opinion of yourself among your fellow-citizens, as of one that is to confer, by his own easy effort, either lucidity or richness, or, at least, polish and order, on what has been handed down by others. How by this you have in no usual degree bound your countrymen in obligation to you, truly they must themselves be ungrateful if they do not perceive. For whoever in a state knows how wisely to form the manners of men and to rule them at home and in war with excellent institutes, him in the first place, above others, I should esteem worthy of all honour; but next to him the man who strives to establish in maxims and rules the method and habit of speaking and writing received from a good age of the nation, and, as it were, to fortify the same round with a kind of wall, the daring to overleap which let a law only short of that of Romulus be used to prevent. Should we choose to compare the two in respect of utility, it is the former alone that can make the social existence of the citizens just and holy; but it is the latter that makes it splendid and beautiful, which is the next thing that is desired. The one, as I believe, supplies a noble courage and intrepid counsels against an enemy invading the territory; the other takes to himself the task of extirpating and defeating, by means of a learned detective police of ears, and a light band of good authors, that barbarism which makes large inroads upon the minds of men, and is a destructive intestine enemy to genius. Nor is it to be considered of small consequence what language, pure or corrupt, a people has, or what is their customary degree of propriety in speaking it—a matter which oftener than once was the salvation of Athens; nay, as it is Plato's opinion that by a change in the manner and habit of dressing serious commotions and mutations are portended in a Commonwealth, I, for my part, would rather believe that the fall of that city and its low and obscure condition followed on the general vitiation of its usage in the matter of speech; for, let the words of a country be in part unhandsome and offensive in themselves, in part debased by wear and wrongly uttered, and what do they declare, but, by no light indication, that the inhabitants of that country are an indolent, idly-yawning race, with minds already long prepared for any amount of servility? On the other hand, we have never heard that any empire, any state, did not at least flourish in a middling degree as long as its own liking and care for its language lasted. Therefore, Benedetto, if only you proceed to perform vigorously this labour of yours for your Re-

public, behold clearly, even from this, what a fair and solid affection you will necessarily win from your countrymen. All
which is here said by me, not because I suppose you to be ignorant of any of it, but because I persuade myself that you are
much more intent on the consideration of what you yourself
can do for your country, than of what your country will, by
the best right, owe to you. I will now speak concerning foreigners; for obliging whom, if that is at your heart, most certainly
at present an ample opportunity is offered—seeing that who
among them is there that, happening to be more blooming than
the rest in genius or in pleasing and elegant manners, counts
the Tuscan tongue among his chief delights, and does not also
consider that it ought to have a place for him in the solid part
of his learning, especially if he has imbibed Greek and Latin
either in moderate tincture or not at all? I, certainly, who have
not wet merely the tips of my lips with both these tongues, but
have, as much as any, to the full allowance of my years, drained
their deeper draughts, can yet sometimes willingly and eagerly
go for a feast to that Dante of yours, and to Petrarch and a good
few more; nor has the Attic Athens itself, with its pellucid
Ilissus, nor that old Rome with its bank of the Tiber, been
able so to hold me but that I love often to visit your Arno and
these hills of Fæsule. See now, I entreat, whether the reason
has been sufficient that has given me to you, for these some days
your latest guest from the ocean, and so great a lover of your
nation that, as I think, there is no other more so. On which account you may, with more reason, remember what I am wont
so earnestly to request of you—to wit, that to your work already
begun, and in greater part finished, you would, to the utmost
extent that the case will permit, add yet, in behalf of us foreigners, a certain little somewhat more concerning the right
pronunciation of the language. For, with other authorities in
your tongue to this day, the intention seems to have been to
satisfy only their own countrymen, caring nothing for us. Although, in my opinion, these would have consulted not a little
more certainly both their own fame and the glory of the Italian

tongue, if they had so delivered their precepts as if it concerned all mankind to acquire the knowledge of that language, yet, in as far as depended on them, you might seem, you Italians, to recognise no space save within the Alps. This praise, therefore, untasted by any one before you, will be wholly your own, is kept till now untouched and entire for you; nor that other less, if, in so great a crowd of writers, you should not consider it too much trouble to give information separately on such points as these—who can justly claim for himself the second place, next after the universally celebrated authors of the Florentine tongue; who is illustrious in Tragedy; who happy and sprightly in Comedy; who smart or weighty in Epistles or Dialogues; who noble in History: by which means it would not be difficult, for a student wishing it, to select one of superior merit, and, as often as he chose to range more widely, there would be ground on which he could step intrepidly. In this matter you will have, among the ancients, Cicero and Fabius to imitate; but, of your own men, I know not whether any. And, although I seem already (unless my memory deceive me) to have made this demand of you as often as we have fallen on the mention of that affair, (such is your politeness and kindly disposition!) I am unwilling that that should be in the way of my considering that I ought to entreat the same in set phrase, so to speak, and in an express manner. For, whereas your virtue and candour assign the lowest value and the lowest estimation to your own labours, I, for my part, would desire that, as their inherent dignity, so also my respect should set a just and exact value upon them; and certainly this is but fair everywhere, that, the more easily one yields himself to a request, the less defect should there be of due honour to his compliance. For the rest, should you perchance wonder why, in this argument, I use the Latin rather than your tongue, this is that you may understand that, in this tongue which I am desirous to have cleared up for me in precepts by you, I do plainly confess in Latin my poverty and want of skill; and by this very method I have hoped to prevail more with you,—besides that, by bringing with me that hoary and venerable mother from Latium as my helper in her daughter's cause, I believed that there would be nothing that you would deny to her authority and reverend character and majesty august through so many ages. Farewell.

At Florence, Septemb. 10, 1638.]

Masson, I, 738-741 (789-792).

SEPTEMBER 16. READS A LATIN POEM IN THE SVOGLIATI ACADEMY IN FLORENCE.

A di 16. di Settbro

I Sīg Accad^e. ragunati in numero competente furono lett' alcune composⁿⁱ. e particolarmz il Giovanni Miltone Inglese lesse una poesia Latina di versi esametri molto erudita.

Atti dell' Accademia degli Svogliati, Bibliotheca Nazionale, Firenze, MSS. Magliabecchiana, cl. IX, cod. 60; Stern, I, ii, 499.

[September 16. To the members of the Academy gathered in considerable numbers some compositions were read, and particularly John Milton, an Englishman, read a very learned Latin poem in hexameters.]

OCTOBER (?). REACHES SIENA.

Florentia Senas . . . profectus.

Milton, *Defensio Secunda*, 1654, p. 84; CM, VIII, 122.

[From Florence I came to Siena.]

From *Florence* he took his Journey to *Siena*.

Phillips, p. xiii; Darbishire, p. 57.

. . . from thence he went to *Sena* and *Rome*, in both which places he spent his time among the most learned there.

Wood, I, 880; Darbishire, p. 37.

OCTOBER-NOVEMBER (?). VISITS ROME.

. . . inde Romam profectus, postquam illius urbis antiquitas & prisca fama me ad bimestre ferè spatium tenuisset (ubi & Luca Holstenio, aliisque viris cum doctis tum ingeniosis, sum usus humanissimis.)

Milton, *Defensio Secunda*, 1654, pp. 84-85; CM, VIII, 122.

[Then I came to Rome. After the antiquity and ancient fame of that city had kept me for almost the space of two months (and where also I enjoyed the highly cultivated Lucas Holstenius and other men not only learned but also ingenious. . . .)]

Translated by the present editor.

From Florence hee went to Rome, where, as in all places, hee spent his time in the choicest company; and amongst others there, in that of Lucas Holstein.

The "earliest" biography, fol. 140v; Darbishire, p. 20. After "Holstein" in the manuscript follows the phrase, "Library keeper at the Vatican." This in turn has been cancelled, and the following phrase added as a note: "for I am not certain that he was Library keeper."

. . . thence to *Rome*; where he was detain'd much about the same time he had been at *Florence*; as well by his desire of seeing all the Rarities and Antiquities of that most Glorious and Renowned City, as by the Conversation of *Lucas Holstenius*, and other Learned and Ingenious men; who highly valued his Acquaintance, and treated him with all possible Respect.

Phillips, p. xiii; Darbishire, p. 57.

. . . to *Sena* and *Rome*, in both which places he spent his time among the most learned there, *Lucas Holstenius* being one. . . .

Wood, 1, 880; Darbishire, p. 37.

OCTOBER-NOVEMBER (?). VISITS LUCAS HOLSTENIUS AT THE VATICAN.

Cum enim tui conveniendi causâ in Vaticanum ascenderem, ignotum prorsus, nisi si quid forte ab Alexandro Cherubino dictum de me prius fuerat, summâ cum humanitate recepisti; mox in Musæum comiter admisso, et conquisitissimam Librorum supellectilem, & permultos insuper Manuscriptos Authores Græcos, tuis Lucubrationibus exornatos, adspicere licuit: quorum partim nostro sæculo nondum visi, quasi in procinctu, velut illæ apud Maronem,

—penitus convalle virenti
Inclusæ animæ, superumq; ad limen ituræ;
expeditas modo Typographi manus, & μαιευτικὴν poscere vide-

bantur; partim tuâ operâ etiamnum editi, passim ab eruditis avide accipiuntur; quorum & unius etiam duplici dono abs te auctus dimittor.

Milton, letter to Lucas Holstenius, March 30, 1639, *q.v.* See also the preceding group of entries.

[For, when I went up to the Vatican for the purpose of meeting you, you received me, a total stranger to you (unless perchance anything had been previously said about me to you by Alexander Cherubini), with the utmost courtesy. Immediately admitted with politeness into the Museum, I was allowed to behold both the superb collection of books, and also very many manuscript Greek authors set forth with your explanations —some of whom, not yet seen in our age, seemed now in their array, like those in Maro,—"souls enclosed within a green valley, about to go up to the threshold above"—to demand the active hands of the printer, and a delivery into the world; others of whom, already edited by your care, are eagerly received everywhere by scholars; I myself, too, being dismissed by you, richer than I came, with two copies of one which you presented to me.]

Masson, I, 749-750 (802), except that the Latin verses, simply quoted in Masson, are translated by the present editor. No trace has been found of the presentation volumes described here.

October (?). Attends cardinal barberini's concert.

Tum nec aliter crediderim, quam quæ tu de me verba feceris ad præstantissimum Cardin. Franc. Barberinum, iis factum esse, ut cum ille paucis post diebus ἀκρόαμα illud Musicum magnificentiâ vere Romanâ publice exhiberet, ipse me tanta in turba quæsitum ad fores expectans, & pene manu prehensum persane honorifice intro admiserit.

Milton, letter to Lucas Holstenius, March 30, 1639, *q.v.* It has recently been contended that the entertainment which Milton saw must have been Rospigliosi's *Che soffre speri*, a secular composition, which was presented in February, 1639, and of which the manuscript is still to be found in the Vatican library (Gertrude L. Finney, "Chorus in *Samson Agonistes*," *PMLA*, lviii [1943], 649 ff.; see also *Modern*

Language Review, VIII [1913], 91-92). But the wording of Milton's letter makes it seem almost certain that this entertainment took place only a few days after his first meeting with Holstenius. If this meeting took place on his first visit to Rome, as seems certain from the descriptions of it already quoted, then February, 1639, is an impossibly late date for the concert. Raymond (38) gives the date as March 1, 1639.

[Then I could not but believe that it was in consequence of the mention you made of me to the most excellent Cardinal Francesco Barberini, that, when he, a few days after, gave that public musical entertainment with truly Roman magnificence, he himself, waiting at the doors, and seeking me out in so great a crowd, nay, almost laying hold of me by the hand, admitted me within in a truly most honourable manner.]

Masson, I, 750 (802).

OCTOBER-NOVEMBER (?). CALLS ON CARDINAL BARBERINI.

Quâ ego gratiâ cum illum postridie salutatum accessissem, tute idem rursus is eras, qui & aditum mihi fecisti, & colloquendi copiam; quæ quidem cum tanto viro, quo etiam in summo dignitatis fastigio nihil benignius, nihil humanius, pro loci & temporis ratione largiuscula profecto potius erat, quam nimis parca.

Milton, letter to Lucas Holstenius, March 30, 1639. From the wording of this passage, Milton's call on the Cardinal must have been made on the day after the sumptuous concert at the Barberini palace.

[And when, on this account, I went to pay my respects to him next day, you again were yourself the person who both made access for me, and obtained for me an opportunity for conversing with him at leisure, such as, with so great a man (than whom, on the topmost summit of dignity, nothing more kind, nothing more courteous), was truly, considering the place and the time, too ample rather than too sparing.]

Masson, I, 750 (802-803).

OCTOBER-NOVEMBER (?). MEETS ENGLISH MINISTER THOMAS GAWEN (?).

[Gawen] travelled, was at Rome, and accidentally sometimes fell into the company of John Milton the antimonarchist.

Anthony Wood, *Athenæ Oxonienses*, ed. Bliss, IV (1820), 130. The wording of this note would seem to mean that Milton and Gawen met at Rome, and it has therefore been filed under the date of Milton's first visit to Rome. It might conceivably not refer to the Roman visit at all, however. Thomas Gawen, the son of a minister of Bristol, was fellow of New College in 1632 at the age of 22, and took his A.M. soon after and went into holy orders. He was later chaplain to the Bishop of Winchester and rector of Exton, Hampshire. After traveling to Rome, he turned towards Roman Catholicism, entered the family of Queen Henrietta after the Restoration, returned again to Rome, married an Italian woman, and died in London in 1684. See also Masson, I (1881), 798.

OCTOBER 30. ENTERTAINED IN THE ENGLISH COLLEGE AT ROME.

Octobris die 30, Pransi sunt in Collegio Nostro Illustrissimus D. N. Cary frater baronis de Faukeland, Doctor Holdingus, Lancastrensis, D. N. Fortescuto, et Dominus Miltonus, cum famulo, nobiles Angli, et excepti sunt lauté.

From the Travellers' Book of the English College, quoted in Milton's *Commonplace Book*, Publications of the Camden Society, New Series, XVI (1876), xvi. I have not seen the original entry. See also Masson, I (1881), 800.

[On October 30 were entertained in our college the illustrious Lord Cary, brother of the Baron Falkland, Dr. Holding of Lancaster, Lord Fortescue, and Lord Milton, with his servant, English nobles, and they were magnificently received.]

Translation by the present editor.

1638 . . . Cary, Mr., the Hon., brother of Lord Falkland, an English gentleman, October 30. Dined in the College.

Holling, Dr., Lancashire. *Id.*

Fortescue, Mr. *Id.*

Milton, Mr., with servant. *Id.*

From the transcripts of the Pilgrim Book in *Records of the English Province of the Society of Jesus*, ed. Foley, VI (1880), 617.

NOVEMBER 3. RECEIVES INTEREST ON COPE BOND (?).

. . . neyther ye s'd principall debt of 150^{li} nor any pte thereof nor any Jnterest due for ye forbearance of the same since November 1641 hath been paid or satisfied. . . .

Milton's bill against Lady Elizabeth Cope and Sir Anthony Cope, June 16, 1654, *q.v.*; see entry under May 3, 1638.

NOVEMBER 9. THIRD PROCLAMATION OF SALE OF LONDON TENEMENT MADE.

T'cia pclam' fca' fuit nono die Novembr' t'nno' eod' Michī Anno quartodecimo Regis infrascr'.

From the Milton-Lyster concord of fine, April 15, 1638, *q.v.*

[The third proclamation was made on the ninth day of November in Michaelmas term in the said fourteenth year of the king written below.]

DECEMBER (?). COMES TO NAPLES.

... Neapolim perrexi. ...

Milton, *Defensio Secunda*, 1654, p. 85; CM, VIII, 122.

[I came to Naples.]

[From Rome he went to] Naples, which was his next remove....

The "earliest" biography, fol. 141; Darbishire, p. 20.

From *Rome* he Travelled to *Naples*, where he was introduced by a certain Hermite, who accompanied him in his Journey from *Rome* thither. ...

Phillips, p. xiii; Darbishire, p. 57.

... from thence he journied to *Naples*.

Wood, I, 880; Darbishire, p. 37.

DECEMBER (?). MEETS MANSO; MANSO GIVES HIM GIFTS; PLANS ARTHURIAN EPIC AND ANTICIPATES LITERARY FAME; ENGAGES IN NUMEROUS ARGUMENTS ABOUT RELIGION.

Mansus. Joannes Baptista Mansus Marchio Villensis vir ingenii laude, tum literarum studio, nec non & bellicâ virtute apud Italos clarus in primis est. Ad quem Torquati Tassi dialogus extat de Amicitiâ scriptus; erat enim Tassi amicissimus; ab quo etiam inter Campaniæ principes celebratur, in illo poemate cui titulus Gerusalemme conquistata, lib. 20. ... *Is authorem Neapoli commorantem summâ benevolentiâ prosecutus est, mul-*

taque ei detulit humanitatis officia. Ad hunc itaque hospes ille antequam ab eâ urbe discederet, ut ne ingratum se ostenderet, hoc carmen misit. . . .

Ergo ego te Cliûs & magni nomine Phœbi
Manse pater, jubeo longum salvere per ævum
Missus Hyperboreo juvenis peregrinus ab axe.
Nec tu longinquam bonus aspernabere Musam,
Quæ nuper gelidâ vix enutrita sub Arcto
Imprudens Italas ausa est volitare per urbes.
Nos etiam in nostro modulantes flumine cygnos
Credimus obscuras noctis sensisse per umbras,
Quà Thamesis latè puris argenteus urnis
Oceani glaucos perfundit gurgite crines. . . .
O mihi si mea sors talem concedat amicum
Phœbæos decorâsse viros qui tam bene norit,
Si quando indigenas revocabo in carmina reges,
Arturumque etiam sub terris bella moventem;
Aut dicam invictæ sociali fœdere mensæ,
Magnanimos Heroas, & (O modo spiritus ad sit)
Frangam Saxonicas Britonum sub Marte phalanges.
Tandem ubi non tacitæ permensus tempora vitæ,
Annorumque satur cineri sua jura relinquam,
Ille mihi lecto madidis astaret ocellis,
Astanti sat erit si dicam sim tibi curæ;
Ille meos artus liventi morte solutos
Curaret parvâ componi molliter urnâ.
Forsitan & nostros ducat de marmore vultus,
Nectens aut Paphiâ myrti aut Parnasside lauri
Fronde comas, at ego securâ pace quiescam.
Tum quoque, si qua fides, si præmia certa bonorum,
Ipse ego cælicolûm semotus in æthera divûm,
Quò labor & mens pura vehunt, atque ignea virtus
Secreti hæc aliquâ mundi de parte videbo
(Quantum fata sinunt) & totâ mente serenùm
Ridens purpureo suffundar lumine vultus
Et simul æthereo plaudam mihi lætus Olympo.
Milton, *Poems*, 1645, part ii, pp. 72-76; CM, I, 284 ff.

[MANSO. Joannes Baptista Mansus, Marquis of Villa, is a man illustrious in the first rank among Italians by the reputation of his genius, as well in the study of letters as also in warlike valour. There is extant a Dialogue of Torquato Tasso "On Friendship," addressed to him; for he was Tasso's most intimate friend; by whom he is also celebrated among the princes of Campania in the poem entitled *Gerusalemme Conquistata*, book XX. . . . This nobleman honoured the author, during his stay in Naples, with every kindness in his power, and conferred on him many acts of courtesy; to him, therefore, his guest, before leaving that city, to show himself not ungrateful, sent the following piece of verse. . . .

I, therefore, also, in the name of Clio and of great Phœbus, wish thee, my father Manso, a long age of health—I, a foreign youth, sent hither from the polar north. Nor wilt thou, in thy goodness, scorn the far-off Muse, which, lately nourished scarce to maturity under the Arctic cold, has dared, indiscreetly, to fly through the Italian cities. We also believe ourselves to have heard, through the obscure shades of night, the song of the swans in that stream of ours, where Thames, broad and silvery from its pure fountains, bathes with its tide the blue hairs of Ocean. . . .

O that *my* lot might yield me such a friend, one who should know as well how to decorate Apollo's children, if perchance *I* shall ever call back into verse our native kings, and Arthur stirring wars even under the earth that hides him, or speak of the great-souled heroes, the knights of the unconquered Table, bound in confederate brotherhood, and (O may the spirit be present to me!) break the Saxon phalanxes under the British Mars. Then, when, having measured out the period of a not silent life, and full of years, I shall leave the dust its due, he would stand by my bed with wet eyes; it would be enough if I said to him standing by, "Let me be thy charge;" he would see that my limbs, slacked in livid death, were softly laid in the narrow coffin; perchance he would bring out from the marble our features, wreathing the hair either with the leaf of Paphian myrtle or with that of Parnassian laurel; but *I* should repose in secure peace. Then, too, if faith is aught, if there are assured rewards of the good, I myself, withdrawn into the ether of the heaven-houséd gods, whither labour and the pure mind and the fire of virtue carry us, shall behold these things from some part of the unseen world, as far as the fates allow, and, smiling serene, with soul entire, shall feel my face suffused with the purple light, and applaud myself the while in the joy of ethereal Olympus.]

Masson, 1, 765-768 (816-819).

Hæc tibi servabam lentâ sub cortice lauri,
Hæc, & plura simul, tum quæ mihi pocula Mansus,
Mansus Chalcidicæ non ultima gloria ripæ
Bina dedit, mirum artis opus, mirandus & ipse,
Et circùm gemino cælaverat argumento:
In medio rubri maris unda, & odoriferum ver
Littora longa Arabum, & sudantes balsama silvæ,
Has inter Phoenix divina avis, unica terris
Cæruleùm fulgens diversicoloribus alis
Auroram vitreis surgentem respicit undis.
Parte alia polus omnipatens, & magnus Olympus,
Quis putet? hic quoque Amor, pictæque in nube pharetræ,
Arma corusca faces, & spicula tincta pyropo;
Nec tenues animas, pectúsque ignobile vulgi
Hinc ferit, at circùm flammantia lumina torquens
Semper in erectum spargit sua tela per orbes
Impiger, & pronos nunquam collimat ad ictus,
Hinc mentes ardere sacræ, formæque deorum.

Milton, "Epitaphium Damonis," *Poems*, 1645, part ii, pp. 85-86; CM, 1, 312-315.

[These I was keeping for thee, wrapt up in the rind of the
    laurel,
These and other things with them; and mainly the two
    cups which Manso—
Manso, not the last of Southern Italy's glories—
Gave me, a wonder of art, which himself, a wonder of nature,

Carved with a double design of his own well-skilled
      invention:
Here the Red Sea in the midst, and the odoriferous summer,
Araby's winding shores, and palm-trees sweating their
      balsams,
Mid which the bird divine, earth's marvel, the singular
      Phœnix,
Blazing cærulean-bright with wings of different colours,
Turns to behold Aurora surmounting the glassy-green
      billows:
Obverse is Heaven's vast vault and the great Olympian
      mansion.
Who would suppose it? Even here is Love and his cloud-
      painted quiver,
Arms glittering torch-lit, and arrows tipped with the
      fire-gem.
Nor is it meagre souls and the base-born breasts of the vulgar
Hence that he strikes; but, whirling round him his
      luminous splendours,
Always he scatters his darts right upwards sheer through
      the star-depths
Restless, and never deigns to level the pain of them
      downwards;
Whence the sacred minds and the forms of the gods ever-
      burning.]

Masson, II, 92. The precise meaning of the passage about the cups has been much debated. Masson, in a note at the foregoing reference, assumes that "the whole of this passage is a poetical description of the designs on an actual pair of cups or chased goblets which Milton had received as a keepsake from Manso at Naples, and had brought home with him." He then queries: "Where are they now?" No such articles have been found since Milton's lifetime. On the other hand, it has been suggested with considerable plausibility by M. de Filippis (*PMLA*, LI [1936], 745 ff.: "Milton and Manso: Cups or Books?") that the language used here may be a rhetorical way of describing some other object, perhaps books. In one of Manso's books there is a poem on the Phoenix which might substantiate such a theory.

Illic per Eremitam quendam, quîcum Româ iter fecerem, ad

Joannem Baptistam Mansum, Marchionem Villensem, virum
nobilissimum atque gravissimum, (ad quem Torquatus Tassus
insignis poeta Italus de amicitia scripsit) sum introductus; eo-
démque usus, quamdiu illic fui, sanè amicissimo; qui & ipse me
per urbis loca & Proregis aulam circumduxit, & visendi gratiâ
haud semel ipse ad hospitium venit: discedenti seriò excusavit
se, tametsi multò plura detulisse mihi officia maximè cupiebat,
non potuisse illa in urbe, propterea quòd nolebam in religione
esse tectior.

Milton, *Defensio Secunda*, 1654, p. 85; CM, VIII, 122-124.

[Here I was introduced by a certain hermit, with whom I
had come from Rome, to John Baptista Manso, Marquis of
Villa, a very noble and important man, to whom the famous
Italian poet Torquato Tasso wrote about friendship. By him
I was treated in the most friendly fashion as long as I stayed
there. Indeed he took me himself through the whole city and
the court of the Viceroy, and more than once he came himself
to my hotel to see me. When I left, he seriously excused himself because, though he had been most desirous of showing me
much greater attention, he had not been able to do so in that
city because I had not been willing to be more guarded in religion.]

Translated by the present editor.

At Naples, which was his next remove, hee became acquainted wth Marquis Manso, a learned Person, and so aged
as to have bin contemporary and intimate wth Torquato Tasso,
the famous Italian Heroic. This Noble-man oblig'd him by
very particular civilities, accompanying him to see the rarities
of the place, and paying him Visitts at his lodging; Also sent him
the testimony of a great esteem in this Distich

Ut Mens, Forma, Decor, Facies, Mos, si Pietas sic,
Non Anglus, verum herclè Angelus ipse fores.

Yet excus'd himself at parting for not having bin able to do him
more honour, by reason of his resolute owning his Religion:
This hee did whensoever by any ones enquiry occasion was of-

fred; not otherwise forward to enter upon discourses of that Nature. . . . Before his leaving Naples hee return'd the Marquis an acknowlegement of his great favors in an elegant Copy of Verses entitled Mansus wch is extant amongst his other latin Poems.

The "earliest" biography, fol. 141; Darbishire, p. 20. The distich, which was printed by Milton at the beginning of his Latin poems in the 1645 volume, may be translated as follows: "If your piety were equal to your mind, form, grace, face, and manners, then by Hercules you yourself would be, not an Englishman, but an angel."

From *Rome* he Travelled to *Naples*, where he was introduced by a certain Hermite, who accompanied him in his Journey from *Rome* thither, into the Knowledge of *Giovanni Baptista Manso*, Marquess of *Villa*, a *Neapolitan* by Birth, a Person of high Nobility, Vertue, and Honour, to whom the famous *Italian* Poet, *Torquato Tasso*, Wrote his Treatise *de Amicitia*; and moreover mentions him with great Honour in that Illustrious Poem of his, Intituled, *Gieruemme Liberata*: This Noble Marquess received him with extraordinary Respect and Civility, and went with him himself to give him a sight of all that was of Note and Remark in the City, particularly the Viceroys Palace, and was often in Person to Visit him at his Lodging. Moreover, this Noble Marquess honoured him so far, as to make a Latin Distich in his Praise, as hath been already mentioned; which being no less pithy then short, though already in Print, it will not be unworth the while here to repeat.

Ut Mens, Forma, Decor, Facies, si* Pietas, sic,
Non Anglus Verum Hercle Angelus ipse foret.

In return of this Honour, and in gratitude for the many Favours and Civilities received of him, he presented him at his departure with a large Latin Eclogue, Intituled, *Mansus*, afterward's Published among his Latin Poems. The Marquess at his taking leave of him, gave him this Complement, That he would have done him many more Offices of Kindness and Civility, but

* This word relates to his being a Protestant not a *Roman*-Catholick (Phillips's note).

was therefore rendered incapable in regard he had been over-liberal in his speech against the Religion of the Country.

Phillips, pp. xiii-xiv; Darbishire, pp. 57-58.

. . . he journied to *Naples*, where he was introduced into the acquaintance of *Joh. Bapt. Mansus* an Italian Marquess (to whom *Torquatus Tassus* an Italian Poet wrot his Book *De amicitia*) who shewed great civilities to him, accompanied him to see the rarities of that place, visited him at his Lodgings, and sent to, the testimony of his great esteem for, him, in this Distich,

> *Ut mens, forma, decor, mos, si pietas sic,*
> *Non Anglus, verum herculè Angelus ipse fores.*

And excus'd himself at parting for not having been able to do him more honour, by reason of his resolute owning his (Protestant) Religion. . . . Before he left *Naples* he return'd the Marquess an acknowledgment of his great favors in an elegant copy of Verses entit. *Mansus*, which is among the Latin Poems.

Wood, I, 880-881; Darbishire, pp. 37-38.

DECEMBER 12. RECEIVES INTEREST PAYMENT FROM RICHARD POWELL.

. . . the growing Jnterest for the forbearance of the said Principall debt was for some yeares then following likewise payd And soe continued to bee paid vntill June Jn the yeare of our Lord One Thousand six hundred ffortie and ffower. . . .

From Milton's answer to Elizabeth Ashworth, February 22, 1653/4, *q.v.*

1639

ALLEGED PORTRAIT.

Dr. Williamson (*Milton Tercentenary*, 1908, p. 36) mentions briefly an alleged portrait of Milton exhibited at Christ's College in 1908. By an unknown artist, it was said to be of Milton at the age of 31. Earlier in the collection of a Mr. Peed of Canterbury, a collector of

Miltoniana who died in 1820, it was lent by Dr. Hill, some time master of Downing College. There is no further information about it.

Hears of the Death of His Friend Charles Diodati.

Thyrsis animi causâ profectus peregrè de obitu Damonis nuncium accepit. Domum postea reversus. . . .

Milton, "Epitaphium Damonis," *Poems*, 1645, part ii, p. 77; CM, I, 294. The date might even be late in 1638, since Diodati died in August of that year.

[Thyrsis, having set out to travel for mental improvement, received news when abroad of Damon's death. Afterwards at length returning. . . .]

Masson, II, 85-86.

January (?). Rejects plan of visiting Greece.

In Siciliam quoque & Græciam trajicere volentem me . . . .

Milton, *Defensio Secunda*, 1654, p. 85; CM, VIII, 124.

[I wished also to cross over to Sicily and Greece.]

He had entertain'd some thoughts of passing over into *Sicily* and *Greece*, but was diverted by the News he receiv'd from *England*.

Phillips, p. xv; Darbishire, p. 58.

. . . from thence [Naples] he thought to have gone into *Sicily* and *Greece*, but upon second thoughts he continued in *Italy*.

Wood, I, 881; Darbishire, p. 38.

January (?). Decides to return home because of war.

. . . tristis ex Anglia belli civilis nuntius revocavit: turpe enim existimabam, dum mei cives domi de libertate dimicarent, me animi causâ otiosè peregrinari.

Milton, *Defensio Secunda*, 1654, p. 85; CM, VIII, 124.

[The sad news of the English civil war recalled me; for I thought it shameful, while my countrymen were fighting for their liberty at home, that I should be peacefully traveling for culture.]

Translated by the present editor.

... News he receiv'd from *England*, that Affairs there were tending towards a Civil War; thinking it a thing unworthy in him to be taking his Pleasure in Foreign Parts, while his Countreymen at home were Fighting for their Liberty.

Phillips, p. xv; Darbishire, p. 58.

JANUARY (?). RECEIVES WARNING LETTERS IN NAPLES FROM FRIENDS.

Roman autem reversurum, monebant Mercatores se didicisse per literas parari mihi ab Jesuitis Anglis insidias, si Romam reverterem; eò quod de religione nimis liberè loquutus essem. Sic enim mecum statueram, de religione quidem iis in locis sermones ultro non inferre; interrogatus de fide, quicquid essem passurus, nihil dissimulare.

Milton, *Defensio Secunda*, 1654, pp. 85-86; CM, VIII, 124.

[As I was about to return to Rome, merchants warned me that they had learned by letters that if I returned to Rome, plots were being prepared against me by the English Jesuits, because I had spoken too freely about religion. For I had made up my mind never to begin an argument about religion myself in those parts; but if questioned about my faith, not to conceal anything, whatever I might suffer.]

Translation by the present editor.

... he had bin advis'd by letters from som friends to Naples, that the English Jesuits design'd to do him mischief on that account [religious discussion]. . . .

The "earliest" biography, fol. 141; Darbishire, pp. 20-21.

... the Merchants gave him a caution that the Jesuits were hatching designs against him, in case he should return thither, by reason of the freedom he took in all his discourses of Religion. . . .

Phillips, p. xv; Darbishire, p. 58.

JANUARY-FEBRUARY (?). REVISITS ROME.

Romam itaque nihilo minùs redii: quid essem, si quis interrogabat, neminem celavi; si quis adoriebatur, in ipsa urbe Pontificis, alteros prope duos menses, orthodoxam religionem, ut antea, liberrimè tuebar. . . .

Milton, *Defensio Secunda*, 1654, p. 86; CM, VIII, 124.

[And so nevertheless I returned to Rome. If anybody questioned what I was, I concealed it from no one. If any one attacked me, I defended the orthodox religion most freely, as before, for almost two months more, in the Pope's own city itself.]

Translation by the present editor.

. . . tua . . . perpetua . . . mendacia . . . qui scripsisse me ais *Romæ martyrii fuisse candidatum; structas ab Jesuitis vitæ meæ insidias.* Ad quod utrūque mendacium diluendum opus est nihil aliud, nisi ut quis locū ipsū libri inspiciat.

Milton, *Defensio Pro Se*, 1655, p. 124; CM, IX, 182.

[It is your everlasting lies when you say that I wrote that at Rome I was a candidate for martyrdom and that plots for my life were laid by the Jesuits. To destroy both of these lies nothing else is needed but to look at the place in the book itself.]

Translation by the present editor. Obviously, More is merely quoting Milton's own account as regards the Jesuit plot. Milton's objection seems to be that the way in which More quotes it gives the wrong impression. He contrives to make Milton seem to be posing as a martyr, whereas Milton wishes to avoid any such impression.

Nor did hee decline its defense [*i.e.*, that of the Protestant religion] in the like circumstances even in Rome it self, on his return thether. . . .

The "earliest" biography, fol. 141; Darbishire, p. 20.

But first resolv'd to see *Rome* once more. . . . to *Rome* the second time he went, determining with himself not industriously to begin to fall into any Discourse about Religion; but, being ask'd, not to deny or endeavour to conceal his own Sentiments; Two Months he staid at *Rome*; and in all that time never flinch'd, but was ready to defend the Orthodox Faith against all Opposers; and so well he succeeded therein, that Good Providence guarding him, he went safe from *Rome* back to *Florence*.

Phillips, p. xv; Darbishire, pp. 58-59.

. . . which resoluteness [as in Naples] he using at *Rome*, many there were that dared not to express their civilities towards him, which otherwise they would have done: And I have heard it confidently related, that for his said Resolutions, which out of policy, and for his own safety, might have been then spared, the English Priests at *Rome* were highly disgusted, and it was question'd, whether the Jesuits his Countrymen there, did not design to do him mischief.

Wood, 1, 881; Darbishire, pp. 37-38.

JANUARY-FEBRUARY. LEGENDARY MEETING WITH ANDREW MARVELL IN ROME.

I am inclined to think, upon this excursion to Italy, that our author [Marvell] made his first acquaintance with Milton, who was at that time abroad. . . . It is most probable that this intimacy was made abroad; it was natural that two such native luminaries should unite in Rome, when they observed the eyes of the conclave turned upon their learning, which Milton partially drew, by disputing against the superstition of the church of Rome, within the very verge of the Vatican.

The Works of Andrew Marvell, ed. Captain Edward Thompson, III (1776), 442-443. This is the earliest occurrence of this tradition which I have noticed. It is entirely impossible, because whereas Milton returned home in 1639, Marvell did not leave England for his tour of Italy and other European countries until about 1642. But the legend occurs so often that it is mentioned here simply as a matter of record. Even Pierre Legouis (*André Marvell*, Paris, 1928, p. 176), who shows that the chronology does not admit of such a meeting, repeats the account of the meeting of the two poets, "tous deux maudissant de concert le pape aux portes du Vatican."

It is probable that, during this excursion into Italy, Marvell made his first acquaintance with the immortal JOHN MILTON, who was at that time abroad. They met in Rome, and associated together, where they publicly argued against the superstitions of the Romish Church, even within the verge of the Vatican.

John Dove, *Life of Andrew Marvell*, 1832, p. 6. Though Dove gives no authority for his statement, he is obviously paraphrasing Thompson's earlier account.

JANUARY 25. FOURTH PROCLAMATION OF SALE OF
LONDON TENEMENT MADE.

Quarta ꝓclam' fca' fuit Vicesimo quinto die Januarij t'nno'
eod' hillerij Anno quartodecimo Regis infrascr.

From the Milton-Lyster concord of fine, April 15, 1638, *q.v.*

[The fourth proclamation was made on the twenty-fifth day
of January in Hilary term of the said fourteenth year of the
king written below.]

FEBRUARY OR MARCH (?). REVISITS LUCAS HOLSTEN-
IUS (?).

Jam illud vero quod mihi negotium dedisse videbare, de inspiciendo codice Mediceo, sedulo ad amicos retuli, qui quidem
ejus rei efficiendæ spem perexiguam in præsens ostendunt. In
illa Bibliotheca, nisi impetratâ prius veniâ, nihil posse exscribi,
ne stylum quidem scriptorium admovisse tabulis permissum.

Milton, letter to Holstenius, March 30, 1639, *q.v.* The general interpretation of the letter which seems to me most likely is that the earlier
meetings with Holstenius described in it took place during Milton's earlier visit to Rome, but that this commission to inspect a Medicean codex
probably was given to the poet just as he left Rome for Florence. The
chronology, however, is very uncertain.

[The commission which you seemed to give me as to the inspecting of a Medicean codex, I have already carefully reported
to my friends; who, however, hold forth for the present very
small hope of effecting that matter. In that library, I am told,
nothing can be copied, unless by leave first obtained; it is not
permitted even to bring a pen to the tables.

Masson, I, 770 (822).

FEBRUARY (?). HEARS LEONORA BARONI SING.

Milton's three poems to Leonora seem to be reasonably adequate proof
of his having heard her sing. The date, however, and the circumstances
of the concert are highly debatable. It has frequently been argued (e.g.,
Masson, I, 751 [803]) that Milton heard Leonora sing at the Barberini
concert. Some doubt has been cast on this interpretation by Gertrude L.
Finney ("Chorus in *Samson Agonistes*," *PMLA*, LVIII, 1943, 658),
who asserts that no women were allowed to sing in such performances,

and that no women were allowed to attend at all unless accompanied by their husbands. The poems themselves are sufficiently vague so that no light on the date of the event described can be gleaned from them. The concert is therefore placed at this date simply for lack of more definite information. It is probable that the poems were composed within a brief time after Milton heard Leonora sing.

FEBRUARY (?). WRITES THREE POEMS TO LEONORA BARONI.

[1] *Ad Leonoram Romæ canentem.*

[2] *Ad eandem.*

[3] *Ad eandem.*

Milton, *Poems*, 1645, part ii, pp. 42-43; CM, I, 228-231. The date here given to these poems is only approximate, but it is generally agreed upon by most editors and biographers. It is thought that Milton may have composed the verses for the complimentary volume of poems printed in honor of Leonora in 1639 under the title of *Applausi poetici alle glorie delle signora Leonora Baroni*, but no poem of Milton's appears in the volume; see CM, XVIII, 538, 641.

[1. "To Leonora singing at Rome"; 2. "To the same"; 3. "To the same."]

FEBRUARY (?). ASCRIBED POEM TO ITALIAN LADIES.

A FRAGMENT OF MILTON.

FROM THE ITALIAN.

NOT IN HIS WORKS.

When in your language, I unskill'd address. . . .

The New Foundling Hospital for Wit, 1773, VI, 32-33; CM, XVIII, 596. There is very little likelihood that this is an authentic composition of Milton's, but since it has been ascribed to him, and since it resembles the Leonora poems slightly in circumstances, it is here mentioned with them. It is accompanied in the 1773 volume by the following note: "When Milton in his youth was at Florence, he fell in love with a young lady; and, as she understood no English, he writ some verses to her in Italian; of which the above is the sense." These lines may also have some sort of connection with the Italian poems of Milton given earlier, especially that beginning "Ridonsi donne e giovani amorosi."

MARCH (?). RETURNS TO FLORENCE.

Deóque sic volente, incolumis Florentiam rursus perveni;

haud minùs mei cupientes revisens, ac si in patriam revertissem. Illic totidem, quot priùs, menses libenter commoratus.

Milton, *Defensio Secunda*, 1654, p. 86; CM, VIII, 124-126.

[Thus, God willing, I reached Florence again safe and sound, revisiting those who were no less glad to see me than if I had returned to my own country. There I gladly stayed the same number of months as previously.]

From Rome hee revisited Florence for the sake of his charming friends there. . . .

The "earliest" biography, fol. 141; Darbishire, p. 21.

. . . he went safe from *Rome* back to *Florence*, where his return to his Friends of that City was welcomed with as much Joy and Affection, as had it been to his Friends and Relations in his own Countrey, he could not have come a more joyful and welcome Guest. Here, having staid as long as at his first coming. . . .

Phillips, pp. xv-xvi; Darbishire, p. 59.

MARCH 17. READS A LATIN POEM IN THE SVOGLIATI ACADEMY.

A di 17. di Mar.

Nell' Accad* si trovarono li ss*ri* . . . Miltonio. . . . Furon portati dal sesto, dal X. e dall' und*mo*. e letti alc*i* nobili versi latini.

Records of the Accademia degli Svogliati, Bibliotheca Nazionale, Firenze, MSS. Magliabecchiana, cl. IX, fol. 52; Stern, I, ii, 499. Milton's name is tenth on the list of those present at the meeting. The meaning seems to be that three of the spectators or guests, 6, 10, and 11, read poems.

[March 17. There were present in the Academy Messrs. . . . Milton. Some noble Latin verses were brought and read by the sixth, tenth, and eleventh.]

MARCH 24. READS LATIN VERSES AGAIN IN THE SVOGLIATI ACADEMY.

A di 24. Mar.

Si ragunò l'Accad*. nella q*lt* furono li ss*ri* Al°. P. Pr*e* Buōm-

mattei Cons⁵ Cavalcāti Cenᵉ. Bartⁱ. Segᵒ. Cavʳ. Valori il Residēte
dᵃ. Serᵐᵃ'. Rep. Miltonio Doni Rena Girolami Gaddi Il 4ᵗᵒ.
lesse et esplicò un cap. dell' etica, a cui fece alcⁱ. estēporanei
argomenti l'ultimo.

Furon recitate oltre un elogio et un sonetto dal Sʳ. Cavalcāti diverse poesie Toscane delli ssʳⁱ. Bartolommei, Buommattei
e Doni, che lesse una scena dᵃ. sua Tragedia, e diverse poesie
latine del Signor Miltonio e un epigᵃ. dal Sʳ. Girolami.

Atti dell' Accademia degli Svogliati, Bibliotheca Nazionale, Firenze,
MSS. Magliabecchiana, cl. IX, cod. 60, fols. 52-52v; Stern, I, ii, 499.
Stern gives full names.

[March 24. There was a meeting of the Academy, in which
there were present Messrs. Pitti, President; Buonmattei, Counsel; Cavalcanti, Censor; Bartolommei, Secretary; Cavaliere
Valori, the Resident of the most Serene Republic; Milton;
Doni; Rena; Girolami; Gaddi. The fourth read and explained
a chapter of the Ethics, on which the last presented some ex-
temporaneous remarks. Then an elegy and a sonnet were recited by Signor Cavalcanti, various Tuscan poems by Signors
Bartolommei, Buonmattei, and Doni, who read a scene from his
tragedy, and various Latin poems by Signor Milton, and an
epigram by Signor Girolami.]

MARCH 26. BROTHER CHRISTOPHER'S SON BURIED.

1639 . . . An infant sonne of Christopher Milton gent':
buryed March yᵉ 26ᵗʰ ♂ .

Horton parish registers; Masson, II, 72; *Notes and Queries*, XI, vii
(1913), 21. The figure at the end is the sign of Mars.

MARCH 30. LETTER TO LUCAS HOLSTENIUS AT ROME.

Lucæ Holstenio Romæ *in* Vaticano.
9. Tametsi multa in hoc meo Italiæ transcursu multorum in me
humaniter & peramice facta, & possum, & sæpe soleo recordari;
tamen pro tam brevi notitia, haud scio an jure dicam ullius
majora extitisse in me benevolentiæ indicia quam ea quæ mihi
abs te profecta sunt. Cum enim tui conveniendi causâ in Vaticanum ascenderem, ignotum prorsus, nisi si quid forte ab Alex-

andro Cherubino dictum de me prius fuerat, summâ cum
humanitate recepisti; mox in Musæum comiter admisso, et conquisitissimam Librorum supellectilem, & permultos insuper
Manuscriptos Authores Græcos, tuis Lucubrationibus exornatos,
adspicere licuit: quorum partim nostro sæculo nondum visi,
quasi in procinctu, velut illæ apud Maronem,

——penitus convalle virenti

    Inclusæ animæ, superumq; ad limen ituræ;

expeditas modo Typographi manus, & μαιευτικὴν poscere vide-
bantur; partim tuâ operâ etiamnum editi, passim ab eruditis
avide accipiuntur; quorum & unius etiam duplici dono abs te
auctus dimittor. Tum nec aliter crediderim, quam quæ tu de me
verba feceris ad præstantissimum Cardin. Franc. Barberinum,
iis factum esse, ut cum ille paucis post diebus ἀκρόαμα illud
Musicum magnificentiâ vere Romanâ publice exhiberet, ipse me
tanta in turba quæsitum ad fores expectans, & pene manu prehensum persane honorifice intro admiserit. Quâ ego gratiâ cum
illum postridie salutatum accessissem, tute idem rursus is eras,
qui & aditum mihi fecisti, & colloquendi copiam; quæ quidem
cum tanto viro, quo etiam in summo dignitatis fastigio nihil
benignius, nihil humanius, pro loci & temporis ratione largiuscula profecto potius erat, quam nimis parca. Atq; ego (Doctissime Holsteni) utrum ipse sim solus tam te amicum, & hospitem
expertus, an omnes Anglos, id spectans scilicet quod triennium
Oxoniæ Literis operam dederis, istiusmodi officiis etiam quoscunq; prosequi studium sit, certe nescio. Si hoc est, pulchre tu
quidem Angliæ nostræ, ex parte etiam tuæ, διδασκάλια per-
solvis; privatóque nostrûm cujusq; nomine, et patriæ publico,
parem utrobiq; gratiam promereris. Sin est illud, eximium me
tibi præ cæteris habitum, dignumq; adeo visum quîcum velis
ξενίαν ποιεῖσθαι, & mihi gratulor de tuo judicio, & tuum simul
candorem præ meo merito pono. Jam illud vero quod mihi
negotium dedisse videbare, de inspiciendo codice Mediceo, sedulo ad amicos retuli, qui quidem ejus rei efficiendæ spem perexiguam in præsens ostendunt. In illa Bibliotheca, nisi impetratâ
prius veniâ, nihil posse exscribi, ne stylum quidem scriptorium

admovisse tabulis permissum; esse tamen aiunt Romæ Joannem
Baptistam Donium, is ad legendas publice Græcas Literas Florentiam vocatus indies expectatur, per eum ut consequi possis
quæ velis facile esse; quanquam id sane mihi pergratum acci-
disset, si res tam præsertim optanda quæ sit, meâ potius opellâ
saltem aliquanto plus promovisset, cum sit indignum tam tibi
honesta & præclara suscipienti, non omnes undicunq; homines,
& rationes, & res favere. De cætero, novo beneficio devinxeris,
si Eminentissimum Cardinalem quantâ potest observantiâ meo
nomine salutes, cujus magnæ virtutes, rectíq; studium, ad pro-
vehendas item omnes Artes Liberales egregie comparatum, semper mihi ob oculos versantur; tum illa mitis, &, ut ita dicam,
summissa animi celsitudo, quæ sola se deprimendo attollere di-
dicit; de qua vere dici potest, quod de Cerere apud Callimachum
est, diversâ tamen sententia, ἴθματα μεν χέρσω κεφαλὰ δὲ ὅι
ἅπτετ' ὀλύμπω. Quod cæteris fere Principibus documento esse
potest, triste illud supercilium, & aulici fastus, quam longe à
vera magnanimitate discrepantes & alieni sint. Nec puto fore,
dum ille vivit, Estenses, Farnesios, aut Mediceos, olim doctorum hominum fautores, ut quis amplius desideret. Vale, Doctissime Holsteni, & si quis tui, tuorúmq; studiorum amantior
est, illi me quoque, si id esse tanti existimas, ubicunq; sim gen-
tium futurus, velim annumeres.

Florentiæ, Martii 30. 1639.

Milton, *Epistolarum Familiarium Liber Unus*, 1674, pp. 25-28; CM,
XII, 38.

[To Lucas Holstenius in the Vatican at Rome.

Although I both can, and often do, remember many courteous and most friendly acts which I have experienced at the
hands of many in this my passage through Italy, yet, for so
brief an acquaintance, I do not know that I can justly say that
from any one I have had greater proofs of goodwill than those
which have come to me from you. For, when I went up to the
Vatican for the purpose of meeting you, you received me, a total
stranger to you (unless perchance anything had been previously
said about me to you by Alexander Cherubini), with the utmost

courtesy. Immediately admitted with politeness into the Museum, I was allowed to behold both the superb collection of books, and also very many manuscript Greek authors set forth with your explanations—some of whom, not yet seen in our age, seemed now in their array, like those in Maro, "souls enclosed within a green valley and about to go to the threshold of the upper world," to demand the active hands of the printer, and a delivery into the world; others of whom, already edited by your care, are eagerly received everywhere by scholars; I myself, too, being dismissed by you, richer than I came, with two copies of one which you presented to me. Then I could not but believe that it was in consequence of the mention you made of me to the most excellent Cardinal Francesco Barberini, that, when he, a few days after, gave that public musical entertainment with truly Roman magnificence, he himself, waiting at the doors, and seeking me out in so great a crowd, nay, almost laying hold of me by the hand, admitted me within in a truly most honourable manner. And when, on this account, I went to pay my respects to him next day, you again were yourself the person who both made access for me, and obtained for me an opportunity for conversing with him at leisure, such as, with so great a man (than whom, on the topmost summit of dignity, nothing more kind, nothing more courteous), was truly, considering the place and the time, too ample rather than too sparing. I am quite ignorant, most learned Holstenius, whether I am the only one of my country who have found you so friendly and hospitable, or whether, in respect of your having spent three years in study at Oxford, it is your express habit to confer such obligations also on all Englishmen. If the latter, truly, on your part, you are paying back finely to our England the benefits of your schooling there, and you eminently deserve equal thanks, both on private grounds from each of us, and on public grounds for our country. If the former is the case, then that I should have been accounted by you distinguished beyond the rest, and should have seemed worthy so far that you should wish to form a bond of friendship with me, I both congratulate myself on this opinion of yours, and at the same time put *your* good nature in the place of *my* merit.

The commission which you seemed to give me as to the inspecting of a Medicean codex, I have already carefully reported to my friends; who, however, hold forth for the present very small hope of effecting that matter. In that library, I am told, nothing can be copied, unless by leave first obtained; it is not permitted even to bring a pen to the tables. But they tell me that Giovanni Battista Doni is now in Rome; he, having been invited to Florence to undertake the public lectureship in Greek, is daily expected; and through him they say it will be easy for you to compass what you want. Still it would have been truly a most gratifying accident for me, if a matter of a kind so eminently desirable had advanced somewhat farther by my little endeavour, rather than otherwise; seeing that it is disgraceful that, engaged as you are in work so honourable and illustrious, all men, methods, and circumstances, should not everywhere be at your bidding. For the rest, you will have bound me by a new obligation, if you salute the most eminent Cardinal with all possible observance, in my name; whose great virtues and anxiety to do right, singularly ready also for the promotion of all the liberal arts, are always present before my eyes, as well as that meek, and, if I may so say, submissive loftiness of mind, which alone has taught him to raise by humbling himself; concerning which it may truly be said, as is said of Ceres in Callimachus, though with a turn of the sense: "*Feet to the earth still cling, while the head is touching Olympus.*" Herein might be a proof to other princes how far asunder and alien from true magnanimity, is that sad superciliousness of theirs, and that courtly haughtiness. Nor do I think that, while he is alive, men will have to miss any more the Este, the Farnesi, or the Medici, formerly the favourers of learned men. Farewell, most learned Holstenius; and, if there is any one more than ordinarily a lover of you, and of your studies, I would wish you to reckon me along with him, if you think that of so much consequence, wheresoever in the world my future may be.

Florence, March 30, 1639.]

Masson, I, 749, 770 (801, 822). Masson divides his translation into two sections, marked in the present transcript by the beginning of a new paragraph. The translation of the two lines of Latin verse near the beginning is by the present editor, since Masson simply quotes it without English equivalent.

MARCH 31. ATTENDS FLORENTINE ACADEMY.

A di 31.

Nell Accad^a. si trovarono li ss^{ri}. . . . G. Miltonio.

Atti dell' Accademia degli Svogliati, MSS Magliabecchiana (Florence), cl. IX, cod. 60, fol. 52v; Stern, I, ii, 499.

[March 31. At the Academy were present Messrs. . . . J. Milton.]

Although this entry is not dated as to the month, there is little doubt about its being March, since the last previous entry is for March 24.

APRIL (?). VISITS LUCCA.

. . . ad paucos dies Lucam excucurri.

Milton, *Defensio Secunda*, 1654, p. 86; CM, VIII, 126. This follows the second visit to Florence.

[I visited Lucca for a few days.]

. . . an excursion of a few days to *Luca*.

Phillips, p. xvi; Darbishire, p. 59.

. . . went to *Luca*.

Wood, I, 881; Darbishire, p. 38.

APRIL (?). PASSES THROUGH BONONIA.

. . . transcenso Apennino, per Bononiam.

Milton, *Defensio Secunda*, 1654, p. 86; CM, VIII, 126.

[. . . crossing the Apennines, through Bononia.]

. . . crossing the *Apennine*, and passing through *Bononia*. . . .

Phillips, p. xvi; Darbishire, p. 59.

. . . went to . . . *Bononia*. . . .

Wood, I, 881; Darbishire, p. 38.

APRIL (?). PASSES THROUGH FERRARA.

... per ... Ferraram.
Milton, *Defensio Secunda*, 1654, p. 86; CM, VIII, 126.

[... through Ferrara.]
... passing through ... *Ferrara.*
Phillips, p. xvi; Darbishire, p. 59.

... went to ... *Ferrara.*
Wood, I, 881; Darbishire, p. 38.

APRIL (?). COMES TO VENICE; SHIPS BOOKS HOME.

Venetias contendi. Cui urbi lustrandæ cum mensem unum impendissem, & libros, quos per Italiam conquisiveram, in navem imponendos curâssem.
Milton, *Defensio Secunda*, 1654, p. 86; CM, VIII, 126.

[I arrived at Venice. When I had spent a month in examining the city and had taken care to have the books which I had collected through Italy loaded on the ship. ...]
... then proceeded to Venice, where hee shippd what books he had bought. ...
The "earliest" biography, fol. 141; Darbishire, p. 21.

... he arriv'd at *Venice,* where when he had spent a Month's time in viewing of that Stately City, and Shipp'd up a Parcel of curious and rare Books which he had pick'd up in his Travels; particularly a Chest or two of choice Musick-books of the best Masters flourishing about that time in *Italy,* namely, *Luca Marenzo, Monte Verde, Horatio Vecchi, Cifa,* the Prince of *Venosa* and several others. ...
Phillips, p. xvi; Darbishire, p. 59.

[He came] to *Venice;* where continuing a month. ...
Wood, I, 881; Darbishire, p. 38.

MAY (?). PASSES THROUGH VERONA.

... per Veronam. ...
Milton, *Defensio Secunda*, 1654, p. 86; CM, VIII, 126.

[through Verona.]
... he took his course through *Verona.* ...
Phillips, p. xvi; Darbishire, p. 59.

[From Venice] he went and visited *Verona*.

Wood, 1, 881; Darbishire, p. 38.

MAY 3. RECEIVES INTEREST ON COPE BOND (?).

... neyther ye s'd principall debt of 150^ll nor any pte thereof nor any Jnterest due for ye forbearance of the same since November 1641 hath been paid or satisfied ....

Milton's bill against Lady Elizabeth Cope and Sir Anthony Cope, June 16, 1654, *q.v.*; see entry under May 3, 1638.

MAY (?). PASSES THROUGH MILAN.

... per ... Mediolanum. ...

Milton, *Defensio Secunda*, 1654, p. 86; CM, VIII, 126.

[... through Milan.]

... he took his course through ... *Milan*. ...

Phillips, p. xvi; Darbishire, p. 59.

... he visited ... *Millan*. ...

Wood, 1, 881; Darbishire, p. 38.

MAY (?). TRAVELS THROUGH LOMBARDY.

... after he had ship'd the books and other goods which he had bought in his travels, he returned thro *Lombardy* ...

Wood, 1, 881; Darbishire, p. 38.

... through the delicious country of Lombardy. ...

The "earliest" biography, fol. 141; Darbishire, p. 21. Before "delicious" in the manuscript comes the adjective "pleasant," later cancelled with a line through it.

JUNE (?). ARRIVES IN GENEVA.

... per ... Pæninas Alpes, Lacu denique Lemanno, Genevam delatus sum.

Milton, *Defensio Secunda*, 1654, pp. 86-87; CM, VIII, 126.

[... by way of the Pennine Alps and then Lake Leman I was brought to Geneva.]

... over the Alps to Geneva. ...

The "earliest" biography, fol. 141; Darbishire, p. 21.

... he took his course through ... the *Pœnine Alps*, and so by the Lake *Leman* to *Geneva*. ...

Phillips, p. xvi; Darbishire, p. 59.

... over the *Alpes* to *Geneva.* ...
Wood, 1, 881; Darbishire, p. 38.

JUNE (?). ALLEGED MISBEHAVIOR IN ITALY.

Eunuchum deinde vocas. Vir esto sane; sed, si Eunuchi omnes fuissent, qui domum tuam frequentabant, uxorem fortasse non repudiasses. Tu, quem olim Itali pro fœmina habuerunt, cuiquam audeas, quod parùm vir sit, objicere? ... Haud sic te decet, pulchellum hominem, inclementem esse; cui Itali olim, apud se peregrinanti, testimonium, & laudem, formosuli adolescentis dederunt. ... Si, quia formosus es, ideo te magni fieri postulas: hoc Itali tui viderint, qui pulchritudinem tuam, cum apud eos esses, deprædicarunt. Haud scio an etiam pædicarint, ipse scis.

Claudius Salmasius, *Ad Johannem Miltonum Responsio, Opus Posthumum,* London, 1660, pp. 23, 94, 107. Though not published until 1660, this answer to Milton's first Defense was written during 1652 and 1653. The passages quoted are typical of many others that could be added. The pun on "deprædicarunt" and "pædicarint" in the last two sentences should not be overlooked. Since these accusations of immorality were made by a bitter enemy of Milton's in an elaborate paper warfare in which truth was incidental and the chief aim was to hurt or disgrace the opponent by any means whatever, they should not be taken seriously. They are included simply as one known instance of the unpleasant gossip about him which was probably known to a good many others at the time. Though filed here under a specific date, this note obviously refers, as does the succeeding one, to the whole Italian journey.

[Then you call him (*i.e.,* Salmasius) a eunuch. Be a man yourself, if you like; but, had they been all eunuchs that used to frequent your house, perhaps you would not have repudiated your wife. Do you, whom formerly the Italians used as a woman, dare to object to any one that he is too little of a man? ... It hardly becomes you, handsome little man, to be harsh. For formerly, when you were traveling among the Italians, they expressed their praise of you as a pretty youth. ... If, because you are handsome, you ask that you should therefore be highly esteemed, your Italian friends saw this, who, when you were among them, extolled your beauty. I don't know whether they also debauched you; you yourself know.]

[417]

Masson (VI, 209) translates part of the first section, though he carefully retains the "quem olim Itali pro fœmina habuerunt" in its safer original language. He gives none of the rest.

JUNE (?). PURITY OF LIFE THROUGHOUT FOREIGN TRAVELS.

Quæ urbs [Geneva], cùm in mentem mihi hinc veniat Mori calumniatoris, facit ut Deum hìc rursus testem invocem, me his omnibus in locis, ubi tam multa licent, ab omni flagitio ac probro integrum atque intactum vixisse, illud perpetuò cogitantem, si hominum latere oculos possem, Dei certè non posse.

Milton, *Defensio Secunda*, 1654, p. 87; CM, VIII, 126.

[As for this city of Geneva, when I am reminded from it of Morus the slanderer, it causes me here again to call upon God as my witness that in all these places where there is so much moral laxity, I lived pure and untouched by all crime and profligacy, always bearing in mind that if I could hide from the eyes of men, I certainly could not from God.]

. . . iisdem conceptis verbis . . . rursum Deum testem invoco, me illis omnibus in locis, ubi tam multa licent, ab omni flagitio ac probro integrum atque intactum vixisse, illud perpetuò cogitantem, si hominum latere oculos possem, Dei certè non posse.

Milton, *Defensio Pro Se*, 1655, p. 121; CM, IX, 178. Since the passage is repeated almost verbatim from that in the *Defensio Secunda*, a translation seems unnecessary.

JUNE (?). VISITS JOHN DIODATI IN GENEVA.

Genevæ cum Joanne Deodato, Theologiæ professore doctissimo, quotidianus versabar.

Milton, *Defensio Secunda*, 1654, p. 87; CM, VIII, 126.

[At Geneva I talked daily with John Diodati, the most learned professor of theology.]

. . . Geneva, where hee liv'd in familiar conversation with the famous Diodati.

The "earliest" biography, fol. 141; Darbishire, p. 21.

. . . *Geneva,* where he staid for some time, and had daily converse with the most Learned *Giovanni Deodati*, Theology-Professor in that City.

Phillips, p. xvi; Darbishire, p. 59.

At Geneva he contracted a great friendship wth the learned Dr Diodati of Geneva [vide his Poems.] Had Sr H. Wottons comendatory lr̄s.

Aubrey, fol. 63; Darbishire, p. 2. The last sentence is written above the last part of the preceding one, though without a caret to indicate its position. The phrase "the learned Dr Diodati" is preceded by the cancelled phrase "Carolo Diodati, son of."

. . . *Geneva*, where spending some time, he became familiar with the famous *Joh. Deodate* D.D.

Wood, 1, 881; Darbishire, p. 38.

June 10. Writes in Camillo Cardoyn's album at Geneva.

——if Vertue feeble were
Heaven it selfe would stoope to her.

Cœlum non animū muto dū trans mare curro
                                        Joannes Miltonius
Junij 10°. 1639.   Anglus./

Cardoyn's album is in the Harvard College Library, the gift of Charles Sumner. There is a facsimile of Milton's autograph in Sotheby, facing p. 98. See also *Notes and Queries*, II, iv (1857), 287; Masson, I, 779 (833); CM, XVIII, 271, 553; French, "The Autographs of John Milton," #81. The English verses are from "Comus"; the Latin from Horace.

[I change the sky but not my mind when I cross the sea.]

July (?). Returns through France.

Genevæ . . . Deinde eodem itinere, quo priùs, per Galliam . . . in patriam revertor.

Milton, *Defensio Secunda*, 1654, p. 87; CM, VIII, 126.

[From Geneva I returned to my native land by the same route as before through France.]
. . . through France. . . .

The "earliest" biography, fol. 141; Darbishire, p. 21.

... returning through *France*, by the same way he had passed it going to *Italy*. ...

Phillips, p. xvi; Darbishire, p. 59.

Thence, going thro *France*, he returned home.

Wood, I, 881; Darbishire, p. 38.

JULY (?). RETURNS TO ENGLAND.

... post annum & tres plus minus menses in patriam revertor; eodem ferme tempore quo Carolus, cum Scotis, ruptâ pace, bellum alterum quod vocant Episcopale, redintegrabat; in quo fusis primo congressu regiis copiis. ...

Milton, *Defensio Secunda*, 1654, p. 87; CM, VIII, 126. Milton's chronology must be taken as rather general. If he refers to the First Bishops' War, it must have been virtually over by the time of Milton's arrival home, since the so-called Pacification of Birks was signed on June 18, 1639, and Charles I was back in London on August 3. If, as his language intimates, he has in mind the Second Bishops' War, he is decidedly wrong, since the Scots did not cross the Tweed until August 20, 1640, and the encounter at Newburn came on August 28. Yet Milton's phrases, "ruptâ pace," "bellum alterum," and "redintegrabat," seem to point to the renewal of hostilities after the Pacification of Birks rather than to the opening skirmishes of 1639. Probably by 1654, when Milton wrote his *Defensio*, the two sets of events had become somewhat hazy in his mind. For the chronology see Masson, II, *passim*.

[After a year and three months, more or less, I came back to my native land, almost at the same time as Charles renewed the second war which they call Episcopal after the breaking of the peace. In it the royal troops were routed in the first meeting.]

... hee returnd home, having, with no ill management of his time, spent about fifteen moneths abroad.

The "earliest" biography, fol. 141; Darbishire, p. 21.

... he, after a Peregrination of one compleat Year and about Three Months, arrived safe in *England*, about the time of the Kings making his second Expedition against the *Scots*.

Phillips, p. xvi; Darbishire, p. 59.

He was severall yeares beyond sea, q̄. how many Resp. two yeares, & returned to England just upon the breaking out of the Civill warres.

Aubrey, fol. 63; Darbishire, p. 2. This entry has been much changed in the writing. The query "how many?" and the response "two yeares" have been added above the line, as has the phrase "to England." Before "the Civill warres" is the cancelled first draft "a bra little before," and after it is a corresponding cancelled "brake out."

. . . he returned home, well fraught with Knowledge and Manners, after he had been absent one year and three months.

Wood, 1, 881; Darbishire, p. 38.

INDEX